UNSHOOK TILL THE END OF TIME

A History of relations between Britain and Oman,
1650-1970

ROBERT ALSTON AND STUART LAING

GILGAMESH
PUBLISHING LTD

Unshook till the End of Time

Published by Gilgamesh Publishing in 2012
Email: info@gilgamesh-publishing.co.uk
www.gilgamesh-publishing.co.uk

ISBN 978-1-908531-07-0

CIP Data: A catalogue for this book is
available from the British Library

TABLE OF CONTENTS

MAPS & ILLUSTRATIONS

Illustration Credits

We acknowledge the following, and express our thanks, for illustrations reproduced in this volume: The Arcadian Library, for four pictures from *Richard Temple's Sixteen Views of Places in the Persian Gulph* (1811); Shawqi Sultan, for additional help on Richard Temple's lithographs; Bait al-Zubair Museum, Muscat, for ten illustrations from the 19th and early 20th century; Clara Semple (Maria Theresa dollar); Wilberforce House Museum, Kingston-upon-Hull (T Perronet Thompson); Sulivan, *Dhow Chasing in Zanzibar Waters*, 1873 (slave-carrying ships); Royal Botanical Gardens, Kew (Sir John Kirk); Worsfold, *Sir Bartle Frere*, (Sir Bartle Frere); Coupland, *The Exploitation of East Africa* (Frere mission in Cairo); Goradia, *Lord Curzon, the Last of the British Moghuls*, (Curzon); Hugh Willing (Cemetery Bay); Ian Buttenshaw of the Royal Army of Oman for six military pictures; the Royal Geographical Society (Bertram Thomas); Colin Richardson, *Tales from a Desert Island* (three pictures of RAF Aircraft); Wilfred Thesiger, *Arabian Sands* (Wilfred Thesiger); Peter Allfree, *Warlords of Oman* (Suleiman bin Himyar and Imam Ghalib); Petroleum Development Oman, taken from Terence Clark, *Underground to Overseas* (Muscat and Oman Field Force and Patrick Bannerman); Edward Henderson, *A strange eventful history* (Fahud); John Akehurst, *We won a war* (Said Hof); Peter Thwaites, *Muscat Command* (Midway Road and Sultan Qaboos 1972); Rowland White, *Storm Front* (Strikemasters); Middle East Centre Archive, St Antony's College, Oxford – Charles Butt Collection (Brigadier Maxwell); The Commanding Officer 22 SAS Regiment (The Battle of Mirbat); Getty (HM The Queen and HM Sultan Qaboos).

Map 1. Oman*

* These maps are for illustrative purposes only, and do not convey endorsement of the international boundaries marked on them. The spelling of place names is taken from the National Survey Authority of Oman, and does not in every case coincide with the spellings in the text of the book.

x

Map 2. The Arabian Sea

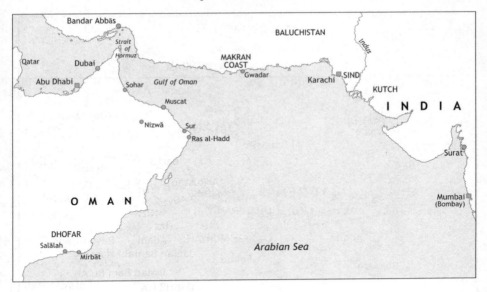

Map 3. The Gulf and Eastern Arabia

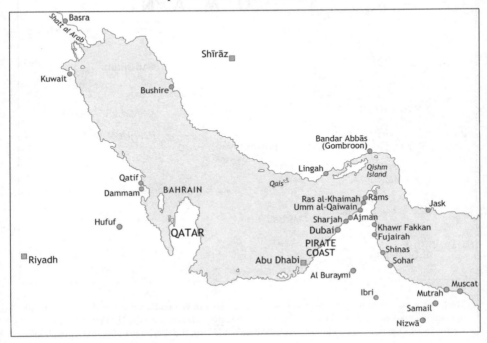

Map 4. East Africa

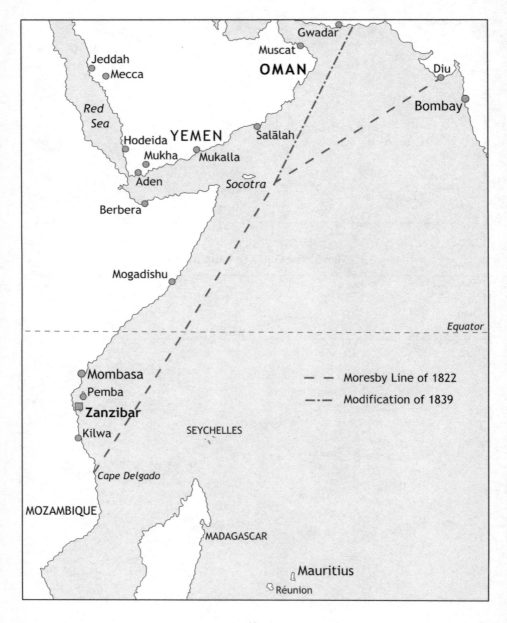

Map 5. The Dhofar War

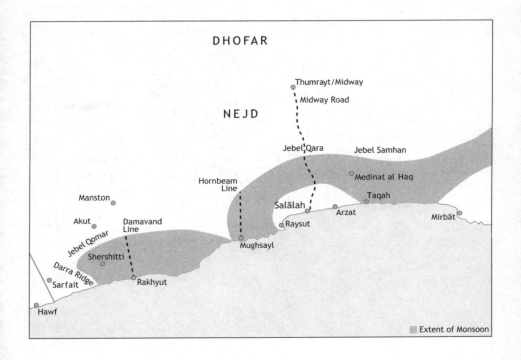

Map 6. Oman's oil industry

Map 7. Travellers' routes across the Empty Quarter

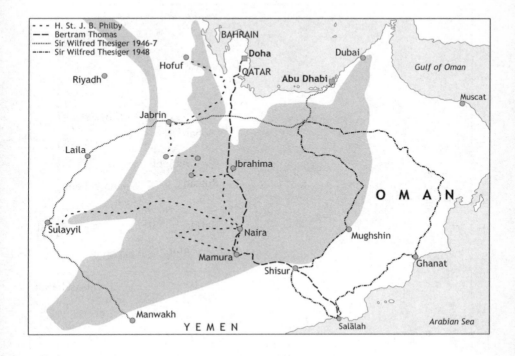

Legend:
- - - H. St. J. B. Philby
— Bertram Thomas
.... Sir Wilfred Thesiger 1946-7
-··-··- Sir Wilfred Thesiger 1948

BAHRAIN
Doha
QATAR
Hofuf
Dubai
Gulf of Oman
Riyadh
Abu Dhabi
Muscat
Jabrin
Laila
Ibrahima
O M A N
Sulayyil
Naira
Mughshin
Mamura
Ghanat
Shisur
Manwakh
Y E M E N
Salālah
Arabian Sea

Map 8. Eastern Arabia – boundary claims

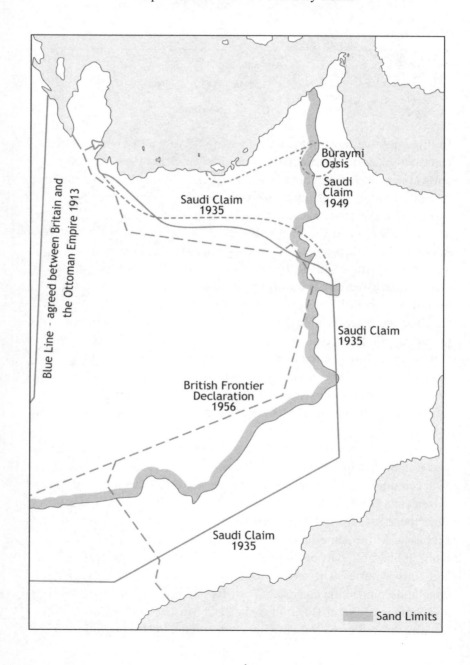

Blue Line - agreed between Britain and the Ottoman Empire 1913

Buraymi Oasis

Saudi Claim 1949

Saudi Claim 1935

Saudi Claim 1935

British Frontier Declaration 1956

Saudi Claim 1935

Sand Limits

Foreword

In this book we have not sought to write a history of Oman, but have chosen to focus on a particular relationship which has been of importance and value to both protagonists over more than three and a half centuries. Although we have checked sources where possible, and consulted records and archives, it is not so much a work of academic scholarship as a narrative which we hope will appeal to any reader with an interest in Oman. The title is taken from the wording of one of the earliest British agreements with a Gulf Ruler, when John Malcolm and Sayyid Sultan bin Ahmad agreed in 1800 that "the friendship of the two States may remain unshook till the end of time, and till the sun and moon have finished their revolving career." We have chosen to end the general narrative with the accession of Sultan Qaboos in 1970. Thereafter what had hitherto been a more or less uniquely exclusive relationship became, though still close, one among a number for a rapidly modernising state. We have however chosen to relate the story of the campaign against rebels in Dhofar, which began in the mid 1960s, to its military conclusion in 1975.

Oman's fortunes fluctuated widely over these centuries. At times she was a major trading power in the Indian Ocean, in the first half of the 19th century with an extensive 'empire' of her own in East Africa. Oman was never a British colony, nor even a protectorate. The Union Jack never flew there, except over the British Agency and then Consulate and Embassy. At the same time she was, with her neighbours in the Lower Gulf, indubitably part of the British Indian imperial system of the 19th and 20th centuries. The security of India's maritime trade was above all what underpinned the consistent British policy of support for the Rulers and Sultans of the al-Busa'idi dynasty in Muscat from 1800 onwards. Equally this policy was always pursued with the lowest possible level of direct involvement. Down to the mid-20th century, with one aberration in the 1820s, British involvement was limited to coastal areas. Interior Oman was off limits. Like many other relationships, that between Britain and Oman got caught up in the tidal wave of change after the Second World War. Oil and other British interests ensured that Britain did not turn her back on the Arabian peninsula and the Gulf after Indian independence in 1947. Oman became a terrain where Arab nationalist and ultimately communist aspirations clashed with Britain's interests from the early 1950s. As a society Oman changed little till oil revenues were available to spend from around 1970. Since then the country itself, and the relationship with Britain, have been transformed.

Inevitably a book of this kind, drawing mainly on secondary sources in English and selectively on British Indian and British documents, tells the story of the relationship from a British perspective. We are very conscious that there were, and are, Omani perspectives also on the episodes we narrate. We have tried to be sympathetic to their existence. No-one would be happier than we if this book were to enthuse and encourage Omani historians to review them through their own eyes.

One point on terminology, the use of the term "Oman". For most of the period covered by this book, the control or influence wielded by the Sultan or Ruler in Muscat fluctuated wildly. At times he had control only over Muscat itself and the coastal plain, the Batinah. At others his influence would spread into the mountainous areas, and he would command loyalty from the tribes and villages north and west of the Hajjar mountains; and he also had control over his overseas possessions, of Gwadar, islands in the Gulf, and his dominions in Zanzibar, Pemba and East Africa. After the truce of 1853, which established peace between the Shaykhs of places and tribes now in the United Arab Emirates, "Trucial Oman" was used to refer to that area also. After the conclusion of the Jebel Akhdar campaign in 1959, and the final expulsion of Imam Ghalib in 1956, Sultan Sa'id took the style "Sultan of Muscat and Oman", acknowledging the historic differentiation between Muscat and the coastal area on the one hand, and the interior – "Oman" – on the other. Early in the reign of Sultan Qaboos it became simply 'the Sultanate of Oman'. In this book we have used "Oman" and "Omani" to refer to the present area of the country, and those inhabiting all of it, including the province of Dhofar in the south. This risks anachronism, since an inhabitant of Muscat in the 19th century would probably not have thought of himself as "Omani"; but it is clear and understandable.

Numerous friends in Britain and Oman have discussed aspects of this book with us. In Muscat, Sayyid Badr, Muhammad Zubair, Salem al-Maskari, Yahya Nasib and Shawqi Sultan, among many, have offered insights and advice. Ruth Hawley, Julian Lush and Terry Clark have kindly loaned books to enable us to work on the text away from libraries. Ian Buttenshaw provided compilations of material prepared for the Royal Army of Oman on the Jebel Akhdar and Dhofar campaigns, as well as helping identify relevant illustrations. Julian Lush, Terry Clark, and Nigel Knocker read and commented on individual chapters. Our wives have supported the project throughout, and helped with proof-reading and improving the narrative. To all of these we are grateful. The text as a whole is however our responsibility alone.

In 1800 John Malcom and Sayyid Sultan also agreed that "an English gentleman of respectability ... shall always reside at the port of Muscat". As two of those gentlemen, recalling with pleasure the periods we resided there, we hope you find this account interesting and enjoyable.

Stylistic conventions

References to books are given in the footnotes by title and author; publishing details are in the Notes for further reading.

We have wanted to make this book accessible to the general reader, and so we have not used an academic style of transliterating all Arabic words and names, and have minimised diacritical markings – ie lines above letters or dots above/below them. Familiar Arabic names, of people and places, are spelt in the way used normally in English writing (eg Oman, not 'Uman; Ras, not Ra's; Seeb, not Sīb). The sect of Islam predominant in Oman is given as Ibadi, correctly Ibāḍī, though often spelt Ibadhi. One of the commonest names in the Omani ruling family is given as Sa'id throughout, though correctly Sa'īd. We have written the name of the ruling family as al-Busa'idi, although it is also found in the form Al Bu Sa'idi, and with other variants. We have not written the long i (ī) for the masculine adjectival form. Less familiar Arabic names and words are spelt with diacritical marks on their first occurrence, and without them thereafter. The letter 'ain is shown as ' throughout, but omitted in names beginning with 'Abd or 'Abdul (which are normally shown in the form Abdul Rahman, Abdul Karim, etc, and not 'Abd al-Rahmān, etc), and in other words with widely accepted familiar transliterations. The hamza is shown as an apostrophe, thus '.

We have normally used bin for "son of ...", rather than ibn (which is equally correct) or b. (often used in scholarly writing).

Names of Indian places are given with the spelling conventionally used before 1947, eg Bombay not Mumbai, Calcutta not Kolkata.

For plurals of Arabic words or names, we have used a final s, and not the Arabic inflected plural, eg the al-Busa'idis.

CHAPTER 1

Friends on the Passage to India (17th century)

Early British links with Oman arose from Western European interest in trading with India, South East Asia and the Far East. Initially the British found themselves involved in struggles for supremacy with the Portuguese and Dutch, the policy and strategy being driven by the East India Company, after its foundation in 1600. Travellers on East India Company business visited Muscat, and recorded interesting impressions.

* * * * * * *

The British connection with Oman goes back to the middle of the 17th century. But they were not the first Europeans to have substantive dealings with the country: nearly 150 years before the British signed their first treaty with the Sultan of Muscat, the Portuguese asserted themselves in the region, and the Dutch – as traders rather than warriors – also preceded the British. The Portuguese story is relevant to the British connection with Oman, first because this episode is a strong part of Omani historical memories, and secondly because the British – with the Dutch – helped drive out the Portuguese in the mid-17th century.

The Portuguese story begins with the discovery by Vasco da Gama of the route to the East round the Cape of Good Hope, in 1498 CE. The Portuguese had for some time been interested in eastward expansion, taking advantage of their growing skill in seamanship, inspired from the days of the 15th century King Henry the Navigator, and motivated by

1

hopes of gaining a share in the spice trade that had been dominated by Arab merchants since the early days of Islam. In addition to well-built and well-armed ships, the Portuguese had some fine leaders and commanders, of whom three stand out in this era of expansion in the Indian Ocean – the famous general Afonso de Albuquerque (1453-1515), the navigator and diplomat Tristão da Cunha (1460-1540), and the statesman Francisco d'Almeida (c 1450-1510). In 1505 an expedition of over twenty ships, under Almeida, was sent out with orders to establish military settlements in an arc stretching from South-East Africa to South-West India; and the next year another fleet, of 14 ships, with Albuquerque and Tristão da Cunha in command, pressed on with the campaign.

Albuquerque's main aim was to assert his claim to the position of Viceroy of Portuguese possessions in India (here he may have been in competition with Almeida), but he also had instructions from King Manoel to blockade the Red Sea and so break the Venetian-Egyptian monopoly of the Eastern spice trade. Albuquerque adopted the sensible strategy of aiming to block the Straits of Hormuz and the Gulf as well, and this led him to feel he needed to occupy or at least suppress the ports of Oman.

Albuquerque acted with great speed and energy. He first asserted Portuguese authority in Mozambique, Zanzibar, and other parts of the East African coast, in part in the face of opposition from Arab colonists, who originated in present-day Yemen and Oman, and who had lived there as traders for some time. Moving north, and overcoming resistance from Arabs based on the mainland, Albuquerque captured the island of Socotra, where he built a fort aimed no doubt at exercising control over the mouth of the Red Sea. But there was too little to support the garrison, and not long afterwards the troops were withdrawn and the fort pulled down.

Proceeding up the coast, Albuquerque's force first engaged the Omanis by burning a fishing fleet off Ras al-Hadd. On making land, Albuquerque recorded his favourable impression of the Omani ports – Sohar, Qalhat and Muscat – which clearly at the time were active in handling trade in a wide range of agricultural products from a prosperous hinterland. The rainfall may have been higher then than it is now. Possibly because of his earlier experiences (he had taken part in an expedition against the Turks in 1481), or simply in order to demonstrate unquestioned supremacy, Albuquerque used extreme force in suppressing the Omani ports. He sacked and burned Qurayyat, Muscat, and Khūr Fakkān[1] on his way to Hormuz, the strategically important island which gives its name to the Straits where it lies. It is generally thought that he made a treaty with Qalhat, but later reneged on it and destroyed the town. The modern tourist can see the ruins where archaeologists are revealing the extent of the ancient city.[2]

Albuquerque's campaign prospered. He went on to capture Hormuz in October 1506, and destroyed a large combined Muslim fleet of Egyptian, Persian and Arab ships at the battle of Diu in 1509. This and other battles at sea enabled the Portuguese to establish themselves on the Omani coast, from where they sought – with varying success – to control trade in the Gulf and the Northern Indian Ocean. The Portuguese made little attempt to establish their influence inland. They found that old alliances and trading patterns were not entirely easy to change or subdue; in 1521, for example, they faced an uprising in Hormuz itself and in its dependencies on the Omani coast. Nevertheless, the Portuguese managed to enforce a system of passes or licences for shipping in the Gulf and the northern Indian Ocean, for over a hundred years, at the same time developing their possessions in India and the East African coast. To secure their position in Oman, particularly against opposition from the Ottoman Turks, operating from Egypt, they built a series of fine forts, many of which were taken over and maintained, and often altered or developed, by later occupiers and then by the Omanis. Probably the best known are the twin forts of Mirani and Jalali, high on the hills on each side of Muscat harbour: the Portuguese started building them in 1527, but completed them – in much the form in which they can be seen today – in 1587-88. These forts, originally known as Fort Capitan and Fort San João, are a distinctive memorial of the Portuguese era in the region, however much we regret the level of savagery which the invaders employed. For 150 years after they left Muscat, Portuguese buildings were the only structures of note there. When Sayyid Ṣulṭān bin Ahmad emerged as the victor of the civil wars of the end of the 18th century, he

---

1 Also Khawr Fakkān, henceforth referred to in its common spelling *Khor Fakkan*
2 Just nearby is the lovely and lonely ruin of the mausoleum of Bibi Miriam, a princess who reigned in Qalhat in the 14th century CE, and according to legend had a romance with the architect of a mosque being built during her husband's absence in the wars.

lived initially in a church built by the Portuguese occupiers, before he had his own palace constructed.[3]

Realising the fortunes to be made from the Eastern trade, the Dutch, French and British began from the late 16th century to create and exploit new opportunities for commercial expansion, backed up by use of force – especially naval power. Portuguese influence faded in the face of this competition, compounded by Persian determination to oust them from Hormuz, and a resurgence of anti-occupation sentiment, led by the new Ya'rubi dynasty, in Oman. In London, the foundation of the English East India Company in 1600 began the process which eventually led to the growth of the British Indian Empire, itself the reason for continued and at times intense British concern for hegemony in the Gulf.

The first British involvement with the Gulf was connected with the opening of trading links with Persia. And this exercise in commercial diplomacy seems also to have resulted in the first British footfall in what is now Omani territory. The East India Company, their attention drawn to Persia by the arrival at King James's court of an envoy from the Shah who was actually an Englishman called Sir Robert Sherley (who had spent some years in Persia), sent a vessel to Persia in 1613. On board were Sherley and his Circassian wife, plus also the man named by King James as Ambassador to the Shah, Sir Thomas Powell, his wife and their entourage. The ship, *Expedition*, called at Dhofar, the first British ship recorded as having done so. From this point plans began to go awry: *Expedition* somehow missed the mouth of the Gulf, and nearly landed the English travellers in Gwadar, in Baluchistan, a territory which later came into Omani possession – see box on p 15. This would have been a mistake, since the Baluchis were then at war with the Shah of Persia and would have liked to kill the two Ambassadors; but *Expedition* managed to put out to sea before disaster intervened. As the ill-fated journey proceeded, the Powells both died, but the Sherleys eventually arrived at the Shah's court in Isfahan. Soon afterwards, in 1619, the British were granted a trading-post on the island of Jask, just up the coast from Hormuz.

---

3 Sayyid Sultan may have lived in the former Portuguese Governor's residence; Skeet: *Muscat and Oman*, p35.

* * * * * * *

The Powell-Sherley landing may not have been the earliest British footfall on what later became Omani territory. That honour may go to Sir John Mandeville, who records in his *Travels*

> "Men travel through India by way of many countries to the Great Sea Ocean. Then they come to the isle of [Hormuz], … But it is so hot there that the men have their testicles hanging down to their thighs because of the violent heat, which weakens their bodies. Men of that country … bind them up and use certain astringent ointments to hold them up – otherwise they could not live..."[4]

There follow other intriguing details of life in Hormuz – Omani territory in the 17th and 18th centuries, but now Iranian. The problem is that it is not at all certain who Sir John Mandeville was, or whether he himself actually travelled to Hormuz, or indeed anywhere. His book circulated in the middle of the 14th century, so this would easily make him the first Englishman in the area if his account is true. It is however equally likely that his *Travels* is a compilation of travellers' tales, beautifully and wittily constructed, but probably not based on what we would call verifiable fact.

* * * * * * *

We return to the 17th century. The Dutch were also among those Europeans who showed an interest in expanding their trade eastwards in this period, and became best known for their trading enterprises in what is now Indonesia. They leased an office in Muscat in 1670, probably to ensure passage of their mail to points further east; and an envoy of the Lord General of Batavia (now Jakarta) visited Muscat on a commercial visit in 1672. The Dutch may also have had a loose naval alliance with the Omanis for some years in the 17th century.

---

4 Moseley, C W R D: *The Travels of Sir John Mandeville*, p 120.

For a while, British interests (related to expanding commerce, and maintaining safe and secure communications) coincided with those of Shah Abbas of Persia, who made great efforts to drive the Portuguese out of Oman, and particularly out of Hormuz. English trading ships of the East India Company joined forces with Shah Abbas in attacking Hormuz in 1622, successfully driving out the Portuguese.[5] Possibly thinking they had gone too far in this act of belligerence, the East India Company held back from further support, and allowed the Persians to push forward on their own to expel the Portuguese from Khor Fakkan and Sohar. The Portuguese recovered both the latter places, and also managed to strengthen the fort at Khasab (known to them as "Cassapo") in what is now the Omani enclave at the far north of the Musandam peninsula. But their position was steadily growing weaker, and eventually it was the Omani Imam Sultān bin Saif who mounted a successful attack on the Portuguese in their strongholds in Muscat in 1649, and took their surrender. The Omani expulsion of the Portuguese added greatly to their regional prestige, and did in reality reflect their growing power and confidence. Particularly apparent was their strength at sea, which is hardly surprising given their long coast-line of 1700 km (nearly 1000 miles) and the very great difficulties of communication with inland Arabia, guarded as their country is by the huge and inhospitable desert of the Empty Quarter to the north and west.

---

5 The Persians allowed Hormuz to waste away, and established a new base on the mainland at a fishing village called Gombroon – which was later named Bandar Abbas after the great Shah. Later, in 1794, Sayyid Ṣulṭān bin Aḥmad leased Bandar Abbas from Persia, having obtained the loyalty of the Bani Ma'in tribe who controlled it.

"Imam", "Sayyid" and "Sultan"

The term Imam is generally used to mean the one who leads the faithful in prayer, and who often preaches the Friday sermon. In several Muslim societies, and particularly in the Ibāḍī sect (the branch of Islam followed by the majority of Muslim believers in Oman), the Imam has been the chosen leader in government and war, reflecting the people's wish to be led by someone who had spiritual and religious leadership qualities. Ibadi doctrine was that the Imam should be elected, and that there was no right of inheritance; and for much of Oman's history after the coming of Islam, the Imam was indeed elected, although it could and did happen that successive Imams could come from one family. The power and influence of Omani Imams was notably strong among the tribes of the interior. There were also Ibadi imamates in strongholds of the sect in North Africa. Leaders in Oman took the title and responsibilities of Imam until and through the 17th and much of the 18th century. All the members of the Ya'ruba dynasty (1624-1728) used the title, as did two of the al-Busa'idi who took power in the middle of the 18th century. After the civil wars of the late 18th century, al-Busa'idi rulers did not think it appropriate to use the title, and called themselves "Sayyid" (meaning "Lord"), a title still used by close members of the Sultan's family today. Through the 19th century, British officials often transcribed this as Syud. Up to and including the early 1800s, British writers, including officials in Government correspondence, continued to use "Imam" (or often "Imaum") when referring to the ruler, and then "Sultan" from about the middle of the 19th century: "Sultan" was first used in an official document in the Anglo-Muscati Treaty of May 1839, and it has since become the customary title of the Ruler.

The title "Imam" was revived by opponents of the ruler in the late 19th and early 20th centuries. Azzan bin Qays, who forced his way to the throne in 1868, was Imam during his 3-year rule; and the title was also held by Salim bin Rashid al-Kharūsi in 1913, from 1920 to 1954 by Mohammad bin Abdullah bin Sa'id bin Khalfān al-Khalīli, and finally by Ghālib bin Ali, who escaped to Saudi Arabia in 1954 after Government troops' victory in the Jebal Akhdar war (see chapter 15).

The visible influence of the Portuguese lies in the remains of the magnificent forts they built in Oman, although we should not forget that Omani indigenous fort-building continued, notably in the late 17th and early 18th centuries, and it is sometimes difficult for the non-expert to distinguish between them. The Portuguese may also have contributed by bringing improved ship-building techniques and skills to the Omanis, and their occupation certainly aroused feelings of Omani national pride and brought to the fore a spirit of national independence – factors which in the end helped bring about the removal of the Portuguese from the Omani scene.[6]

It was in fact Sultan bin Saif's predecessor and cousin, Nāsir bin Murshid, who both established the Ya'ruba dynasty and also took the initiative which was to provide the spur to opening the Omani relationship with Britain. In 1624 Nasir had been called upon by the religious leadership of the tribes in the coastal area to accept the responsibility of the Imamate and seek to unite the country, then suffering from one of its periodic rounds of civil strife. He built a solid body of support in the mountainous areas round Nizwa, and in the Dhāhirah region, and then moved against the Portuguese, recovering ports such as Sūr and Qurayyat (although Muscat fell only in 1649, to Imam Sultan). In 1645 Imam Nasir seems to have taken the initiative to write to the East India Company, and offer them trading facilities at Sohar.[7] We can only surmise his motives. Perhaps the Portuguese, despite the rough way in which they had dealt with the local people on their first arrival, had at least provided a level of peace and organisation in commercial matters which worked to the advantage of traders in Omani ports, and Nasir thought that a British presence could bring similar benefits to fill the vacuum created by the decline or expected removal of the Portuguese. Or he may have calculated that a British commercial connection could help in his campaign against the Portuguese.

---

6 McBrierty and Zubair: *Ancient Civilisation: Modern Nation, p 23.*

7 Looking at the geographical setting of the town, it is difficult to see why Sohar was so prominent in medieval times. Ibn Hawqal, an Arab geographer of the 10th century, mentions it as "the most developed and wealthy town in Oman". John Wilkinson, in *The Imamate Tradition of Oman,* p44, stresses its prosperity, reaching its apogee in the 10th century. Perhaps, as Ian Skeet suggests (in *Muscat and Oman: The end of an era,* pp 64-65), it owed its position to a favourable situation near one of the main passes through the mountain range; or possibly the nearby *khūr* (inlet), now silted up, was formerly navigable. Sohar is now developing as a major port and industrial centre.

Regions of Oman
The reader will find in this book references to regions of Oman, as well as its cities and towns. These are shown in the maps, but some explanation may be useful. Some regions bear names according to points of the compass, for example Sharqiyah (Eastern), Shamaliyah (Northern) and Gharbiyah (Western). The names Dhāhirah and Bāṭinah reflect the physical shape of the country, meaning "back", or "spine", and "stomach" respectively – the spine being the Hajjar mountains and the stomach the coastal plain which runs North and West from Muscat. Dākhiliyah means "interior", and is the part of the country inland from the Hajjar mountains. Ja'alān is the flat desert plain south of Sūr inland from the Eastern coast, the area of the Bani Bu 'Ali and the Bani Bu Hasan (see chapter 6).

The East India Company, since its founding in 1600, was by now reasonably well established with trading posts on the West Coast of India, and it was from Surat (a port north of Bombay) that in 1646 they sent Philip Wylde to negotiate an agreement, the first of what was to be a long line of Treaties and other agreements between the Omanis and the British. Since it is not long, it is worth quoting in full:

Agreement and conditions of peace propounded by Philip Wylde ... to the people of Sohar, for them to keep, and observe, without breach.

1. That we may be granted and permitted free trade within the dominions of this kingdom, without prohibition of any commodity to be brought, bought or exported out of the kingdom: neither limitation, confining to a certain quality of merchandise: in lieu of which, being sold, to receive such coins as may stand with our liking; – carrying it where and whither we please.
2. That if any of our goods shall be stolen, the King shall be liable to make satisfaction.
3. That we shall pay no Custom for any Goods or Merchandise brought or imported out of the kingdom.

4. That no man shall engross to himself, in the way of merchandising such commodities as the English bring: - but that all Merchants, without exception, may have free liberty to buy, at such rates as they can agree for.

5. That we may have licence to exercise our own Religion.

6. That if any, it should so happen, broils and offences betwixt the English and these Country people: - the Governor of the same place shall punish the Mussulmen; and the Chief of the English shall do justice among his own people.

7. That the English shall be tolerated to wear the Arms ashore.

8. That no Christian shall have license, in any part of this kingdom, besides the English: – on which performance, they enjoin themselves to supply this Port, yearly, with Ship, or Ships, bringing such commodities as India, etc, adjacent ports, afford, suitable to what be demanded.

There are several interesting features in this agreement. First, it comes over as very informal, certainly by comparison with later similar texts. Second, we note a lack of precision in the parties to the agreement: it was of course known that Wylde was acting for the East India Company, but the text does not say so; and that side of the agreement seems to give obligations and rights to "the English" – the other party being "the people of Sohar". Overall, the freedoms given to the English traders seem very wide by modern comparison: a trading monopoly, freedom to practise their own religion, and jurisdiction over their own affairs. But such concessions were then common, and presumably served both sides' interests. The question of foreigners exercising self-jurisdiction, which later became a basis for much law and conduct in the Gulf, re-appeared nearly 200 years later, when the Omani Treaties with the USA and the UK included such clauses, in 1833 and 1839 respectively.

In 1650 a British ship, the *Fellowship*, called at Muscat, and the captain was offered "the best house in town" in the hope or expectation that the East India Company would set up a trading "factory", ie a store and office for commerce. A further advance for the English was registered when in 1659 Imam Sultan bin Saif negotiated a new treaty with the Company, represented by Colonel Henry Rainsford. The Company committed itself to providing a garrison of 100 soldiers, and to sharing the customs revenues with the Omanis, in return for being able to occupy one of the forts and for having a part of the town designated for their accommodation. However, Colonel Rainsford died soon after the conclusion of the negotiations. A renegotiation was required, and by the time a successor to Rainsford could be sent the Imam seems to have gone back on his undertakings. Possibly this was under pressure from the Dutch, who were themselves seeking to enhance their already strong trading position in India and the Gulf; or perhaps Sultan bin Saif, or his successors, had second thoughts about allowing new European settlements on Omani soil – which, in the light of their experience of the Portuguese, was understandable. The outcome was that the East India Company did not establish their factory in Muscat, although their ships called regularly there.

* * * * * * *

We may assume that a good number of British sailors and traders came to Muscat in this period on their way to and from India and Persia. Lorimer's account of the period suggests there was steady trade in the Gulf, especially in silk and woollen textiles.[8] Two writers in particular have left vivid accounts. One, John Ovington, was born in Yorkshire in 1653, and in April 1689 (he proudly records the date of sailing as being that of the coronation of King William III and Mary) embarked on an East India Company vessel *Benjamin*, as Chaplain. He spent a few years in Bombay and Surat, and returned to England in 1693. He records in detail the pattern of life – and high incidence of death and disease – in India, and also records favourable descriptions of the people of Muscat, laying stress on their abhorrence for alcohol. In one passage, as evidence of the gentle nature of the inhabitants of Muscat, he describes their method of capital punishment:

> "If murther or theft .. is .. committed, the Malefactor is never
> punished with sudden death, nor does any fatal hand touch
> him, but his Sentence is, to be Immur'd, where he leisurely

8 Lorimer, J G: *Gazetteer of the Persian Gulf, Oman and Central Arabia,*

dies, between two walls. For they hate by a violent direct Death, to take away the life of any Offender."

More congenial to modern taste is Ovington's general description of the Muscati character:

"These Arabians are very courteous in their Deportment, and extremely Civil to strangers; they offer neither Violence nor Affront to any; and tho' they are very tenacious in their own Principles, and admirers of their own Religion, yet do they never impose it upon any, nor are their Morals leven'd with such furious Zeal, as to divest them of Humanity and a tender Respect …. In fine these are a People naturally Temperate and Just, and imbued with those excellent Qualities which *Grecian* Philosophers and *Roman* Moralists endeavoured to inspire into their Subjects..."[9]

Those who have the privilege of knowing the present-day inhabitants of Muscat will say that these judgements remain valid over 300 years later.

It is possible that Ovington did not personally visit Muscat. His near-contemporary, the traveller Alexander Hamilton (see below), certainly thought he had not. The account of his voyage to and from India suggests that he crossed the Indian Ocean by the direct route from Mozambique and the Comoro Islands, without making landfall in Arabia.[10] Ovington's book gives an account of Mukha[11] and the Red Sea – neither of which he could have visited – in a style similar to that of his description of Muscat. Probably he noted down accounts heard orally from other sailors and traders, possibly including one Captain Edward Say, whose ship

---

9 Ovington, J: *A voyage to Surat*, London, 1696, pp 430 and 432. A modern edition, edited by H G Rawlinson, was published by Oxford University Press in 1929, in which these quotations are on pp 250-51.

10 The arguments for and against Ovington's having visited Muscat are set out in Alastair Hamilton's *An Arabian Utopia: The Western Discovery of Oman*, Oxford and London, 2011.

11 Also Mocca. Its extensive exports of coffee resulted in its name being used for the coffee-chocolate drink.

Merchant's Delight was ship-wrecked on the island of Masirah (nowadays a short ferry-ride from the coast between Duqm and Ras al-Hadd) in 1684. The Arabs living on the island helped Say and his crew-mates ashore, and Ovington gives a charming description of bargaining by mime and with props: gesturing to the rescued cargo, the Arabs made a pile of sand, and divided it into two, in the proportion 2:1 – which Say refused, insisting on equal shares. The deal was done, and half the cargo (but all the crew) were delivered to Muscat, the other half being retained as the price of rescue.

Our second writer was an East India Company sailor and trader: Alexander Hamilton, born in lowland Scotland in about 1668, travelled to India in 1688, and became captain of a small trading ship working for the Company out of Surat to the East Indies. Even less than Ovington does Hamilton record in his book[12] his own voyages and experiences: it is a handbook, not a diary. But it is clear that he has personally visited – probably more than once – the places of which he writes, including Muscat, Mukha and other ports. He tells the story of Say's shipwreck, with some differences (he claims to have known an interpreter who was on board, so no need for bargaining in sand-language), and describes the boats in which they were taken to Muscat as "Trankies (or barks without decks)" – perhaps some kind of dhow, although elsewhere Hamilton describes them as small rowing vessels. Hamilton's narrative is littered with humorous asides, many of them in a style that would now be unacceptable, since he cannot resist gentle mockery of groups such as priests, Roman Catholics and Muslims. But he was obviously taken by Muscat: he describes in terms which would still be accurate today the Muscat customs of hospitality:

> "... As soon as everyone is seated, a Servant brings a pot of coffee, and serves it about in small cups, that contain not a Quarter of a Gill; but as soon as one Cup is out, they fill again and perhaps a third Time. Then a Pipe of Tobacco is presented, their Pipes differing much from ours in Europe,

---

12 British Sea-Captain Alexander Hamilton's *A new account of the East Indies*, ed J Corfield and I Morson, 1727. The quotations are from the reprinted edition of 2001, Edwin Mellen Press, New York, USA.

in Shape and Magnitude, which service lasts till near the Time of breaking up company, when comes in a little pot of hot burning coals, on which they throw some chips of Agala-wood [agala or aloe], or some Powder of Benjoin, Myrrh or Frankincense, which produce a thick Smoke, that incenses or perfumes the whole Room. And, as I observed before, it is the Custom of wearing very great Sleeves to their Garments. They open their Sleeves as wide as they can, and hold them over the Smoke, which perfumes their Arms, Shoulder, neck and beard. And the last course is some Rose-water to besprinkle the company, which is the Signal to be gone every one about their Business; so, without any Forms of Ceremony, everyone walks off".

Hamilton sums up: "The Muskat Arabs are remarkable for their Humility and Urbanity", and justifies his assessment by giving a couple of examples he has witnessed of their civility and cool tempers.

In contrast to the inhabitants' coolness, these early British travellers do however – almost all – comment on Muscat's heat. Another writer of this period, John Fryer, a doctor and Fellow of the Royal Society who came to the region, described how he

"saw Muscat, whose vast and horrid Mountains no Shade but Heaven does hide, though they cover the City with a horrid one; reflecting thence the Heat scorching us at Sunsetting, and aboard ship; within their fiery Bosom the Pilots find secure Harbour for their weather-beaten ships"[13]

and Hamilton reports that from May to September "none appear on the Streets from 10 in the Morning till 3 or 4 after Noon", that "every Body lodges on the [roof terraces] in the Nights, for below Stairs they cannot sleep for the heat", and like Fryer he attributes the intense heat to the storage-heater qualities of the mountains that surround Muscat:

---

13 Fryer, J: *A New Account of East India and Persia, in eight letters*, 1698, quoted in Bidwell, R: *Travellers in Arabia*.

"the Sun heats [the mountains] to such a Degree, that between 10 and 11 in the Forenoon, I have seen the Slaves rost Fish on them. And the Horses and cattle, who are accustomed to that Food, come daily, of their own Accord, to be served their Allowance, and when they have breakfasted, retire again to Shades built for them, and yet their Beef and Mutton, that are partly nourished by that Sort of Food, have not the least Savour of Fish."

We shall see later how the heat and health hazards of Muscat affected British officials sent there on service.

Gwadar and Makran

Gwadar (or Gwadur) was for nearly 200 years an Omani enclave on the Makran coast, now in Pakistan, near the border with Iran. The first Omani connection with Gwadar was during the civil wars of the 18th century, when some al-Busaʻidi leaders took refuge there. Previously, men from Baluchistan – the mountainous area inland from the Makran Coast – had been recruited as mercenaries for Omani armies since the 1730s. In the 1780s, the local ruler conferred Gwadar (at that time an insignificant fishing village) on Sayyid Sultan bin Ahmad, then in exile there. When in 1792 he became Imam, Sultan bin Ahmad annexed Gwadar to Oman and sent Saif bin ʻAli with troops to govern it and build a fort.

The al-Busaʻidis did not always find it easy to maintain their control of Gwadar, which came under attack from the Qawasim, Afghanis and others. But the port prospered nevertheless. It became important to the British when they set about constructing the telegraph cable in the 1860s, and the Khan of Kalat – whose ancestor had ceded Gwadar to Sultan bin Ahmad – revived his claim to the place, hoping that the British Indian Government would do a deal favourable to himself. But the Government of India respected the ancient possession by the Sultan of Muscat; and in the end, but only after another Persian claim to the Makran Coast had been raised and then waived, the cable was laid. During this time, a British Agent was appointed there – Lt E C Ross, later Political Resident in Bushire. Gwadar remained under Omani sovereignty until 1958, when Sultan Saʻid bin Taymur sold it to Pakistan for £3 million.

CHAPTER 2

Civil war and emergence of the al-Busa'idis (18th century)

From this point forward – and it could perhaps be said even from Philip Wylde's Treaty – until well into the 20th century, the relationship between Britain and Oman (or, more accurately, the leaders variously in Muscat, Rustaq, and other towns and areas that make up the modern Sultanate) has to be seen through the perspective of Britain's interests in India, and the protection of trade in and out of Britain's Indian possessions. However, despite this being a period of often controversial British expansion in India, the relationship with Oman remained quiet. Reasons included prolonged periods of civil strife in Muscat and Oman, and priority given by the British to trade with Persia.

* * * * * *

While British trade with Persia flourished in the 18th century, largely due to demand for English woollens, the British relationship with Oman developed very little for more than 100 years after the contacts made by Wylde and Rainsford. On the Omani side, this can be attributed to the intervention of one of the turbulent periods that have marked their history. Mention has been made of the appeal made to Nasir bin Murshid to unite warring factions in the Batinah region in the early 17th century, and the success of his cousin Sultan bin Saif in ousting the Portuguese. Nasir and

Sultan were the first Imams of the Ya'ruba dynasty;[1] they and their immediate successors Bil'arab and Saif (both sons of Sultan), and Sultan (son of Saif),[2] not only united areas in the northern parts of the Batinah and Dhahirah, but also set the country on the path towards peace and prosperity; the two often go together. The Arab historian Salil ibn Razik records, in a celebrated passage about Imam Sultan bin Saif I (ruler 1649-1668), translated by the Rev George Percy Badger:[3]

> To sum up, Oman revived during his [Sultan bin Saif's] government and prospered: the people rested from their troubles, prices were low, the roads were safe, the merchants made large profits, and the crops were abundant. The Imam himself was humble towards his subjects, condoning their offences when such condonation was lawful, and never keeping himself aloof from them.

Sadly this idyllic picture was of short duration. Feuding broke out in the ruling family during the later stages of the reign of Sultan's son Bil'arab, perhaps presaging the more serious civil war which was to break out in the 1720s. The reigns of Saif bin Sultan (1692-1711) and his son Sultan bin Saif II (1711-1718) were successful for Oman: the struggle against the Portuguese was taken outwards to India and to East Africa, and the period marked the start of Oman's establishment as a naval force to be reckoned with. Hamilton (whose new *Account of the East Indies* was mentioned in the previous chapter) lists the impressive Omani fleet in 1715:

---

1 also spelt Yaaruba
2 See the list of Imams and Sultans, at Annex B; to the European reader the names are often confusing because of the Arab tendency to name sons after their grandfathers. Thus the sixth Imam of the Ya'ruba dynasty was Saif bin Sultan bin Saif bin Sultan.
3 Salil ibn Razik, tr Badger: *History of the Imams and Seyyids of Oman*, London 1871. A better transliteration of the author's name is Salīl bin Ruziq or Ruzayq. Badger was a member of the Commission mandated by Canning to resolve the dispute following the death of Sayyid Sa'id bin Sultan in 1856. See also the note on this book in the Notes for Further Reading, Annex A.

> ... one Ship of 74 Guns, two of 60, one of 50, and 18 small
> Ships from 32 to 12 Guns each, and some Trankies or
> rowing Vessels from 4 to 8 Guns each, with which Sea
> Forces they keep all the Sea-coasts in Aw, from *Cape
> Comorin*[4] to the Red Sea.

Despite the period of destructive civil war which followed during the
Imamate of Saif bin Sultan (actually several Imamates, since he was
elected, deposed and re-elected more than once), this naval strength was
destined to endure. It should be added that the end of the 17th and start
of the 18th centuries were also marked by increasing lawlessness at sea
in the region. Not only the Omanis, but also the Europeans, engaged in
privateering. Strictly speaking, this means the use of privately-owned
but publicly licensed warships cruising against an enemy in time of
declared war, but often such ships' captains were more interested in the
pursuit of their own personal or national trading interests, by force, even
in peacetime; and their activities amounted to nationalised piracy. In the
1690s, Whig political interests and the authorities in New York quietly
encouraged Anglo-American piracy including in the Indian Ocean, where
they based themselves in Madagascar or other islands, and preyed on
Indian shipping. This caused deep embarrassment to the East India
Company, who depended on the goodwill of "The Great Moghul" –
Aurangzeb, emperor of India – for their trading licenses.

To seek to reduce this, in 1698 the British, Dutch and French agreed
to police the Indian Ocean, the Red Sea and the Gulf respectively. The
arrangement was never properly implemented, but by 1701 it became
politically expedient and necessary to put down this kind of piracy, and
the menace seems to have faded away. A century later piracy in different
forms would engage the British in the Gulf up to their necks (see below,
chapter 5).

It may seem curious that the peaceful people described by Ovington
and Hamilton in the late 17th century should resort to bitter civil war
only 30 years later. It can perhaps be attributed to the weakness of
institutions, or the ambiguity surrounding what was expected of an Imam.
The strength of tribal loyalty may also have been a contributing factor,

---

4 at the Southern tip of India.

especially in the interior – whereas Ovington and Hamilton were commenting on the more cosmopolitan communities of coastal towns. Saif bin Sultan (sometimes referred to as Saif bin Sultan II, to distinguish him from his grandfather) was only 12 years old when his father died in 1718, and immediately there was dispute over whether one so young could be elected Imam. Disputes over power broke out first among the family, and then the civil war became a struggle between factions of the two main tribes, the Hinawi and the Ghafiri. Through to the 19th and 20th centuries we shall see outbreaks of rivalry and hostility between these tribal groups (see box below). This conflict continued through the 1720s and 1730s, including periods of a "split Imamate" – ie when there were two Imams, usually Saif bin Sultan and one other. Matters reached a crisis in the early 1730s, at the initiative of Saif bin Sultan, about whose abilities opinions differ. By some accounts, now mature and with political experience beyond his years he showed at this stage decisiveness and determination to bring the civil war to an end. He was also a fine horseman if we are to believe an anecdote of his having successfully tamed and ridden a powerful horse sent by Shah Nadir of Persia. In about 1730 Shah Nadir sent Saif a horse which the Persians themselves had not been able to ride, and challenged him to tame it. Saif had the horse saddled, and rode it at speed down Wadi Kabir near Muscat with stones flying in every direction from the horse's hooves. When he reached the gate of the city, the horse leapt the wall, and Saif jumped off, landing erect on the wall. Sadly the horse had broken its legs and died; but Saif became famous for his equestrian feat.[5]

5 The story is told graphically by Salil ibn Razik, in *History of the Imams and Seyyids of Oman*, pp 132-3.

Tribes in Oman

Oman's inhabitants today almost all live in cities, towns and villages; there are only very small numbers of bedu living a nomadic Arab life. Nevertheless, tribal feelings and loyalties remain strong, particularly in the interior of Oman, going back to the times when tribes from elsewhere in Arabia came to settle in this area. Tribal connections are inherited through the father's line but cemented by marriages that for centuries were contracted only within the tribe. Names sometimes reveal the tribe, though many Omanis use simply their own name, their father's name, and the family name. Tribal names, and some family names, are generally prefixed with al- . References to two major tribal groupings recur in this book: the Bani Hina ("sons of Hina", Hinais or Hinawis) and the Bani Ghāfir (Ghāfiris). The origins of these groupings are lost in early history, but it is generally thought that the Hinawis were the descendants of immigrants into Oman from Yemen and the south. They settled in the south-east of Oman, and were loyal to Ibadism. The Ghafiris were later arrivals, settled more in the north-west, and were more prone to embrace other Islamic movements, including Wahhabism (see Chapter 3). The rivalry between the Hinawis and Ghafiris reached a climax in the early 18th century, causing a civil war which engulfed almost every Omani tribe. Peace was brought to the country in 1749, but the competition simmered in the background. Later al-Busaʻidi rulers found that, to stay in power, they needed always to take account of the perpetual Hinawi-Ghafiri tension; and they were most threatened when, as in 1915, the two groups came together.

Those less sympathetic to Saif bin Sultan claim that he was an incompetent ruler, and also lost the allegiance of the stricter Ibadi adherents because of his reputation for immoral behaviour;[6] the Danish traveller Carsten Niebuhr records him as "a voluptuary, a lecher, and a smoker of tobacco".[7] Saif bin Sultan brought in mercenaries from the

6 Kelly, J B: *Britain and the Persian Gulf, 1795-1880*, Oxford 1968; p 9
7 Niebuhr, C: *Description de l'Arabie*, Copenhagen, 1773, p 258

Makran coast in Baluchistan, and then appealed to the Persians for assistance, to help him get the upper hand in the civil war. The Persians landed an army in Northern Oman. However – unfortunately for Saif – they did not satisfy themselves with assisting him defeat the latest contender for the Imamate, Bil'arab bin Himyar, but they occupied the Dhahirah region and imposed taxes. In 1742 the Persians extended their control, occupied Muscat and Matrah, and attacked Sohar. Here they came up against Ahmad bin Sa'id, who was commander of the fort and later became the founder of the al-Busa'idi dynasty. Following the deaths of both the legitimate and the alternate Imam, Saif bin Sultan and Sultan bin Murshid, Ahmad bin Sa'id led the resistance to the Persians on his own. After organising the murder of 50 Persian officers at a dinner in Barka, and then a wholesale massacre of the occupying force, Ahmad was elected Imam. His path was not initially smooth – the effects of the civil war took time and effort to dissipate – but he succeeded in imposing peace on the troubled nation; and, coming from a family with strong commercial and maritime interests on the east coast of Oman, he also maintained the tradition of maritime strength.

During this troubled period of the early-mid 18th century the annals reveal virtually no contact between the British and Oman. We have a record of a factor of the English Levant Company passing through Muscat in 1755, whose report suggests that eventually a high degree of law and order, and of prosperous trade, had by then come to benefit Oman:

> "There are at present such immense quantities of goods in this town that, as there are not warehouses to contain half of them, they are piled up in the streets, and lie night and day exposed, without any watch or guard, yet there never happens an instance that such goods are robbed, or even pilfered, of the least part."[8]

The East India Company established a brokerage in Muscat in about 1758, but the trade between the Gulf and India was being conducted by

8 Parsons, Abraham: *Travels in Asia and Africa*, London 1808, p 207

Arab, Persian and Indian traders; the Company probably saw little advantage in investing in engagement with a territory where inter-tribal strife was rampant, and over seas where piracy was an ever-present risk. The British Government and British Navy, preoccupied with internal politics, European wars and (later in the century) the War of American Independence, would not have given priority to sending envoys or ships to Oman or elsewhere on the southern side of the Gulf. Although ships of the Bombay Marine (the East India Company's naval force) were present to protect traders from India, no ship of the Royal Navy visited the Gulf before 1769, when the Bombay Government asked the Commander-in-Chief East Indies for help against the Ka'b tribe of Khuzistan and pirates operating from the Persian coast. On the Omani side, the early al-Busa'idi rulers seem to have wanted to maintain neutrality as between the French and the British, whose mutual aggression was becoming a growing feature of the scene in the Indian Ocean through the 18th century; and they turned down all requests for further European "factories" in their ports.

There was however some British attention to Persia, and the Gulf's north-eastern shores. This is relevant to the British relationship with Oman, because later the East India Company's representative in Bushire (now Bushehr, or in Arabic Abu Shahr, a port some 200 km WSW of Shiraz) became responsible for British dealings with Muscat. Back in 1619 East India Company representatives had set up a "factory" (trading post and depot) at the harbour of Jask, having landed a consignment of goods there in 1616, as well as inland at Shiraz and Isfahan. Their purpose was to find a market for English cloth, and also to buy Persian luxury products such as silk. They must have been a novelty in the region, being the first Europeans to establish themselves in the Gulf after the Portuguese – who had chosen the route of occupation rather than trade. The Persians had for some years been aiming to remove the Portuguese from the area. Shah Abbas forced them out of Bahrain in about 1602, and from Ras al-Khaimah in 1619-20. As we have seen, the English followed up their establishment at Jask by helping the Persians oust the Portuguese from Hormuz in 1622, and were allocated revenues in Gombroon, then renamed Bandar Abbas. These factories seem to have flourished, or at least maintained a steady trade, through the 17th century – despite the unpopularity of the place with sailors ("Only an inch of deal stands between Gombroon and Hell", as a naval saying had it) – a dislike that went back to the late 16th century, according to the merchant Ralph Fitch, who wrote: "The air you breath [sic] seems to be on fire; mortal vapours continually exhale from the bowels of the earth; the fields are black and dry as if they had been scorched with fire".[9] The factories nevertheless came to be considered by the Persians as quasi-official British representatives; and in 1699 the Shah is reported to have made a formal visit to the factory in Isfahan.

Conditions worsened between 1700 and 1760, due to the difficulties of trading in the chaotic environment resulting from the fading of the Safavid dynasty and the ensuing invasions of Persia by Afghans and Turks. Other discouraging elements were the extortions of local officials and attacks on shipping by pirates. The Isfahan factory had to be closed down, and then – in a rare extension to the Gulf of hostilities in the Seven Years War (1756-63) – the French destroyed the factory at Bandar Abbas, in 1759. The East India Company decided to make Bushire its headquarters in the Gulf. Despite a break from 1770-73, when Basra (often referred to in contemporary writing as Bussora) became a temporary headquarters, Bushire was from then on – in Curzon's words – "the principal British centre, both commercial and political, in the Persian Gulf". This remained the case right until the opening of the British Residency in Bahrain, and the transfer of the Bushire duties to the Resident there, in 1946. Through the years, arrangements changed with changing political circumstances: the Bushire office was a "Residency" of the East India Company when it opened in 1763, it continued under that name when its Residents were appointed by the Governor of Bombay and later the Governor-General and then Viceroy, for a time it was both Political Residency and Consulate-General, and it became a Consulate with the changes in 1946. We shall later see how the personality of the Resident in Bushire was important for the conduct and development of relations between Britain and Oman, since the Political Agent in Muscat, while ultimately responsible to senior officials in India, reported to Bushire in the first instance.

9 Fitch: *The Voyage of Ralph Fitch by way of Tripolis in Syria,* London, 1598, p 106; quoted in *British Missions around the Gulf,* p 61, drawing on Curzon: *Persia,* vol 2, p 421

Bushire had been developed by Persian rulers as a naval base as well as commercial centre. But British writers of the time found it far from attractive, whatever its acknowledged importance. Wellsted, an officer of the Bombay Marine writes of "the dust, the dirt, the wretchedness which its narrow streets expose to view", and of the contrast with the "richness and verdure" of India;[10] and the trader-traveller James Silk Buckingham, visiting in1816, has some uncomplimentary remarks about the inhabitants: "a disagreeable mixture of the Arab and the Persian, in which, whatever is amiable in either character seems totally rejected, and whatever is vicious in both is retained and even cherished".[11]

It was not only the prospects of trade with Persia which drew the East India Company to man these uncomfortable and unpopular places in the Gulf. Increasingly the route though Syria, known as the "desert" or "direct" route – in contrast to the usual passage by sea round the Cape – had become important as a way of travelling to and from India, and of communicating between London and the growing number of settlements first on the West coast (eg Surat and Bombay) and then on the East (centred on Madras and Calcutta, now Chennai and Kolkuta). The agent in Basra played an important part in arranging couriers for mail, which went overland via Aleppo in Northern Syria, Baghdad and Constantinople, and would also help Company employees who chose this route for travel home. The whole journey between Bombay and London took 10-12 weeks. As far back as the 1640s the English had traded with "Turkish Arabia", meaning present-day Iraq, over which the Ottoman Empire claimed suzerainty, and the East India Company set up a factory there in 1723. When the Bandar Abbas factory was closed in 1763, the office at Basra became an Agency, and controlled all the Company's trade in the Gulf; and in 1764 the Ottoman administration (often referred to as "the Porte"[12]) recognised it as a Consulate. Basra was by this time an important trading port. Niebuhr, writing of his visit

---

10 Wellsted, J: *Travels to the City of the Caliphs,* London, 1840, Vol 1, p 130-1

11 Buckingham, J S: *Travels in Assyria, Media and Persia*, London, 1829; vol 2, pp 108-9

12 An abbreviation of "the Sublime Porte", the conventional translation of the Arabic *al-bāb al-a'lā*, Turkish *Babiâli*, a reference to the "high gate" of the palace where justice in the Sultan's court was administered.

there in 1765, thought it the dirtiest and most insanitary town he had seen. But Abraham Parsons, who was there a little later, describes it as "the grand mart for the produce of India and Persia, Constantinople, Aleppo and Damascus"[13] and quantities of goods were traded there to and from India. Basra was struck by an onset of bubonic plague in 1773, and was occupied by the Persians, 1776-79; and from then on its place as a primary trading hub was taken by Bushire, Bahrain and Muscat.

Later in the century the route through Egypt became the preferred one. Leaders in India, such as Warren Hastings (who became Governor General in 1772), were keen to develop trade between Egypt and India, and on the back of that developed the most rapid route, through Suez, of sending despatches and mail to and from India and London.

One other product and its trade route developed in Arabia at this period; this was coffee. Planting and cultivation of coffee had been extended in Yemen, which may have been the original source of the plant, in the 15th and 16th centuries, and the drink had become popular in Europe in the 17th. The Dutch realised the commercial importance of this and took the plant to their colonies in South-East Asia (where it became particularly successful in Java), while the French laid the foundations for the American coffee trade through a cutting taken to Martinique. It seems to have been merchants from Turkey who made the drink popular in London, where coffee-houses became so fashionable as gathering-places for political gossip that King Charles II tried to suppress them by a decree issued in 1675. The plantations were mainly on Yemeni mountain slopes, notably at Bait al-Faqih (nicknamed "Beetlefuck" by East India Company officials), about 50 km from the modern port of Hodeida, and about 150km from the port of Mukha (Mocca) which was then used for the export of coffee, and which has given its name to a flavouring of mixed coffee and chocolate. The coffee trade seems to have had its ups and downs, with Arabian (ie Yemeni) coffee meeting stiff competition in the European market from coffee grown in the West Indies and South East Asia. English merchants lived and traded in Mukha, and market conditions forced them in the 18th century to ship the product to India, some of it through markets in Muscat.

13 Parsons, Abraham: *Travels in Asia*, p 154

Nowadays the coffee plantations have given way to the more easily cultivated mild narcotic known as *qat*, consumed mainly within Yemen itself; and so, sadly, a valuable export cash crop has virtually disappeared.

At the end of the 18th century the outlook for the British in Oman, and indeed in the rest of the Gulf, was not promising. There was no obvious reason to build on the opening made by Philip Wylde in 1659. East India Company trade had dropped back for a number of reasons, including that of trading competition in Persia from the Russians. Indeed, with trade on its own account having fallen, much of the Company's raison d'être in the Gulf, and the maintenance of its Residency and Agencies, lay in the protection of ships trading to and from India – a few of these ships owned and run by British merchants, but most of them by Persians, Armenians, Arabs and of course Indians. But any idea that the Company, or the British Government, could turn its back on the area would soon be dispelled: political, strategic, commercial and security factors would converge as the century went on, to lead to a prolonged period of intense interest and involvement.

CHAPTER 3

French-British rivalry (1750-1800)

The world had been changing, if imperceptibly, for Muscat and Oman in the last quarter of the 18th century. The factors that played a part in producing a changed relationship for the British and the Omanis included the increasing importance of India in the British global perspective, the growing rivalry between the British and the French in the Middle East and the Indian Ocean, the need to counter the rise of piracy, and Muscat's need to defend itself against attack from the Wahhabis from Central Arabia. Later would be added a fifth element: the British determination to end the slave trade, and the institution of slavery, in countries and oceans where they had power or influence.[1]

* * * * * * *

The French Connection

While the Portuguese invaded and occupied, and the British and Dutch traded, the French began their involvement in the Gulf with an ecclesiastical appointment – that of the exotic-sounding Latin Bishop of Babylon in 1638. They maintained a religious representative in Basra, who often acted as French Consul; and when the consul at Basra became a lay appointment in about 1740, a Carmelite priest was appointed as French consul in Baghdad, simultaneously holding the revived post of Latin Bishop of Babylon. The French established a Resident in Basra in 1755, but their trade shrank to virtually nothing by the end of the century.

1 For more detail on events covered in this chapter, see: J B Kelly: *Britain and the Persian Gulf, 1795-1880;* and R Coupland: *East Africa and its Invaders.*

Further south, however, in the Indian Ocean, the French were pushing hard to consolidate and expand their trading and strategic position. In 1662 they had established a colony on Réunion (then named Bourbon), and in 1715 they had occupied Mauritius (then Île de France) – the two principal islands in the Mascarenes group, named after a Portuguese explorer and lying about 500 miles east of Madagascar. They established a lively business in spices, sugar and other exports based on slave-labour plantations. Trading in slaves became important to the economy of both Île de France and Bourbon. In 1735 the French Governor of Île de France, Vicomte de la Bourdonnais, took steps to revive the slave trade which the Dutch had started with Madagascar and Mozambique, in order to ensure a steady flow of new slaves for the plantations, the surplus to go to the West Indies. But Bourdonnais was really concerned to strengthen Île de France as a fortress and naval base for action against the British in the Indian Ocean. In 1746 he took a fleet to the Bay of Bengal, fought an indecisive sea battle against an English squadron, and later forced Madras into surrender. But he became the victim of politics in France, and of the weather in India (some of his ships were wrecked by monsoon winds), and was recalled.

The Mascarene Islands

The Mascarenes are a group of islands east of Madagascar, named after the 16th century Portuguese navigator Pedro de Mascarenhas. The Portuguese claimed the whole group during the 16th century, and used them as ports of call for reprovisioning on their eastern trade routes. The main two islands are now Mauritius (an independent republic) and Réunion (an overseas department of France). The Dutch occupied Mauritius in 1598, giving it that name after Maurice of Nassau, then chief magistrate of the Netherlands. The Dutch left in 1710, and the French took possession of the group of islands in 1715, naming the largest two Île de France and Bourbon. In 1793 the French Revolutionary leadership renamed Bourbon as Réunion. The British gained control over the islands during the Napoleonic wars in the early 19th century, but in 1815 returned Réunion to the French, keeping Île de France but giving it back its earlier Dutch name. On both islands the cultivation of sugar, as well as spices, was widespread in the 19th century. Mauritius gained independence from the British in 1968; Réunion became an Overseas Department of France in 1946.

Competition between the British and the French turned to confrontation, and then took the form of active hostilities during the Seven Years War of 1756-63, when they fought for colonial supremacy in Canada and India, as well as fighting in the West Indies and elsewhere. Clashes in the Indian Ocean were bound to involve Oman sooner or later. As we have seen, British trading with Oman was at a negligible level at this time, although we must assume that East India Company ships sailing to and from India would have used Omani ports for water, provisions and shelter, as they passed the coast on the way either to agencies in Basra and Bushire, to the Red Sea, or to the Cape. The French were interested in attacking shipping on any of these routes.

Omani rulers at this time, emerging from the civil war, preferred to maintain neutrality as between the two major European powers; but this luxury proved in the end to be unsustainable. They seem to have given some limited privileges to the French, probably under the influence of those in Oman who valued the trade from Île de France, since exporters from the Mascarenes found in Muscat a ready market for their sugar and other plantation products. The outcome was that French privateers were able to use Muscat as a base for attacking British shipping in the Indian Ocean through the period of the British wars with France. But in 1759 they pushed their luck, by attempting such hostilities too far inshore: when French privateers attacked a British merchant ship taking shelter at Muscat, the Omani forts opened fire and drove them off. Other similar incidents occurred in 1778 and 1781; and the outcome of the second was the capture by French privateers of an Omani ship, the *Saleh*, and then Omani counter-capture of a French vessel, *La Philippine*. The incident ended with the return of *La Philippine*, accompanied by a stiff protest from the ruler in Muscat, Sayyid Ḥamad bin Saʻid, to the Governor of Île de France. Sayyid Hamad could have taken things further, for example by banning French ships from Muscat; he may have exercised restraint because of those Omani trading interests with Île de France.

Lord Nelson at Muscat

In 1999 or 2000, Sir Ivan Callan (then British Ambassador in Muscat) did some research into the question of Admiral Lord Nelson and Muscat. It was believed that HMS *Seahorse*, on which Nelson served as a midshipman in the 1770s, had visited Muscat, in the course of the growing interest that Britain had at that time in protecting the trade route to India from the depredations of the French and of local pirates. Sir Ivan asked if it could be checked on the ship's log. It could, and it was. The outcome was proof that *Seahorse* had indeed called at Muscat, and during the time when Nelson served in her. This was in July 1775, when the frigate – of 20 guns, commanded by Captain Farmer – anchored at Muscat while sailing to/from Bushire, and stayed for two months. (HMS *Seahorse*, or a successor ship of the same name, was incidentally Nelson's flagship at the attack on Santa Cruz in the Canary Islands in 1797.)

This corroborated the story told in Jan (then James) Morris's book "Sultan in Oman", a finely-written account of the journey by Sultan Sa'id bin Taymur, the present Sultan's father, from Salalah in Dhofar through the interior all the way to Muscat, in 1955. In this short extract, Morris is talking to Sultan Sa'id about the ships' names painted on the rocks above Muscat harbour along from Fort Jalali.

"I liked the inscriptions, for they reminded me of the Greek travellers who carved comments upon the Colossi of Memnos at Thebes,…; and anyway an honest British naval name never disfigured anything. The Sultan liked them too. He called the anchorage "my visitors' book". When I mentioned my sympathy for the midshipmen who had climbed those rugged rocks in the heat of the Muscat sun, the Sultan told me that Nelson had visited Muscat as a midshipman in 1775 and spent two months there… Who could know? Perhaps Nelson had himself climbed the rock to record the name of HMS *Seahorse*. He was "stout and athletic" then, according to his biographer Southey, and would have been admirable for the job."

We cannot tell how Sultan Sa'id had this information about Nelson, Seahorse, and the date of 1775. But all three are noted in a brief reference (page 274) in *The Countries and Tribes of the Persian Gulf*, the masterly account – with considerable focus on Oman – by S B Miles, who was Agent in Muscat, 1872-1886. His book, one of very few then written about Oman and the Gulf, was published posthumously by his widow in 1919, and would have been accessible to Sultan Sa'id.

French interest in recovering their weakened position in India after the disastrous outcome of the Seven Years War continued both before and after the Revolution in 1789. Manifestations of this included suggestions for a French-Persian alliance, investigations on routes to India through Egypt and Iraq, a treaty actually concluded by the French in 1785 with the Mamluks in Cairo, and a successful French request to Sayyid Hamad bin Sa'id for permission to set up a "factory" in Oman. No other European nation secured this concession at this time. However, the French did not exercise this right, and two years later, in 1787, British officers calling at Muscat were assured that the Omanis – still maintaining what neutrality they could – were keeping in force the ban on all European factories. In a further attempt to woo Sayyid Hamad, after the *contretemps* over *La Philippine*, in 1790 the French presented the Ruler with a ship, and secured the additional concession of a welcome for the appointment of a French Consul, plus the assurance that his hosts would pay for his office. But there were slips twixt cup and lip: although in 1795 the Committee of Public Safety appointed M. Beauchamp, a scientist and traveller, as Consul, there were problems about his taking up the post (see p 39 below).

The British watched carefully. At the strategic level, losing the American War of Independence (1783) caused policy-makers to look more to the East than the West for the gains of empire. At the same time, and reflecting the developments in public opinion towards the governance of India – exemplified in the India Act which Pitt navigated through parliament in 1784 – the British public mood was in favour of consolidating and improving government in the wide areas already under British control, rather than in targetting new conquests. There was also a feeling that British representatives should hold back from involvement with "native princes". In this atmosphere, maintaining good and safe communications with India both by sea (round the Cape, and across the Indian Ocean) and by the "overland route" (now via Egypt) was vital. At about this time, administrators and traders in both Bombay and Calcutta became interested in links between India and Egypt, satisfying the needs of both commerce and communication.

In the early 1790s, and despite the al-Busa'idi rulers' neutrality, the Bombay Government managed to secure permission for an Indian broker to be stationed at Muscat to arrange for the East India Company's mails and goods to be forwarded. They won this concession in exchange for permission granted by the British Government of Bengal to allow limited imports of salt by ships from Muscat.

At this time too, the British noted with concern that Omani traders to Île de France were carrying intelligence about movements of British ships. This Omani trade in any case amounted to breaking a blockade of the Mascarenes currently being attempted by the British. No doubt worried – with good reason, as it turned out – that French designs on Egypt were aimed at creating a base for renewed and more serious aggression against the British presence in India, the Bombay Government decided to check out the Omani position. In 1796 the Governor sent a message to the Ruler, Sayyid Sultān bin Aḥmad, asking about his attitude to the East India Company and to the French. Sultan bin Ahmad's reply is a superb example of diplomatic language of the era:

> "As from former times the chain of friendship and amity
> has been so firmly established between our Sirkars[2] that by
> the blessing of God as long as breath remains in the body
> the garden of love and unanimity will be kept afresh by the
> water of affection and sincerity. For this reason the friends
> of the Hon'ble Company are mine and their enemies mine."[3]

2 A word from Persian via Urdu meaning originally "court" or "palace", and then "state" or "government".
3 State Papers, Bombay; quoted by Kelly in *Britain and the Persian Gulf,* p66

In 1797 the idea of an eastward invasion, for some years germinating in French minds, took reality. Talleyrand, appointed Foreign Minister in September that year, believed that Egypt offered France "the means of ousting the English from India by sending a body of 15,000 troops from Cairo by way of Suez",[4] consciously or unconsciously following up an idea which Magallon, the French consul in Cairo, had reported two years previously to the Directory (the revolutionary cabinet in Paris). Magallon had even submitted a schedule for conveying an army to India – Muscat being an essential element in the plan. Napoleon picked up the ball and ran with it: in July 1798 he landed at Cairo with his Army of the East – and, it should be added, a smaller but considerable army of scientists.

Since much has been written of Napoleon's expedition to Egypt, and its lasting effect there in terms of French influence and culture, despite its short duration, there is no need to do more here than to summarise. Within a few weeks of landing, Napoleon's army had broken the power of the Mamluk rulers of Egypt, and set about reforming the country on French models. But the real purpose of the invasion was not to secure the control of Egypt for its own sake: before setting out, Napoleon had said, "To ruin England utterly we must seize Egypt; through Egypt we come in touch with India",[5] and once secure there he set about putting in place the pieces necessary to support the move to the East. As well as writing to the Sharif of Mecca to declare his friendship, he informed the Governor of Île de France, Malartic, of the stationing of two French garrisons in Egypt, at Suez and Cosseir (now al-Qusayr, on the Red Sea coast about 100 miles south of Ghurdaqa). Malartic, quick on cue, sent Sayyid Sultan bin Ahmad a useful present of artillery and ammunition.

The British response

Napoleon's position in Egypt soon turned shaky, notably after his lines of supply from France and his means of communication were shut off as a result of Nelson's heavy defeat of the French fleet off Abu Qir, at the Battle of the Nile, in August 1798, just a month after the French landing. But Napoleon's occupation of Egypt was of high concern to the British in India, whose forces were under heavy pressure – from engagements

4 Quoted by Coupland, in *East Africa and its invaders*, p 87
5 Quoted by Coupland: *East Africa and its invaders*, p 88

with Tippoo Sultan in South India, defence against Afghans in the north-west, and the naval blockade of the Mascarenes in the Southern Indian Ocean (above, p 32). So it was not surprising that Jonathan Duncan, the Governor of Bombay, thought this a good moment to test Sayyid Sultan's assurances of "the garden of love and unanimity". In September 1798, Duncan instructed Mehdi Ali Khan, a Persian employee of the East India Company who had just been appointed Resident at Bushire, to call in at Muscat en route to taking up his post. Mehdi Ali Khan was to request Sayyid Sultan bin Ahmad to exclude the French and the Dutch (then French allies) from his territories while the war continued, and to give permission for an East India Company "factory" in Muscat. He was also to find out if it was true that the Ruler had a French doctor in attendance on him; and, if it were the case, to request Sayyid Sultan to get rid of him and take "a regular bred surgeon" in his place.

Mehdi Ali Khan fulfilled his commission completely. He was received by Sayyid Sultan on a number of occasions over a few days, and secured his agreement to signature of a written engagement known as a *qawlnamah* (from a Persian word meaning "written promise"), whose picturesque text ran as follows:

Translation of the Cowlnamah, or Written Engagement from the Imam of Muscat – 1798

Deed of Agreement from the State of the Omanian Asylum, under the approbation of the Imam, the Director, Syud Sultan, whose grandeur be eternal! to the High and Potent English Company, whose greatness be perpetuated! as comprehended in the following Articles:

Article 1
From the intervention of the Nawab Etmandi Edowla Mirza Mehedy Ally Khan Bahadoor Hurhmut Jung never shall there be any deviation from this Cowlnamah.

Article 2
From the recital of the said Nawab my heart has become disposed to an increase of the friendship with that state, and from this day forth the friend of that Sircar is the friend of

this, and the friend of [this][6] Sircar is to be the friend of that; and, in like manner, the enemy of that Sircar is the enemy of this, and the enemy of this is to be the enemy of that.

Article 3

Whereas frequent applications have been made, and are still making, by the Dutch and French people for a Factory, i.e. to seat themselves in either at Maskat or Goombroom, or at the other ports of this Sircar, it is therefore written that, whilst warfare shall continue between the English Company and them, never shall, from respect to the Company's friendship, be given to them throughout all my territories a place to fix or seat themselves in, nor shall they even get ground to stand upon within this State.

Article 4

As there is a person of the French nation, who has been for these several years in my service, and who hath now gone in command of one of my vessels to the Mauritius, I shall, immediately on his return, dismiss him from my service and expel him.

Article 5

In the event of any French vessel coming to water at Muscat, she shall not be allowed to enter the cove into which the English vessels are admitted, but remain without; and in case of hostilities ensuing here between the French and English ships, the force of this State by land and by sea, and all my people, shall take part in hostility with the English, but on the high seas I am not to interfere.

Article 6

On the occurrence of any shipwreck of a vessel or vessels pertaining to the English, there shall certainly be aid and

---

6 Aitchison's text gives "the".

comfort afforded on the part of this Government, nor shall the property be seized on.

Article 7
In the port of Abassy (Goombroom) whenever the English shall be disposed to establish a Factory, I have no objection to their fortifying the same and mounting guns thereon, as many as they list, and to forty or fifty English gentlemen residing there, with seven or eight hundred English Sepoys, and for the rest, the rate of duties on goods on buying and selling will be on the same footing as at Bussora and Abushehr.

Dated 1st of Jenmadee-ul-Awal 1213 Hegira, or 12th of October 1798

From Article 3 we note that Sayyid Sultan could agree to prohibit the French and the Dutch from establishing a "factory"; but at the same time was not prepared to grant the English that privilege – at least (so the reports of the negotiations show) not unless the East India Company were prepared to enter into a kind of defence pact with Oman, to protect Muscat itself, and its shipping, against the French. Article 7, however, allows the Company to set up a factory at Bandar Abbas ("Goombroom"), which was now under Sayyid Sultan's control. In 1794 he had led an expedition against the Bani Ma'in, the Arab tribe who ruled the islands of Hormuz and Qishm (on the straits separating the Gulf from the Indian Ocean) and controlled Bandar Abbas, which they leased from the Persians. Sayyid Sultan had a new *firman*, or decree, issued, transferring the lease to him. In fact, the East India Company might have claimed that no new article in a *qawlnamah* was necessary to give them the right to have a factory at Bandar Abbas, since Persian *firmans* had been issued in their favour to this effect going back to 1622, and the transfer of the lease should not have affected this right. Nevertheless, Mehdi Ali Khan clearly thought it useful to have it enshrined in the new document, with the new lessee.

Other points in the *qawlnamah* are worth noting. Article 4 must be a reference to the French doctor mentioned above, which turned out to be significant when the first British agent in Muscat was appointed. Having the right people in close contact with the Ruler has been consistently important in relations with Oman. Note also the implications of Article 5: Sayyid Sultan engages himself to assist the Company's ships close inshore, but not to "interfere" on the high seas; and English ships are allowed into a special "cove" – presumably better sheltered, or more easily defended – where the French are not. Article 6 may reflect a concern of the Company's during the 1790s, when goods stolen or captured from British ships seem to have been traded in the Muscat market.

Not recorded in the *qawlnamah*, but apparently important to Sayyid Sultan, were two demands that he made as recompense for his assistance against the French and Dutch. He requested that his ships be given wood and water, without charge, when in Bombay and Calcutta, the East India Company's ships receiving this treatment when provisioning at Muscat. He also asked for an increase in the quantity of salt that Omani ships could land at Calcutta, from 1000 maunds annually to 5000. (A maund was equivalent to about 37kg or 82 lb.) This had for some time been a significant Omani trading interest – it had played a part in the establishment of the Indian broker's residence in Muscat granted in the early 1790s.

Overall, the signature of the 1798 *qawlnamah* represented a significant shift on the part of Sayyid Sultan. He had moved over from a position of stated neutrality (but actual favouritism towards the French) to a firm placement of his eggs in the British basket. The reasons for the turn-around are not clear. J W Kaye, the biographer of Sir John Malcolm (who negotiated the 1800 Treaty, see below), writing in 1856, believed that it was due to the French having "lately captured one of his vessels"; but if this was a reference to the incident of the *Saleh* and *La Philippine*, in 1781, the timing hardly fits, and there is no evidence of such naval hostilities with the French in the 1790s. It is more likely that Sayyid Sultan took note of the growth in British naval power, evidenced by their victory at the Battle of the Nile in 1798, and reckoned that he could achieve a stronger alliance and better protection from the British than he could from the French.

* * * * * * *

When Sayyid Sultan signed his *Qawlnamah* with Mehdi Ali Khan, Napoleon was still in Egypt, and planning his next move eastwards. In January 1799 he wrote a letter to Sayyid Sultan:

> À l'imam de Muscat
> Je vous écris cette lettre pour vous faire connaître ce que vous avez déjà appris sans doute, l'arrivée de l'armée francaise en Égypte. Comme vous avez été de tout temps notre ami, vous devez être convaincu du désir que j'ai de protéger tous les bâtiments de votre nation et que vous engagiez à venir à Suez, où ils trouveront protection pour le commerce. Je vous prie aussi de faire parvenir cette lettre à Tippo-Saib par la première occasion qui se trouvera pour les Indes.
>
> BONAPARTE
>
> (Author's translation:)
> To the Imam of Muscat
> I am writing to let you know what you have doubtless already learnt, the arrival of the French Army in Egypt. Since you have always been our friend, you must be aware of my wish to protect your nation's vessels, and that you should commit yourself to coming to Suez, where your ships will be given protection for trade. I ask also that you arrange to have the enclosed letter delivered to Tippoo Sahib at the first occasion possible for the Indies [ie when transport to India is first available].[7]

Tippoo Sahib, also known as Tippoo or Tipu Sultan, the Muslim ruler of Mysore, was at war with British forces in Southern India. In his letter to Tippoo, Napoleon refers to his army then in Egypt as being "filled with the desire to deliver you from the iron yoke of England", and invites Tippoo to send a representative to meet with him at Suez.

---

7 Both this and the letter to Tippoo Sultan are quoted by Coupland in *East Africa and its Invaders,* p 89

However, neither of these letters reached the addressees. The original plan was for Beauchamp, who had been appointed French Consul in Muscat in 1795 but had not yet taken up his post, to deliver the letter to Sayyid Sultan. But he was sent on a mission to Constantinople (where he was arrested and imprisoned), and the letters were sent by less secure means – and were intercepted, as bad luck would have it, by a British agent at Mukha. No doubt readers in Bombay and London scanned them with glee – tempered with concern at this evidence of contact between the French and Sayyid Sultan. In addition, Sultan was known to be in touch with Tippoo Sultan, still the enemy of the British. In the event, Napoleon's failure to establish personal contact with Sayyid Sultan bin Ahmad and with Tippoo Sultan may not have mattered substantially, since the Egyptian expedition packed up in failure late in 1799, and Napoleon himself returned to France. But the whole episode was far from reassuring to the British Governor and his staff in Bombay, who watched carefully to see if Sayyid Sultan was standing by his commitments in the 1798 *Qawlnamah*.

And they were not entirely satisfied. Reports reached India of signs of wavering on Sayyid Sultan's part. By now the system of government in India had become more formalised, with a Governor-General operating from Calcutta. For a while, the Calcutta headquarters had effectively taken over responsibility for Gulf and Arab affairs from the Governor's office in Bombay. Richard Wellesley[8] took up his post as Governor-General in May 1798, and quite soon became involved in Persian and Arab diplomacy. Towards the end of 1799 Wellesley judged it necessary to despatch a senior officer to the court of the Shah of Persia, Fath Ali Shah, in Tehran. The objectives of this mission were complex: they were to persuade the Shah to engage in diversionary activities in Western Afghanistan that would both help him, the Shah, recover some lost territory from the Afghan ruler Zaman Shah, and prevent Zaman Shah from persisting in hostile incursions into Northern India. In instructing the envoy, Wellesley thought it sensible to include orders to reinforce the 1798 *qawlnamah* with Sayyid Sultan in Muscat, to remind Sayyid Sultan

---

8 Wellesley, the older brother of Arthur Wellesley who later became Duke of Wellington, had by this time succeeded his father as Earl of Mornington, but is generally referred to as Wellesley in historical writing about the period.

of the obligations he had entered into, and to point up – to the Shah as well as to Sayyid Sultan – the advantages of sticking with the British as allies rather than incline towards the French. As an additional issue, of lesser importance, the British also wanted Sayyid Sultan to patch up his quarrel with Sulaiman Pasha of Baghdad, an irritant to the British Indian authorities because of their alliance with the Ottoman Turkish Government in Istanbul. After all, according to the *qawlnamah* the friends of one state were to be the friends of the other.

The envoy chosen for this mission was John Malcolm, who at the time held the rank of Captain and was stationed in Hyderabad. Later he undertook further missions to Persia, was knighted, and became Governor of Bombay. Wellesley gave "Boy Malcolm", as he was nicknamed, careful instructions. The part of them which touched on the French – ie to persuade the Shah to obstruct any French effort to get to India through Persia or the Persian Gulf – came in second place after matters concerning India's freedom from attack by Zaman Shah, and building a commercial relationship between Persia and India. And it was clearly the aim to impress the Shah with British India's power and wealth: Malcolm had with him six British officers, 100 sepoys,[9] and other support staff making a total of 500 in his entourage.

Malcolm left Bombay at the end of December 1799, and arrived in Muscat on 8 January 1800. Sayyid Sultan was in the Gulf, perhaps near the Straits of Hormuz, in action against pirates. In an account based on Malcolm's journal, his biographer Kaye records his meeting with the Governor of Muscat, who himself knew British India well – he had visited Bombay 16 times and Calcutta once. Malcolm painted a graphic picture of British strength and French weakness, and the pointlessness of Omani attempts to pursue their trading interests in the region without British support. Malcolm's journal may have been self-serving, since he would have needed to carry back forceful accounts of his mission to impress his superiors in Bombay and Calcutta. In addition, through a biographer's admiration of his subject, Kaye may have chosen to add colour to the narrative; but nevertheless the description comes over powerfully:

9 An Indian soldier under British command, from an Urdu word meaning "horseman" or "soldier".

"[Malcolm] told them how we had beaten the French in the East; how we had deprived them of all their possessions there except the Mauritius, "an unproductive island and no object of conquest"; and how the Dutch had lost almost everything in Asia, except Batavia,[10] where they were shut up by their apprehension of the English cruisers. Then he told them how the French "seized upon Egypt .."; .. "By [God's] mercy, " added Malcolm, "the French have sustained such signal defeats that the miserable remnants of their army are now anxious only for a safe retreat from Egypt." Then he spoke of the great victories we had achieved in Mysore ...; how the reduction of Tippoo's power placed us in possession of the whole coast of Malabar, and how, with the exception of the islands of Ceylon, Malacca and Amboyna, there was not a port from Surat to Calcutta in which a vessel could anchor without the consent of the English. What then, he asked, was to become of the famed commerce of Muscat if the harbours of the whole Indian peninsula were to be closed against the merchant-ships of Muscat by the fiat of the paramount power?"[11]

Malcolm sailed on into the Gulf, and caught up with Sayyid Sultan off Hanjam Island (itself off Qishm Island) on 17 or 18 January 1800. Again Malcolm is reported to have given full reign to his rhetoric; and this time Kaye records his interlocutor's response, in words and body language:

"Then Malcolm spoke of the regret with which the Governor-General had perceived the recent disposition of the Imaum to league himself with the French, and expressed a hope that he was now convinced that it was his true policy to enter into and observe such covenants with the English Government as would tend not only to the political security but to the commercial prosperity of the country under his

10 now Jakarta
11 Kaye, J W: *Life of Sir John Malcolm*, Vol 1, pp 107-8

rule. And to this end he proposed to establish at Muscat an English gentleman of respectability as the agent of the East India Company. Malcolm paused, and the Imaum asked if he had anything else to request. Receiving an answer in the negative, the Arab placed his hand upon his head, and then on his breast, and said that he consented to the proposal from his head and his heart; that he was willing to sign and seal the agreement at once, and would be equally willing if it stipulated the establishment of a thousand gentlemen instead of one at Muscat."[12]

Either then (according to some accounts), or previously while in Muscat (as Kaye relates), Malcolm arranged for the placing of the person intended for the post of "English gentleman of respectability: Surgeon Archibald Bogle, from the medical establishment in Bombay – who could therefore conveniently fill the bill of being "a regular bred surgeon", as Jonathan Duncan, Governor of Bombay, had suggested to Mehdi Ali Khan at the time of the 1798 *qawlnamah*. Sayyid Sultan accepted Bogle as he accepted Malcolm's other proposals; he had in any case been recently reported as having preferred to have an English physician attending him. He put his signature to the Agreement of January 1800, with its picturesque language emphasising the perpetuity of the friendship between Oman and Britain:

Agreement entered into by the Imam of the State of Oman with Captain John Malcolm Bahadoor, Envoy from the Right Honourable the Governor-General, dated the 21st of Shaban 1213 Hegira, or 18th January 1800

Article 1
The Cowlnamah entered into by the Imam of Oman with Mehedy Ally Khan Bahadoor remains fixed and in full force.

---

12 Kaye, J W: *Life of Sir John Malcolm*, Vol 1, p 109. Both this and the preceding reference are quoted by Coupland in *East Africa and its Invaders*, p 97 and p 98

Article 2

As improper reports of a tendency to interrupt the existing harmony and create misunderstanding between the States have gone abroad, and have been communicated to the Right Honourable the Governor-General, the Earl of Mornington, K.P., with a view to prevent such evils in future, we, actuated by sentiments of reciprocal friendship, agree that an English gentleman of respectability, on the part of the Honourable Company, shall always reside at the port of Muscat, and be an Agent through whom all intercourse between the States shall be conducted, in order that the actions of each government may be fairly and justly stated, and that no opportunity may be offered to designing men, who are ever eager to promote dissensions, and that the friendship of the two States may remain unshook till the end of time, and till the sun and moon have finished their revolving career.

Sealed in my presence,

John Malcolm,
Envoy

Approved by the Governor-General in Council on 26 April 1800

In this way the *qawlnamah* was confirmed and reinforced; the East India Company had a British Agent in Muscat to conduct dealings between the Company and local traders there; the French doctor close to Sayyid Sultan would be sent on his way; and the British alliance with Muscat secured. Like many alliances and friendships, this one would be tested by the passage of time and events; but fundamentally it stayed "unshook", and it was with good reason that in 2000 the British community in Muscat celebrated in grand style the passing of 200 years since Malcolm's Treaty.

CHAPTER 4

Oman under pressure (1800-1810)

If the British had hoped that the signature of the 1800 Agreement would set a seal on the relationship and provide stability for a period, that was not to be. Rivalry with the French for pre-eminence in the Gulf and the Indian Ocean was to continue for several years, and the threat of a major French thrust at India stayed on the agenda. The first decade of the 19th century also saw the rise of two new forces hostile to Oman and to the position of the Ruler of Muscat – one from central Arabia, and the other on the shores and the seas of the Gulf. Struggles lay ahead.[1]

* * * * * * *

Surgeon Archibald Bogle took up his office as the first British Agent in Muscat in 1800; but, sadly, he was not to hold it for long. Before the end of the year he became the first of several Agents to die in the post; over the years, Muscat's intense summer heat, and the rudimentary medical facilities of the era, took their toll (see List of British Residents and Agents, Annex C). Bogle was replaced in 1801 by Captain David Seton.

1 For more detail on events covered in this chapter, see Kelly, J B: *Britain and the Persian Gulf, 1795-1880*; Coupland, R: *East Africa and its invaders*; Miles, S B: *The Countries and Tribes of the Persian Gulf*; Badger, G P and Salil ibn Razik: *History of the Imams and Seyyids of Oman*.

Seton was dealing with a Ruler who faced a range of pressures, which may be summed up in two main problems: how to deal with his European interlocutors, and how to preserve his kingdom. As regards the first, Sayyid Sultan had committed himself to alliance with the British in the 1798 and 1800 agreements, but may not always have found them comfortable partners. Magallon, reporting on Omani affairs from his position as Governor of Île de France, wrote that Sayyid Sultan had written complaining of "the vexatious conduct of the English Government". Even allowing for Magallon's presumed wish to write what his Paris audience wished to read, it does seem that Sayyid Sultan sent signals to the French aimed at keeping his options open, and that the French responded in kind, in the hope (we may assume) of weaning him away from his British attachment. Magallon had been able to send some troops to assist Sayyid Sultan in a campaign aimed at securing the island of Bahrain (a long-term aspiration by this and future Rulers in Muscat); and the two exchanged valuable gifts.

More serious than these thorny issues of political strategy were the commercial and existential threats to Oman posed by the rise in piracy and the attacks from the followers of Muhammad Ibn Abdul Wahhāb in Central Arabia. In these and the years that followed, Sayyid Sultan and his successors would need all their political and military skills to neutralise these risks to their country and their rule.

Piracy and the Qawasim
To understand the problems faced in this period by the Ruler in Muscat, we need to look at the tribal structure of the area north-west of Oman, in the present-day United Arab Emirates. This area was then inhabited by tribes of two main groups: the *Qawāsim* in the North (including Sharjah and Ras al-Khaimah) and the Bani Yas in the South (Abu Dhabi and Dubai, and inland eastwards to the oasis of Buraimi). *Qawāsim* is an Arabic plural, the singular – and adjective – being *Qāsimī*. Because of local variations in pronunciation, many 19th and 20th century writers refer to them as Jasimi and Jawasim, or as Joasmee and Joasim. (The traveller James Silk Buckingham adds that Indian officials called them "Joe Hassim", and nicknamed the Wahhabis the "War Bees". But he may have intended gentle mockery of the pen-pushers in Bombay.)

Neither the Qawasim nor the Bani Yas owed allegiance to the Rulers in Muscat. Both, but especially the Qawasim, relied on earning their living from the sea – from commerce, fishing and pearling – the hinterland being arid sandy or gravel plain with only the occasional oasis where village-dwellers might scratch out a living from dates and primitive agriculture.

In this hard economic and social environment it was therefore not surprising that the Qawasim turned their hands to piracy. By the end of the 18th century they had acquired a fearsome reputation, giving rise – later in the 19th century – to the nickname "The Pirate Coast" by which the stretch from Dubai to Ras al-Khaimah and beyond was called. John Malcolm records the verdict of one of his Persian servants:

> "Their occupation is piracy, and their delight murder; and to make it worse they give you the most pious reasons for every villainy they commit … If you are their captive, and offer you all you possess to save your life, they say, "No! it is written in the Koran that it is unlawful to plunder the living, but we are not prohibited in that sacred work from stripping the dead"; so saying they knock you on the head. But then … that is not so much their fault, for they are descended from a Houl, or monster, and they act according to their nature."[2]

The Qawasim began to be an irritant for Sayyid Sultan at the turn of the century. It has been mentioned that he was not in Muscat when Malcolm came to call on him there in 1800; his presence off Qishm was due to his being occupied in a campaign against the Qasimi pirates. Sultan was also busy at this time trying to capture or recapture Bahrain, which he had failed to win in 1799, taken in 1800, retaken shortly afterwards (when the Al Khalifa, the ruling family there, repudiated an agreement they had reached), and lost in 1803.

---

2 Malcolm, J: *Sketches of Persia*, London, 1845, p 15, quoted by Kelly in *Britain and the Persian Gulf,* p 19

The Wahhabis

The sect known as the Wahhabis (although they prefer the term al-*Muwaḥḥidūn*, the Unitarians) arose in Central Arabia as the followers of Muhammad Ibn Abdul Wahhab, who urged an uncompromising return to the fundamentals of Islam as written in the Qur'an and preached by the Prophet and his immediate companions. His reform movement refused to accept such practices as calling on Saints for protection, respecting the holiness of places or objects, and building funeral markers in cemeteries. Denouncing as heretics those who would not accept this austere return to early Islam, Muhammad Ibn Abdul Wahhab and his followers were prepared to use force, and indeed burst out of the desert of central Arabia in an effort to carry their version of Islam, and their authority, west to the Hijaz, north to Iraq, and south and east to Oman and the Gulf. Muhammad Ibn Abdul Wahhab secured the protection of Muhammad bin Sa'ud, the head of a tribe in the Nejd region of central Arabia, and sealed the alliance by marrying his daughter. Muhammad bin Sa'ud died in 1765, and Ibn Abdul Wahhab in 1787; but by then the political-religious alliance had transformed a small Beduin principality into a legally instituted theocracy, and under the leadership of Abdul Aziz, the son of Muhammad bin Sa'ud, Wahhabi forces moved onwards and outwards. It may be questioned why this political and military force is given a religious name; the answer is probably that they self-identified more by their religious commitment to Ibn Abdul Wahhab's movement than by their allegiance to the Sa'ud family leadership, and officials of the period (and many historians since) invariably refer to them as Wahhabis, not Sa'udis.

In 1801 the Wahhabi forces caused shock in the world of Shi'a Islam by attacking the holy city of Karbala and engaging in extreme pillage and cruel massacre. Their capture of Mecca in 1802 eventually provoked a firm reaction from the Ottoman Turks, who in 1813 recaptured the Hejaz under the forces of Muhammad Ali of Egypt and his son Ibrahim Pasha, and then went on to destroy the Wahhabi headquarters of Dir'iyyah in 1818. Heading towards Oman and the Pirate Coast, the Wahhabis overcame the Bani Khālid in Hasa (now the Eastern Province of Saudi Arabia) in 1795, and in 1800 reached the Buraimi Oasis. This was at the north-western extent of Omani authority, and a place of vital strategic importance: its locality was watered and fertile, with date palms and other agriculture, and its position was (and still is) a commanding one, standing at the cross-roads of various routes between Oman, the Pirate Coast (now the UAE), and central Arabia.

From Buraimi, the commander of the Wahhabi expeditionary force sent a demand to Sayyid Sultan, that he should renounce what the Wahhabis considered to be the heretical beliefs of the Ibadi sect and acknowledge the suzerainty of his Amir, Abdul Aziz. Sayyid Sultan put up fierce resistance, despite the Wahhabis' managing to bring the Qawasim on to their side. But nevertheless he was obliged, at the end of a few months' manoeuvring and fighting, to leave the Wahhabis in possession of Buraimi. J B Kelly, the great historian of Britain in the Gulf, describes this as "the greatest mistake of Sultan's life", and one for which "his countrymen would pay heavily ... in the years to come".[3] But it is hard to see how Sayyid Sultan could have avoided it. He had made every effort to dislodge the Wahhabis from Buraimi, but failed; and his troops had had the worse of it in engagements with Wahhabi cavalry. He needed no telling that it was not good for Oman, or for any Ruler in Muscat, to have hostile forces occupying this strategic point. In due course, the successors of the Amir Abdul Aziz became the rulers of Saudi Arabia; and the early Wahhabi possession of Buraimi would give rise to tension and dispute – in which the British played a significant role (see chapter 14 below).

Back in Muscat, the French started another attempt to win Omani favour, at British expense. Napoleon agreed to a recommendation from Talleyrand to send a serious expedition to the Indian Ocean – a fleet of 7 ships, with 20,000 troops on board, commanded by General Decaen, the new Governor of Île de France, with instructions to assert French supremacy in the region. The man designated to handle the Omani angle of this policy (and also intended as French Resident in Muscat, should things turn out well for the mission), de Cavaignac, wrote to Magallon ahead of his arrival, enquiring about the potential for expansion of French commercial and political influence in India, the Gulf and Arabia, based on Muscat and Île de France; and moving perhaps on to the East African coast. Arriving in Muscat in October 1803, de Cavaignac received some initial encouragement, since Sayyid Sultan was away, fighting the Wahhabis who

3 Kelly: *Britain and the Persian Gulf,* p 102

had made a substantial incursion into the Batinah coast. Seton, the British Agent, was also absent. The notables left in Muscat were of the pro-French persuasion, probably those traders engaged in the trade with Île de France; and they gave de Cavaignac support for the French aims.

But de Cavaignac's success was short-lived. When Sayyid Sultan returned from the Wahhabi campaign, his staff asked him to receive the French representative and to allocate a residence to him in accordance with the agreement of 1790 (p 31 above). No doubt to British relief, Sayyid Sultan agreed to neither request, explaining that this would be contrary to the *qawlnamah* of 1798 – but that he would allow French commerce and French ships to come to Omani harbours.

We have no direct evidence showing why Sayyid Sultan, having toyed with Magallon, then decided to stick with his commitment to the British. The most likely reason lies in his current insecurity, and in a calculation of how best to confront the dangers to his rule. He had just returned from countering a very serious threat from the Wahhabis, and was probably saved only by the unexpected assassination of Abdul Aziz, while at prayer in the mosque in Dir'iyyah, and the resulting confusion in the Wahhabi command. He was conscious too that the Qawasim were growing in strength, and that their piratical activities would soon cause damage to the maritime trade on which Oman depended. And he had hostile relations with the 'Utub tribe, and its Āl Khalifa leadership, in Bahrain. In these dicey circumstances, he may have calculated that he would be safer throwing in his lot with the British, who had established uncontested domination in the Indian Ocean and on much of the sub-continent's coasts, than with the French with an as yet unproven record (or worse). Duncan, the Governor of Bombay, had also threatened him quite specifically that communication between Muscat and India would be closed off if the French were given a footing in Muscat. This would have constituted an added risk for Sayyid Sultan: the Muscat merchant fleet's trade with Indian ports was important. French officials at the time believed it was his belief in the British ability to secure him against the Wahhabi threat that decided Sayyid Sultan against de Cavaignac. But they may have seen only part of the picture. The Wahhabi threat would have weighed heavily with Sayyid Sultan; but probably several factors combined to bring him to his decision to favour the British and – on this occasion – to reject the French.

The start of the piracy campaign

The first decade of the 19th century marked the preliminaries of the anti-piracy campaign which was to dominate British involvement with the Gulf then and for the next twenty or thirty years. Interpretation of the events of this period requires disentangling the complex and sometimes changing relationships between four main players: the al-Busa'idis, the Wahhabis, the Qawasim and the British. The al-Busa'idis suffered one of their periodic turbulent succession disputes. The Wahhabis also came under new leadership, but pursued more or less consistent strategies, including active involvement in Muscat's dynastic affairs. The Qawasim were motivated sometimes by religious zeal, as they were subjected to Wahhabi influence, but were mainly attracted by hopes of plunder and of maritime domination. And the British, focussing on protecting their assets in India and consequently on maintaining the security of trade and communication through the Gulf, increasingly were forced to turn their attention to solving the problem of piracy and Qasimi aggression.

In January 1803, soon after backing off from his attempt to capture Bahrain from the 'Utub and the Al Khalifa, Sayyid Sultan bin Ahmad left Muscat for the Hijaz, to perform the Hajj. He was unhappy to find Mecca in danger of being captured by the Wahhabis, and, once back in Muscat, sent the Sharif of the Hijaz some men and money. This provoked the Wahhabi Amir Abdul Aziz to order the Commander of the garrison at Buraimi to launch a full-blown attack on Oman. Sayyid Sultan and the Omani forces could only just hold their own, and might have suffered complete defeat had it not been for the Wahhabi retreat caused by the news of Abdul Aziz's assassination.

Just under a year later, in the summer of 1804, Sayyid Sultan sailed to Basra for what was supposed to be a joint expedition against the Wahhabis with the Ottoman Turk Pashas of Syria and Baghdad. But preparations were hopelessly inadequate, and Sayyid Sultan decided to go home. An alternative explanation of this expedition has it that Sayyid Sultan was engaged in a sweeping-up operation against the Wahhabis, who were still occupying Basra, at the head of the Gulf. On the way back, in a surprise and probably unplanned attack, possibly launched by Qasimi pirates, he was shot and killed. His death precipitated Oman into one of its periodic bouts of disturbance caused by a disputed succession, enhanced by almost immediate Qasimi attempts to take advantage of the resulting instability, no doubt in the hope of replacing Omani maritime hegemony. The Qawasim took over the islands of Qishm and Hormuz (vital to Omani control of the mouth of the Gulf), and captured Bandar Abbas, still on long lease to the Omanis from the Shah of Persia. This lease was to become a political hot chestnut in later years.

The Qawasim had a history of attacking British shipping. There had been an unpleasant incident in 1797 off Bushire, when one of the Qasimi shaikhs tried to get an assurance from the British Resident in Bushire that the British would not give protection to Omani ships or transport goods in them. The British Resident's response to this was not clear. But the Qasimi shaikh went on to ask for supplies of ammunition. Rather surprisingly, especially in the light of what followed, this request was granted by the captain of a cruiser of the Bombay Marine, the *Viper*, then lying close by off-shore. For no apparent reason – perhaps he was not happy with the reply or non-reply that he had received from the Resident – the Qasimi shaikh used this ammunition to open fire on the *Viper*, whose crew fought off the attack, but with the loss of the Captain and 32 men out of the complement of 65. A protest was lodged, and the paramount shaikh of the Qawasim, Shaikh Saqr bin Rāshid, claimed that the *Viper* had fired first and was interfering in his quarrel with Oman. The incident was considered an act of treachery by the Bombay Marine, whose officers and men long resented their own authorities' unwillingness to pursue it there and then by force with the Qawasim. In the long run, the Qawasim were brought under control; but that came later.

There had been other attacks. Back in 1778 an English "snow" was captured after coming under attack by 6 Qasimi dhows. (See the box below for a description of the terms used to describe vessels in use in the Gulf at this time.) The snow was then held at Ras al-Khaimah, Shaikh Saqr's headquarters, for a ransom. In 1797 another snow was attacked by 22 dhows (the Qasimi tactic seems to have been to attack in numbers), and also held at Ras al-Khaimah. In our current period, two brigs that were the property of Samuel Manesty, then Resident at Basra, were captured late in 1804, and in early 1805 a squadron of 40 dhows dared an attack on the East India Company's cruiser *Mornington*, who fought them off with her 24 guns.

The Qawasim were also in open war with Oman, as evidenced by the "explanation" given by Shaikh Saqr after the *Viper* incident. It seems there were mixed motives for their hostility. Partly, as mentioned above, the tribe were inclined towards piracy for economic reasons; and they may have been encouraged to engage in acts of greater daring as a result of an increased confidence, from about 1780, under the strong leadership of Shaikh Saqr. From his base in Ras al-Khaimah (known to the Persians as Julfar) Shaikh Saqr commanded the allegiance of another Qasimi Shaikh in Sharjah, and of the intervening towns and villages along the coast. But from the late 1790s a religious element seems to have been added. As they pushed eastwards from their base in the Najd, in central Arabia, the Wahhabis had looked for military allies and potential converts wherever they could. A kind of mutual convenience brought together the Wahhabi wish to over-run the perceived heretical Ibadis of Oman, and a Qasimi aim of maritime hegemony in the lower Gulf. And the austere precepts of Muhammad Ibn Abdul Wahhab may have appealed to the Qasimi desert temperament, giving an element of religious fanaticism to their anti-British and anti-Omani warfare.

Terms for maritime vessels

The Bombay Marine used a number of differently-rigged vessels. Ships (including cruisers and frigates were 3-masted, square-rigged; brigs were 2-masted, square-rigged but with one fore-and-aft sail; snows were also 2-masted, having a small mast aft of the main mast; schooners had 2 masts, either with fore-and-aft sails throughout, or with a mix of fore-and-aft and square rigs; sloops had one mast; ketches had 2 masts, with a fore-and-aft mainsail and a second mast with a smaller sail; and hoys were small vessels rigged as sloops.

In 1800 the Bombay Marine complement included 5 ships, 5 brigs, 2 snows, one schooner and 5 ketches; and 277 European officers and men.

Local sailing craft were of more than a dozen types, in most English writing described by the generic term dhow, a word of uncertain derivation, but possibly from a Swahili term used in Zanzibar, originally a warship, which mounted a broadside. The baghlah (which appears as buggala and with other spellings in contemporary writing) was the largest, having two masts, each with a large lateen sail, and decks fore and aft. Some may have had long oars, referred to as sweeps, which enabled them to evade British ships during periods of calm or very light winds. Baghlah means "mule", and was used because the baghlahs were

52

the main transport ships of Arab sailors. A batil was single-masted if built on the Persian coast, two-masted if from Arabia; it was smaller (30-60 feet in length), and had a pointed stern. A baqara was similar to a batil. A boom was single-masted, with a long, straight stem-post. A tranky was a small boat powered by oars. There are also contemporary references to pattamars, lateen-rigged Indian vessels with one, two or three masts, used on the West coast of India, especially for mail or despatches.

The Omani succession

Sayyid Sultan had two sons, and it was assumed – including by the British in India – that one of them would succeed. However, their uncle Qays intervened, and trapped them in Muscat which he put under siege. (See the box below for the *dramatis personae* of this part of Omani history.) While this was going on, Sayyid Badr bin Saif, nephew of the recently deceased Sayyid Sultan, came back from Qatar, where he had been in exile since attempting to overthrow Sayyid Sultan two years previously during his absence on the Hajj. Badr, hostile to Qays, appealed to the Wahhabis in Dir'iyyah, where Abdul Aziz's son Sa'ud had now succeeded his father as Amir. Kelly remarks trenchantly that this appeal was answered "with ominous alacrity". Wahhabi forces moved from Buraimi to lay siege to the port of Sohar in the Batinah, while a marine contingent sailed from Bahrain to Muscat. Badr and Qays reached a settlement; and for these two years, 1805-6, the British dealt with Badr as though he were Ruler; and he did indeed exercise power on the coast. Omani historians however considered that Sālim and Sa'id, sons of Sultan, constituted the legitimate authority, until Salim's death in 1821. Further fighting occurred between Badr and Qays in 1805, and again Badr called in Wahhabi help.

The family strife was brutally ended in July 1806. Sa'id bin Sultan, who is recorded as having hated Badr partly because he had usurped power but more because he had thrown in his lot with the Wahhabis and converted to Wahhabi belief, got together with an anti-Wahhabi tribal chief, Muhammad bin Nāsir, and killed Badr in Barkā'. The British hesitated before recognising a Ruler who had taken power through assassination; but from 1807, when they also assured Sa'id that they would consider Muscat as a neutral party in the context of their own continuing hostility with the French, they gave him recognition. Salim, notionally co-Ruler, seems to have faded from the Muscat scene, partly because of the influence of his aunt, Moza, but also because Sa'id was the stronger personality and Salim was willing to concede power to his brother.

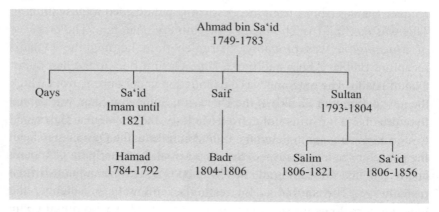

The British response – joint action against the pirates

The British were alternatively on and off the scene through this period. Seton was sent back to Muscat in 1805 to re-open the Agency, which had been closed since late in 1803; but he left again in 1806 or early 1807. Seton's predecessor, it will be recalled, had died in post, and he himself had fallen ill; his superiors in India may have wanted to reduce the risk of further casualties. Seton's skills and regional knowledge were also useful in other contexts: in mid-1806 he commanded a detachment of two cruisers sent to the Red Sea to deal with a pirate named Muhammad 'Aqīl, who exerted some kind of rule over Dhofar and whom the British suspected of assisting French privateers operating off the South Arabian coast.

For his return in 1805, Seton was given careful instructions – and also the use of the cruiser *Mornington*. He was to help one of Sayyid Sultan's sons to succeed to the throne; he was to facilitate action, with the new Ruler, to recover British and Indian ships and cargoes captured by the Qawasim, but using negotiation (or threat) rather than actual force; and in all this he was to ensure that he did not risk the British getting into hostilities with Muscat, the Wahhabis, or the Governments of Turkey or Persia. This last provision might seem a distant contingency; but, as Seton's superiors in Bombay and Calcutta will have been aware, the Qawasim were under pressure from Persia as well as from the Wahhabis, since they used ports on the Northern shore of the Gulf, and sometimes relied on Persian protection.

Seton arrived – in May 1805 – just as Sayyid Badr was setting out to recover Bandar Abbas from the Qawasim, and decided to go with him. This was the first British-Omani joint military operation. The presence of *Mornington* was probably instrumental in helping the Omanis recapture Bandar Abbas and trap a large Qasimi fleet in the harbour at Qishm Island. The outcome was a negotiation under duress, from which the new paramount Shaikh of the Qawasim, Sultān bin Saqr, was forced to return one of the brigs stolen from Manesty, the Resident at Basra, and to sign a *qawlnamah* in February 1806 committing the Qawasim to keep the peace at sea and to respect the property of the East India Company and its subjects – meaning, it must be supposed, British and non-British residents of British India. Interestingly, and with prescience, the *qawlnamah* allows for the contingency that the Qawasim might come under pressure from the Wahhabis to break the peace, in which case they were to give three months' notice of their intention to do so. On the plus side for the Qawasim, the last article gives them the right of access to "English ports from Surat to Bengal as before", once the previous provisions have been confirmed and ratified by both parties. The agreement, which is reproduced in Aitchison's collection,[4] was approved by the Governor-General in Council in April 1806.

Seton seems not to have stayed long in Muscat after this excursion. He was not there when Sayyid Sa'id and Muhammed bin Nasir killed Sayyid Badr, and in 1807 the British Indian authorities decided to leave the Agency vacant for a while, partly to save money but also in order to avoid getting involved in Omani affairs. This doctrine of non-intervention came to be oft-quoted in an Omani context, notably in the correspondence on the Bani Bu Ali campaign (see chapter 6 below); but circumstances often contrived to bring British officers to honour the doctrine more in the breach than the observance, and later in the century

4 Aitchison: *Collection of Treaties*, Vol 12, p 164, of the 1909 edition

Curzon thought he foresaw a time when Oman would come totally under British protection.

Seton was back in Muscat in 1808. As had been the case nearly 10 years earlier, it was concern about the French which lay behind the move to reinstate him in the Agency. Russia and Turkey had become Napoleon's allies, and Seton was instructed to watch for French attempts to re-establish themselves in the Gulf, since the danger of an attack on British possessions in India had risen again. But he was also to keep an eye on the new young Ruler, to report on the security of his rule and to ensure that he abided by his father's commitments of 1798 and 1800. Soon after his usurpation of power through the murder of Sayyid Badr, and in the absence of Seton, Sayyid Sa'id bin Sultan had entered into correspondence with Jonathan Duncan, Governor of Bombay. He was seeking to resolve an issue that had arisen with the French early in 1806, when a French privateer, *La Vigilante*, had put in at Muscat but been ordered out by the port authorities at the request of the captain of a British frigate, the *Concorde*, lying off nearby. The captain had been invoking the 1800 Treaty, since the Muscatis had gone further than to supply the French ship with water and supplies, but had also lent men to repair the rigging. As soon as she left the safety of Muscat harbour, *La Vigilante* was captured by the *Concorde*, taken to Bombay and later sold, despite Duncan's contention to the Vice-Admiralty Court that *Concorde*'s captain had perhaps been a little tough in his interpretation of the 1800 Treaty. Soon afterwards, a flotilla of Omani merchantmen fell victim to an attack by another French privateer, whose commander explained that the Omani-French *entente* had been wrecked on the rocks of the rejection of de Cavaignac and the *La Vigilante* incident. Sayyid Sa'id sought to make things up with General Decaen, the Governor of Île de France, but received a stiff reply, demanding the return of *La Vigilante* – an awkward request for Sayyid Sa'id, since the ship was out of his hands, and his letters to Duncan, the Governor of Bombay, were not being answered. By the end of the year he must have been seriously concerned that he had lost out with both his powerful European friends. This was not a desirable position to be in, given the continued pressures on his northern land and sea borders, from the Wahhabis and the Qawasim. In December 1806 he decided to send his *Waqīl* (confidential minister) to Duncan. The Waqil carried a letter reaffirming Sayyid Sa'id's wish for renewed friendly relations with the British, and an oral message asking specifically for British protection against the French.

Sayyid Sa'id had been right in suspecting that the British non-response to his earlier letters had been because of doubts as to whether they should recognise an assassin as Ruler, and lack of reliable information (because of Seton's absence) about Sa'id's security on the throne. By the end of 1806 Duncan seems to have swallowed his scruples on the former, and been satisfied on the latter. In addition, exaggerated reports of Sa'id's contacts with Decaen had reached Bombay, and Duncan wanted to probe Sa'id on whether it was true that he was intending to receive a French Resident in Muscat and to send a mission to Port Louis, the Île de France capital (and still today capital of Mauritius). Duncan wrote in friendly manner to Sa'id, through the Waqil; and, while referring the question of British protection to the Governor-General in Calcutta, he used some subtlety in dealing with the French question, saying that he assumed that the reports of an Omani link with France were not true, since Sa'id could not expect his trading ships to be welcomed in India if the link were confirmed.

A British review of policy

Duncan's referral of Sayyid Sa'id's request for protection gave rise to a thorough review of British India policy towards Muscat and Oman. The acting Governor-General, Sir George Barlow, reflecting a change in public opinion in England, considered that policy should revert to the line taken at the time of the passing of the India Act in 1784, namely that British representatives should avoid involvement with (or commitments to) native states, whether in India or in the Gulf, except with the express agreement of authorities in England.

The result of Duncan's referral was a highly reserved response to Sayyid Sa'id's appeal. The British were prepared to protect Muscat's neutrality, but at the same time wanted to insist on it; they hoped that Sa'id would reach an accommodation with the authorities in Île de France, but would intervene if the French tried to force Sa'id out of his neutrality into a new pro-French alliance. They were also prepared to help him protect his trade against French privateers; possibly there was some self-interest in this, if the British wished to promote freedom of trade in the Indian Ocean, and growth of commercial activity in Indian ports. But "permanent protection" of Oman would lay too much of a burden on British and Indian naval forces, and any obligation of that kind could be entered into only with agreement from London.[5]

The outcome of this policy review was transmitted through Seton to Sayyid Sa'id, who – very reasonably – interpreted it as a refusal of a British alliance, and an encouragement to restore or create a good relationship with the French. He quickly despatched a senior adviser to start negotiations in Port Louis, and a Treaty of Amity and Commerce was signed with Decaen in June 1807. Unlike the 1798 and 1800 agreements with the British, which had consisted mainly of commitments by Sayyid Sultan, this Treaty was genuinely bilateral, with mutual reciprocity of engagement. That being said, the practical commitments (for example, that ships of either party could use the ports of the other) were principally of benefit to the French. Provisions allowed Omani ships to trade with ports in British India. This was in fact in breach of the French policy in Europe aimed at blockading British ports. But Decaen was keen to resume the forward march of French power that had been blocked by de Cavaignac's failure in 1806. By this time, the extension of Omani maritime power had resulted in their establishing themselves in several coastal locations in East Africa, and Decaen may also have had in mind the need to secure continued or enhanced access to these Omani ports. The East Africa littoral was of increasing importance to France's possessions in the Mascarene Islands, because of the trade in slaves, ivory and gold.

It might be assumed that Sayyid Sa'id would have been content with his balanced neutrality between the French and the British. But then he seems to have been concerned about his distance from the British. In a somewhat surreal conversation recorded by the Italian traveller Maurizi (who may have been working for the French), Sa'id is recorded as having rejected the temptation of doing a deal with the Wahhabis, and even of adopting their faith, in favour of "[relying] upon the assistance which the East India Company were bound to yield him, both by policy and good faith". Later, when Maurizi suggested that an alliance with the Ottoman Turks or the Persians might be more advantageous to him, Sa'id "observed that a Treaty with the Governor of Bombay would render him more respectable in the eyes of the whole English nation".[5]

5 Maurizi, V: *History of Seyd Said, Sultan of Muscat*, 1984, p 75

British fears of renewed French designs on Oman

At this time there occurred a spurt of British activity aimed at countering the revival of Napoleon's interest in the East. Its focus was more on Persia and Ottoman Turkey than on Muscat, but the episode naturally had its effects all down the Gulf. The French set out by seeking to establish an alliance with Turkey and Persia against Russia; but Napoleon and Talleyrand hoped to go a step further, by marching on India. They made good diplomatic progress through 1806, weaning the Turks away from the British, and in May 1807 Napoleon concluded a secret treaty of alliance with an envoy of the Shah at Finkenstein in Poland. This treaty (sometimes also referred to as the Treaty of Friedland) placed a range of constraints on the Shah regarding his dealings with the British, and required the Shah to give assistance to any French expedition despatched against India. Napoleon appointed General Gardane to be his ambassador to the Shah, and instructed him to research ports on the Gulf which could supply a fleet large enough to carry 20,000 men. This treaty was followed, in July 1807, by an agreement with Tsar Alexander at Tilsit, making the spectre of a French-Persian-Russian invasion of Asia all too vivid. Back in Île de France, Governor Decaen believed he could contribute by recommending the possibility of an attack on India from the sea, an idea which his brother René promoted personally with Napoleon in January 1808. And, to ensure Omani compliance or support should it be necessary or useful, Decaen agreed to a request from Sayyid Sa'id to amend the June 1807 agreement, giving Omani ships enhanced trading permissions in British India, again in defiance of the French blockade.

Malcolm's mission

The British authorities in India reacted by planning a high-level diplomatic mission to Persia and Turkish Arabia aimed at persuading both out of alliance with the French. The mission was led by John Malcolm, the negotiator of the 1800 Treaty with Sayyid Sultan, now promoted Brigadier-General. Malcolm was to call in at Muscat on his way to Persia, and had instructions from Jonathan Duncan, Governor of Bombay, to have an interview with Sayyid Sa'id and explain to him British actions in the Gulf. A short while earlier, there had been reports that Bandar Abbas and Hormuz had been ceded to the French, for the preparations of their India-bound fleet. It will be recalled that both ports were under Persian sovereignty but under long lease to the Ruler of Muscat. Sayyid Sa'id had replied that since both places were under his rule he would not allow either the French or the Persians to use them as bases. Governor-General Minto wished to know – through Malcolm's mission – if Sayyid Sa'id would accept British assistance and the stationing of British ships and troops there, if necessary, in order to keep the French out of Bandar Abbas. But Malcolm never got round to carrying out either Minto's or Duncan's instructions. Anchored off Muscat at the end of April 1808, he received Sayyid Sa'id's *wazir* (Minister), and engaged in a not altogether friendly discussion, with Malcolm insisting that the Omanis should not give the French any aid, and that "if his master was not found to be a decided friend he would most undoubtedly be treated as an enemy", while the *wazir* reminded Malcolm that the British had decided to regard Muscat as neutral. Malcolm refused to wait for an opportunity to clarify all this personally with Sayyid Sa'id, and sailed for Bushire. It is difficult to avoid suspecting a patronising attitude on Malcolm's part: he had dealt in 1800 with Sa'id's father, when Sa'id himself was only 10 or 11 years old, and (as he records in his journal) he had given him a model ship as a present. Perhaps he under-estimated the value of treating with the 18-year-old son. He adds, on the present occasion, that Sa'id had "[given] promise of good temper and intelligence; but this promise has not, I understand, been fulfilled".[6]

Malcolm's failed diplomacy in Muscat was then duplicated in Persia. Through a subordinate officer he laid down threatening conditions for a meeting with the Shah, and – when the Shah refused to concede – he had to return to India, in July 1808, mission unaccomplished. Meanwhile a second delegation to Persia was under way, under Sir Harford Jones (who later took the name Brydges), former Resident in Basra and Baghdad. Jones had been appointed by Canning, recently appointed Foreign Secretary, as ambassador to Persia, but had generously agreed to hold off approaching the Shah until the outcome of Malcolm's mission was known. Now, in the autumn of 1808, Jones reached Bushire and was eventually allowed to go on to Tehran. In March 1809 he concluded a

6 Quoted by Coupland: *East Africa and its Invaders,* p130

treaty of alliance (known as "the Preliminary Treaty"), a success due mainly to a change of heart on the part of the Shah, not least because of French failure to give him protection from threatening Russian attacks on his northern border. With the Persian alliance now lost, and events in Europe (particularly in Spain) putting pressure on Napoleon, French plans for operations in the East now faded. Although Napoleon was still considering the composition of a large-scale expedition to India in May and June 1808 (56 ships, 30,000 men), by August he had dropped the plan in favour of the despatch of just 20 frigates to prey on British shipping world-wide – and only one pair to make for Île de France. Any hopes for a further revival of the plan for Indian Ocean supremacy would have been destroyed by the British capture of Île de France (from then on to be known as Mauritius) in December 1810. It was now time for the British – and Sayyid Sa'id – to focus on the threats to Oman's north posed by the Wahhabis and the Qawasim pirates.

CHAPTER 5

1809-1820: Campaigns against the Pirate Coast

We have seen that the British had for some years been concerned about the losses to shipping in the Gulf from actions of piracy by the Qawasim. In 1807 there were no acts of piracy against British shipping in the Gulf, partly because of the recent (1806) treaty with Sultan bin Saqr, and partly because a naval squadron of HMS *Fox*, accompanied by eight cruisers of the East India Company, could be spared for patrolling. Despite the despatch of a new squadron in February 1808, Qawasim aggression revived, and by late 1808 acts of piracy had reached the point where the British authorities in India decided that firm and decisive action needed to be taken.[1]

* * * * * * *

The lead-up to the anti-pirate expedition of 1809

Seton was back in Muscat in January 1808, and reported with little optimism on the inexperienced Sayyid Sa'id, whose government he said was unpopular and whose power was limited to the coastal area. In the interior the people paid revenue to the Wahhabis, to whom Sa'id had to submit in order to avoid their making further inroads.

---

1 A detailed account of the early 19th century campaign against the Gulf pirates, often graphic in its descriptions, is given in Moyse-Bartlett, H: *The Pirates of Trucial Oman*, Macdonald, London, 1966.

Seton had to leave Muscat again soon afterwards; but the authorities in India hardly needed on-the-spot reporting to know that the situation was deteriorating, with regard both to the Qawasim and to the Wahhabis. Trouble had begun seriously in mid-1807 when the Wahhabi forces under a particularly able commander, Mutlaq al-Mutairi, arrived in Buraimi. Mutairi started building a large fort with an obviously aggressive profile, made agreements with tribal leaders across northern Oman, and – in early 1808 – replaced Sultan bin Saqr of Ras al-Khaimah as chief of the Qawasim with someone more compliant, Husain bin Ali from the more northern coastal town of Rams. He ordered Husain to cruise the Gulf with hostile intent against all non-Wahhabis, and to remit to Dir'iyyah one-fifth of all the plunder they took. He also increased the annual tax (*zakat*)[2] payable by the Qawasim to the Wahhabi leadership in Dir'iyyah from 4000 to 12,000 Maria Theresa dollars (see box below for a description of this currency); this was on top of the revenue paid to the Wahhabis by the people of the interior.

In discussing piracy in the Gulf, it should be added that there is another explanation, possibly explaining Qawasim policy, if not exactly condoning their violent implementation of it. This is that they derived much of their revenue from tolls levied on shipping coming in and out of the Gulf, and that the British either misunderstood the system, or chose to do so, and refused to pay the tolls. Hence the Qawasim attacks.[3]

2 Normally the religious tax, one of the Five Pillars of Islam, payable by individual Muslims to the poor as alms, or to travellers, or to the state. Thus Qasimi acquiescence in paying *zakat* implied a subservient relationship to the Sa'udi/ Wahhabi polity.
3 Onley, J: *The Arabian Frontier of the British Raj*, p 44

The Maria Theresa thaler or dollar (abbreviated in this book to $MT) was first minted in the middle of the 18th century, and named after the Empress Maria Theresa who ruled Austria, Hungary and Bohemia from 1740 to 1780. The word thaler, which is the origin of dollar, comes from St Joachimsthal, or the Valley of St Joachim, the site of an early silver mine in Bohemia.

The coin became a standard for commerce in Europe, and then, in the 19th century, in the Arab world and in Indian Ocean trade. It weighed just over 28 grams, was known to have a reliably high silver content, and was difficult to forge or to clip – the edge is embossed and not simply milled and contains the words "Justitia et Clementia" ("Justice and Mercy"), the motto of Maria Theresa's reign. The coins continued to bear Maria Theresa's image and the date of her death, 1780, for as long as they were minted. The explorer Sir Samuel Baker thought that "the effigy of the Empress with a very low dress and profusion of bust is ... the charm that suits the Arab taste".

The $MT remained a common unit of currency throughout the Arab world, in North Africa and in the Sudan or Sahel long after it ceased to circulate in Europe. Both the $MT and Indian rupee were Oman's currency from early in the 19th century until the Omani riyal was introduced in 1970. Mainly the system worked well, but after 1870 the cost and therefore the value of silver dropped. This was damaging to the Omani economy, whose cash receipts (notably the Zanzibar subsidy – see chapter 10) were in $MT.

The coin became so popular that demand for it outstripped Austrian capacity to supply. In the 20th century several European countries minted their own. British-supervised mints produced the $MT in London, Birmingham, and Bombay. In 1960 the Austrian Government asked foreign governments to cease production; the British were the last to do so, in 1962.

Visitors to the Arab world will be aware of the ubiquitous nature of this coin. For many years, and until late in the 20th century, thalers were melted down to make jewellery, and often actually incorporated into head-dresses, belts, anklets and bracelets. One of the authors saw one used as a weight (in order to value an anklet) in the souq in Nizwa in Oman in 2005.

By the middle of 1808, the Qawasim were reported as cruising in squadrons of 15-20 dhows, capturing their prey by coming in close, surrounding them and pelting them with stones and boulders (despite defence by guns), and then boarding. They were also merciless in dealing with the crews, whether European or Indian. Wellsted, the English naval officer who wrote most graphically about his travels in the area at that time, comments:

> ... I must confess, with a people who are not naturally cruel, I am somewhat surprised that they should have adopted the savage and revolting principle of sacrificing their captives. ... After a ship was taken, she was purified with water and with perfumes; the crew were then led forward singly, their heads placed on the gunwale, and their throats cut, with the exclamation used in battle of "Allah akbar!" – God is great![4]

The number of ships that the Qawasim had available for war is difficult to calculate, since contemporary reports enumerate a fleet of 63 *baghlas* (large vessels), 800 smaller ones, and 19,000 men; but a large proportion of these, perhaps the majority, would have been normally used for fishing, pearling and commerce. Nevertheless, it was a powerful force; and the small brigs and schooners of the Bombay Marine would have felt overwhelmed in size and number by the high-pooped and well-manned dhows. The Marine were also constrained by standing orders which forbade commanders to open fire until actually attacked – a measure which was presumably designed to reduce the risk of provoking open hostilities with Sa'ud, the Amir of the Wahhabis. East India Company and British naval resources were under strain because of campaigns in India and elsewhere, and could not afford war on another front. When attacked, the British ships had to rely on superior seamanship, greater manoeuvrability, and stronger fire-power in order to escape or to mount an effective counter-attack.

British records carry accounts of a series of attacks in the summer and autumn of 1808, interrupted only by the pearling season. In May 1808

---

4 Wellsted, J R: *Travels to the City of the Caliphs*, vol 1, p 101. There is a similar account in Fraser, J B: *Narrative of a journey into Khorasan* – except that Fraser says that purification of the vessel occurs after the executions.

an East India Company cruiser was attacked off Muscat by two dhows whom she eventually repelled. Later the same month, a ship belonging to Samuel Manesty, Resident at Basra, met a large fleet off Ras Musandam, and was captured after a running fight lasting two days. Many of the crew and passengers were murdered, but some were kept as captives, including a Mrs Taylor, wife of an officer in the Residency in Bushire. When later released, she was bought by a Bahraini for $MT (Maria Theresa dollars) 670, and ransomed in October 1809 for $MT 1,000. She must have had an interesting story to tell.

There were other attacks. When Sir Harford Jones had sailed from Bombay to Bushire in September 1808 (p 60 above), he had been on board a Royal Navy (RN) frigate, HMS *Nereide*, accompanied by another RN ship and a cruiser, the *Sylph*. The convoy separated, due to the varying speeds of the three ships. The *Sylph* fell a long way behind and was captured by two large dhows who had attacked her off Ras Musandam. By happy coincidence, HMS *Nereide*, who by now had disembarked Sir Harford Jones at Bushire and was on her way back to Bombay, witnessed the attack and managed to recapture the *Sylph* (but not before nearly all of her crew were killed in action or murdered) and escort her to Muscat.

In November 1808 the Qasimi fleets trespassed yet further, into Indian waters. 40 dhows started attacking the coastal trade off Kutch, and that month captured 20 Indian merchant vessels. Responding to a request from a delegation of distressed local merchants, Governor Duncan instructed the Superintendent of Marine to prepare a force to clear the coast of pirates. But no action appears to have been taken until reports in early 1809 from Seton – now back in Muscat – convinced Malcolm that Muscat would fall completely under Wahhabi domination if the British held back any longer. Malcolm, recently returned from his failed mission in Persia, nevertheless retained the confidence of Governor-General Minto, who gave him a supervisory role in British Indian interests in the Gulf. The Amir Sa'ud had demanded that Sayyid Sa'id should join forces with the Qawasim in attacking Basra and in plundering Indian shipping; and was threatening to visit Oman in person if Sa'id did not comply. Both Sa'id and Malcolm assumed sinister intent in this proposed "visit", no doubt with good reason, and Malcolm recommended Minto to approve an expedition aimed at quashing the power of the Qawasim and protecting the independence of Muscat and Oman.

The expedition against the Qawasim, Autumn 1809

Minto gave his approval in April, and instructed Duncan to prepare the force. It was to be a combined operation, since it was clear that bombardments from ships lying off-shore would not be enough to destroy the forts in which the Qawasim took refuge; armed landings, in strength, would be required. The expedition would therefore draw on ships of the Royal Navy and of the Bombay Marine, and troops of the British Army as well as of the East India Company's Bombay Army. The main focus was nevertheless to be naval: the aim was to destroy Qawasim capacity for continued piratical operations, and – even though it was known that they were in alliance with and partly under instructions from Amir Sa'ud in Dir'iyyah – the expedition would not conduct more than the minimum of action on land.

Indeed, the instructions were careful and specific on this point. Minto told Duncan "that the crews of the ships and the troops employed on them should not be employed on shore against any land forces in the service of the Wahabee chiefs".[5] The authorities in India were still determined not to risk provocation of all-out hostility in the Peninsula. As regards the second aim of the expedition, ie to protect Sayyid Sa'id and give him time to strengthen his internal position and build up his defences against Mutlaq al-Mutairi in Buraimi, Minto and his staff may also have calculated that assertion of supremacy at sea and the destruction of a number of pirate dhows would be sufficient.

The more detailed instructions given in September to the joint commanders, Captain J Wainwright RN and Colonel Lionel Smith, made it clear that the main target was to be the Qawasim headquarters and their ships at Ras al-Khaimah, while the expedition was also to clear them from other ports from Rams southwards on the Pirate Coast. Operations were also to be conducted against Qasimi bases on the Persian Coast and on the island of Qishm in the Straits of Hormuz. It was hoped that it would be possible to bind the Qawasim by a new treaty to ensure their future peaceable behaviour; but, as will be seen, this proved to be elusive.

Despite the long history of the connections between the British Indian authorities and the Gulf, and the frequency of sailings from Bombay and

---

5 Bombay records, India Office; quoted by Kelly: *Britain and the Persian Gulf*, p 114

Surat to Gulf destinations, the expeditionary force actually lacked good local information or experience appropriate for this kind of operation. No proper marine survey of the Pirate Coast had been carried out, and both the ships and the troops to be employed were not trained for, or accustomed to, this kind of operation. David Seton succumbed to Muscat's fierce climate in August, and so his valuable local knowledge was not available to the expeditionary force. On the positive side, the Bombay Infantry had been remodelled during the later decades of the 18th century; a Marine Battalion had been recruited for service at sea; the "King's Troops" (regiments of the regular British Army, who had been sent out to India in the late 18th century to reinforce the East India Company's forces) were of high quality; and the whole detachment was equipped with small arms and heavy guns which far surpassed anything the Qawasim could draw on.

Seton's death was followed by a long gap in staffing the Agency in Muscat. Four Agents or Deputies had died in post in the nine years since it had been opened. From this point the Residency in Bushire took responsibility for political affairs in the Gulf, reporting to Bombay; and the member of the Bushire staff appointed to take the lead on these issues was Lieutenant (later Captain) William Bruce of the Bombay Marine.

In the summer months of 1809 there was some dispute among the leadership as to whether the expeditionary force should set out immediately or wait until the cooler weather in the autumn or winter. Seton and Duncan argued for a speedy attack, in order to avoid the unfavourable winds of the South-West monsoon and to catch the Qasimi boats in harbour over the summer. Delay was favoured by John Malcolm, who was still in Bombay; he had been arguing for the establishment of a British base at Kharaq, an island at the head of the Gulf off Bushire, but this idea had been discarded. He thought that the interval could be used to gain more information about the area and intelligence about the enemy's strengths and weaknesses. Wainwright and Smith accepted Malcolm's recommendation for delay, and the expedition sailed from Bombay in September.

It had inauspicious beginnings. A munitions and artillery transport ship, which had probably been unseaworthy in any case, sank early in the voyage, which was made slower by bad weather. The unexpected longer duration of the voyage also caused the convoy to run short of water. Wainwright ordered some ships to break off to take on water on the Makran coast, but his attempt to get the whole convoy to meet up off Ras Musandam failed, and he was obliged to gather most of the force together at Muscat – so reducing the likelihood of being able to spring a surprise on the Qawasim. Nor were they much encouraged in Muscat: Sayyid Sa'id thought that a much stronger force would be required to storm the well-defended fort at Ras al-Khaimah, and that the ships' cannons would be of limited effectiveness.

The convoy sailed from Muscat early in November (1809), assembled off Ras Musandam with two cruisers who had been detached earlier, and soon all reached Ras al-Khaimah. After some initial bombardment of the Qawasim defences on 12 November, the attack was launched at dawn the next day. Fighting was fierce, the Qawasim defending each house, but by mid-morning the British had captured the town and the Qawasim had taken refuge on the other side of the creek. While the troops battled, the seamen began burning the pirate dhows and destroying the ammunition and other stores, including stolen merchandise. The only loot available for the troops was a small quantity of jewellery and money. Losses on the British side were light – about four killed and 20 wounded. Smith estimated that several hundred of the enemy had died, 70 or 80 in the fighting but a number more in the bombardment and from wounds afterwards.

In the afternoon the British began receiving reports that an Arab force was approaching from inland. Assuming that these would be Wahhabi and hostile, Smith kept his troops prepared to resist a counter-attack. Although none came, Smith was anxious not to run counter to his instructions to avoid direct hostilities with the Wahhabis, and decided to withdraw his forces on the morning of 14 November. Qawasim appeared from their refuges, and, staying out of range, watched the re-embarkation with a mixture of jeers and defiance.

This was in several ways an unfortunate outcome for the British. The capture of Ras al-Khaimah had been total, and the destruction of ships considerable. But the rapid withdrawal had made it clear that the British lacked either the will or the capacity to force the Qawasim into submission; the attack, with its killing, destruction and looting must have seemed to them akin to an Arab desert *ghazu*, or raid, not an invasion or sustainable conquest. As the authorities in India would find out over the next 20 or 30 years, it would need a more comprehensive and overwhelming victory if this resilient people's will to fight and plunder was to be broken.

The expeditionary force sailed across the Gulf to Lingah, on the Persian shore just north-west of Qishm Island. Lingah was attacked and taken (or according to another account it was occupied unopposed), and 20 ships burned. The plan after that was to go for Laft (also spelt Luft), a Qasimi port on the north side of Qishm Island, an attack which required a pincer movement by using ships at each end of the narrow waters between Qishm and the Persian coast. Not without a hitch, Wainwright completed the manoeuvre, forcing the Qawasim to retreat to their fort. Although there are inconsistent reports of what happened thereafter, it seems that the fierce and consistent bombardment from the sea led to the fort's being surrendered. Wainwright left it in charge of a Shaikh who was loyal to Sayyid Sa'id, who considered Qishm one of his possessions.

Cruisers from the expeditionary force then returned to the Pirate Coast, where they destroyed ships at Rams, al-Jazira al-Hamra and Sharjah; and by the middle of December they and all the convoy assembled at Muscat.

The expeditionary force continues to Shinas

Sayyid Sa'id had now revised his opinion of the British expedition, realising that its operations had proved how superior fire-power (and perhaps other qualities) could overcome sheer numbers. He visited the fleet, witnessed a display of artillery practice, and suggested that their joint forces might recapture Shinas, a port just north of Sohar, and clear the Qawasim out of a fort they had built at Khor Fakkan (yet further north, near present-day Fujairah). This would be the second, but not the last, combination of Omani and British forces in military operations, the first having been the recovery of Bandar Abbas in 1805 (p 55 above).

Most of Sayyid Sa'id's troops marched up the coast, though some were embarked on the British convoy, which reached Shinas on the last day of 1809. The fort at Shinas would be a tough nut to crack – tougher than Wainwright and Smith knew, since Mutlaq al-Mutairi had sent Wahhabi reinforcements from Buraimi after the battle at Ras al-Khaimah. In the style of the time (and perhaps because they genuinely wanted to minimise casualties) the besieging force demanded the fort's surrender, but received a derisive and dusty answer. Heavy guns were brought on shore from the ships, and under their bombardment the walls eventually crumbled and a tower collapsed. But the defenders still refused to surrender, and Omani and British troops attacked through breaches created by the artillery. Smith describes graphically how, despite a hopeless situation and with the walls breaking up, "the enemy still kept up fire and seemed determined to be buried under [the towers'] ruins".[6] Finally a surrender was achieved, and Smith reckons that over 700 lives were saved, that being the number of prisoners they took. Considering the fierceness of the fighting, British losses were light (one killed, 11 wounded), though Omani losses were much higher; and there was no assessment of Wahhabi-Qasimi casualties, which must have been heavy.

The victors held the fort for three days, expecting a counter-attack, though none came, probably because the commander of the Wahhabi relief force, arriving from Buraimi near Shinas, died suddenly in his camp. Though offered a lift in Wainwright's fleet, Sa'id took his troops back south overland, but was severely harried en route, probably by this relief force, and arrived at Muscat in some disarray. As a result of this, he appealed again to the British in Bombay for protection, claiming that it was only because of his having been in alliance with the British that he had been exposed to danger. He may have over-stated his case. The Bombay authorities suspected that Sa'id's intention was to set the Wahhabis against the British, and thereby to provoke a war so as to obtain the aid that he wanted. Minto, advised by Duncan and possibly abetted by Malcolm, was having none of this, and sent back a firm reply which made clear that the British were sticking to the policy of non-interference in local affairs, and non-provocation of the Wahhabis. As an addition, he advised Sa'id to come to terms with the Wahhabis, provided such terms were "consistent with the honour and security of the State of Muscat".[7]

Wainwright kept his fleet on the Pirate Coast through the month of January 1810, destroying pirate dhows where he could find them. But a number would have escaped his searches, since the Qawasim were adept at concealing them in inlets and khors (bays formed at the mouths of dry river-beds, where often there is semi-saline water behind a sand-bar).

6 Smith's report to the Governor-in-Council, written at sea on 8 January 1810, quoted at
  greater length in J B Kelly *Britain and the Persian Gulf*, p 120
7 Quoted by Coupland: *East Africa and its invaders,* p 146

Those who have visited the highly indented coast-line of Musandam will have seen how many such hiding-places there are.

Assessment of the 1809 campaign

Governor-General Minto seems to have been highly satisfied with the campaign, and commended Wainwright and Smith for their success. But a realistic assessment would give a more cautious verdict. It is true that the expeditionary force had demonstrated superiority over the enemy, had destroyed a large number of pirate ships and done considerable damage to Qasimi forts and towns, had restored possessions in Qishm Island to Sayyid Sa'id, and had done all this with ships, crews and troops relatively unused to this kind of warfare; but these gains were only tactical. The strategic aims, those of forcing the Qawasim to agree to a compact to keep the maritime peace and abstain from piracy, and of getting the Wahhabis off Sayyid Sa'id's back, were barely approached. Amir Sa'ud could afford to look down his nose at the whole episode. Nicholas Hankey Smith, the Resident in Bushire, had written to him in the spring of 1810, requesting him to restrain a notorious pirate operating out of Qatar, named Rahmah bin Jabir; and in his reply, which was relatively conciliatory (he agreed to "interdict the followers of the Moohumedan faith and their vessels from offering any molestation to your vessels"), he told Hankey Smith that the British should not "be elated with the conflagration of a few vessels" and that they had been duped by Sayyid Sa'id into interfering where they had no right to.[8] The British failure to take this opportunity to deal with these twin enemies would continue to be of concern to them and to Sayyid Sa'id for some time.

Sayyid Sa'id under pressure

From his base in Buraimi, Mutlaq al-Mutairi must have thought, with some justification, that he had Sayyid Sa'id on the run. He continued his attacks on the towns of the Batinah, but the effect was more of destruction than of consolidation. The Omani forts and towns mainly stood up to his attacks. But Sa'id could not on his own rid the country of the Wahhabi menace; his troops were inferior when opposed to Mutairi's in open battle.

---

8 Bengal Records, India Office; quoted by J B Kelly: *Britain and the Persian Gulf*, p 124

Realising that he would not get help from the British, he decided to appeal to Persia, using his brother Salim as an emissary. The Persians agreed to help, and Sa'id soon had 1500 Persian mercenaries as an addition to his forces. With these he did battle with the Wahhabis and their sympathisers such as Muhammad bin Nasir, paramount chief of the Bani Jabir tribe. Mutlaq al-Mutairi re-entered the field, responding to a request from Muhammad bin Nasir, who had been expelled from the fortress of Samail, a crucial point on the pass from the coast to Nizwa. Mutairi collected troops from sympathetic tribes from central Oman, and severely defeated Salim and his force of Persians and loyalists. This was late in 1810. For the next two years fighting continued sporadically, and occasionally intensely, between Sayyid Sa'id and the Wahhabis. Twice Sa'id launched successful attacks on Bahrain, but does not seem to have been able to hold on to his gains on a sustained basis. Amir Sa'ud reacted with a mixture of military measures (when he had resources to spare) and diplomacy. By now he was himself facing external threats – from the West, since Muhammad Ali, Pasha of Egypt, had begun to campaign to recover the Hijaz on behalf of the Ottoman Turks and put an end to Wahhabi control of central Arabia. This ended later in the destruction of Dir'iyyah in 1818.

In Eastern Arabia in 1811-13, while Sa'ud was focussing on the western threat, Mutlaq al-Mutairi was again involved in Omani campaigning. He re-captured Sohar, and got close enough to Muscat to be bought off by Sayyid Sa'id for $MT 40,000. But late in 1813 he was trapped while on a raid in the Sharqiyah, the eastern area of Oman, and killed. On the diplomatic front, Amir Sa'ud managed to persuade the Persians not to give Sayyid Sa'id any more mercenaries; and on his way back from Shiraz his Ambassador, Ibrahim bin Abdul Karim, saw the acting Resident at the British Residency in Bushire, asked if the British were planning further operations in the Gulf, and said he was authorised to conclude a commercial agreement. Once again the non-intervention policy was invoked; and, after referral to India, Amir Sa'ud was told that the British preferred no formal relationship with the Wahhabis.

Calm before another storm

Despite the British failure to subdue the Qawasim, Sayyid Sa'id's difficulties in maintaining the security of his rule, and Wahhabi preoccupations with the threat from Pasha Muhammad Ali's armies in western Arabia, piracy in the Gulf calmed down temporarily in the 2-3 years following the 1809 campaign. This was probably due to the time it took the Qawasim to import timber, from areas of India not under British control, and rebuild their fleet. By late in 1812 their ships began to reappear. Sayyid Sa'id reported to the British in Bombay that he planned to restore Shaikh Sultan bin Saqr to his former leadership position in Ras al-Khaimah (it will be recalled that in 1808 the Wahhabis had removed him for being insufficiently compliant to their wishes), and then conclude an agreement with him which would remove or reduce the risk of attacks on Oman. William Bruce, the acting Resident in Bushire, was invited to join the expedition, and did so in the hope of getting a commitment from the Qawasim not to attack British shipping. But the venture did not prosper: the outcome was only that Sultan bin Saqr took possession of Sharjah, an important Qasimi port but not the headquarters.

Over the next 3-4 years more Qasimi attacks on shipping in the Gulf and the seas off north-west India were reported. There were sporadic diplomatic exchanges between the British and the Qasimi leadership – now Hasan bin Rahmah, who had become chief at Ras al-Khaimah in place of Husain bin Ali. At one point the Resident in Bushire accepted an assurance from Hasan bin Rahmah that the Qawasim would not attack British shipping. This later led to disputation as to what constituted "British shipping". In 1814 the Amirs of Sind, in north-west India, appealed for British naval protection against Qasimi dhows, but the Bombay authorities turned it down, reckoning that the East India Company need not concern itself with attacks on ships that were not actually British. The logical outcome of this was that the Company had to acquiesce in piratical attacks on non-Company ships, even in waters which the British liked to believe they controlled – a stance that not all in the British Indian administration were happy with, since it could hardly be said to encourage the growth of trade. But it was difficult to see how they could act otherwise, since neither the Company nor the British Indian authorities had the resources to protect all Indian shipping. Amir Abdullah bin Sa'ud, who had succeeded his father as chief of the Wahhabis in May 1814, certainly interpreted the British policy as meaning that he had unfettered right to attack his enemies, even if (as happened once in 1815 with a Turkish ship) carrying papers issued by the British. He wrote to William Bruce, Resident at Bushire, making clear that he would not molest British shipping; "but you must not mix my enemies" (amongst whom he specifically counted the Turks) "with your people or give them papers".[9] A year later, in 1816, the same question came up with Hasan bin Rahmah, whose men had captured three Indian merchant ships sailing under British colours and carrying valuable cargo, and had murdered nearly all the crews. Hasan bin Ramah replied to the British protest by claiming that the undertaking he had given two years previously to the Resident in Bushire did not apply to Indians but only to "the English of the sect of Jesus who bear with them the British pass and flag".[10]

In 1812 Sir Evan Nepean succeeded Jonathan Duncan as Governor of Bombay. His previous career had been in the Royal Navy and the Admiralty, and his instincts were those of a naval man rather than a bureaucrat. Nepean's approach was to be critical in the campaigns which followed. He now sent a Captain Bridges to recover the cargoes captured by Hasan bin Rahmah, and remind him that the undertaking had to apply to Indian as well as to British shipping. Bridges failed completely in his mission. Indeed, Hasan bin Rahah said that he could not accept Indians as British subjects, arguing ingeniously that if the British took over all of India then the Qawasim would have no victims to plunder! After attempting to damage some Qasimi pirate dhows lying at anchor (unsuccessfully, since the shots fell short), Bridges had to withdraw because of a change of wind, having made no progress at all. Worse than that, the Qawasim now had a low impression of British power. They had rebuilt their own strength; and several ports on the Persian coast – including Laft on Qishm Island, which they had recovered from the Omanis – were in alliance with a Qasimi confederation which stretched all the way down the Pirate Coast from Rams to Sharjah. By 1816 their dhows were operating boldly off the Kutch coast; and in 1817 Nepean felt he had to arrange for both the Royal Navy and the Bombay Marine to cruise on the trading routes off India and Arabia, and in the Gulf, to ensure the safety of British and Indian shipping – both being prey to attacks from the Qawasim.

---

9 Bombay records, India Office, quoted by J B Kelly: *Britain and the Persian Gulf*, p 132
10 India Office Records, quoted by J B Kelly: *Britain and the Persian Gulf*, p 133

The need for another expedition

And so during 1817 it became obvious to the British authorities in India that they would have to mount a fresh attack on the Qawasim, in order to make permanent what they had done only provisionally in 1809. Equally obvious, however, was the risk of provoking the Wahhabis. Writing to the Resident in Bushire in early 1817, Amir Abdullah bin Sa'ud had told Bruce that he would accept no obligation to refrain from attacking what did not belong to Englishmen, and mentioned the people of Oman and the Persian subjects of Sayyid Sa'id (among several others) as his enemies and therefore as people whom he reserved the right to attack and plunder. So the British, knowing that the Qawasim were to a certain extent under the Wahhabi thumb, had to reckon that an anti-pirate expedition might involve them in a wider campaign on mainland Arabia. However, this risk noticeably declined in 1817: late in 1816 Pasha Muhammad Ali had renewed his campaign against the Wahhabis in the Hijaz, the following year his army pressed forward into central Arabia, and in 1818 he besieged and eventually captured Dir'iyyah. Amir Abdullah was captured, taken as a prisoner to Egypt, and later publicly executed in Istanbul.

The Amir Abdullah's preoccupation with resisting this determined attack from the west had mixed effects in the Gulf. While it removed the Wahhabi element from the plundering of shipping, it left the Qawasim with a free hand, and also seems to have removed the religious element from their piratical activities. These became especially serious during the trading season in the winter of 1817-18. Using Muscat as a base, the Bombay authorities made an arrangement for trading vessels to travel in protected convoys; and they also approached Sayyid Sa'id to get his help in ensuring security in the Gulf.

But it was not until mid-1818 that the British began serious planning for the expedition that was to lead to a solution to the piracy problem in the Gulf. They were provided with the motivation and the opportunity partly because of the provocation of the increasing number, and range, of the Qawasim attacks in 1817 and early 1818; but also because military success within India resulted in increased availability of troops for action outside the Indian borders.

Governor Nepean drew on detailed reports that had been submitted to him from the Political Agency in Turkish Arabia (ie Iraq) and the

Bombay Marine. These reports analysed the location of the pirate bases, and the numbers of the dhows (nearly 300) and of their fighting men (about 10,000). He submitted a recommendation to the Governor General, Lord Hastings, together with some options for a solution. These options included another punitive and destructive expedition, like that of 1809; the establishment of British authority in the Gulf, to ensure longer-term security; and the creation of an arrangement with the Ruler of Muscat, making Sayyid Sa'id and his successors responsible for the southern shore of the Gulf, including Bahrain. After some deliberation, the Governor-General replied in November 1818 that a strong force of 5,000 men would be required to subdue the Qawasim in such a way as to remove the possibility of their recovering their strength and requiring yet another attack on them. He added that such a force could not be spared until the following winter's campaigning season, but that in the meantime Ibrahim Pasha (the son of Muhammad Ali and the leader of the Turkish-Egyptian force fighting the Wahhabis) might be asked if he would join an attack on the Qawasim. However, Hastings failed to give a view on the longer-term options submitted to him by Nepean.

Hastings was able to follow up his proposal to involve Ibrahim Pasha when, at the turn of the year, he heard the news of the destruction of Dir'iyyah and the further advance of the Turkish-Egyptian army to the shores of the Gulf. He wrote to Ibrahim Pasha inviting him to join in the suppression of the Qawasim; and Nepean also informed Sayyid Sa'id in Muscat of the way in which Hastings's thinking was going. Predictably happy with Ibrahim Pasha's crushing of Wahhabi power, Sa'id said he was attracted by the plan.

Nepean seems to have interpreted Hastings's plan as implying Turkish-Egyptian control of the whole southern coast-line as a means of ensuring security in the Gulf. Nepean however considered that a better way forward, which would also not involve the British in military obligations, would be to enhance the power of the Ruler of Muscat, while at the same time putting Bahrain under Sayyid Sa'id's control. In putting this to his Council (a body that consisted of the Governor plus three others), Nepean also renewed the idea of a British base on Qishm Island. It will be recalled that this proposal had been advocated previously by John Malcolm; under Nepean's scheme, the base would be partly financed from Muscat, since the possession of Bahrain would give Sayyid Sa'id increased revenues from pearl fishing and taxation. Other members of the Council had reservations, in particular over the strength of Sayyid Sa'id's position in the lower Gulf, and his ability to sustain domination over his own territory (eg the northern coast-line, beyond Sohar, known as the Shamailiya), still less over Bahrain. The outcome was agreement to send an emissary to Ibrahim Pasha, who offered – though orally, and deliberately not in writing – to install his garrison in Ras al-Khaimah, once the British-Egyptian alliance had captured it.

Sadlier's crossing of Arabia

There followed an episode which resulted in the first East-West crossing of Arabia by a European – remarkably by a series of accidents: this was far from being the intention of the mission. Captain George Sadlier (the spelling "Sadleir" is also found) was chosen to travel to meet Ibrahim Pasha in Arabia, in order to carry the message about Ras al-Khaimah, a letter from the Governor-General and a ceremonial sword, a presentation also from Lord Hastings.

Sadlier was instructed to stop at Muscat on the way, and check on Sayyid Sa'id's willingness to participate in a joint operation, with the Turkish-Egyptian force, against the Pirate Coast. Arriving in Muscat in May 1819, he was taken aback to find Sayyid Sa'id quite strongly opposed to the idea – surprising after the positive response he had given earlier in the year to Captain Robert Taylor, the Resident in Bushire. Perhaps he was offended by reports of Ibrahim's troops' brutal behaviour after capturing Dir'iyyah, or he was having second thoughts about having the Turkish-Egyptian force right at his borders – he asked for a guarantee against an attack by them. He may have suspected that Ibrahim might have designs on Bahrain, which he himself hoped to regain. He may even have wondered if the British authorities in India meant serious business, since for four or five years they had been content with half-measures to counter the Qasimi revival. But he did offer to help the British with troops and supplies in any operation against the Qawasim, if the Omani contribution could be kept separate from any Turkish-Egyptian contingent.

Sadlier pursued his mission to meet Ibrahim Pasha, and in late June arrived at Qatif, on the coast near Dammam, north-west of Bahrain. His journey is parenthetical to this narrative, and has been told elsewhere.[11] Suffice it to say that by this stage, in the face of uprisings from beduin tribes, the Turks and Egyptians had decided to withdraw from eastern and central Arabia, and Sadlier felt obliged progressively to pursue or travel with the departing army in the hope of meeting Ibrahim Pasha. By now it was becoming clear that there was no real chance of Turkish-Egyptian co-operation against the Qasimi pirates, but Sadlier judged that he should nevertheless hand over his Governor-General's message to Ibrahim. He met up with the Egyptian regional governor in Hufuf (in the Hasa Oasis), and then joined the Egyptian force as it travelled west. When they arrived in Dir'iyyah, in the blistering heat of August, Sadlier was shocked at the utter destruction wrought on the Wahhabi capital. (The sad ruins may still be seen today.) As he moved on with the Egyptians, it became clear to Sadlier that he would not be able to return to India via the Gulf, but would have to meet Ibrahim Pasha in the Hijaz. This eventually happened: Sadlier met twice with him, first in Madina and then in Jeddah, but the exchanges were unsatisfactory. Sadlier considered that the Pasha's gifts to Lord Hastings (in return for the ceremonial sword) were of such poor quality as to be an intended insult, and sent them back – causing Ibrahim to take offence. Ibrahim prevaricated on the proposed plan for a joint operation against the Qawasim, and then left for Egypt. The unfortunate Sadlier was left on his own in Jeddah for another two months before being rescued by a Bombay Marine cruiser in January 1820.

The expedition of 1819-20
Meanwhile in India preparations for the expedition were going ahead, and the force was ready to sail in October 1819, under the command of Major-General Sir William Grant Keir. The policy disagreement between Nepean and Hastings was still unresolved. The Bombay Government Chief Secretary, Francis Warden, who was a temporary member of the Governor's Council, was at pains to spell out his objections to Nepean's way of thinking. He was particularly opposed to handing over responsibility for lower Gulf security to Sayyid Sa'id, whom he

---

11 His own account is in his *Diary of a Journey across Arabia*. See also Edwards, F M: "George Foster Sadleir", *Journal of the RCAS*, xliv (1957), 38-49.

considered unpopular and unfit for the purpose. In addition, Warden considered that to hand Bahrain over to him would give rise to further instability in the area, actually going so far as to blame Sayyid Sa'id and his father for the fighting of the last couple of decades. When the various arguments were submitted to him, Lord Hastings passed the buck back to Nepean, avoiding any decision – particularly on what to do about Bahrain – until more information was available. As a result, Nepean also postponed giving any political instructions to Major-General Keir: the expedition was to capture Ras al-Khaimah, destroy Qasimi boats and stores, and then deal likewise with any other ports on the Pirate Coast whose occupants were known to be involved in piracy. In accordance with the usual policy of avoiding involvement in the internal affairs of Arabia, Keir's forces were instructed not to operate further from the coast than was necessary for the aims mentioned above.

In advance of the force's departure from Bombay, Nepean sent an emissary to Muscat (there was still no Agent there) to find out if Sayyid Sa'id would assist the expedition. The British wanted Sa'id to let the fleet rendez-vous at Qishm Island, to help with supplies there, and to participate himself in the operation. The emissary, Andrew Jukes, was a surgeon from the Bombay Army who had previously served in the Agency in Bushire. He found Sayyid Sa'id in a positive attitude towards the British requests, promising supplies and stores, the despatch of troops by land to Ras al-Khaimah, and his own presence with three ships and several hundred troops. Major-General Keir followed up Jukes's approach by detaching his ship from the fleet, and meeting Sayyid Sa'id in Muscat in November – receiving confirmation of the earlier promises.

Keir rejoined his fleet off Qishm in late November 1819. Gathering together those ships that had sailed from Bombay, and those already in the Gulf, he had considerable forces at his disposal: three warships of the Royal Navy, and eight cruisers of the Bombay Marine, convoying 20 transport ships which carried nearly 1500 European and over 2000 sepoy troops. These, and the two ships which Sayyid Sa'id had in the event brought from Muscat, hove to off Ras al-Khaimah on 2 December.

The attack on Ras al-Khaimah
A reconnaissance showed that the Qawasim had strengthened the defences of Ras al-Khaimah since Bridges's ineffectual visit in 1816, and

that they had over 4,000 fighting men in the town. British troops landed on 3 December, and advanced close to the town the next day. Starting on 5 December for 3 days and a night, the British used guns which had been landed, and those on board Keir's flagship, HMS *Liverpool*, to bombard the town and its defences, and fought in some small-scale engagements. On the morning of 9 December, the walls were breached enough for an assault to be mounted, but the Qawasim had retreated to the other side of the creek, and both the fort and the town were almost deserted. Qasimi losses were heavy – over 1000 were estimated to have been killed. The British lost one officer and four men, with 49 wounded. The Omani troops arrived two days after Ras al-Khaimah fell, but their marine forces had assisted in landing the guns and equipment.

In other actions, Keir's force occupied Rams (north of Ras al-Khaimah), where Husain bin Ali had been based, and then captured the fort nearby where he had taken refuge. They destroyed the fortifications at Ras al-Khaimah, burnt or sequestered all pirate craft, and searched there and in other ports on the Pirate Coast for stolen property. Keir then brought together all the Chiefs of the Pirate Coast, to ensure their submission.[12] In a series of initial agreements, they undertook to give up all vessels other than fishing craft, and to hand over any Indian prisoners.

Nearly four weeks after the capture of Ras al-Khaimah, and two months since he had sailed from Bombay, Keir had not received the political element of his instructions. He realised that he could not detain the Shaikhs of the Pirate Coast, or the prisoners of war, indefinitely, especially since the initial agreements had been understood to offer early release for the Shaikhs. He therefore took matters into his own hands. He released all the prisoners, and on 8 January 1820 offered Hasan bin Rahmah a draft treaty of peace. This document, the General Treaty of peace for the cessation of Plunder and Piracy, became known as the "General Treaty of Peace with the Arab Tribes", and was the forerunner of the treaty relationship established between Britain and this region, and also of the Truce which caused the region's name to change from "Pirate Coast" to "Trucial Coast" and later "Trucial Oman".

---

12 The Shaikhs of these tribes, towns and villages were called "Chiefs" in British official correspondence.

The General Treaty of January 1820

The General Treaty was a remarkable document, and brought Major General Keir into conflict with the man who had taken over from Nepean as Governor of Bombay not long after the expedition had sailed, the Hon Mountstuart Elphinstone. Although we may assume that Keir subscribed completely to its substance, since he argued fiercely in defence of it in later correspondence with Elphinstone, the Treaty's text was largely drafted by Captain T Perronet Thompson, who was an Arabic-speaking member of Keir's staff and one of those bright stars that shoot across Omani-British history from time to time (see box below.)

The Treaty opened with a preamble "[establishing] a lasting peace between the British Government and the Arab tribes", and went on to declare that "there shall be a cessation of plunder and piracy by land and sea on the part of the Arabs, who are parties to this contract, for ever". Other articles prescribed forfeiture of life and property by anyone committing plunder or piracy, and set out regulations which would allow British Navy and Bombay Marine vessels to check Qawasim and other Arab shipping, and inspect their ports. Finally the Treaty forbade the murder of prisoners, and contained an article prohibiting slavery: "The carrying off of slaves, men, women or children from the coasts of Africa or elsewhere, and the transporting them in vessels, is plunder and piracy, and the friendly Arabs shall do nothing of this nature."[13]

The inclusion of this anti-slavery provision provides some confirmation of Perronet Thompson's claim to have had a major hand in drafting the Treaty: his letters and writings show how much he had been affected by his experience in Sierra Leone. He said that this article had amused the Pirate Coast Shaikhs, presumably because they knew that Sayyid Sa'id's Omani subjects were much more active in slave trading than they were. Yet Thompson also had reservations about the maritime regulations in the text, since a few weeks later he wrote on this subject to Governor Elphinstone. We must conclude that the Treaty was a joint effort by Keir and Thompson, reflecting both men's judgement that a relatively mild treatment of the Qawasim and other pirates was more likely to lead to long-lasting peace than a vindictive settlement.

---

13 The full text of the Treaty is given in Aitchison, C U: *A Collection of Treaties, Engagements and Sanads relating to India and neighbouring Countries.*

Elphinstone did not agree, perhaps sharing the views of the Bombay Marine officers who thought that the Qawasim did not deserve this lenient treatment; and there followed some firmly-worded exchanges between him and Keir. But finally Elphinstone felt he had to recommend the Governor-General to ratify the Treaty.

The Shaikhs of the Pirate Coast dutifully presented themselves to Keir to sign the Treaty. Most had done so by the end of January 1820, the last two (the Shaikhs of Ajman and Umm al-Qaiwain) in mid-March. Sayyid Sa'id felt badly about the Treaty: he had been kept out of the negotiating process, and was among those who believed that the Qasimi behaviour of recent years deserved stronger punishment. In addition, he had been hoping for British help in restoring Bahrain to his rule, and he may also have expected compensation from the Pirate Coast Shaikhs for acts of piracy and plunder against Omani shipping. He left for Muscat before all the signing was done.

Thomas Perronet Thompson

Thomas Perronet Thompson was born to a strongly Methodist family in Hull in March 1783. He was sent to Queens' College, Cambridge, where he graduated in mathematics in January 1802, a little before his nineteenth birthday. He was soon elected a Fellow of the College, but decided on a military career, and joined the Royal Navy in February 1803. After three years' naval service, he took a commission in the Army, and was in the force which sought unsuccessfully to recapture Buenos Aires from the Spanish in 1807. Back in England he fell in with William Wilberforce and the anti-slavery "Clapham Sect", and his name was put forward for the post of the first Crown Governor of Sierra Leone, the colony founded in 1787 as a home for freed slaves. For its first 20 years, the colony was a philanthropic concern administered by the Sierra Leone Company, but in 1807 the Company handed it over to the Crown. Thompson was only just 25 when appointed Governor, and was appalled by the situation in the colony when he arrived: slaves who had been freed were put to work under an apprenticeship scheme which was barely less arduous than slavery, while their white administrators were nearly always drunk. He determined to put things right, and rushed into a series of measures which pleased some of his supporters but which raised antagonism at home. He was recalled in 1810, but with his anti-slavery sentiments undented. In 1812 he rejoined the Army, and served in the Peninsula War. About this time he took up the study of Arabic; and after the end of the Napoleonic Wars asked for a transfer to Bombay, partly to pursue his interest in the Orient and in oriental languages. He found it difficult to continue his studies while serving in India, but was invited to join Keir's expedition against the pirates, and accepted. He was appointed liaison officer to Sayyid Sa'id, and then joined the force besieging Husain bin Ali, translating messages to him from the commanding officer. In his private correspondence he claimed to have drafted the General Treaty, which he probably did; certainly he was central to the negotiations leading up to it. He also claimed – again probably with justification – that he was instrumental in introducing into the text, for the first time, the identification of slavery with piracy, and the first prohibition of slavery in an international agreement. His later career is described below in the account of the action against the Bani Bu Ali. He is the subject of a biography by Leonard G Johnson.

There remained the problem of Sayyid Sa'id and his ambitions in Bahrain. Elphinstone did not like Nepean's preference to place it under the control of the Ruler of Muscat. However he showed inconsistency in putting forward possible solutions. In December 1819 he recommended to the Governor-General a policy of entire neutrality (provided that the Al Khalifa, the ruling tribe of Bahrain, avoided "any indications of a piratical spirit"), and also suggested in a letter to the chargé d'affaires in Tehran that the Al Khalifa could be persuaded to recognise Persian sovereignty and to pay an annual tribute, on condition that they retained possession. Sayyid Sa'id was to be encouraged to focus his attention on consolidating his authority in his territories nearer home. This was all in correspondence between Bombay, Calcutta and Tehran, some of it being copied to Keir, who was still in the Gulf. Sayyid Sa'id asked Keir if the British would object to his occupying Bahrain; he received the reply (in accordance with the neutrality policy) that he could do as he wished, but no encouragement to expect British assistance. Conscious that he could not capture Bahrain unaided, he re-opened discussions with the Persians, who were keen to re-establish their control over the island, and supported the plan for a joint expedition. Husain Ali Mirza, the Prince-Governor of Fars, then brought Keir into the planning process, since he needed Keir's acquiescence at least, and if possible his help in transporting troops by sea. In the event, no expedition was required: in mid-January the Al Khalifa sent a representative to Keir, still at Ras al-Khaimah, to ask if they could be admitted to the General Treaty. After the representative had signed the Treaty on the Al Khalifa's behalf, he went on to Muscat. Sayyid Sa'id still felt ill-used by the Al Khalifa: when Keir had warned him against reviving hostilities in the Gulf, he had replied that he could not ignore the injuries Muscat had suffered at their hands. Nevertheless, he did a deal, whereby the Al Khalifa recognised his sovereignty and paid him an annual tribute of $MT 30,000. The British, in order to secure it, assured the Al Khalifa that they would not help the Persians in any attack on them, and also warned the Shah against enforcing his claim to Bahrain.

As part of the final settlement, and because he had been instructed to leave a military force in the Gulf, Keir set up a base in Ras al-Khaimah, under the command of Captain Perronet Thompson. Sayyid Sa'id, who would have got to know him well during the campaign, wrote to him to express his pleasure at the appointment. The two men were to see more of each other before many months had passed.

Keir returned to Bombay in mid-March 1820. He had achieved considerable success. He had destroyed much of the boats, stores and equipment which the Qawasim used for piratical activities. In the actions against Ras al-Khaimah and other fortified towns he had asserted undoubted British military superiority. Where he had gone much further than Wainwright and Smith in 1809 was in persuading the Pirate Coast Shaikhs to sign a commitment which stood a good chance of ensuring peace on the seas in the Gulf and north-west Indian Ocean for some years to come. In addition, he had left a relatively secure settlement of the question of Bahrain, with Sayyid Sa'id in a position of greater wealth (with the receipt of the Al Khalifa tribute) and security (with the Wahhabi threat removed) than he had been at any time so far during his reign.

We should not leave this episode without some comment on the Qawasim, whom history – or at any rate European historians – may have treated unkindly. They were far from being the only maritime nation who practised piracy in the 18th century; indeed British, Omani, Indian and other Gulf ships had attacked trading vessels from at least the late 1600s. As for their reported brutality, this is not the place to defend Qawasim indiscriminate murder of many of their captives (especially Indians, whom they considered as trade competitors), but it should be said that Portuguese treatment of their Arab enemies not so long before was of extraordinary cruelty. The Qawasim had the misfortune to run up against the British when the latter were at the height of their naval power in the region, and also in a state of high concern to protect the route to India; and Qawasim contacts with the Wahhabis inflamed them to acts of piracy above a level which the British could tolerate. Had this extraneous element been absent, the Qawasim might well simply have developed as a small trading tribe benefitting from commerce with India alongside the Omanis and the 'Utub of Kuwait.

CHAPTER 6

The Bani Bu Ali campaigns, 1820-21

Having, as they thought, resolved the problem of piracy in the Gulf itself, the British next sought to tidy up other pockets of lawlessness. Under the headstrong leadership of T Perronet Thompson, they looked further south and east, and joined forces with Sayyid Sa'id to engage in a campaign in Eastern Oman that carried strategic and personal risks, and coloured Omani and Arab views of the British for decades to follow.

* * * * * * *

After Keir's Pirate Coast campaign, one other piece of unfinished British-Indian business was the question of whether to establish a military base in the Gulf, to watch over British and Indian interests there and to ensure implementation of the 1820 General Treaty. The arrangement in Ras al-Khaimah, with Perronet Thompson as Agent and also force commander, was temporary, given the insistence of both Governor and Governor-General that there should be no mainland base, although a base on an island would be acceptable. The Ruler of Muscat was once more brought into the equation, since the favoured places were Qishm Island and the smaller island of Qais, about 100 miles West of Qishm and equally close to the Persian shore; it is shown as Halah on modern maps. Acting on his naval commander's advice, Keir preferred Qais, for its more sheltered harbour and better water, and hoped that the government of the Shah could be persuaded to allow the British to base there.

Discussion of this proposal in Tehran did not succeed, however. The Persians accepted that Qishm Island fell under the control of the Ruler of Muscat "under the supremacy of Persia", in the same way as he held Bandar Abbas. It was therefore decided to transfer Thompson and his contingent to Qishm, a move that took place in July 1820, after Sayyid Sa'id had given his approval.

Thompson was not destined to stay there long. Almost as soon as he had brought the troops on to the island and set them up in the headquarters at Dairistan, he was called away to deal with an incident of piracy off the southern coast of Oman – an incident (or Thompson's handling of it) which was to colour the British relationship with Oman for decades to follow, and which was to have severe consequences for Thompson himself.

The Bani Bu Ali incident[1]

The Bani Bu Ali are a tribe living in the Ja'lan region, on the coast and inland south and west of Sur, north of the area of dunes known as the Wahiba or Sharqiyah Sands. The coastal area is dry and desolate, but the Bilad Bani Bu Ali (literally "the country of the sons of the father of Ali") has oases where date plantations prosper. In the late 18th and early 19th century, when Wahhabi influence had penetrated deep into Oman, the Bani Bu Ali had adopted Wahhabi practices and then in 1818 had renounced their allegiance to Sayyid Sa'id. Reports were then received that they were engaging in acts of piracy. First, an Indian merchant had complained in Bombay that his vessel had been attacked and captured off Ras al-Hadd, and then abandoned, and in May 1820 Sayyid Sa'id told Captain Bruce, from the Bushire Residency, that the Bani Bu Ali had also taken a Portuguese ketch and two vessels from Muscat. In correspondence with a Captain Maillard, whom Thompson had left in charge in Qishm while he recovered from a fever, Sayyid Sa'id said that he planned to mount an attack on the Bani Bu Ali, and that he hoped it would be a joint expedition with the British. His motives would have been directed towards getting the Bani Bu Ali to give up Wahhabi practices and restore their allegiance to himself. Maillard's aims, on instructions from Bombay (addressed to Thompson, though he had not

1 A detailed account of the lead-up to the incident, and in particular of the battle at Bilad Bani Bu Ali, is in Moyse-Bartlett, H: *The Pirates of Trucial Oman*

yet seen them), were to stop piracy, but his letter to Sayyid Sa'id used language that could have been interpreted as implying British support for restoring his authority in the Ja'lan. This was far from the intention of the Governor's Council in Bombay, who were as keen as ever not to get embroiled in internal Arab affairs.

Thompson returned to Dairistan in Qishm, from Muscat, his health restored, in August 1820. He had the instructions from Bombay to which Maillard had referred earlier; these made it clear that he could engage against the Bani Bu Ali provided that the actions taken had indeed been piracy, and that a letter was first addressed to the Shaikh of the tribe explaining the British Government's purpose in ending piracy and calling on him to abandon such acts. Thompson went ahead, sending the required letter by means of the cruiser *Mercury*, which sailed for Muscat and al-Ashkarah in early September. Even now, al-Ashkharah is a small port on a desolate coast; and *Mercury*'s Commanding Officer, Captain William Collinson, not knowing how to find the place, took on board at Muscat a pilot described in the ship's log as "Shaikh of Ras al-Hadd". It is not certain that this person was chief of a tribe – the usual meaning of "Shaikh" – since the area of Ras al-Hadd, the most easterly point of the Arabian Peninsula, was and is very sparsely populated, without a tribe worthy of the name; and it is more likely that the term "Shaikh" was being used in the sense of "venerable old man".

The *Mercury* sailed past Ras al-Hadd, and came to a point on the coast which this pilot told Collinson was al-Ashkharah, although no boats or buildings could be seen. The next day, 20 September 1820, when the weather was calmer, Collinson sent a small boat ashore, manned by a First Lieutenant (presumably carrying Thompson's letter), the Shaikhly Pilot to act as interpreter, and a small armed crew. However, it was still too rough for the boat to land, and the Pilot swam ashore, where after a short conversation with a local inhabitant (not of course recorded) he was attacked by a group of Arabs who had been hiding behind a sand dune. The boat's crew killed three of the assailants, but could not save the pilot.

Collinson realised that it would not be possible to land safely except in strength, and returned to Dairistan in Qishm to report to Thompson, and to Bombay. Thompson did not feel he needed to wait for further instructions from Bombay: from the murder of the emissary he judged it could be assumed that the Bani Bu Ali admitted guilt for the acts of piracy, and somehow hoped to brazen it out. The instructions sent in June were authorisation enough. Thompson – not without an element of rashness in his temperament – was determined that British prestige in the region, and their anti-piracy policy, should not be undermined. Firm and prompt action was required. He collected together all the ships available to him in Dairistan, and about half his garrison, ie just over 600 troops, and sailed in early October. As a result he did not see the instructions sent by Elphinstone in response to Collinson's report of the pilot's murder at al-Ashkharah. These instructions did indeed confirm that Thompson should join forces with Sayyid Sa'id in his projected expedition against the Bani Bu Ali; but Elphinstone – perhaps with too little knowledge of the topography of Ja'lan, and not realising how far inland were the date plantations and dwellings of the Bani Bu Ali – required Thompson not to move troops into the interior. He must have believed that the anti-piracy objectives could be met by burning boats and buildings on the coast, as had been done at Ras al-Khaimah and Shinas.

By mid-October (1820) Thompson and his fleet arrived in Muscat and assembled the joint expedition with Sayyid Sa'id's forces. Sa'id told Thompson how he had been provoked by the Bani Bu Ali, and how he planned to put his own forts there to ensure loyalty. Thompson wrote again to Bombay, explaining his intention to co-operate with Sayyid Sa'id, in view of the tribe's hostility towards both the Ruler and the British, adding that this would be done without putting the British troops at risk. Further instructions were then sent to him from Bombay, authorising him to co-operate with Sayyid Sa'id if piracy were proved, although only after eliminating any doubt on the matter by directly communicating with the tribe. But Thompson did not see these instructions either, until he returned to Dairistan after the operation.

Thompson and Sayyid Sa'id agreed to land the combined force at Sur, rather than al-Ashkharah, where Captain Collinson thought he had seen defensive forces on *Mercury*'s previous visit, and where the surf was known to make landing difficult. This has been considered by some as a mistake on Thompson's part – he might have been wiser to make the landing at al-Ashkharah. However, although the march from Sur to Bilad Bani Bu Ali is longer than from al-Ashkharah, the route enabled the force to set up camp in Bilad Bani Bu Hasan, the town of a tribe loyal to Sayyid

Sa'id; and, in the event, the march there, though arduous and long (about 70 km, or 45 miles), was accomplished without any losses. But in terms of his tactical position vis-à-vis his superiors, Thompson would have found it easier to justify the short raiding route from al-Ashkharah than the campaign march from Sur into the interior. (From al-Ashkharah to Bilad Bani Bu Ali is only about 35 km, or 22 miles.)

The confrontation, then battle, with the Bani Bu Ali
The Bani Bu Ali had in fact deserted al-Ashkharah, burnt their boats there, and concentrated their fighting men, numbering about 900, in their town and date plantations inland. The British-Omani combined force came to about 1600 men, with an artillery detachment of six guns. It may be understood why they were confident, and why Thompson considered they could press their demands. These were delivered to the Bani Bu Ali on the evening of 8 November, in a letter from Sayyid Sa'id (Thompson did not want to give the impression of a divided command) which made clear that his own presence was because of hostilities against his people, and the British participation was because of their wish to suppress maritime piracy. The requests were for them to surrender their forts and arms, and to hand over those who killed the messenger at al-Ashkharah, ie the pilot "Shaikh of Ras al-Hadd".

In his reply, Shaikh Muhammad bin Ali, the chief of the tribe, not surprisingly refused to agree that the Bani Bu Ali should surrender their arms, although he would have been prepared to comply with the other two conditions. Shaikh Muhammad was worried that, unarmed, his men would have been delivered as prisoners to the British; and we may also assume that he considered it a natural right for his men to possess and carry personal weapons. Thompson did not want to give the impression that he was prepared to bargain with the tribe; and he may also have thought that only complete suppression, followed by a written agreement (as had been done at Ras al-Khaimah), would achieve the ending of piracy on the southern Omani coast. Almost certainly he believed that the combined force was strong enough to force the Bani Bu Ali to come to terms. Sayyid Sa'id accepted his advice to order an attack the next morning.

9 November 1820 was a disaster for the combined force. Both misjudgement and bad luck played a part, combined (if we are to believe

accounts written by Thompson and other British witnesses) with an unusual reluctance of the Indian sepoys to obey orders and fight. Later an enquiry was held, and Thompson brought before a court-martial in Bombay, with the result that detailed descriptions of the battle have survived, though they are not consistent. The smoke of battle, from the artillery and the matchlocks, would have made it difficult or impossible to discern what was actually going on. Thompson's plan was to encircle the town, bombard the far side – as they approached it from Bilad Bani Bu Hasan – and then mount an assault in the hoped-for breach of the walls. But as the combined force was advancing in a column preparatory to surrounding the town, fighting men of the Bani Bu Ali attacked them from the flank. This need not have been fatal to the Omani-British force, but somehow they failed to re-form in such a way as to be able to resist the attack. The Bani Bu Ali drove forward in a wide formation, endangering both flanks of the Omanis and British. At this point, Thompson issued orders which might have provided the necessary resistance – if they had been obeyed. The sepoys, ordered to advance with fixed bayonets, stayed their ground, and fired a few shots; but then – when ordered again to fix bayonets – turned and took refuge by fleeing through Sayyid Sa'id's troops who were immediately behind them.

The rest of the combined force were soon forced (or chose) to leave the field. The artillery detachment, exposed on the right flank, deserted their guns; and then the Omani troops and the remaining sepoys fled in panic, now under fire from the Bani Bu Ali matchlock guns. Thompson and Sayyid Sa'id attempted to stop the rout, but without success. They and the other survivors fell back to the camp at Bilad Bani Bu Hasan, leaving eight British officers, 400 sepoys and several hundred Omanis dead on the battlefield.

Things did not improve much the following day. An attack on the camp by the Bani Bu Ali was beaten off during the night, but in the morning officers and men began to take themselves off back to Sur. With his remaining men Thompson spiked the guns, bundled the barrels of powder down a well, destroyed supplies, and left. He and Sayyid Sa'id, who had been wounded in the battle, decided to make for Muscat overland, fearing that the way back to Sur might be blocked or subject to attack.

They reached the capital a week later. Thompson was reunited with his family: his 5-year-old son and his wife Anne (known as Nancy; he had characteristically eloped with her in 1811 when her family had objected to the marriage) were awaiting him on one of the ships which had taken the British force to Sur. Immediately Thompson, in making his report to Bombay, began to recommend the provision of fresh troops to assist Sayyid Sa'id to restore his position in the Ja'lan and bring the Bani Bu Ali to heel. He did so in terms not designed to reassure his superiors in Bombay that his political judgement was sound, or that he had fully taken on board their determination to avoid political commitment or military engagement in the Arabian hinterland. He reported that he had assured Sa'id that British resources would be at his disposal if required – a great deal more than Bombay, interested only in suppressing piracy, would have been content with.

The British revenge for the Bani Bu Ali defeat
Nevertheless, preparations for a punitive expedition were put in hand. Warden, still Chief Secretary to the Government of Bombay, made an express connection between co-operating with Sayyid Sa'id in reducing the Bani Bu Ali and maintaining the advantage of successes already gained in the Gulf. A sizeable force of 12 companies, plus artillery, was collected, totalling not far short of 2,000; and its commanding officer, Lieutenant-Colonel Warren, sailed on ahead to Muscat to make arrangements with Sayyid Sa'id. His instructions were to get Sa'id to agree to secure the forts from Sur to the Bilad Bani Bu Hasan, but not to allow British-Indian troops to fight as a combined force with the Omanis on the battlefield. This may have been because reports of the battle would have shown that Omanis and the sepoys were very close to each other, and perhaps thereby confused. More probably, the Bombay authorities would have been keen to have it clear that this was a British expedition, with Omani support, and not a combined campaign or one under Sayyid Sa'id's leadership.

By early January 1821 many of the troops were in Muscat, and others were on their way from Qishm. But in mid-January fresh and different instructions reached Warren and Thompson, who were both in Muscat. The Bombay authorities had been re-examining and re-evaluating the reports of the November debacle. They noted that the Bani Bu Ali had shown Wahhabi sympathies, and they may have been concerned about a possible Wahhabi resurgence in Oman. They would have judged that reassertion of British strength and authority was essential, the thought perhaps still in some minds that the settlement with the pirates and the Qawasim had been too soft. After the November defeat of a numerically superior and better-equipped force, they would have been determined not to take any risks. They had concluded that a significantly larger detachment was needed, and that a more senior and more experienced officer was required to lead the expedition – someone who could reliably deal with Sayyid Sa'id and restore British prestige in the lower Gulf. They appointed Lionel Smith, who had been joint commander of the 1809 campaign in the Pirate Coast, and was now Major-General. He was instructed to make clear to Sayyid Sa'id that the Governor could not stand by Thompson's assurance that British Indian resources would always be at his disposal. On the military side, Smith was instructed to have the murderers of Thompson's messenger executed, to obtain the release of prisoners, to recapture lost guns, to ensure "effectual security" against piracy, and to restore Bilad Bani Bu Ali to Sayyid Sa'id. There were also careful instructions limiting Major-General Smith's freedom to take troops further into Oman's interior. His force was of divisional strength, now numbering over 3,000 and with powerful guns and mortars. The whole expedition met up at Sur in late January. It was so large that Sayyid Sa'id, who was supposed to be providing transport camels and donkeys on a large scale, needed more time to assemble the required beasts and to collect together his tribal levies.

Smith decided to wait until they came before advancing to Bani Bu Hasan. At this point the British may have been complacent, confident in their own strength and taking too much comfort from the relative inactivity of the Bani Bu Ali since November. The 10-day wait near the sea, in pleasant climatic conditions, perhaps encouraged them to relax. Certainly the camp was widely spread out. A detachment of the Bani Bu Ali, led by Shaikh Muhammad (who had sent the defiant reply in November to Thompson's and Sayyid Sa'id's demands), attacked the camp by night on 10 February. It was pitch dark, and the surprise and the confusion were total. Contemporary accounts are a mixture of horror and comedy, since some of the British were forced out of their tents in their night-shirts or less. After a while, the British regrouped and the Bani Bu Ali were driven out of the camp; they had lost 12 men, but killed 17 including one British officer, wounded 43, and killed or disabled a number of horses. Smith tightened up the arrangements in the camp.

When the Muscat levies arrived, the fighting contingent set out for Bilad Bani Bu Hasan, and marched on to Bilad Bani Bu Ali, where they arrived on 2 March (1821). They found themselves advancing over the gruesome remains of November's battlefield. Once in front of the fortified town, the British advanced slowly, careful to maintain formation in case of a flank attack such as that which had brought about Thompson's downfall. The Bani Bu Ali charge, when it came was of intense ferocity, and caused one British officer to write later that their bravery made Thompson's disaster look less surprising. The Bani Bu Ali broke through the British line, but were forced back by the counter-attack, and eventually the town fell to Smith's small army and the British regiments' flags were flown from the battlements. Casualties were high: of the Bani Bu Ali force of about 1000 fighting men, over 200 were killed (Smith thought considerably more, since bodies were removed from the field) and nearly 300 injured. British-Indian losses were 29 killed and 169 wounded.

Meanwhile one of the ships of Smith's fleet, the *Psyche*, sailed from Sur to al-Ashkharah, and destroyed a number of boats and then the village.

After the battle
The aftermath of the short campaign was untidy, and came later to fall under criticism from the Court of Directors of the East India Company in London. Smith was left holding over 300 prisoners, whom Sayyid Sa'id refused to take, on the grounds that he could not ensure their safety – although it is not clear why not. Eventually he did agree to take nearly 200, but persuaded Smith to take the rest, including the two principal shaikhs, back to Bombay. Both lots of prisoners suffered badly in their internment. Those taken by Sayyid Sa'id were shut up in Fort Jalali overlooking Muscat harbour, where it was reported that 80 of them died of starvation. As for those embarked on Smith's fleet, Salil ibn Razik reports that "when they reached India they were unbound and well cared for, the wounded received the best professional treatment, and all lived in great comfort in Bombay";[2] but Muhammad bin Ali wrote to the Court of Directors a petition which they described as "most afflicting", at the

---

2 Salil ibn Razik: *History of the Imams,* p 344

same time judging that the removal of the prisoners to Bombay was unjustifiable. After some months (and in fact before he was ordered to do so by the Directors), Governor Elphinstone released the prisoners, returned them to Ja'lan, and also arranged for aid to be given to the Bani Bu Ali to rebuild their town and destroyed plantations.

This was necessary because Smith, after the battle, set about wholesale destruction of the fort, the town, the date palms, and their *falaj* irrigation system. This was because Sayyid Sa'id, for unexplained reasons, as well as declining (at first) to take charge of the prisoners, also refused to occupy the Bani Bu Ali territory. The women and some of the children – since even boys had been taken as prisoners to Muscat – were allowed to go free, but had no means of support and took refuge with the Bani Bu Hasan.

The campaigns assessed

Assessment of these campaigns is a gloomy task. None of the protagonists comes out of the episode with much credit. Even the Bani Bu Ali, to whom later writers have ascribed remarkable courage on the battlefield, badly misjudged their adversaries – initially in killing the "Shaikh of Ras al-Hadd" (why this purposeless murder?) and later in not making more effort to come to terms either, first, with Thompson and Sayyid Sa'id, or secondly with Smith. On the British side, Thompson clearly made a series of errors, both political and tactical, in the November campaign. He acted with precipitate haste in organising a punitive expedition after the murder of the "Shaikh of Ras al-Hadd", and would have done better to check with the Bani Bu Ali (as he had been instructed) for answers to the questions in the letter which was being carried in the boat by the First Lieutenant and which was never delivered. He miscalculated badly in landing at Sur, and making the long journey inland to Bilad Bani Bu Hasan and Bilad Bani Bu Ali: he knew well the long-established doctrine of not venturing far from the coast in the anti-pirate campaign, a doctrine based on the British Indian authorities' determination not to get involved in local politics and especially not to risk provoking the Wahhabis into hostility. This doctrine was of long standing: it goes back to the instructions issued to the Political Agent Seton on his return to Muscat in 1805 (see page 54 above). By 1820 the direct Wahhabi threat from the Al Sa'ud in Dir'iyyah had largely receded;

but the memory of it would still have been fresh, and those in charge in Bombay may (rightly) have feared that pockets of this highly driven group of religious puritans could have survived. Further, in taking the long route via Sur instead of the short route inland from al-Ashkharah, Thompson laid himself open to accusations of rashness and neglect of duty.

Once the campaign was launched, Thompson compounded his errors. Although he was probably correct in reckoning that the wrong signals would be given to the Shaikh of the Bani Bu Ali if there were twin leadership of the expedition, his decision to pass the initiative to Sayyid Sa'id (who, it will be remembered, signed the letter of demand sent to Shaikh Muhammad on the eve of the battle) instantly allowed the Arabs both there and elsewhere to conclude that the campaign was an action taken by the Muscat Ruler to assert his supremacy over a recalcitrant and disloyal tribe. Whatever might have been written in Sayyid Sa'id's letter of demand, few would have known about the careful explanation in it, that the British presence was because of the Bani Bu Ali's alleged acts of piracy. Thompson had lost the opportunity to switch the balance, or to make clear that the expedition was a logical continuation of the British anti-piracy campaigns of the previous year, with Muscat's support because of the Omani interest in maritime peace and security.

It is more difficult to make judgements on Thompson's conduct of the battle, even though the events of 9 November 1820 were gone through in great detail later, in the court-martial at Bombay at which Thompson was charged. He may have been at fault in allowing the column to be exposed to attack from the flank, although he does appear to have given himself time to turn the troops to defend themselves against the Bani Bu Ali charge. He certainly fought with great personal courage, moving from one place to another on the battlefield to try to bring the sepoys to order, co-ordinating with Sayyid Sa'id, and not leaving the scene until absolutely necessary. The letter he wrote to his wife the day after the battle makes clear his disappointment with the sepoys; he was later accused of disgraceful conduct in blaming them for the defeat, but he seems to have had no doubt on the matter.

Nor can Thompson's superiors in the Bombay Government be entirely absolved from censure. Their instructions and actions contained internal inconsistencies. For example, they instructed Thompson to engage in joint action with Sayyid Sa'id against the Bani Bu Ali, and then blamed him for giving the tribesmen the impression that he was supporting Sa'id in putting down a revolt. They compounded this inconsistency by mounting the second expedition, on its huge scale: however much it may have been intended to demonstrate – to borrow from the motto of the Order of the Thistle – that no-one could provoke the British with impunity, the conclusion naturally drawn by the Arab on-looker, and by the Bani Bu Ali themselves, would have been that the British wished to suppress the tribe and assert Sayyid Sa'id's supremacy in the area.

This conclusion would have been strengthened by Major-General Smith's actions after the battle in March. By taking prisoner all the males (including many of the old men and boys), and by destroying the date palms and *aflaj*, Smith took away the livelihood of all the tribe; it cannot have been easy for the women and remaining children to take refuge with the Bani Bu Hasan: that tribe were their only near neighbours, but they had been loyal to Sayyid Sa'id and would in a sense be tribal enemies. We have seen what pitiful outcomes awaited the male prisoners, about half in the awful dungeon of Fort Jalali and the rest far from home in Bombay.

Some justice was done in the months that followed. Thompson, who had been relieved of his post as Political Agent at the time of the start of Smith's 1821 punitive expedition, was brought before a court martial in Bombay in May (1821). He was found partly guilty on two of the four charges against him, and acquitted of the other two; and sentenced to a public reprimand. Thompson himself saw this as more than a partial vindication of his actions, especially when the Commander-in Chief of the forces in Bombay, Lieutenant-General Sir Charles Colville, sought to get the Court to reconsider its verdict and have Thompson acquitted. But this appeal was brushed off. Despite Colville's attempt to intervene on his behalf, and the letters of congratulation and support which he received from his brother officers in the 17th Light Dragoons, Thompson had lost the confidence of the authorities in Bombay, and his career in the Gulf was over. He returned to England independently and rejoined his regiment for a while, and later became a political writer and then a Member of Parliament. He remained technically gazetted in the Army, though not on the active list, and was given a series of promotions, becoming a General in 1868, aged 83.

The Court of Directors of the East India Company in London made mature and sober judgement of the affair. They criticised the Governor and his staff in Bombay for instructing the co-operation with Sayyid Sa'id, Thompson for his conduct, Smith for his treatment of the Bani Bu Ali after the battle, and Sayyid Sa'id for the destruction of the plantations and *aflaj*. They ordered the return of the prisoners from Bombay (though in fact Governor Elphinstone had already taken this measure by the time the order arrived), and some assistance to restore the livelihood of the defeated tribe. The Bani Bu Ali accepted all this graciously: a few years later Shaikh Muhammad travelled to Bombay to thank the Governor personally, and in 1835 Lieutenant Wellsted of the Bombay Marine visited the area and was given a warm welcome.

An overall assessment of the Bani Bu Ali incident is bound to leave us with mixed feelings. The British allowed themselves unnecessarily to be trapped in an awkward corner, then used a sledge-hammer to crack a nut, and afterwards were excessively firm, even brutal, in dealing with the conquered enemy. They suffered losses of 9 British and over 300 Indian men, for a simple assertion of power which achieved marginal success, if that, in its primary objective, that of suppressing piracy: before long the Bani Bu Ali seem to have been at it again. But British determination on the piracy issue would have been clear to all those on the Indian Ocean coast as well as in the Gulf; and Sayyid Sa'id would have been left in no doubt as to the strength of his alliance with the British, a factor which may have played a part in his decision to allocate resources and energy to the development of his colonial possessions in East Africa in the decades that followed. His confidence in his position in Oman may have been a factor in his decision to travel to Mecca in 1824 to perform the Hajj, so displaying to fellow-Muslims the sureness he must have felt – a happier voyage than his father Sa'id's pilgrimage in 1803 (p 50 above). He made it into a grand affair, sailing in a 74-gun ship (named the *Liverpool*, curiously) that had been specially prepared in Bombay;[3] and he was welcomed in the Hijaz in grand style. He was received by the Sharif, given lavish gifts sent by Muhammad Ali, Pasha of Egypt, and welcomed home in Muscat with celebrations that lasted several days. He may however have failed in one ambition: according to

3 Probably the same ship which Sa'id later presented to King William IV

Owen, a British naval commander whom we shall meet in the context of Mombasa, Sa'id showered gifts on religious personages in Mecca in the hope of winning their support for his claims to the Imamate, but without success.

But in the meantime his closeness to the British, and developments in Britain which extended quickly to Bombay, brought Sayyid Sa'id into tension with his allies over the subject of that little clause which Perronet Thompson had introduced into the General Treaty of 1820 – the slave trade.

CHAPTER 7

1820-1840: Opening moves in the campaign for abolition of the slave trade

The period of 1820-1840 was one of growing prosperity for Muscat and Oman, and for Sayyid Sa'id bin Sultan personally. Maritime power and commercial success were increasing, the Eastern African possessions became more significant, and revenue from Zanzibar grew. But for the British, whose position in India was now more stable, and the administration more settled after the changes of the 1780s, the issue of abolition of the slave trade became the centre-piece of the relationship with Muscat and its Ruler.

* * * * * * *

The Eastern African slave trade

The slave trade from east African ports, and on the mainland, is of great antiquity. For centuries, and for much longer than the slave trade from west Africa to the Americas, traders had taken men, women and children from their villages in east and south-east Africa and traded them north and east. The markets were widespread and diverse: demand for east African slaves ran from Egypt, to the Gulf, into Persia, and even into India. The uses to which they were put were also more diverse than in the Caribbean and North America, where by far the majority of slaves went to plantations of sugar, cotton and tobacco. The east African trade took slaves for plantations, public works (a famous slave revolt took place in the late 9th century among slaves who were draining salt

101

marshes in lower Mesopotamia, present-day Iraq), and pearling, among other occupations; some fought in Ottoman and other armies; some captained and crewed ships; some were castrated and employed in harems; and probably the majority – some males, but mostly females, some of whom became concubines – went into domestic service. Plantations of cloves and other spices, mainly in Zanzibar and its sister-island Pemba, and in the Mascarene Islands (see box on p 28), became significant in the early-mid 19th century, and employed large numbers of slaves captured on the mainland. Sayyid Sa'id was instrumental in bringing cloves from Indonesia, and himself owned large estates planted with them. Date plantations in Oman and elsewhere in Eastern Arabia were also maintained through slave labour.

Researchers have sought to quantify the trade, but records are scarce; much deduction has to be done from imperfect records of taxes and duties paid on slaves passing through ports, and anecdotes from travellers' accounts. As a broad generalisation it has been estimated that from earliest times to the end of the 19th century some 12 million people may have been taken from their homes and sold into slavery from east Africa – that is, about the same number as were traded on the west African route to the Americas, though over a shorter period. But the number may be higher, perhaps as high as 20 million, on each of the two routes. There was also a significant trade in slaves across the Sahara, to markets in north Africa, from villages in the area near Lake Volta and across the Sudan (a term used in this context to describe the area stretching west from present-day Sudan). This trade, though numerous, did not impact on Omani and British interests in east Africa.

The east African slave trade was complex and changed over time, responding to supply and demand and other factors, such as the ease of moving people through certain areas. As well as the central east African trade centred on Zanzibar and ports on the mainland, there was also trade through present-day Ethiopia to ports from where slaves were taken to markets in the Red Sea, for onward sale to the Gulf and India. That the numbers were large is shown by evidence that significant areas of east and south-east Africa were denuded of their population by the direct and indirect effects of the slave trade – the indirect effects including, for example, the destruction of villages during raids and the decline of agriculture when raiders or traders took the able-bodied away for slavery.

In addition, the incidence of death from disease seems to have been high among the slave population, particularly among those employed on plantations. Morbidity and mortality figures for these societies in this period are hard to come by; and so it is difficult to make a comparison between slave and free populations. Some tried: for example, when abolition of slavery was about to be enacted in Zanzibar in 1896, the Sultan's First Minister estimated the slave numbers at 140,000 out of a total population of 208,000. But the continued high rate of trafficking, even when markets were not expanding (eg when numbers employed on clove plantations were static), can be accounted for only by the employers' need to replace those who had succumbed. In some places the annual replacement rate was around a third or a quarter; in other words, the average life expectancy on some plantations may have been only three or four years. Given that employers would have had to pay good money for each slave, it may seem surprising that they did not make more effort to keep them alive and in good health; but replacement seems often to have been the preferred option.

Some writers have sought to ease the reader's conscience by suggesting that the lot of slaves in the Arab or Muslim world was an easy one, or at least not as harsh as elsewhere. Such comments need to be approached with caution. There were some mitigating factors: slaves in domestic service – once they had survived their brutal removal from the villages and the grim journey to their ultimate destination – may have been treated with consideration, and many were guaranteed food and clothing; Islam lays down a number of rules that encourage masters to treat slaves with kindness, and both the Qur'an and the *hadith* (accounts of sayings and deeds of the Prophet Muhammad) contain many such injunctions, notably on manumission, the release of slaves; some slaves could rise to positions of power and responsibility; and in some circumstances (for example among pearl fishers in the Gulf, even into the 20th century) there was not much difference in the conditions of life of slaves and free men. But these factors cannot take away from the shocking nature of the trade: the extreme violence of the raids on villages, the suffering and loss of life during the journey to the coast and to market, the cruelty of castration of boys and the appalling death rate that accompanied it, the hazards of the voyage to the secondary market or employer, the humiliation of being treated as a chattel, and the abuse (including sexual abuse) which too often went with slave status.

Apart from the commands to Muslims on how to treat slaves, which of course dated back over a thousand years, and were themselves a considerable advance, in moral terms, on the previous practices of the societies with whom early Muslims came in touch, these ethical considerations about slaves and slavery were new at the opening of the 19th century, and far from widely accepted, even in Europe and North America. It was only in 1807 that the prolonged political campaign in England, spear-headed by Clarkson and Wilberforce, led to the passage of the law making the trading and transport of slaves illegal in British vessels. Despite a court judgement in favour of an escaped slave in 1772 (the "Somerset judgement"), it was not until 1833 that the institution of slavery became illegal in Britain's homeland and dependencies, and even then the slave-owners were given five years before they actually had to release their slaves into freedom. For well-known reasons, the process (and the change of attitudes) was even slower in North America: the 13th Amendment to the Constitution, abolishing slavery throughout the United States, was passed in December 1865, shortly after the end of the Civil War.

If this was the situation in Europe and North America, where a large proportion of society was educated, communications were good, there had been abolitionist movements since the 1780s (but little before then), and the dictates of religion were different, it should not be surprising that attitudes towards slavery took longer to change in the Ottoman Empire, in the Gulf, in India, and in East Africa. So, in looking at the issues surrounding slavery and the slave trade in the Indian Ocean and the Gulf in the early 19th century, we should make some attempt to do so through contemporary moral spectacles if we are to understand the reasoning behind what the protagonists did and wrote.

The Omani presence in East Africa

There had been Arab colonies on the East African coast for some time before the Portuguese occupation which began around 1500. These early settlements were by Arabs from the coastal areas of what is now Yemen, the Hadramawt and southern Oman. The Omanis – including some from Muscat – established themselves there in a more systematic and dominating way as an extension of their campaign to expel the Portuguese from their homeland between 1650 and 1700. Following up their success in Oman itself, they ejected the Portuguese from Mombasa, Zanzibar and other ports on the coast of what is now Tanzania and Kenya. The Portuguese staged a brief come-back in the 1720s, but by 1730 the Omanis had recovered, and controlled, nearly all the coast north of Mozambique and its mainland dependencies; that southern area and coast remained Portuguese. The Omanis were by now the dominant naval power in the lower Gulf and western part of the Indian Ocean, and had even ventured to attack Portuguese possessions in India. They used this power to protect their trade, of ivory, timber and metal, spices and foodstuffs, and other goods. But the trade in which the Arabs had a virtual monopoly was that in slaves. Arabs of Omani and Yemeni origin engaged in both inland expeditions to capture slaves and transport them to market, and in trading them where they were in demand. Zanzibar developed as the prime market in the region, where slaves brought from the east African littoral and, later, much further inland, were sold either for local employment or for another long journey to the market in Muscat or Sur. In Oman there was demand for slaves in the date plantations and for domestic use, and large numbers were sold on to dealers, including the Qawasim. We may assume that Perronet Thompson was targeting this aspect of the trafficking when he inserted the anti-slave-trading article into the 1820 agreement.

The beginning of British attempts at abolition of the slave trade

It was a few years before the 1807 Act had its effect in the Indian Ocean. A further Act was passed in 1811 making it illegal for British subjects, or those resident in the East India Company's territories, to transport slaves by sea; and regulations were issued by the Presidencies in Bombay and Bengal, prohibiting the import and export of slaves, as early as 1805 and then in 1807, 1811 and 1813. But the authorities in Bombay do not seem, at first, to have taken the issue at all seriously. True, they brought Sayyid Saʿid's attention to the 1811 Act and Regulation, knowing that Omani vessels were trading slaves into India; and in 1815 Governor Nepean wrote to Sayyid Saʿid suggesting that he could earn the approval of the British Government by ending the slave trade in areas under his control. But no reply was sent, and the subject was not raised again for some years. Even the orders given to the Bombay Marine, after the inclusion of Thompson's clause in the 1820 Treaty, were somewhat half-hearted, since commanders were warned to make sure that a vessel, if detained, was from a tribe that had signed the Treaty. As a result, few if any slaving vessels were detained, since commanders would have known that most of them would have been from Muscat, a non-signatory of the Treaty. In addition, in India as elsewhere, preventing the import of slaves proved difficult: small and medium-sized traders could easily land their illicit cargo at unsupervised ports, including those in independent states not part of the East India Company's empire. Ending the slave trade in the Indian Ocean could be done effectively only through preventing export from the countries of origin or the trading locations.

Change came – which would have direct effect on British dealings with Oman – as a result of the British occupation of Île de France in 1811. Sir Robert Farquhar, the first Governor of Mauritius (the island regained the name given it by the Dutch in 1598), reported to London that agriculture could not survive without a continued supply of slave labour, and asked whether the 1807 Act applied to a newly-acquired colony. The Foreign Secretary put him right in unambiguous language – sending multiple copies of his letter so that there should be no risk of the message not getting across. Farquhar took the point, and made efforts to reduce smuggling of slaves into Mauritius and the (still French) island of Réunion from Madagascar, Zanzibar and Kilwa.

By 1821 it was clear that the best way of stopping the trade was to involve Sayyid Sa'id. The ideal solution would have been to prohibit the trade in Omani vessels and Omani ports. This proposal came to Elphinstone, Governor of Bombay (1819-27) from the East India Company Court of Directors, following a memoir submitted to them by the African Institution in London. Elphinstone knew this was impractical: Sayyid Sa'id had already protested against the detention of two Omani traders, and Elphinstone had begun to realise the economic importance (to Oman) of the business. He knew that already Sa'id was getting much of his revenue from the slave trade; and in later years, as clove plantations (including large ones belonging personally to him) grew up in Zanzibar and Pemba dependent on slave labour, this revenue would increase. For the first time, the question arose of financial compensation – a buy-out.

Short of the ideal solution, it seemed feasible to consider a proposal, submitted by Farquhar, that Sayyid Saʻid might agree to prohibit Europeans from purchasing slaves in any of his ports. This might not incur Saʻid in such high losses of revenue. Elphinstone transmitted this request in August 1821, mentioning another issue that would become important as the attempts to end the slave trade in this region continued – the question of searching vessels: he assured Saʻid that the British would not infringe his sovereignty by searching Omani vessels on the high seas. Farquhar had in fact put the question to Saʻid a few months before, offering Omani vessels trading concessions in Mauritius in return. Saʻid's reply to Elphinstone was positive, although he could not meet the maximum request (of total abolition) for reasons which he said would be "as clear ... as the Sun and Moon". (Was this wording intended to echo the poetic language in the 1800 Agreement, or was it just a customary turn of phrase?) Saʻid explained to Bruce, the Resident in Bushire, that he would lose $MT 40,000-50,000 in annual revenue, from loss of import and export duties in ports owing him allegiance. Bruce also thought there was a political-religious interpretation to be given to Saʻid's "Sun and Moon" comment: he considered that since slavery was permitted under Islam, Saʻid would find his authority undermined if he were to acquiesce in any attempt to make it illegal. The political, religious and financial factors were in fact probably linked: losing revenue would make it more difficult for Saʻid to pay subsidies to tribes in Oman, which was the time-honoured way of securing loyalty, and agreeing to prohibit a practice that was sanctioned in the Qurʾan might have been viewed as a betrayal of religious and traditional values. Both of these would have reduced Saʻid's support among the tribes and their leaders, and put his position at risk.

The Moresby Treaty of 1822

Farquhar however wanted to go further, and recommended that Sayyid Saʻid should sign up to ending slave-carrying by both Arab and European vessels from Africa to the Mascarenes and elsewhere. Elphinstone demurred, fearing that Saʻid would demand financial compensation and perhaps even protection from other Arab rulers affected by the proposed ban. The outcome of this policy debate in British circles was that Sayyid Saʻid was presented, in August 1822, with a proposal for a prohibition of the export of slaves from any of his possessions to any British or European possession, with the additional provision that no Arab vessels could carry slaves south and east of a line drawn from Cape Delgado (south of Zanzibar) to Diu Head (north of Bombay) via a point near the island of Socotra (see map 4 on p xii). The negotiator was Captain Fairfax Moresby, and the line became known as the Moresby Line. The agreement effectively allowed Arab slaving vessels to trade in coastal waters off east Africa, and along the south Arabian, Persian and north-west Indian littoral. Sa'id squeezed one concession out of Moresby, and this was on the right of search: Sa'id insisted that only ships of the Royal Navy could search vessels sailing east of the Moresby Line, and refused to allow the right to be enjoyed by ships of the East India Company, ie the Bombay Marine. Moresby believed that Sa'id insisted on this restriction partly out of irritation with the Bombay Marine, one of whose ships had detained the two Omani traders the year before, and partly because he knew that Royal Navy ships patrolled the region less frequently than those of the Marine.

Why did Sayyid Sa'id agree to this British demand so readily, and without financial compensation for the revenue he expected to lose? He may have felt subject to *force majeure*, since the British were by now the only power of significance in the Indian Ocean; and he probably thought it worth cementing his alliance with them. But there were positives for him too. First, British acknowledgement of his authority on the east African littoral (by reference to his "possessions" and "dominions" as far south as Cape Delgado) amounted to recognition of more control than he actually had. And secondly, the trade concessions for Omani ships landing in India and Mauritius may have gone a long way to make up for the loss in taxation of the slave trade out of his ports.

The continuation of the coastal trade, after signature of the Moresby Treaty, then gave rise to closer examination of the famous clause that Perronet Thompson had inserted in the 1820 General Treaty with the Pirate Coast shaikhs. Soon after he took over as Resident in Bushire, John Macleod noticed that the Qawasim were still trading in slaves, and referred to the 1820 text. On closer examination the English wording seemed deficient: "The carrying off of slaves .. and the transporting them in vessels, is plunder and piracy, and the friendly Arabs shall do nothing of this nature."[1] The Indian authorities' priority in this period was to

---

1 The text is given in Aitchison's compilation, and reproduced as Appendix B(iv) in Moyse-Bartlett's *The Prates of Trucial Oman*

suppress piracy; and their (and Macleod's) fear was that to focus too hard on anti-slavery measures on the basis of this text might have led to further confrontation and blood-letting with the Qawasim, who appear to have been now trading peacefully. Elphinstone agreed that action would be taken only against kidnappers, ie those engaged in "carrying off ... slaves". This hardly applied to the Qawasim, who left it to others to do the raiding in Africa and the trading in Zanzibar. So Thompson's well-intentioned efforts became more or less a dead letter.

William Owen and the occupation of Mombasa

There followed an episode which bears only marginally on the relationship between Britain and Oman, but which is worth relating nevertheless, because of its curiosity value and because of the light that it sheds on British efforts to end the slave trade in Sayyid Sa'id's area of control and influence. It relates to the temporary occupation of Mombasa, one of those Omani "possessions" where Sa'id's authority was challenged, the result of opportunistic and independent action by a Royal Navy officer, Captain William Owen.[2]

Owen arrived off East Africa in 1823, tasked with a maritime survey. As he sailed up the coast, he observed the continuation of the slave trade (including in waters where it was forbidden under the Moresby Treaty), and on arrival in Bombay suggested to Elphinstone ways of stiffening the Treaty's provisions. Not deterred by having his suggestions dismissed, Owen chose to use an audience of Sayyid Sa'id, in December 1823, to threaten him with the loss of British friendship if he did not move towards the complete abolition of the slave trade, and to warn him that he expected soon to give British protection to Mombasa where he would suppress "that hellish traffic".[3] Owen would have known that since the 1740s, but particularly over the last 10 years, the Mazru'i clan had effectively ruled Mombasa and posed specific challenges to Sa'id and his predecessors. Twice in 1823 the Mazru'i chief in Mombasa had asked the Governor of

---

2 A detailed account of Owen's exploits and the Mombasa episode is given in Coupland: *East Africa and its Invaders*, which draws on Admiralty and India Office records and on Owen's own account in his *Narrative of Voyages to explore the shores of Africa, Arabia and Madagascar,* London 1833.

3 Owen's report to the Admiralty, March 1824 quoted by Coupland, R: *East Africa and its Invaders*, p 232

Bombay for protection under the British crown. In reply to Owen, Sa'id made it clear that he would respect the Moresby Treaty, but could not be expected to put down the slave trade with Muslims. At the same time he may have held back from an open quarrel with Owen, and gave orders to the Omani ships' commander off Mombasa to leave the Mazru'i clan alone. But he sent to Bombay a letter of protest about Owen's behaviour, where Elphinstone – not sure about the strength of Sa'id's claim to Mombasa – prevaricated and referred the question to London.

When Owen arrived at Mombasa, in February 1824, using more initiative than might be expected even from an ambitious officer of the Royal Navy, he concluded with the Mazru'i leadership a convention establishing a British protectorate, covering not only the town itself but also the littoral north 250 km to Lamu and Pate, and south 100km to Pemba Island. Sovereignty was to be exercised by the Mazru'i Chief; customs revenue was to be divided between the two contracting parties; and – of course – the slave trade was to be abolished at Mombasa.

In his reports to the Admiralty of March 1824 Owen justifies his extraordinary action mainly by reference to the immediate need to abolish the slave trade in East Africa. In language containing a level of emotion not often to be found in official annals he advocates extending British protection over the whole coast from Mogadishu to Cape Delgado, offering Sayyid Sa'id compensation equal to the net revenue he received from it: "It is to me as clear as the sun that God has prepared the dominion of East Africa for the only nation on earth which has public virtue enough to govern it for its own benefit."[4] He adds that the retention of the protectorate over Mombasa would have commercial and strategic benefits for the British; and that it was important to deny it to the French.

In between his surveying, Owen pursued his political path, partly out of his obligations towards the Mazru'i clan, and partly from his personal anti-slavery convictions. His activities caused some understandable concern among Omani Governors, who reported back anxiously to Muscat as Owen hoisted British flags at ports on the coast near Mombasa, called at Pemba to press Mazru'i claims, and in Zanzibar sought to do a deal with the Governor, Ahmad bin Sayf, on slave trade abolition. He left

4 Owen's report to the Admiralty, March 1824, quoted by Coupland, R: *East Africa and its Invaders*, p 237-8

the east African theatre in July 1825, to do more surveying off the Gambia in west Africa, no doubt to the relief of both British and Omani officials.

The British flag was nevertheless still flying over Mombasa. It continued to do so for another two years: a decision had been taken by the Government in London that nothing more should be done in Mombasa,[5] but there was delay in actually sending instructions to withdraw the small garrison, and – when the instructions did come – those in the Navy and at Mauritius who received them found ways of delaying their implementation. Eventually, and because the new Mazru'i leadership in Mombasa themselves saw no advantage in remaining under British protection, the garrison and a small number of freed slaves were evacuated in July 1826. Later, but not until 1837, Sayyid Sa'id reasserted his control over Mombasa and removed the Mazru'i leaders there.

Renewal of the official campaign for abolition

Meanwhile correspondence had been flowing between Zanzibar, Muscat, Bombay and London about slave trade abolition, in part stimulated by the approach made by Owen (true to form, not on instructions) to Ahmad bin Saif in Zanzibar in February 1825. Owen had threatened dire consequences if the slave trade were allowed to continue in Omani ports in Africa, but promised him "the settlements of the Portuguese"[6] (meaning Mozambique) if Sayyid Sa'id were to comply. Colonel Stannus, the Resident in Bushire, discussed Owen's actions and the situation in Mombasa with Sa'id in Muscat in February and May 1825, and the result was a recommendation from Elphinstone to the East India Company Court of Directors in June 1825, that the British Government should either stop interfering in Sa'id's territories or offer him adequate compensation to abolish the slave trade. What level of compensation might be "adequate"? Sa'id's answer to this question, put to him through his agent in Bombay, consisted of elements each one totally unacceptable to Elphinstone: a guarantee of defence against his enemies by land and sea, or the acquisition of Mozambique, or a grant of money sufficient for him to give up Oman and settle in Zanzibar.

5 "It is His Majesty's pleasure that no further measures should be taken upon the subject"; instructions from Lord Bathurst, Colonial Secretary, to Sir Lowry Cole, Governor of Mauritius, November 1824

6 Col Stannus (or Stanners), Resident in Bushire, reporting to Bombay Government, May 1825

These proposals throw interesting light on Sayyid Sa'id's thinking at this time. The request for a defence guarantee is not surprising; the earlier narrative has shown how this was never far from his mind. For Mozambique, we may understand why the offer made by Owen was attractive, since Portuguese revenues from ports in South-East Africa were still considerable; but Sa'id should have known that the British would not have been willing or able to deliver on it. The third request is the first evidence of Sa'id's contemplating what eventually he did of his own accord, without a British subvention; even by the mid-1820s, and even before he had built up his own investments in Zanzibar, he could see the balance of prosperity and revenue-earning in his dominions shifting to the south.

Given the longstanding British policy on avoiding involvement in the security of the Ruler of Oman, we shall not be surprised at Elphinstone's rejection of the first proposition. The second, the acquisition of Mozambique, was impracticable. And the third was also not much to British Indian liking, since the removal of Sayyid Sa'id to Zanzibar would risk re-opening the Gulf to a new era of anarchy. On top of this, there was suspicion in Bombay (for example from Francis Warden, whose involvement in the Bani Bu Ali campaign we saw earlier) that it might be difficult to keep Sa'id to observe any anti-slavery commitment he might make. In London the East India Company's Court of Directors considered Elphinstone's submission, and in a despatch of October 1827 came down against taking up Sa'id's offer, if offer it was. They thought that Sa'id had already made considerable concessions on the slave trade, and that there would be little advantage in abolishing the trade at Muscat and Zanzibar if it were to continue (as surely it would) in other African and Arab ports over which he had no jurisdiction or control. They also considered there were risks to Sa'id's own authority and safety among fellow-Arabs if he were perceived as having been forced into taking unpopular measures – and they found it convenient to British interests at the time to maintain his regional influence. So the practice of the slave trade continued as it had been following the Moresby Treaty: permitted trade north and west of the Moresby line, along the coast, with inspections of Omani ships south and east of it.

During the ten years that followed, the issue of the slave trade remained at the forefront of the minds of policy-makers in Bombay and London. But their concerns were less with putting further pressure on Sayyid Sa'id, and more with resolving problems arising from a continuation – perhaps even a growth – of the trade carried on in ships and in ports of those who were not signatory to the Moresby Treaty. This meant primarily the Qawasim, whose boats were now trading as far as Zanzibar, but also vessels from Kuwait, Bahrain, Mukulla in the Hadramawt, and others. The Bombay authorities were particularly worried about slaves being traded (legally) into parts of North-West India outside British jurisdiction, and about smuggling into Bombay itself. Incidents were reported of Somalis (usually girls) being traded by the Qawasim; and there was even a small trade in Indian women taken from Bombay to Muscat and traded elsewhere in the Gulf.

British officials looked for ways of curbing this trade. The measures they considered included modifying the Moresby Line so as to include more of the Indian coast, persuading the Shaikhs of the Pirate Coast voluntarily to observe the Moresby Treaty, and expanding the Indian Navy's right of search of slave trading vessels. Hennell, the British Resident in Bushire, was especially active in the correspondence.

For Sayyid Sa'id, his relationship with the British in the early 1830s was concerned not so much with prevarication on the slave trade as with securing support in his revived problems with the Wahhabis. Saudi forces had crushed opposition in Hufūf and the Eastern coastal region, and put increased pressure on Sayyid Sa'id – who in 1833 gave way and agreed to pay $MT 5,000 a year to their governor, now in occupation of Buraimi. Kelly judges, probably correctly, that he was by now reckoning that the Zanzibari part of his empire deserved more of his attention, and that he could rely on British Indian support if his Oman possessions came under serious threat. But the East India Company Court of Directors were not in a mood to offer guarantees of this sort, again concerned – as they had been during the pirate campaigns – to avoid commitment in the Arabian interior. To mollify them, Sayyid Sa'id offered to abrogate a commercial treaty he had just signed with the Americans (see below), and to give the Royal Navy his 74-gun ship, the *Liverpool*. The Admiralty did not want to accept the ship, for fear (in consultation with the India Board) that to do so would give rise to greater expectations on Sa'id's part than were warranted. In the end, Sa'id had his way, and in 1835 sent the ship to England as a gift to King William IV. To ensure honour was satisfied, and no obligations incurred, the Navy accepted the *Liverpool*, renamed her the *Imam*, and gave Sa'id a steam yacht named *The Prince Regent* in return.

Gifts

It is worth recalling the strong culture of presentation of gifts in this era. Gifts often had a double intention: to symbolise the friendship between rulers or persons, and the importance of the relationship, while at the same time indicating the wealth and power of both giver and recipient. On his mission to negotiate the 1800 Agreement, Malcolm gave Sayyid Sultan "an elegant watch set with diamonds – a silver ornamented clock – a gold enamelled creese (dagger) – a double-barrelled gun – a pair of pistols – a spying-glass", according to his biographer Kaye. ("Creese" is presumably a corruption of the Malay kris.) Discussing the next part of his mission, in Persia, Kaye attributes Malcom's liberality as an appeal not only to the cupidity of the Persians, but also to the importance of impressing them with "an idea of the wonderful power and the immense resources of our English civilisation". Not all gifts were suitable, some caused offence if deemed inadequate, and sometimes errors occurred in despatch and presentation. For example, Lord Clarendon gave Sayyid Sa'id a snuff-box after his kindly ceding the Kuria Muria islands to Queen Victoria (see chapter 9) – not very suitable for a Muslim ruler to whom tobacco was forbidden. As an example of an inadequate gift, we recall the insult given to Col Sadlier in the Hijaz after his crossing of Arabia (see p 78). Among impractical gifts, *The Prince Regent* was a fine steam yacht, but of no use to Sayyid Sa'id, and he passed it on to the Governor-General of India. In 1842 Queen Victoria gave him a state carriage, which Hamerton reported could never be used in Zanzibar because there were no roads suitable for it; and this was given (with permission) to the Nizam of Hyderabad. In 1844 Victoria sent a silver-gilt tea service to Sa'id. Hamerton assumed it was in a large packing-case which arrived in early 1845, and arranged to have it opened in the presence of Sa'id; but unfortunately what emerged from the case was a tomb-stone. Hamerton reported that "His Highness took this affair in the highest good-humour". When the tea service did arrive, Sa'id was pleased with the gift but asked Hamerton to keep it at the Consulate – probably because he did not want to be seen possessing such a luxury item while pleading poverty in reply to requests for subsidies from Wahhabis from the Arabian peninsula.

The Commercial Treaty, and the Anti-Slavery Treaties, of 1839

The slavery issue then became confused with a separate set of negotiations, concerning a proposed commercial treaty between the British and Sayyid Sa'id. In the summer of 1838 Sa'id sent Ali bin Nāṣir, the Governor of Mombasa, as an envoy to London to offer Queen Victoria congratulations on her accession to the throne the previous year, and to present to her his coronation gift, a fine Arabian horse (see plate 9). At the same time he proposed a commercial treaty. Sa'id was keen to consolidate markets for the growing export products of the two parts of his empire, but especially Zanzibar, which was rising in size and importance. Apart from slaves, Zanzibar was exporting large quantities of spices (mainly cloves), gum-copal (a product used in varnish for European coaches and carriages), and ivory. In quick succession Sa'id signed commercial treaties with his main trading partners, who themselves wanted markets for their goods and minimal customs dues: treaties were concluded with the USA in 1833, the UK in 1839, and France in 1844. The result for Sa'id was an increase in customs revenue, from the 5% he charged on goods from these countries landed at Zanzibar and the ports in all his East African dependencies.

The proposal for a commercial treaty appealed to British ministers who thought that this might be an opportunity to work in some wording on reduction or abolition of the slave trade. However, those drafting the text could not resist the temptation to go too far, suggesting commitments by Sayyid Sa'id to prevent all transport of slaves from his ports to others, particularly India, and to punish anyone buying slaves in his territories. Sa'id's envoy was using as an intermediary a Captain from the Indian Navy, Robert Cogan, who advised the India Board to resist this wording, and to deal with the slavery issue in some other way, not in the context of the commercial treaty. Again, as when the Court of Directors had considered Elphinstone's submission in October 1827, the argument was deployed about the risk to the authority of the Sultan (as Sa'id now begins to be referred to in official correspondence).

Cogan's advice was accepted, and he it was who finally concluded the commercial treaty, in negotiations with Sayyid Sa'id in Zanzibar in May 1839. Just one article touched on the slave trade, with a text that reaffirmed the Moresby Treaty and extended the Indian Navy's rights of

115

search. In commercial matters, most favoured nation status, guarantees of free trade and assurances of assistance to shipping were reciprocally conferred; and British subjects were given the right to buy, sell and hire property in the Sultan's dominions. The British Consul or Resident Agent was given the right to adjudicate in cases between British nationals and those of other Christian nations.

Meanwhile the Indian authorities pursued their anti-slave trade policy in the Gulf. Hennell (from Bushire) put a set of proposals to the Shaikhs of the Qawasim and the neighbouring tribes in July 1839, and within a few days secured commitments from them all, covering three points: to limit their countrymen's slaving activities to areas west and north of the Moresby Line, modified slightly so as to include the northern Indian coast (now Pakistan), to give the Indian Navy rights to search and seize slaving vessels east of the line, and to punish any of their subjects caught enslaving Somalis. Most Somalis were Muslims, and so should not have been enslaved by Muslim Arab traders anyway. It is probable that Hennell wrote in this clause because British Indian officials had been particularly offended by the trade in Somali girls.

The Pirate Coast becomes the Trucial Coast

Achieving this agreement with the chiefs of what had until recently been considered the Pirate Coast was a significant achievement; and Hennell took it one stage further by getting Sayyid Sa'id to make the same commitments in December 1839 – with a small amendment to the modified Moresby Line so that Omani possessions on the Makran Coast would be "inside" (ie west of) the Line, not outside as they had been in the agreement made with the Shaikhs. The original Moresby Line, and its modification, are shown on the map on page xii. Why did these Rulers give in so easily? They may have been genuinely concerned not to incur British anger, which in living memory had brought them violence and destruction; and they will have felt that the British Big Brother was keeping a watchful eye on them. The General Treaty of 1820 had, in a sense, been replaced by the Trucial system introduced in 1835, when Hennell had settled a dispute between the Qawasim and the Bani Yas tribes, and then brought in the other Shaikhs of the Pirate Coast to agree to put an end to a spate of lawlessness which was resulting in attacks once more on British and Indian shipping as well as destructive inter-tribal conflict. All the Shaikhs who had been signatories of the 1820 General Treaty joined in a Truce originally designed to last only for the pearling season of the summer and autumn of 1835, but they then agreed to renew it the following year. This continued annually until 1843, when a ten-year Truce was signed; Hennell played a big part in making the system work, to the economic benefit of the participants, as well to the advantage – in security terms – of the British. In this way the "Pirate Coast" became the "Trucial Coast", although the term did not come into general use until the 1870s. Thus, these tribal Shaikhs would have been conscious of a kind of British supervision. They wished also to keep good relations with Sayyid Sa'id, perhaps for commercial reasons, since Muscat was such a thriving port at this time. In April 1838 Hennell had discussed these matters with the paramount chief of the Qawasim, who told him that he had proposed to Sayyid Sa'id a system for regulating slaving vessels trading to Zanzibar, in order to avoid accusations of misconduct. It was then that Hennell had first suggested to him that "regulation" by the Indian Navy might be better, and indeed had got him and three other Trucial Shaikhs to sign up to a limited agreement later that month.

However much the political officers may have congratulated themselves on having these anti-slaving commitments signed by both Sayyid Sa'id and the Trucial Shaikhs, the effects turned out to be disappointing, at least in the short and medium term. The officer commanding a Bombay Marine cruiser, Captain Nott, made a survey of slaves carried in ships calling at Kharaq (on Qishm island) in a 2-month period in 1840, and found significant numbers of vessels shipping slaves to Muscat and Sur from Zanzibar, Berbera and the Red Sea. From the Omani ports, slaves were carried to ports in the Northern Gulf. Other reports at the time showed that slaves were being smuggled into and out of India in Muscat-based ships.

Palmerston's more determined approach

At this point Palmerston, re-appointed Foreign Secretary in Viscount Melbourne's administration of 1835, decided that the time had come for determined action against the East African slave trade. Under his instruction, in June 1841, the Deputy Under-Secretary at the Foreign Office, Lord Leveson, requested the India Board to instruct the

Government of India to tell Sayyid Sa'id and the Trucial Shaikhs that they were to sign up to a treaty forbidding all the maritime slave trade and allowing British ships the rights of search and seizure. Palmerston offered Sayyid Sa'id £2000 (equivalent then to about $MT22,000) for three years to compensate him for loss of revenue; and he offered the Trucial Shaikhs nothing. Leveson's letter added that, if the Sultan and the Shaikhs did not want a new treaty, the British authorities could simply rely on the existing ones. This was of course not the case: as will be recalled, the existing treaties prohibited trading in Somali slaves, taking slaves from Africa, and carrying them across the Moresby Line. The Indian authorities – who until now had been concerned only to prevent the slave trade in and out of India – thought that the strategy in Leveson's letter was unwise and would not work. Nevertheless, and because fresh reports continued to come in about the slave trade between the Gulf and Bombay, late in 1841 the Governor of Bombay sent instructions that Leveson's letter should be communicated to the Trucial Shaikhs and to Sayyid Sa'id. These instructions went to Lt Col Robertson in Bushire (Hennell, suffering from overwork and poor health, having taken extended leave) and to Captain Atkins Hamerton in Zanzibar. Hamerton, appointed Political Resident in Muscat in 1840, had accompanied Sayyid Sa'id soon afterwards on what turned out to be an almost permanent stay in his East African outpost. Robertson questioned the instructions, arguing that Sayyid Sa'id and the "Arab chiefs" would not make such concessions, and that the only hope of stopping the slave trade was to interdict at the ports of export in Africa. At a meeting in Zanzibar, Hamerton did read the letter to Sa'id, who was horrified; and he threatened to send an envoy to ask Queen Victoria to get her Government to reconsider. In his report to Bombay, Hamerton mentioned the religious element in Sa'id's position – that "slavery is, in the opinion of the Arabs, a right guaranteed them by their religion, and the Imam would not dare to appear to coincide with the wishes of the Government on this subject, unless backed by a force; and even then he would be obliged to make it appear to his people that the English Government compelled him to the measure".[7]

---

[7] Hamerton to Willoughby, 2 Jan 1842; quoted by J B Kelly: *Britain and the Persian Gulf,* p 450-1

This episode, marked by the personal intervention of the Foreign Secretary, represented the surrender by the India Office and India Government officials of the lead in policy-making and action on the East African slave trade. In September 1842 the Court of Directors of the East India Company, in a letter to Bombay, acknowledged that the abolition of the slave trade was a matter of national rather than of Indian policy, and implicitly left it to the Foreign Office to take it forward. When they did so, their dealings would be as much with Sayyid Sa'id and his successors in his capacity of Sultan of Zanzibar, as with the Ruler or Imam of Muscat.

The Egyptian Crisis of 1837-39

Before leaving this period, we should consider how the "Egyptian crisis" of 1837-39 affected the relationship between Britain and Sayyid Sa'id. This crisis arose when the Pasha or Viceroy of Egypt, Muhammad Ali, decided to destroy the power of the Wahhabis in the Nejd, in Central Arabia, in order to clear his way to take over Turkish Iraq. He had already been given the *Pashaliq* (Governorship) of Syria by the Ottoman Sultan Mahmud II, and wanted to add to it the Pashaliq of Baghdad. Egyptian forces soon captured Riyadh, prompting Palmerston to warn Muhammad Ali away from trying to extend his authority to the Gulf or to Baghdad – presumably out of concern to maintain the security of the route to India. The Egyptian move came at a bad time, since just then Palmerston was concerned about the other side of the Gulf, where Persian attacks against Afghanistan risked giving the Russians a position that could threaten India's north-western borders. The British watched anxiously as the Egyptians advanced further across Arabia, reaching the coast late in 1838, and then threatening to occupy Bahrain. On cue, Palmerston sent another warning, hoping that Muhammad Ali would abandon any intention of establishing himself on the Gulf.

So far, none of this had affected Oman. Hennell, Resident in Bushire, was in frequent correspondence with Bombay and the commander of the naval squadron in the Gulf, Sir Frederick Maitland. The crisis took another turn when Egyptian forces defeated a Turkish army in northern Syria in June 1839, making it possible – if he had had the will – for Muhammad Ali to advance on Turkey itself. By now, Bahrain had submitted to (but not actually been occupied by) the Egyptian army commander, Khurshid Pasha. In the Trucial Shaikhdoms, Sa'ad al-Mutlaq – who had been the Wahhabis' acting governor in Buraimi but had now allied himself with the Egyptians – actually got Khurshid Pasha to appoint him governor in the Trucial Coast region. These developments made Hennell worry that the Trucial Shaikhs, and perhaps Muscat too, were at threat from the invading force. Hennell met up with the Shaikhs, and warned the Egyptians against interfering in Buraimi, now held by the Na'im tribe. He then went on to Muscat, where he saw Sayyid Sa'id's son and nephew, acting as joint regents in the Ruler's absence in Zanzibar. They agreed that Khurshid Pasha should be prevented from extending his influence further south and east, though (for reasons of internal family rivalry) they were unwilling to take concrete action to support the Na'im tribe in Buraimi.

Returning to Muscat two months later, in November 1839, Hennell discussed the situation with Sa'id, now back from Zanzibar. He found Sa'id curiously negative – not believing that either his own or Trucial Shaikhs' forces could stop Khurshid Pasha without British help, and not willing to lend support to the Na'imis in Buraimi. In fact he asked Hennell if the British would send troops to Buraimi, and if they would also occupy Bahrain – which he would do himself if they preferred not to.

A stalemate continued for a few months into 1840, with Khurshid Pasha still in position in Eastern Arabia, the British engaging in correspondence between Hennell, Bombay, Calcutta and London over whether to use force to eject the Egyptians from Hasa or to prevent Khurshid Pasha from actually occupying Bahrain, and Sayyid Sa'id sitting tight in Oman. At this point Hennell decided he wanted better information about Buraimi, and arranged for Captain Atkins Hamerton, then still in the Bombay Infantry, to visit there. Hamerton, who later came to prominence as Agent in Zanzibar, arrived in Buraimi in January 1840, the first European to see the oasis. He reported afterwards that it was of some size, but he was unimpressed with the state of repair of the defences, forts and guns. An earlier visit to the interior of northern Oman (this time in peace, unlike Perronet Thompson's incursion in 1820) had been undertaken by two Indian Navy officers, James Wellsted and F Whitelock, who left a remarkable account of their travels in late 1835 and early 1836. Wellsted travelled from Sur, through the lands of the

Bani Bu Ali to Samad, where he met Whitelock who had come from Muscat through the mountains. They visited Nizwa, trecked up narrow paths to the heights of the Jebel Akhdar, came down to the coast near Seeb, recrossed the Northern Hajjar to Ibri where they were threatened by a large group of Wahhabi tribesmen, and from where they packed up quickly and returned to Muscat.[8]

In late May 1840, news started coming through that the Egyptian forces were withdrawing. They had been experiencing difficulties with their lines of supply across Arabia, and then encountering active resistance to their presence, and by the summer of 1840 had evacuated nearly all their regular troops. With the end of the Egyptian crisis, Hennell resumed discussion with Sayyid Sa'id about the future of Bahrain: the British did not want to occupy it for themselves (they had considered it as a military base, but decided it was unsuitable), but would not prevent Sa'id from taking it. (We may marvel nowadays at what seems a casual attitude towards acquisition of territory by force.) Sa'id countered by saying that he would be happy to acquire Bahrain, but would need British help to do so – preferably by the loan of the garrison then at Kharaq on Qishm island. Hennell put to Bombay a strong recommendation that this support should be provided, even though during the previous year or so his despatches had revealed more than slight hesitation about the value to Britain of the alliance with Sayyid Sa'id. Sir James Carnac, Governor of Bombay, was inclined to agree to Sa'id's request, but held back because there were not enough forces in Bombay to spare for the venture; and Lord Auckland, Governor-General, who had other worries such as instability in Afghanistan, thought likewise. Sa'id did not wait to hear the end of these deliberations. He had already told Hennell, in August 1840, that he would stay in Muscat for as long as he thought there was a chance of his getting help to occupy Bahrain, but would otherwise leave again for Zanzibar. During the autumn he must have concluded that the odds were too long, and sailed south.

Several questions arise from the narrative of this crisis. Some – relating to Muhammad Ali's motives in invading Arabia and then not ensuring

8 A more detailed account of the Wellsted/Whitelock journey is in Kelly: *Britain and the Persian Gulf*, pp371-3. Wellsted's own description is in his *Travels of Arabia* and *Travels to the City of the Caliphs* (see Notes for further reading).

adequate support for his forces, and Khurshid Pasha's rather leisurely advance and then unconvincing occupation – lie outwith the scope of this book. As regards Oman and Britain, we may ask why Sayyid Sa'id was so equivocal about his defence of Oman and at the same time so keen to acquire Bahrain. It would be natural to consider that the status quo in the northern part of his territory was unsatisfactory: Buraimi, normally thought of as of strategic importance for Oman's interior, was under direct or indirect Saudi authority, and the Governor of Sohar almost in active hostility towards the al-Busa'idi ruler. But in fact this situation carried few disadvantages to Sayyid Sa'id, and to attempt to change it would have been risky. As for Bahrain, the 'Utub occupants were weak, and the potential gains from acquisition were high, since Bahraini ships were taking valuable quantities of pearls from the banks off Qatar, and the port was doing good trade with India and other destinations in the Gulf. Sa'id would have seen prospects of useful revenue, mainly from customs dues. This is why, in a sense, Zanzibar was an alternative: by 1840 the clove and other spice plantations which had been started some years previously were bearing fruit, and Sa'id would have judged it necessary for him to be there to supervise the development of his own estates and the administration of the customs and other revenues accruing from Zanzibar's growing importance as a trading centre.

Sayyid Sa'id's move to Zanzibar in autumn 1840 coincided with a change in British representation to the Omani Ruler. Under the 1839 Commercial Treaty the British were committed to place a Consul in Sayyid Sa'id's territory. Late in 1840 or in 1841, Atkins Hamerton, now given a Consular Commission by the Foreign Office in addition to his Indian Government position as Agent, followed Sa'id to Zanzibar, where for 16 years he played a major part in the relationship. From this point until Sa'id's death in 1856 Zanzibar, and not Muscat, would be his capital, and British dealings with him would be as much focussed on East African issues as with those of Oman and the Gulf.

15. Rescuing slaves from a wrecked dhow, late 1860s

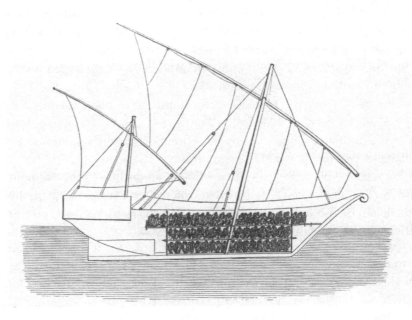

16. Diagram of a slave-carrying dhow

CHAPTER 8

The end of Sayyid Sa'id's rule (1840-1860)

From 1840 until his death in 1856, Sayyid Sa'id spent most of his time in Zanzibar, and his relationship with the British was coloured by London's continued determination to see the slave trade ended, and in maintaining the stability in the Gulf created by the Trucial arrangement of 1835. This led to British intervention to help resolve a further threat from the Wahhabis from central Arabia, and then to arbitrating on the dispute over the succession to Sa'id. Their strategy of non-involvement in Arabian affairs was becoming impossible to maintain.

* * * * * * *

Another anti-slavery Treaty
We have seen that in 1839 the British secured significant commitments from Sayyid Sa'id and the Trucial Shaikhs to restrict slave trading, but that the trade continued to flourish nevertheless. In the early 1840s Palmerston and the Foreign Office took forward the process that had been started by Lord Leveson's letter to the India Board – the letter which had caused such a violent reaction from Sa'id when Hamerton had read it to him in Zanzibar. Sa'id carried out his threat to send an envoy with instructions to discuss the matter personally with Queen Victoria and Lord Aberdeen, now Foreign Secretary. This emissary, 'Ali bin Nāṣir, fought Sa'id's corner with persistence, and came back to Zanzibar with

answers from the Queen and Lord Aberdeen; but these replies showed no flexibility. And, although the issue seems to have gone quiet for two years after 'Ali bin Nāṣir's mission, Sa'id must have seen that he would have to make concessions. These came in the form of the Treaty of 1845, which followed an exchange between Sa'id and Lord Aberdeen in 1842. Sa'id had set out the conditions on which he would abolish the slave trade in his area of control, and Lord Aberdeen had sent back a draft treaty with some explanations (for example, of why he could not agree to Sa'id's request for assistance in acquiring Bahrain). Sa'id negotiated with awkward obstinacy, especially on financial compensation, but in the end agreed to Aberdeen's draft with only minor modifications, even though it contained no clause on finance. He was still asking Hamerton to sort this out with London more than a year later, well after he had actually signed the Treaty, but still without success.

The 1845 Treaty was a significant advance for the British. It superseded that of 1822, and rendered the Moresby Line otiose, for by it Sayyid Sa'id was to prohibit the export of slaves from his African possessions, to prevent the import of slaves from anywhere in Africa into his possessions in Asia (ie Muscat and Oman, Gwadar and Bandar Abbas), and to give Royal Navy and East India Company ships the right to search and seize his or his subjects' vessels carrying slaves beyond his dominions. He was however allowed to continue carrying slaves within his African possessions, meaning in practice from the mainland to Zanzibar and Pemba.

It is not clear why Sayyid Sa'id conceded this Treaty. Certainly he would have felt under general pressure from the British, who evinced a number of signs (including visits by ships of the Royal Navy) that they meant business on abolition. He may have been concerned that he was mishandling his relationship with the French, who he feared might have designs on his possessions further up the African coast, and so thought that a nod in the British direction could be helpful. It is also possible that, in his negotiations with Hamerton, Sa'id had inflated the estimate of his loss of revenue from the trade. He had claimed to Hamerton that he would lose $MT35,000-40,000 a year if the trade were abolished. But if, as is possible, his actual losses were short of this, then a relatively small subvention from the British, if he could get it, would compensate him adequately. He may have thought he had reasonable expectation of receiving some subsidy, since a tentative offer of £2000 a year for three years had been included in Leveson's letter of June 1841; but nothing came of it. The Foreign Office had for some time claimed that Sa'id would soon make up, in legitimate trade, any shortfall experienced from ending the slave trade; perhaps they were right.

It is also possible that Sayyid Sa'id cynically decided to enter into the Treaty reckoning that he could get away with minimal change in current practice. In other words, he may have judged that he could get the British off his back by putting his signature to a document he had little or no intention of implementing. He might reasonably have reckoned that the British had inadequate naval resources to patrol the slave trading routes, and that he could with impunity allow all or most of the traffic to continue. While we hesitate to impute such motives to Sayyid Sa'id, it is notable that he made only weak or token efforts to fulfil his obligations under the Treaty, and it was even reported that one of his own ships was carrying slaves from Zanzibar.

The 1845 Treaty came into effect in 1847. At least, that was the intention. But in September 1847 the arrest of some Muscat dhows off Bushire revealed that the necessary enabling legislation in India had not been passed, and so there were no courts before whom to bring alleged offenders. Whether because Sa'id's officials were less than enthusiastic in implementing the Treaty, or because traders became adept at avoiding enforcers, numbers of slaves traded appear to have been barely affected in the early 1850s. The port of Sur increased in importance and activity in the trade, developing a strong trans-shipment business to points further north on the Omani coast. Indians living in Zanzibar and elsewhere in East Africa (known as banyans), who had long dominated trading activities and during the 19th century began owning plantations, managed to continue to own slaves without restriction, and with some diminution to trade in them, despite many of them being British Indian subjects. And in this period a new trend developed: a decrease in the number of slaves being exported to the Gulf from Sa'id's African possessions was made up for by expansion of the trade from Abyssinia through Red Sea ports into Muscat and further up the Gulf.

It should be added that the British did not only target the Sultan of Muscat in their efforts to restrict or end the trading of slaves to the Gulf. For example, in 1847 they negotiated with the Ottoman Government the issue of a firman prohibiting the carrying of slaves in Turkish ships, and an undertaking in 1856 by the Trucial Shaikhs that they would hand over slaves caught in their territories. But neither of these arrangements had much practical effect. The confusion that followed Sayyid Sa'id's death in 1856 cannot have helped. As we shall see, in the late 1850s the British had to deal with separate Sultans in Muscat and in Zanzibar, each with distinct political and financial agendas.

Renewal of the Wahhabi threat

While suppression of the slave trade was an important policy objective for the British in their relationship with Oman in the early 1840s, for the Ruler of Muscat different and potentially existential issues were at stake. After the Egyptian forces had withdrawn from central Arabia in 1840 (see p 121 above), the Saudis began to re-establish Wahhabi power there, and then to renew their threat to the north-western borders of Muscat's territory. Faisal bin Turki Al Sa'ud, who had formerly been Amir in Riyadh, was released from captivity in Cairo in May 1843, and soon took back power in the Najd. Before long he was building links to the Trucial Shaikhs, and early in 1845 sent a substantial force eastwards to retake Buraimi. In this the Wahhabis were successful, and the force's commander Sa'ad bin Mutlaq became governor of Buraimi for a second time. This offensive caught the Omanis on the wrong foot. Sayyid Sa'id had gone back to Zanzibar in December 1844, leaving in charge his son Thuwaini, who is generally considered to have been a vacillating character and barely fitted for rule in such turbulent times. Later he was to inherit the sultanate in Muscat. Kelly delivers this verdict on him: "Indulgent when he should have been ruthless, indecisive where he should have been assertive, his rule was characterised more by inertia than by energy."[1]

Faced with this serious Saudi/Wahhabi threat, Thuwaini consulted Hennell, the British Resident in Bushire, who advised him not to provoke Faisal bin Turki unnecessarily, and to make concessions provided they did not compromise Omani independence. When Sa'ad bin Mutlaq made large demands of cash payments from both Thuwaini in Muscat and his cousin Hamūd bin 'Azzān who was the virtually autonomous governor

---

1 Kelly, J B: *Britain and the Persian Gulf,* p 530

of Sohar, Thuwaini appealed to the British in Bombay for help. The British were in two minds: on the one hand they felt tied by the doctrine of non-interference in internal Arabian affairs and of avoidance of commitments that could lead to deployment of troops on the mainland, while on the other they thought they had obligations to Sayyid Sa'id because of the concessions he had already made on the slave trade and the complete ban that they were currently asking him to agree to.

While Bombay were still dithering, events moved forward. In June or July 1845 Sa'ad bin Mutlaq forced Sayyid Hamud bin 'Azzan to concede the demanded cash payment, and gathered more forces from the tribes in the Dhahirah to march on Muscat. Hennell, despite reporting that Thuwaini's Government was acting with "weakness and imbecility", with hardly enough troops to man the defences, brought in two cruisers to patrol the coast and wrote letters of protest and warning to both Sa'ad bin Mutlaq and his Amir in Riyadh, Faisal bin Turki. Possibly as a result of this British intervention, Thuwaini escaped with a deal with Faisal that substantial but not ruinous payments – $MT 5,000 annually, and presents to the value of $MT 2,000 – be given to Sa'ad bin Mutlaq. In London, the East India Company Court of Directors approved of what Hennell had done, but expressed reservations about the risk of involvement in land operations in Arabia. Writing to Bombay, they criticised Sayyid Sa'id for not paying more attention to the Omani end of his dominions, failing to realise that such comments came too late – by now he had decided to give top priority to handling his East African affairs.

A new problem for Sayyid Sa'id and Sayyid Thuwaini arose the following year. This time the threat came from their kinsman Sayyid Hamud bin 'Azzan in Sohar. He gathered support from some of the religious conservative elements among the Ibadis, who were discontent with Sa'id's neglect of affairs in Oman and his concessions to unbelievers on issues such as the slave trade. They were of course aware of the latest agreement signed in Zanzibar in October 1845. But Hamud did not manage to launch a direct attack on Thuwaini in Muscat, being distracted by fighting in and around Buraimi. Sa'ad bin Mutlaq had lost control of the oasis in 1847, and Hamud became involved in the confused disturbances which followed, and which ended with Buraimi falling to Sa'id bin Tahnūn, shaikh of Abu Dhabi, and Sayyid Thuwaini in 1850. Shortly afterwards Thuwaini captured Sayyid Hamud by a trick, and imprisoned him in Muscat, where he died. Hennell, whose main concern at this time was to maintain the Trucial system and peace at sea and on the coast, was indirectly involved in these events. Back in 1839 he had mediated an agreement between Sayyid Sa'id and Sayyid Hamud, and it was clear that Thuwaini's attack on Sohar, and his murder of Hamud, was in breach of that agreement. Now Hennell received instructions from Lord Falkland, the Governor of Bombay, to try to bring about a settlement between Muscat and Sohar and to get compensation for Hamud's family. He spoke to Thuwaini to no avail. The situation was exacerbated when Sayyid Sa'id arrived in Muscat from Zanzibar in May 1851. Hamerton, the Consul in Zanzibar, was with him, and was pretty certain that Sa'id had given Thuwaini the orders to attack Sohar and capture Hamud. Hamerton was probably right, since later in the year Sa'id moved on Sohar, where Qais bin 'Azzān, Hamud's brother and governor of Rustaq, had taken over; and early in 1852 Thuwaini took a strong force up the coast, captured Sohar and Shinas, and took Qais prisoner. Sohar was now back under Muscat's control.

The Wahhabis return
Faisal bin Turki in Riyadh was however not going to accept the loss of Buraimi lying down. As soon as Sayyid Sa'id left Muscat in late 1852 to return to his preferred Zanzibar, Faisal despatched his son 'Abdullah with a very large force, of over 3000 men, to Oman. The Na'īmi tribesmen occupying Buraimi quickly surrendered, and Abdullah sent absurdly extravagant demands to Thuwaini (who was regent again), at the same time summoning the Trucial Shaikhs to Buraimi to make sure that none of them was tempted into alliance with Muscat. An extraordinary – but critical – stand-off then took place between the new British Resident, Captain Kemball (who had recently replaced Hennell), Thuwaini and Abdullah bin Faisal. Kemball had arrived off Sharjah, and summoned the Trucial Shaikhs to meet him in order to negotiate the renewal of the maritime truce, which this time the British wanted to make permanent. Abdullah twisted the Shaikhs' arms to make them stay with him, and also sent a fresh demand to Thuwaini to surrender Sohar to him. Kemball sent stiff letters to Abdullah and the Shaikh of the Qawasim, and arranged for two cruisers to patrol the Trucial and Batinah coasts. Abdullah agreed to send an envoy to negotiate with Thuwaini in Sohar. A tense two weeks followed. At stake

was not only the future of al-Busa'idi control of Muscat and Oman, but also the survival of the Trucial system. If Abdullah had decided to take his forces down the Batinah to Muscat, Thuwaini would have found it very difficult to mount effective resistance. It is difficult to calculate the results for the Trucial Shaikhs; it is likely that they would have been reduced to a kind of fiefdom to the Saudis, but one at such a distance as to leave them free to resume their former ways of piracy, slave trading and mutual rivalry. In other words, the Trucial system would have collapsed.

Kemball was waiting at Basidu, a port on Qishm Island. There in April 1853 he received word that a settlement had been reached, whose terms were harsh for Thuwaini – but better than the subjugation of the Sultanate to Riyadh. The deal obliged him to pay substantial cash sums to Abdullah, and allow that large parts of what is modern Oman, including Buraimi and much of the land south and west of the Western Hajjar, owed allegiance to the Amir Faisal. But al-Busa'idi authority over Muscat, the Sharqiyah and Ja'lan was recognised.

Abdullah bin Faisal left Buraimi very soon afterwards. Kemball crossed the Gulf back to the Trucial Coasts in order to manage the unfinished business of the maritime truce. In less than a week, in May 1853, he persuaded the five Shaikhs to sign the Treaty of Maritime Peace in Perpetuity, a significant and lasting achievement. By it they agreed that they and their subjects would not attack each other, and that if any attack did take place the matter would be referred to the British for obtaining reparation. Although Kemball clinched the final deal, the Maritime Peace was in fact the legacy of Hennell, who had worked adroitly, since his first appointment as Assistant Resident in 1826, aged 26, to maintain peace in the area, and secured the survival of the al-Busa'idis, as Sultans of Muscat and Oman, against Wahhabi/Saudi threats. It may seem curious, given his achievements, that he was not honoured by the British Government; but in the long line of Residents in Bushire, only Percy Cox was given a knighthood, and perhaps it is only with the passage of time that we can see how valuable was Hennell's contribution to Gulf peace and security, and the reduction of the slave trade there.

Sultan Sa'id's closing years

Sayyid Sa'id paid only one more visit to Muscat. He came in 1854 to resolve a problem with the Persians, who had decided to end the lease of

Bandar Abbas, without informing the "tenant", the ruler of Muscat, of their intentions. Thuwaini retook the port from the (re)occupying Persians, but the Omanis were then expelled once more in November 1854, with considerable violence and Omani loss of life. The British tried to keep out of the dispute, and also ensured that the Trucial Shaikhs stayed clear as well. Where they did get involved, for example when Sa'id asked the British Minister at Tehran to intercede with the Shah, they either could not or would not. In Tehran they could do nothing because relations had just been broken. Then in 1856 the new Resident, Captain Jones, prevented the Trucial Shaikhs from joining in alliance with Sa'id to recapture Bandar Abbas by force. In the end, Sa'id had to settle for an expensive re-occupation: he was allowed to take back the port and its dependencies for a rent more than double what he had been paying before, with various other conditions attached. These included the requirement that the Persian flag was to be hoisted on the citadel and salutes fired on festivals and the Shah's birthday.

Sayyid Sa'id left Muscat a few months later for the last time. He died on the journey to Zanzibar on 19 October 1856, off the Seychelles. He seems to have had a premonition of his death, since he arranged for planks of wood to be loaded on to the vessel (a frigate named *Queen Victoria*), and gave instructions that if anyone were to die on the voyage he should not be buried at sea but his body put in a coffin and taken to Zanzibar. His death caused great distress among his people. Salil ibn Razik records that the news in Muscat caused "such a wailing throughout the town that the hills were almost shaken by it".[2]

Sa'id's was a lengthy and successful reign. He came to the throne – as did so many of the al-Busa'idis – in circumstances of confusion and with doubtful prospects. He had to face a number of threats, notably in the form of attacks from the north-west, any of which could have unseated him. His dealings with the British were not always smooth and straightforward. As we have seen, on several occasions he was obliged or forced by them to make moves which were bound to put his popular support at risk – notably over his concessions on restricting the slave trade. Indeed, to some of the more strongly conservative Ibadis, the very fact of his dealing with the British on close terms was a reason for

2 Badger: *History of the Imams and Seyyids of Oman*, p 261

suspicion. Yet he managed to adopt policies that avoided damaging confrontation with either the British Indian imperium or his own countrymen's religious conservatism. He built up the maritime power of Muscat and Oman, protecting trade routes which his merchants exploited with considerable success, creating prosperity which peaked under his rule. He left an empire which included a substantial corner of the Arabian peninsula, Zanzibar and Pemba, plus the strip of colonies down the East African coast. That his sons could not hold it together is not entirely his responsibility.

The succession to Sayyid Sa'id

Fifteen of Sayyid Sa'id's 25 sons were alive at his death, of whom four played major roles in the intrigues over the succession: Thuwaini and Turki, who were in Oman, and Mājid and Barghash, who were in Zanzibar. None of them was on good terms with the others. Thuwaini, who once again was Regent in Oman in Sa'id's absence, kept the news of his father's death secret from Turki, to give him time to round up pledges of loyalty from garrison commanders. In Zanzibar Barghash tried to seize power, but Hamerton, the Consul, managed to get Majid acclaimed Sultan.

Sayyid Sa'id had anticipated problems over the succession, and interestingly he seems also to have realised that it would be difficult or impossible to keep the disparate parts of his empire together. In 1844 he had written to Lord Aberdeen, the Foreign Secretary, to make clear his intentions: Thuwaini to be ruler over Oman and the possessions in the Gulf, and his son Khālid to be ruler of the possessions in Africa. But Khalid died in 1854, and, during his absence from Zanzibar that year, Sa'id had appointed Majid governor of Zanzibar and the other African possessions.

It may have seemed that Sayyid Sa'id's intentions were clear. But the sons were not going to accept the arrangement in its simple form. The major dispute was over money, since it was Zanzibar revenue that kept Muscat afloat. Thuwaini managed to get Majid to agree to an annual payment of $MT 40,000 to make up for the disparity, but Majid failed to pay, and Thuwaini threatened an invasion of Zanzibar in late 1858. The Government in Bombay were seriously concerned about the possibility of civil war, and in February 1859 succeeded in intercepting Thuwaini, who had already set sail with his fleet, with a letter from Lord Elphinstone.[3] In the letter the Governor asked Thuwaini to call off the invasion and submit the quarrel to arbitration by the Governor-General.

Disorder broke out in Zanzibar, partly because Sayyid Barghash was still threatening Majid, but mainly because numbers of ruffians of various types – mostly Arab – had come to the island either pursuing slave trading activities or in the hope of plunder in the event of fighting breaking out if/when Thuwaini's ships arrived. (They are referred to in correspondence from Zanzibar, and so by historians, as the "Northern Arabs" – to distinguish them from Omanis and other Arabs living in Zanzibar – despite their origins being in southern and eastern Arabia, ie Oman and Hadramawt.) A few ships did make it, and the addition of the thousand men on board them did not help stability or security in Zanzibar. Worse, two French warships then arrived, intent on supporting Barghash. However, the new Political Agent and Consul, Rigby, had three British warships in port, and the support of the American Consul, and the situation subsided when the French ships sailed away and the Arab mischief-makers also left on the south-west monsoon.

The negotiation of the Canning Award
Detailed correspondence now took place between Bombay, Calcutta and the Political Agents in Muscat and Zanzibar about the proposed arbitration. Lord Canning, the Governor-General, at first declined to undertake the task, reckoning that Sayyid Thuwaini had decided in advance not to abide by it. He preferred a negotiated settlement between the brothers, with Majid making a voluntary payment to Thuwaini to compensate for the difference in income-generation between the two halves of the empire. This solution did not run, however, and the Bombay Government instead extracted a grudging commitment from Thuwaini to abide by the outcome of an arbitration supervised by the Governor-General, and sent a two-man commission to inquire into the dispute and come up with a solution. The leader was Brigadier Coghlan, Political Resident in Aden, and he was assisted by the Revd Percy Badger, who was chaplain in Bombay but noted as an Arabic and Persian scholar. We

---

3 John Elphinstone, 13th Baron, Governor of Bombay 1853-59, was nephew of the Hon Mountstuart Elphinstone, Governor of Bombay 1819-27.

have come across him indirectly in this history as the translator and editor of Salil ibn Razik's *History of the Imams and Seyyids of Oman*, a useful source-book for Omani history; and Badger's lengthy introduction and appendices provide informative commentary.

Coghlan and Badger received careful instructions from the Governor-General in Calcutta and from Bombay, where officials had gone into detail on the legal and historical claims of both contenders, eg on questions such as whether Sayyid Sa'id had the power to bequeath his empire, and whether it should be kept as one or allowed to split. They had sessions with Thuwaini in Muscat in June 1860, and with Majid in Zanzibar in September.

The outcome was curious. Coghlan and Badger found that, on legal and historical grounds, Majid had no real claim in favour of making Zanzibar a separate or independent state. But on grounds of justice and expediency – ie, that Zanzibar had the right to independence, and that stability and prosperity depended on its being separate – Coghlan recommended the division of the empire and an annual payment of $MT 40,000 from the ruler of Zanzibar to the ruler of Muscat. The payment was called a "subsidy", presumably to get away from any idea either that it was tribute from an inferior to a superior, or that it was a form of *zakāt*, the term for the religious tax or tithe paid by all Muslims, and incidentally the term which the Wahhabis had used in demanding payment from rulers of Muscat. Coghlan's recommendations were submitted through the Governor of Bombay to Lord Canning, who issued his award in April 1861. He wrote identical letters to Thuwaini and Majid, and within two months they both accepted. At this time the British Indian authorities stopped using the title "Imam" (which they often wrote *Imaum*) for the ruler of Muscat, and referred to both rulers as "Sultan". There had in fact been no Imam in Oman since the death of Sa'id bin Ahmad early in the century,

One postscript to the Canning Award should be mentioned. In talks in Paris in March 1862, the British and French Governments agreed a joint declaration committing each to respect the independence of the two Sultans. This may have been inspired by British concern that renewed French interest in Zanzibar might lead on to something more acquisitive. The odd thing about this "declaration" is that it was not openly declared! More than that, although it was published in 1868, its existence was apparently not at the time communicated to British representatives in Muscat and Zanzibar, nor to Indian Government authorities in Calcutta or Bombay.[4] This happened only in 1872, and even then the Declaration seems to have been neglected or ignored. Only in 1890, when British officials in India were considering the possibility of declaring Oman a British Protectorate, and when work was in progress on what became the commercial treaty of 1891, was the 1862 Declaration brought to officials' attention – bringing with it the realisation that it prevented them from taking any action that infringed Omani independence without first securing the agreement of the French Government. They certainly did not want to go down that path, and so dropped the protectorate idea.

Very quickly the British realised that the Canning Award did not represent closure; instead it soon began to create new problems and responsibilities. In the short term, the British had to (or chose to) intervene in Omani internal affairs, contrary to all the doctrine of the first half of the century. Sultan Thuwaini thought that Sayyid Turki, his younger brother, might try a breakaway on the Zanzibari model, and secede with Sohar, of which he was governor; and the new Political Agent became involved in arranging talks between them to prevent violence. The arrangements broke down, and Turki soon found himself imprisoned in Fort Jalali in Muscat. Under British pressure Thuwaini released him a few months later. But the episode showed that through the Canning Award the British had incurred an undefined obligation to sustain Thuwaini in power. As we shall see, obligations arose also on the Zanzibari side, when Majid and his successors could not or would not pay the subsidy. Eventually, as part of the deal that was to lead to the end of slavery in Zanzibar, responsibility for payment was taken over by the British Indian Government, and later by the Treasury in London, ending only in the late 1960s.

Although the relationship between the two halves of Sayyid Sa'id's empire remained edgy or outrightly hostile for some time, until at the turn of the century they went their different ways, the Canning Award nevertheless removed the likelihood of actual war. The idea of the subsidy should have been a practicable solution, but – not having been

4 according to Coupland, *The Exploitation of East Africa,* London, 1939; p 399 footnote

forged on an anvil of goodwill between the two sides – it never really worked. The problem was that the Sultan of Zanzibar had adequate but not lavish revenue, resented having to pay the subsidy, and was not short of reasons or excuses to avoid payment; while the ruler of Muscat needed this boost to his revenue to counter the economic decline which followed Sa'id's death, and to maintain an authority which rested largely on gratuities paid to restless tribes and Shaikhs in Oman. When the Zanzibari subsidy was absent or delayed, his own position was put in peril. This awkward mixture of circumstances was to lead to an ever-increasing dependence on external support, which the British – for reasons of their own – found it expedient to supply.

CHAPTER 9

The Kuria Muria Islands

The 19th and 20th century story of the Kuria Muria islands is an example of the curiosities that can arise – and have arisen – in the course of imperial history. It must be admitted that the early parts of the story do not show the British Government in a good light, though it could also be said that the story has a happy ending.

* * * * * * *

The Kuria Muria is a group of five islands (named Hallānīyah, Jibliya (also called Kiblia), Soda, Haski and Gursond) lying about 25 miles (40 km) off the coast of Dhofar, north east of Salalah. They are about 800 miles by sea from Aden, and about 500 from Muscat. Their total area is 30 sq miles (78 sq km) – ie, a little more than the island of Guernsey. Hallaniyah, the largest, is the only one that is inhabited; the small number of residents there support themselves through fishing.

The meaning of their curious name is uncertain. Buckingham, the early 19th-century traveller, says that the name had been Qurtan or Kurtan, and been corrupted to Quryan/Kuryan because of the closeness of the letters t and y when written in Arabic. He goes on: "By Kurian-Murian would be meant the island of Kurian, and others round it, as it is common in Arabic, Persian and Hindoostanee, when speaking of several things of the same or similar kind, to add a word exactly like the name of the thing expressed, except its always beginning with an

M, as Bundook-Mundook, for musket and all accoutrements thereto belonging..."[1]

It is not clear when the British first stepped on the islands. The Dutch geographer Dapper wrote in the late 17th century that they had been discovered by English pirates operating against Muslims voyaging to Mecca for pilgrimage. More certain and more honourable contact was made in the early 19th century, during the period of surveys of the lower Gulf coasts in the 1820s and 1830s. Buckingham seems to have sailed past the Kuria Muria in 1815, but does not report having landed. Captain William Owen, commanding *HMS Leven*, gave a brief description of the islands, plus Masirah, after his voyage of 1823. Twelve years later, S B Haines, Captain of the brig *Palinurus*, landed there: and in early 1835 and again in 1836 his assistant surgeon, J G Hulton, spent a couple of months on the islands. Both Haines and Hulton left accounts which are less than complimentary (or, it could be said, patronising) about the then inhabitants.

In 1853 occurred the visit that was to start off this entertaining episode in Omani-British history. It was by a Captain Ord, master of a Liverpool-owned merchant ship. He probably called to take on water, and found that, although the poor rainfall and terrain of barren rock did not permit agriculture, some of the islands were covered in a thick layer of guano – accumulations of wild birds' droppings known for their value as fertiliser. It happened that, at this time, the only easily available market in guano – Peru – had been cornered by a monopolising group of merchants who kept the price artificially high.

Ord saw a commercial opportunity. He suggested to the Foreign Office that Britain should occupy the islands, and that he should be given a licence to exploit the guano, as a reward for having discovered it. The initial Foreign Office (FO) reaction was negative: Lord Clarendon, then Foreign Secretary, thought that Britain had no right to the islands, and that it was not clear who had. Sayyid Sa'id had at best a tenuous claim to Dhofar, the nearest mainland. But later, perhaps under the influence of the British agricultural community (who were interested in a cheaper source of guano), FO officials decided to follow it up after all, and to make enquiries in Zanzibar – ie to ask Hamerton, then British Agent in

1 Buckingham, J S: *Travels in Assyria, Media and Persia*, London, 1830, p 434

Zanzibar, whether Imam Sa'id claimed sovereignty or jurisdiction over the islands. But no mention was made of the guano.

In February 1854 the FO took things a stage further. They persuaded the Admiralty to instruct Captain Fremantle, commanding *HMS Juno*, who was about to sail for Australia, to call in at Zanzibar and to propose to Sayyid Sa'id, if he claimed the islands, that he should cede them to Britain for a price that Fremantle was authorised to negotiate, up to £10,000 – on the grounds that they would be useful to Britain as a coaling station between Bombay and Aden. Again he was not to mention the guano. If Sayyid Sa'id did not claim the islands, Fremantle was to go to the Kuria Muria, attempt to identify the "sovereign" in order to conclude a similar deal with whoever it might be and, if that failed, to take possession of the islands in the name of Queen Victoria.

Meanwhile, Hamerton replied to the FO's despatch. He explained that Sa'id claimed them as a dependency of Oman, although at times neighbouring chiefs had also claimed them. But, just as importantly, he added that the existence of the guano was well known, that French merchants from Bourbon (Réunion) and Mauritius, and Arab merchants, regularly called to take some away; and that Sa'id had turned down French requests for cession of the islands.

Fremantle arrived in Zanzibar, on *Juno*, in June 1854, and saw Hamerton. Sayyid Sa'id was not there, but in Muscat. Hamerton wrote a letter to Sa'id for Fremantle to deliver to him; and reported to the FO that he expected Sa'id to see through the "coaling station" story, but he thought Sa'id might nevertheless do a deal with the British.

Fremantle sailed on to Muscat, calling at the Kuria Muria on the way. He also wrote a patronising description of the islanders. In Muscat he delivered Hamerton's letter, and was given not only a most warm and courteous reception but also an immediate and positive reply to the request for the cession of the Kuria Muria islands. Fremantle reported: "[Sa'id] seemed rejoiced to have in his power the means of conferring the smallest obligation on a nation for whose friendship he entertained so much respect". Nor did Sa'id ask for compensation. On 14 July 1854 Sa'id signed the Deed of Cession, which Fremantle witnessed.

Why did Sa'id give in so quickly to the British request, especially when he had turned away the French? No evidence on this has come to light. Perhaps he calculated that he did not have the resources to exploit the guano; and that maintaining friendly relations with the British would strengthen his security – he had good cause, living mostly in Zanzibar, to be concerned about the stability of his home base.

There followed some tense exchanges between the FO (who had driven this process leading to cession) and the Colonial Office, who took over responsibility for administration of the islands. Sir George Grey, Colonial Secretary, was concerned that concealment had been used with Sa'id, and that the British should share with him the profits of the guano exploitation. Hamerton was instructed accordingly, but Sa'id wanted nothing. Lord Clarendon later presented him with a snuff-box as a token of gratitude! As Liesl Graz has pointed out in *The Omanis, Sentinels of the Gulf*, this was not an appropriate gift for someone to whom tobacco was as forbidden as alcohol, but perhaps it was intended as an ornament rather than for use.

In 1855 Ord got his licence, and the next year started exploiting the guano. He had hoped that a British warship would call by periodically, to protect him against foreign or unlicensed guano-merchants. But the Admiralty had other uses for its ships, and the Bombay Government – who might have sent ships from the Bombay Marine – kicked up rough, objecting strongly that the FO had actually acquired territory from an Arab ruler without consulting them. It was the Government of Bombay which was responsible for British relations with the Arabs, or at least from the Gulf to the Red Sea. So no ship was forthcoming from that source.

Ord's initial guano-farming ran into trouble within a few months. In October 1856 a group of Arabs from the mainland surrounded him and his men, and forced them to leave. Back in London, Ord naturally complained that this was because of his lack of Admiralty protection. Questions were asked in parliament. Eventually, Ord secured an escort for his return to the islands in October 1857, and – using workers recruited in Muscat – began digging and shipping the guano. He extracted over 26,000 tons of guano in the winter of 1857-58, and just less than 15,000 tons the following year; but the venture cannot have been as successful as Ord had hoped. Mortality and illness among the imported labour was high. Ord sought relief from the royalty he was supposed to pay to the British Government as a condition of his licence, and in fact ended up paying none. The licence was terminated in May 1861.

1. British ships in Muscat Harbour

2. British troops landing at Ras al-Khaimah

3. Sayyid Saʿid bin Sultan

T. Perronet Thompson

Presented to the Subscribers to **THE NEWS** Sept.ʳ 30.ᵗʰ 1838.

LONDON PUBLISHED BY J. THOMPSON, 28, BRYDGES STREET, COVENT GARDEN.

4. *T Perronet Thompson*

5. Storming Ras al-Khaimah

6. Sack of Ras al-Khaimah

7. Ships at Elphinstone inlet (Telegraph Island)

8. Cable-laying ships at Muscat

PURE ARABIAN.

PRESENTED TO HER MAJESTY BY THE IMAUM OF MUSCAT.

9. Horse given to Queen Victoria

10. *"Cemetery Bay", near Muscat*

11. *Shell liaison representative to the tribes 1961*

12. *Brigadier Colin Maxwell*

13. *"The Battle of Mirbat" by David Shepherd*

In 1883 two British officers visited the islands, and found all traces of the earlier British occupation vanished. There had been an attempt in 1861 to use the islands for a telegraph cable repeating station, but it had broken down and was abandoned. The number of inhabitants was down to that recorded by Fremantle in his visit on *Juno* in 1854 – about 25 adults and 11 children, subsisting on fish, shell-fish and goat's milk. For the next 80 years the Kuria Muria received occasional visits from the Political Agent in Muscat.

Britain retained possession of the islands, and then faced a dilemma when considering the future of Aden in the late 1960s – since by that time the Kuria Muria were administered from Aden. In 1965, Sir Gawain Bell produced a report on the future of Aden, and included the Kuria Muria as part of Adeni territory. But it was obviously going to be embarrassing for the British Government to give to a third party (the new Government of Aden) a territory which had been given to Queen Victoria by an ancestor of the current Sultan of Muscat and Oman. So, at risk of irritating the new Government of South Yemen – with whom relations were in any case not going to be easy – the British Government decided to return the islands to Sultan Sa'id bin Taymur. This duly took place in 1967.

CHAPTER 10

From partnership to dependence (1861-1888)

The Canning Arbitration Award secured a peaceful settlement to the problem of the succession to Sayyid Sa'id; but it left Muscat and Oman in an economic situation from which the Sultanate never properly recovered for over 100 years, and with political uncertainties that also had damaging effects for the people of the country. Over the two decades that followed the Canning Award, the rule of Sayyid Sa'id's branch of the al-Busa'idis was nearly lost to a revived Imamate, run by a strongly conservative arm of the Ibadi sect. This pattern of events helped set a path towards what became increasingly direct British control of Omani affairs, in the closing years of the 19th century.

* * * * * * *

Sayyid Thuwaini's unsteady rule

In 1861 Sayyid Thuwaini, third son of Sayyid Sa'id bin Sultan, was confirmed as Sultan of Muscat. The Canning Award also gave him what seemed at the time a useful supplement to his income from customs dues and other revenue, the promised annual payment from his brother in Zanzibar of what later became known as the "Zanzibar subsidy", of $MT 40,000, as recommended by Lord Canning's small Arbitration Commission. But for various reasons the promise was often not fulfilled, and the periodical non-payment of the subsidy added to the difficulties faced by the Muscat exchequer and so to Oman's economic hardship in the 1860s and 1870s.

Sayyid Thuwaini had effectively exercised the powers of Sultan since the death of his father in 1856, but the situation that he faced was far from ideal. The country was exposed to hostile activity by the Wahhabis in the north-west, who still maintained strength in Buraimi. Internally, Thuwaini faced rivals to his throne from both within his own branch of the family, and also from the Qais branch, of whom Hamud bin Azzan (the leader of opposition to Thuwaini back in 1845) had been a member. In addition, he had yet to win the support of the strong tribal groupings of the Hinawis and Ghafiris, without which he could make little progress. And on top of that, the forces of conservative Ibadism were gathering, and considering a revival of the Imamate in order to bring back theocracy to Muscat and Oman.

But it was his younger brother Sayyid Turki who was the first to mount a direct challenge. From his position as *wālī* (governor) of Sohar, and soon after the announcement of the Canning Award in 1861, Turki declared the independence of his district, an act which provoked intervention by Lt Pengelley, who had only that year been appointed British Agent in Muscat. It was not to be a long appointment. Although he succeeded in bringing together the Sultan and the Governor, to the extent that the two brothers agreed on a truce and a peace conference at Seeb, an arrangement for a safe-conduct for Turki broke down, and Thuwaini captured and imprisoned him. The authorities in Bombay thought that Pengelley had acted injudiciously, putting at risk future assurances of British protection, and removed him from his post as soon as they could. The implementation of this was delayed, because of the shortage of Arabic speakers available in the Bombay administration. But the outcome, even if unplanned, was probably satisfactory to the British: Thuwaini was able to confirm his authority all the way along the Batinah coast.

This settlement was however far from permanent. Thuwaini had to put down a revolt from the Al Sa'd, a large tribe in the Batinah, over a taxation issue, and for 3-4 years was engaged in a number of battles in territory which he might reasonably have thought his own. Opposition to him was now being led by 'Azzān bin Qais, a strong leader from the Qais branch of the al-Busa'idi family. The Qais branch, operating from their base in the magnificent fort of Rustaq, had long exercised power and influence in that area where the coastal plain meets the Western

Hajjar mountains. Rustaq had been the capital of conservative Imams in the past, and 'Azzan built his power from conservative Ibadi elements and by alliance with Turki al-Sudairi, the commander of the Wahhabi/Sa'udi garrison in Buraimi.

A change in British leadership on Gulf policy

This serious danger to Sayyid Thuwaini was naturally spotted by the British, this time by the able and wilful Lewis Pelly, who in 1862 had moved from Zanzibar to become British Resident in Bushire. This promotion was due largely to the intervention of Sir Bartle Frere, who – also in 1862 – took office as Governor of Bombay. Frere, and his protégé Pelly, represented a new, firmer and more expansive British policy in the Gulf. They saw the Gulf not only as a channel of communication between England and India, but as part of a defensive belt surrounding India's frontiers – stretching across Persia and Afghanistan and over to Burma and Siam. Just as Governors of British Indian territory saw it as their duty to maintain relations (often of a controlling kind) with the princely states bordering them, so Frere and Pelly considered it necessary to have the rulers and chieftains in the Gulf settled and stable internally and helpfully disposed towards Britain. As Governors organised cavalry patrols on and outside their borders, so Frere and Pelly placed value on naval patrols in the Gulf and Indian Ocean. In other words they saw the Gulf as an extension of – perhaps even part of – the British Indian Empire.[1] All this required – and during Pelly's tenure led to – a decisive change in the Rulers' and Shaikhs' relationships with the British, such that by the early 1870s significant moves even in their internal administration could be achieved only with British approval. Most obviously this was true of Muscat.

We should place this in context by recalling that big changes had taken place in British Indian administration following the suppression of the Indian Mutiny in 1857. The Government of India Act of 1858 discarded the East India Company as the agent of British control and administration, and put in its place a system which reported to a Secretary of State for India (a Minister in the Cabinet) who was supported by an

---

1 This argument is developed by James Onley in *The Arabian Frontier of the British Raj*.

advisory Council of India. This shift in administrative power (no doubt facilitated by better communications by telegraph and steamer ships) was accompanied by a London-driven wish to improve and modernise the Indian territories for which the British had acquired responsibility. In addition, the British became more sensitive than ever to the importance of maintaining internal and external security for the Indian Empire. Yet, awkwardly, the British Indian Government was badly in debt, after the costs of dealing with the mutiny. One result of this was the disbandment of the Bombay Marine in 1862, and the decision that its tasks would be taken on by the Royal Navy. But – at least in the 1860s – the Navy's resources were under pressure; and between 1863 and 1870 there were only three visits to the Gulf by Royal Navy gunboats. This reflected a tension between Frere and Pelly on the one hand (wanting a strengthened British presence in the Gulf) and the Governor-General's administration in Calcutta on the other, the latter wishing to avoid new or added commitments.

Sir Bartle Frere was in the vanguard of the movement to use British power to improve and modernise. He believed in the ability of the British to spread an influence (not necessarily through direct rule) that would get local Governments to "conform to the civic standard of right and wrong [of the British]",[2] spread modern concepts of thought and technology, and convert people to Christian ethics and morality through the medium of West European modernisation. To achieve this it was necessary to have men of his own way of thought in key positions, and accordingly engineered the removal of the then Resident in Bushire, Captain Felix Jones (a Bombay Marine officer of the old school), and his replacement by Pelly.

Thuwaini's campaign to recover Buraimi
In 1864 Sayyid Thuwaini faced a dangerous alliance of Wahhabi/Saudi forces invading down the Western (inland) edge of the Hajjar from Buraimi and conservative Ibadis led by 'Azzan bin Qais, his kinsman. In March the next year Pelly actually undertook the arduous journey to Riyadh, where he thought he had persuaded the Saudi leader, Faisal bin

2 Landen: *Oman since 1856*, Princeton, 1967; quoting Martineau: *The Life and Correspondence of Sir Bartle Frere*, London, 1895.

Turki, to "turn over a new leaf".[3] But he was mistaken: Wahhabi/Saudi forces joined with those of the Bani Bu Ali (the same tribe as had had the contretemps with Captain T Perronet Thompson in 1820-21; see chapter 6) and attacked and looted the port of Sur, hoping to throw off what little rule was then exercised by Sayyid Thuwaini in Muscat. Pelly, partly angered by this Sa'udi deception (as he saw it), partly feeling that the British position in the Gulf was under challenge, argued to Bombay that maritime peace was being threatened. As a result of his persuasion, two gunboats were sent out, and one bombarded Saudi positions in Qatīf and Dammām. British warships also visited Sur, but by then Sayyid Thuwaini had paid off the Wahhabis and got them to withdraw.

This episode persuaded Sayyid Thuwaini that he should take more positive action to clear the Wahhabi/Saudi presence out of Buraimi. Pelly gave this strong support. The British pressured Sayyid Majid in Zanzibar to pay arrears owing from the Zanzibar subsidy, and gave Thuwaini two field guns and ammunition. He managed to assemble a coalition that included tribal levies from the Hinawis, and even support from his formerly rebellious brother Turki (now released from captivity).

Thuwaini assassinated

But the planned attack to recover Buraimi did not take place. In January 1866, in a murky incident in the fortress at Sohar, of which the details have not been convincingly recorded, Sayyid Thuwaini was killed by his son Sālim, who seized power – to the alarm of the merchant community in Muscat, who feared or suspected that he was at the least a conservative Ibadi, and possibly a Wahhabi sympathiser. (It was thought that the Wahhabis might have helped him kill his father.) The British hesitated over recognising Salim as Sultan; Frere and Pelly entertained deep doubts – parricide was presumably not in their list of "civic standards of right and wrong". Salim sent envoys to Bombay and Calcutta; the Viceroy was sufficiently persuaded that Salim would be a moderate and safe in power, and granted him recognition, late in 1866.

3 Pelly, L: "A visit to the Wahabee Capital, Central Arabia", *Journal of the Royal Geographical Society*, xxxv (1865), 169-91

Britain, Oman and the telegraph

Visitors to the Musandam peninsula, the Omani enclave north of the United Arab Emirates, frequently visit Telegraph Island, in Elphinstone Inlet (now Khūr al-Shaʻam). The telegraph station was installed in 1863, and was the occasion of lengthy negotiations involving the Ottoman Turkish authorities, the government of the Shah of Persia, and rulers and governors on the Makran coast, as well as the Sultan of Muscat and the Bombay Government.

Following the suppression of the Indian Mutiny in 1857, improvement of communication between London and India received high level official attention. Telegraphic communication already existed as far as Egypt, and in 1859-60 a cable was laid to complete the connection to India using a submarine route down the Red Sea and along the south and east Arabian coast via Aden, the Kuria Muria Islands, and Muscat, ending at Karachi. Experience and skill in undersea cables was limited, and this one soon failed. The British investigated alternative routes, and decided on a mainly land-based route: the cable would go through Turkey to Iraq, and along the Persian and Makran coast to Karachi.

This decision occasioned lengthy and complex negotiations. The coastal areas through which the cable would pass included several regions where the Persians were anxious either to claim or to preserve their sovereignty. Bandar Abbas, for example, was leased to the Sultan of Muscat, under arrangements confirmed by a Treaty in 1856. The Sultan of Muscat also exercised sovereignty over certain ports east from Bandar Abbas, including Gwadar. Areas of the Makran coast were ruled by Baluchi chieftains. Negotiations which began with an apparently simple request for permission to lay the cable soon became tortuous discussions about sovereignty and ownership, with the Bombay Government resisting any Persian pretensions to rights east of Gwadar.

Eventually, but not until 1870, agreement was reached on the definition of the Makran boundary. Meanwhile, however, enough was agreed for work on the cable to begin through Gwadar in 1863, and from there to Cape Jask and across the Gulf of Oman the following year. The cable route went by land over the Musandam Peninsula, from Malcolm's Inlet on the east to Elphinstone's Inlet on the west, and on via submarine cable to Bushire. The final connections to the Turkey-Iraq cable were quickly made, and the Indo-European telegraph service opened in January 1865. Unfortunate officials were tasked with manning the station on the island in Elphinstone Inlet, whose ruins may still be seen, after turning a corner on the boat passage there. This corner, and the loneliness and frustration of the posting, are said to be the origins of the expression "being sent round the bend".

It was not for long, however. By late 1868 the Musandam route was abandoned, being considered too hazardous, and a new cable was laid from Jask to Bushire, via Hanjam Island, off Qishm. By the end of 1869, when a new convention had been signed with Persia, the route from Bushire to Karachi was secured by new cables via Jask and Gwadar.

Financial and other pressures on Sultan Salim

The Viceroy had misjudged. Like his father, Sayyid Salim ascended a throne that rested on shaky foundations. His finances relied heavily on the Zanzibar subsidy, which Sultan Majid now decided to withhold. He claimed that the Canning Award applied to Sayyid Thuwaini personally, and that he should not be obliged to support a parricidal Ruler – presumably he had some residual loyalty to the memory of his brother, despite their having come near to blows over the inheritance. The British agreed to act as intermediaries for the payment, so that uncle and nephew did not have to come into direct contact; but even so, it was more than a year before the next payment came through, leaving Salim seriously short of funds in the meantime. He set a dangerous precedent when he took loans from Indian merchants in Muscat after failing to get subsidies from the British.

Pelly did however help with difficulties that Salim had with the Persians over Bandar Abbas and Gwadar. These places were important for trade (and the revenue from customs thus generated), and the more so after Zanzibar was split off from Muscat following Sayyid Sa'id's death. Bandar Abbas (and the islands of Qishm and Hormuz), it will be recalled, were rented by the Ruler of Muscat from the Persians, who since the mid-1850s had shown signs of wanting to resume its administration. During Sayyid Thuwaini's reign they had claimed the port of Chahbar and even Gwadar itself; and in 1866 the Persians claimed that the leases were void because of Salim's having illegally seized power from his father. Salim threatened a naval attack on the Persians, who asked for British mediation. Together Pelly and Salim's *wazīr* (ministerial adviser) went to Shiraz and sorted it out: the lease was extended, but (as tends to happen when leases are renewed) the rent was put up – to the equivalent of $MT 75,000 a year. It must have pared to the bone the profit for the Muscat exchequer.

Worse than his precarious financial situation was Sultan Salim's exposure to the same range of threats as his father's rivals within the family (one in particular), continued Wahhabi presence in Buraimi, and rebellion from conservative Ibadis. The particular rival was Salim's uncle, Turki bin Sa'id, whom we have already seen in contention for the Sultanate, in 1861, and whose persistence eventually paid off. Presumably as a precautionary measure, but also because Turki had been supporting Thuwaini just before he died, Salim had Turki locked up on his accession. The British asked for him to be released, successfully; but they soon had grounds to regret it. Turki went travelling in the interior, collected forces to oppose Salim, and in August 1867 actually occupied Matrah, just a couple of miles from Salim in Muscat. Before Turki's forces could attack Salim, in which they might well have succeeded, Pelly arrived to rescue the (narrowly legitimate) Sultan. Turki was persuaded to accept a pension from Salim and go off to exile in India.[4]

Salim may have concluded from this that, with British backing, he was invulnerable. But in fact any Sultan's rule in 19th century Muscat and Oman depended on a careful construction of support from the various tribes and religious interests. This Salim failed to build. The British Agent, Atkinson, could only watch as a conservative coalition was assembled, led by Sa'īd bin Khalfān al-Khalīlī, who for long had hoped for a revival of the ancient Imamate, and 'Azzan bin Qais, who had led the rebellion against Sayyid Thuwaini in 1864. In September 1868 the combined forces arrived near the capital, and offered Salim a deal – that he might continue as Sultan provided that the conservative Ibadis exercise power. Salim, noting that the Hinawi tribes were well

---

4 Atkinson gives a graphic account of these events in his despatch of 16 May 1868, India Office Records R/15/6.

represented in the conservative coalition, thought he might get help from Ghafiri tribesmen, and also from the British, and so turned down the offer. Again Pelly arrived at the last minute, but this time it was too late. Muscat had already been captured, and Salim had taken refuge in the forts above the harbour. Pelly received instructions from Bombay prohibiting him from intervening, the expected help from Ghafiri tribes was not forthcoming (some of them were busy fighting each other), and Salim was forced to accept exile. He sailed off to Bandar Abbas, from where he continued to plot in the hope of his restoration, leaving Muscat and much of Oman in the undisputed control of the forces of conservative Ibadism. Within a few weeks, in October 1868, 'Azzan bin Qais was elected Imam, though under arrangements which left much of the power with Sa'id bin Khalfan al-Khalili.

The revival of the Imamate
It was during the Imamate of 'Azzan bin Qais, which lasted just three years (1868-71), that the rivalry between the Hinawi and Ghafiri tribal groupings – always a fault line in Omani society – showed most clearly. In the year after his election, Imam 'Azzan campaigned to suppress Ghafiri opposition, with considerable success. By the summer of 1869 he could claim control over all the Batinah and most of the inland region, and had even recovered Buraimi from the Saudis. This prompted a short if masterly letter from the Saudi leader: "From 'Abdallah bin Faysal, Imam of the Muslims, to Sayyid 'Azzan bin Qais, Imam of the Robbers. We have heard what you have done. We intend to pay you a visit with 20,000 men. We hope you will receive us suitably." In fact, and luckily for 'Azzan, the "visit with 20,000 men" did not materialise, because of Saudi civil war; but the letter caused some alarm in Imam 'Azzan's camp.

However, this political and military supremacy was accompanied by the same financial troubles as had beset Sultans Thuwaini and Salim, and Imam 'Azzan – once more made worse by Sultan Majid's refusal to pay the Zanzibar subsidy. Indeed, he came under no pressure to pay it, since the British never recognised Imam 'Azzan's Government, presumably because of the force used to eject Salim. The British also resented the treatment given to Hindu merchants in Muscat (who had hitherto been able to live peaceably and prosperously there). Overall, Imam 'Azzan's Government's conservative flavour did not match the modernising trend which the British hoped for in their Gulf protégés. Late in 1870 Pelly felt he should accept the *fait accompli*, and recommended recognition, but 'Azzan's Government fell before this could be implemented.

Political, religious and economic factors combined to make things worse for Imam 'Azzan. In bringing the Ghafiris to heel, he humiliated them so that they were too ready to join opposition when the chance came in 1871. In Muscat itself the conservative elements of the régime, led by the pious but fundamentalist Khalili (now appointed Chief *Qāḍī*, ie head of the juridical system but with wide-ranging influence), imposed strict puritanical rules on the normally easy-going populace. Here the difference became apparent between the maritime and trading society of the coast, with its international outlook and mixed ethnic composition, and the austere ethos of the folk from the interior. Khalili was supported by groups of *muttawwi'ūn*,[5] who enforced rules against dancing, the use of liquor or drugs, and music and drums. In some cases violence was used against Hindu traders, despite their notionally being protected as British Indian citizens. The port's business, which was in decline anyway for other reasons (see p 153 below), was further reduced as members of the Indian community took their business elsewhere, for example to Zanzibar or other Indian Ocean ports.

All this had a direct effect on the stability of Imam 'Azzan's Government. Reduced commerce led to lower tax revenue. Khalili, in charge of Government finance, attempted to boost income by confiscation of property, with predictable consequences for the esteem in which the régime was held.

The conservatives' fanaticism helped to worsen relations with Sultan Majid in Zanzibar, since groups travelled to Zanzibar in order to inspire revolution and/or to take over the island for Imam 'Azzan. Majid, however, despite his scratchy relations with Thuwaini and Salim, preferred to see one of his branch of the family restored in Muscat, if he could not have the Sultanate there himself. He made contact with Sayyid Turki, his younger brother, still in exile in India, and later gave him funds to help his bid for power.

---

5 Also given as *mutawwi'* or *mutawwa'*; and some historians refer to this episode in Omani history as the Mutawwa' Revolt. The word can be translated as "volunteers" (*muṭṭawi'ūn*) or "enforcers of obedience" (*muṭawwi'ūn*).

The al-Busa'idi counter-coup

Opportunity came in 1870. Turki sailed to Bandar Abbas in March of that year, and toured the Trucial States looking for support, claiming to have British backing. This was not true: the British had actually warned him not to upset the maritime truce in the Gulf, eg by attacking Muscat. But after receiving promises of the Zanzibari money, a second tour, lubricated with bribes or promises of bribes, enabled Turki to assemble a considerable force with whom he marched south, taking an inland route, all the way to Sur. At this stage Pelly reported that Turki had exhausted his Zanzibari subsidy and his ability to proceed. But somehow Turki regrouped, sent part of his force straight up the coast from Sur while leading the main part inland via the Sharqiyah province, and in January 1871 – after Imam 'Azzan was killed in fighting at Matrah – captured Muscat as well.

Pelly was again on the scene, intervening in an attempt to minimise loss of life and damage to property. Khalili had taken command of the Imamate forces, though not elected Imam himself, and Pelly persuaded him to surrender after Turki had agreed to a number of conditions, including protection for Khalili, under Pelly's guarantee. But the deal was honoured only in the breach: two months later Khalili died in dubious circumstances. It has been suggested that Atkinson, the Agent in Muscat, shot himself out of depression and dismay at this failure to respect a British guarantee. An alternative version has it that Atkinson had been told he was to be posted as Agent and Consul in Zanzibar, and was devastated by the prospect. Both explanations are speculative. Either way he seems to have been prey to serious depression.

Overview of the 1860s

This was a turbulent decade for Oman; and much of the political uncertainty was due to the economic decline which began with the death of Sayyid Sa'id and continued – sadly – until well into the 20th century. Sa'id's rule had left Muscat and Zanzibar operating happily in combination and at a level of prosperity which neither would see again for 100 years, if then. It has been described as an empire, but this may need some qualification, since for much of his lifetime Sayyid Sa'id's direct rule extended only over the coastal areas of what is now Oman, and over Zanzibar and its dependencies; on the East African coast those towns owing allegiance to the Sultan did little more than pay his taxes and accept his jurisdiction. But traders in the ports of Muscat and Sur, and up the Batinah coast, in Zanzibar, and Pemba, in Mombasa, Kilwa and others, prospered through commerce carried in Omani sailing ships over waters kept safe both by the Omani navy and through British supervision, both naval and by treaty.

Decline set in quickly after Sa'id's death, for a range of reasons which made an unfortunate combination for Muscat and Oman. The division of Zanzibar from Muscat itself was seriously injurious: Pelly thought it the most damaging factor second only to the introduction of steamer vessels. These ships came into the Indian Ocean exactly at this time, British engineers constantly working to improve the efficiency of the engines and the design of the ships, paddle-driven at first and then with screws. Traditional dhows could not compete, for scale, efficiency or reliability. This in turn damaged Muscat's leading position as a commercial port: Oman itself was producing virtually nothing for export – the trading prosperity of Matrah and Muscat depended on turn-around traffic, accepting cargoes large or small, and breaking them down or building them up into new cargoes small or large. With the advent of steam, ships no longer required this service, or only to a reduced extent. Muscat saw further contraction during the régime of Imam 'Azzan bin Qais, as we have seen. All this contraction of trade led to reduction in revenue from taxes and customs dues, as well as a drop in actual commercial earnings for the Sultan, who (at least in Sayyid Sa'id's case) had traded on his own account through his possessions of spice and other plantations.

In addition, British action to reduce the slave trade had a direct and indirect negative effect on Muscat prosperity. Omani traders in Zanzibar, Sur and Muscat principally, but also in other ports, made significant profits on the trade, which were whittled away as the Treaties of 1822, 1839, 1845 and 1873 were implemented. At the same time, the Sultan's revenue from the duty paid on slaves was also steadily reduced.

Two other factors in economic decline should be mentioned, although they came into play really only after 1870. First, the Maria Theresa dollar, in which much of Muscat's trade (and all the Zanzibar subsidy) was denominated, suffered a serious drop in the last quarter of the century – from about 5 to the Pound Sterling in 1870 to 11 to the Pound in 1900.

This was because of a global drop in the cost and value of silver. Thus, trade figures quoted in $MT appear to increase between 1874 and 1902, but actually stayed the same in real (Pound Sterling) terms. Second, in contrast with actual possessions or dominions in the empire, the British had no incentive to expand the Omani economy or to invest there, since the legal system was not as familiar as in (for example) India, no taxation revenue accrued to the British exchequer, and British merchants had no special advantage, beyond legal protection.

It would be wrong to lay the blame for instability in Muscat and Oman in the 1860s on economic factors alone. Traditional rivalries – between the Hinawi and Ghafiri tribal groups, between coast and interior, between moderate and conservative Ibadis, and between the two branches of the al-Busa'idis – also came to the fore. The combination of these factors produced a damaging mix, which left the people notably worse off than in the heady days of Sayyid Sa'id's rule. This situation also opened the way for an even closer British involvement in the affairs of Muscat and Oman in the last quarter of the century.

Turki at last becomes Sultan

Turki bin Sa'id was about 30 when in early 1871 he became Sultan. He had fought long and hard for it, since before the Canning Award of 1861 (when he had been Governor of Sohar), through rivalry with his brother Sayyid Thuwaini, and then through exile in India for three years after his failure to overthrow Sayyid Salim. He was seen as energetic and with some political acumen – which he was certainly going to need if he were to consolidate his power in the face of the disparate forces in the Sultanate. We may wonder why these successive Rulers of Oman expended such effort in securing their ascent to the throne, when such difficulties awaited them even when success was attained. In Turki's case the problems were similar to those of his predecessors: the rivalries just mentioned were still simmering, and the financial problems were without apparent solution – especially since payment of the Zanzibar subsidy had not been resumed by Sultan Majid's successor, Barghash. This was crucial to Turki's survival, since it was expected that he would continue, as his predecessors had done, to pay subsidies to the tribes of the interior to maintain their loyalty and to keep together the coalition that had brought him to power.

Lewis Pelly, having been present at Sultan Turki's assumption of power, was almost immediately called on to help keep him there. Turki faced resistance in the northern Batinah, from the brother of 'Azzan bin Qais, Ibrahim. In June 1871 Turki wrote to Pelly to ask him to persuade Zaid bin Khalīfah, Shaikh of Abu Dhabi, to give up supporting Ibrahim – which he did. This would have enabled Turki to mount an attack on Ibrahim, were it not for his having to spend most of 1872 in dealing with a flank attack from tribes in the Sharqiyah who threatened not only to support Ibrahim bin Qais but also to put back on the throne the ex-Sultan Salim, who was still in Oman, and did not leave until the end of 1872, eventually to die of smallpox in Sind.

Renewed – and final – efforts to end the slave trade

At this stage, in early 1873, there came into play another factor – or actually an old one in new form. The British had decided to bring to a head the issue of ending the East African slave trade. We have seen that since the 1845 Treaty with Sayyid Sa'id the number of slaves traded on these routes had barely decreased. The situation, unsatisfactory in the 1850s, worsened in 1861 and 1862, when groups of "Northern Arabs" (mostly from Sur, or Qawasim) descended in large numbers on Zanzibar to purchase as many slaves as their boats could hold. Sultan Majid, presumably reckoning that this trading was too blatant a breach of the 1845 Treaty, actually took measures to restrict the trade in Zanzibari markets. But the trade continued, despite British efforts to increase patrolling and redirect efforts towards the ports of export rather than in the Gulf. This burden fell entirely to the Royal Navy after the Bombay Marine was disbanded in 1862. The Navy had barely enough ships for the business, but attempted more systematic patrolling in 1868 and 1869, years in which again the Northern Arabs had caused disturbance in Zanzibar during the trading season. This time it was probably exacerbated by the trouble in Muscat following Sayyid Salim's murder of his father Sayyid Thuwaini, and the growth in power of the *muṭṭawi'ūn* supporters of Imam 'Azzān bin Qais.

At this point in British policy-making the issue of the Canning Award subsidy became connected with the determination to take decisive action to end the slave trade out of Zanzibar. Sultan Majid argued that he had to continue the trade in order to earn enough to pay the subsidy, but the

British did not want him to stop payment for fear that the Ruler of Muscat, deprived of income, would resort to force to reunite the Sultanate. For the British, and especially the British administration in India, maintenance of the status quo was of paramount importance. The status quo was interpreted as keeping someone from the moderate Ibadi branch of the al-Busa'idis on the throne at Muscat, and sustaining the maritime Truce in the Gulf. Protracted discussions took place, during which differences emerged between the Foreign Office (determined to abolish the slave trade) and officials in India (concerned not to upset the Canning Award), as well as concern over which treasury – the Imperial or the Indian – would bear the cost of any removal of the subsidy obligation and the consequent need to make good the amount ($MT 40,000, or about £8,000, per year) to Muscat. However, a Select Committee of Parliament formed in 1871 reported without dealing adequately with the subsidy question, resulting in further argument between the Prime Minister (Gladstone) and the Foreign Secretary (Earl Granville[6]); and it was not until 1872 that Sir Bartle Frere was sent to Muscat and Zanzibar with the aim of negotiating a conclusive agreement. Frere had now concluded his term as Governor of Bombay, and was in London on the India Council. His brief was comprehensive, and included consultation of both Sultan Turki at Muscat and Sultan Barghash in Zanzibar. The British had at last recognised that the nettle needed to be grasped: it was no good aiming to stop the trade through prohibition of imports or through interception of traffickers – the only solution was to prevent exports of slaves from East African ports. Frere was therefore instructed to get Barghash to agree to prohibit all export of slaves from his African mainland possessions, to close slave markets, to protect liberated slaves from re-enslavement, and to forbid Indian subjects of Britain to acquire slaves. He was also to persuade Turki to commit to honouring the 1845 Agreement. And as a sweetener, he could offer payment of the Canning Award subsidy, at the joint expense of the Imperial and Indian Treasuries.

The procedure was successful, though not much credit for it is due to Frere. He encountered an initial blank refusal from Barghash, who used political and religious arguments to justify continuing the trade, but may

6 Formerly Lord Leveson, who as Deputy Under-Secretary had been the author of the June 1841 letter that led to the 1845 Treaty

also have been put off by Frere's haughty style and inflexible negotiating approach. Frere had more luck with Turki – but this is not so surprising, since the Muscat Sultan had more to gain from compliance than his Zanzibari brother. As we have seen, he was in severe need of money to enforce his rule and deal with Ibrahim bin Qais. On Frere's return to London (Frere seems to have been more effective in Whitehall than with the Sultans), Earl Granville embarked on a policy of brazen threat: Zanzibar would be blockaded by the Royal Navy if Barghash did not follow his brother and comply. This he did, at the instigation of Dr John Kirk, the astute British Agent in Zanzibar, signing the Treaty on 5 June 1873.[7]

This time, though not immediately, the Treaty arrangement worked; trading and owning slaves steadily declined. Complete eradication was to take decades: slavery was still an issue in the late 1880s during the confrontation between the British and the Germans in East Africa which led later to the British take-over in Zanzibar, and it was not until 1889 that Sultan Khalid, under German-British pressure, issued a declaration that anyone entering his dominions would be free. This was to ensure, the British hoped, that as existing slaves died, the institution of slavery would be extinct in Zanzibar within a matter of a few years.

Growth in British involvement in Omani affairs

To return to Oman: Sultan Turki now had the finances necessary to pursue his objectives in the Batinah. The sweetener offered by Frere actually enabled him to draw $MT40,000 immediately, and $MT20,000 three months later from the British Agent at Muscat. With this he was able to pension off Ibrahim bin Qais, and quieten potential resistance from tribes in the interior; and he might well have consolidated his rule still further, and longer, had he not fallen seriously ill, possibly from a stroke, in 1873. He never fully regained his strength, suffering from other illness later which forced him to use crutches. In the short term, this gave an opportunity to Ibrahim bin Qais and others to resume resistance to his rule.

In 1872 E C Ross was moved from Muscat and appointed Resident in Bushire, on promotion from Captain to Major, and replacing Lewis Pelly. In the same year Colonel S B Miles took over in Muscat. Ross stayed in

7 A detailed account of the negotiations is in Alastair Hazell's The Last Slave Market, effectively a biography of Kirk.

office until 1892, and Miles – with some intermissions – until 1887; and together these two men played a large part in shaping British policy towards Muscat and Oman for this important period in the nation's history. Ross was less outgoing than Pelly, and less interested in the imperial mission; he was a sound administrator, careful to preserve the imperial interests, but with a more intellectual approach. He is known to scholars as the translator and editor of an important chronicle of Oman (details in Notes for further reading). Miles bore some similarities to his superior: he established good relations with Sultan Turki and his son Faisal, and was allowed to travel extensively in the interior – which enabled him to write his distinctive *Countries and Tribes of the Persian Gulf.*

In a number of ways Ross and Miles raised the level of their involvement in Omani affairs. Under instructions from Bombay, they kept Turki in power, using force on occasion – for example in 1874 when British gunboats bombarded lands of the al-Sa'd tribe on the Batinah coast, and thus ensured that the Sultan's edict ran there for the rest of his reign. The same year Miles warned off two of Turki's nephews against making trouble: the two sons of former Sultan Thuwaini took the hint and made peace with Turki. Ross and Miles also eased the process whereby Turki appointed his half-brother Abdul 'Aziz as *wazīr* (minister or adviser) to help the Sultan when he was at his weakest after his illness. For most of 1875 Turki took leave in Gwadar. The British did not much like the conservative rules which Abdul 'Aziz introduced as regent in his absence, and continued to pay the Zanzibar subsidy personally to Turki in Gwadar, so that he had the money to resume rule when he was fit again. Abdul 'Aziz fell away from Turki, and even participated in the revolt against him in 1877 (see below); he later set himself up as a pretender to the Sultanate, but ended his days in exile in India.

The British also helped Sultan Turki establish his authority in Dhofar. Sayyid Sa'id had occupied the district in 1829, but Muscat's control had been allowed to lapse; and Turki re-occupied Dhofar in 1879 and appointed a Governor there. He encountered opposition, mainly from the Ottomans (who at this time had designs on all the Arabian peninsula), and – after minor outbreaks of disorder in the early 1880s – the British intervened to counter the Ottoman threat in 1886. Omani domination remained dubious for a while, and it was only in the early 20th century that the province was secure.

More significant British intervention occurred in 1877 and 1883. On both occasions conservative forces gathered and attacked Muscat, but the assaults were repelled, with the assistance of bombardments from British gunboats, HMS *Teaser* in 1877 and HMS *Philomel* in 1883. These successes, aided also by a punitive expedition into Wadi Samail led by Turki's son, Sayyid (later Sultan) Faisal, helped secure Turki's prestige and reduce the risk of continued opposition from the interior. As a seal of approval of his régime, in 1886 the British issued to Turki a declaration whereby they undertook to uphold him as Ruler in all eventualities. The context was a plan initiated by Ross aimed at consolidating the treaty arrangements in the Gulf, to counter threats to British primacy there from the Ottomans and the Persians. Ross's plan led eventually to a new British-Omani commercial treaty in 1891; but this was under the rule of Turki's son, Faisal, who inherited the throne peaceably when Turki's illnesses overcame him and he died aged less than 50, in 1888.

The succession of Sultan Faisal bin Turki

That the succession passed smoothly – the first time that power had transferred without violence since the al-Busa'idis had taken over more than 100 years before – is a tribute to the relative success of Sultan Turki's administration. The judgement has to be qualified, since his power barely extended beyond Muscat and Matrah, and the towns and villages of the Batinah, and the economic decline which had begun in the 1860s was only slowed, not reversed. Financially and politically Turki became increasingly dependent on British protection: Ross and Miles ensured the security of his position, both by active intervention and by arranging the exile to India of potential rivals, and of course by arranging British payment of the Zanzibar subsidy. They were well aware of the fragility of Turki's authority: writing in 1883, five years before Turki's death, Ross mentions "several attempts ... to capture Muscat", and says, "Who will eventually establish his power in succession to the present Sultan cannot with any confidence be predicted", adding his view that Turki's sons were then young and inexperienced. Nevertheless, with British backing and relatively secure financially, Turki could afford the cost of retaining the loyalty of those tribes and tribal shaikhs who might otherwise have been tempted to cause disruption. In return, Turki (who for the last 12 years of his rule was assisted by a pro-British wazir, Sa'id bin Mohammed) had to subscribe to the British view of lower Gulf security, and in particular go along with their intention to end slavery in the region. These issues would become even more stark under the rule of his son Faisal.

17. Sir John Kirk   *18. Sir Bartle Frere*

19. The Frere mission, 1873

CHAPTER 11

Division and dependence (1888-1920)

S ultan Faisal bin Turki and his son Sultan Taymūr had the misfortune to assume power during a period of economic decline in Muscat and Oman, and also faced religious conservative opposition that had greater intellectual strength and organisational capacity than the movement that brought about the Imamate of 'Azzan bin Qais. Sultan Faisal also found himself the victim of renewed and acute rivalry between France and Britain. Outcomes included a Sultanate in a 'client state' relationship with the British, a revival of the Imamate, and – in 1920 – formal separation of the interior ("Oman"), under the Imamate, from Muscat and the coastal plain, under the Sultan.

* * * * * * *

Sultan Faisal seeks less dependence on the British

Sayyid Faisal bin Turki succeeded as Sultan in 1888, aged 24. During the early part of his rule, the relationship with the British deteriorated sharply. An early portent was his decision to sack his father's pro-British *wazir*, Sa'id bin Mohammed, a move perhaps simply intended as a signal of his determination to be less dependent on the British than his father. Nevertheless, he allowed resumption of the negotiations begun by Ross, still Resident in Bushire, for a bilateral treaty. Ross's purpose had been to establish a complete network of treaties through the Gulf. He may in part have been motivated by a wish to counter growing French interest

161

in the Gulf (see p 165 below). But his main aim was to get commitments on paper to what had become implicit, and indeed the practice, since the 1853 Trucial arrangements – namely that Britain would take responsibility for the Trucial States' foreign affairs. The position was a little different in Oman, where matters rested with the Commercial Treaty of 1839; but Ross clearly thought that some up-dating with Muscat was required as well.

In 1887 Ross concluded negotiations on exclusive agreements with each of the Trucial Shaikhs, but it was found that they could not be ratified since he had not been given plenipotentiary powers. It was not until 1892 that Lt Col A C Talbot (who had succeeded Ross the year before) presented revised treaties to them all; and these were duly ratified by the Viceroy. But in Muscat the process was less straightforward. Ross had suggested a new Treaty to Sultan Turki, who died before the negotiations were concluded. When they were resumed in 1890 officials in India considered – not for the first time – the possibility of declaring a protectorate over Oman. There were several arguments in favour. Primarily, stability in Oman and the maintenance of a régime in Muscat that was favourable to British and British Indian interests was important to London and Calcutta. But in addition, it seemed to British Indian policy-makers that a virtual protectorate existed already: Britain was responsible for guaranteeing the Canning Arbitration, the Indian Treasury was paying the Zanzibar subsidy, the British had several times intervened to keep the Sultan on his throne and to tidy away rivals or pretenders into exile, and the British Resident had handled the negotiations for the Omani-Netherlands Commercial Treaty in 1877.

Lord Salisbury (Prime Minister and also Foreign Secretary) was naturally consulted about the proposed policy, and engaged in correspondence about it with Lord Lansdowne (Viceroy of India) in the autumn of 1890. He drew officials' attention to the Anglo-French declaration of 1862, which committed the Governments in London and Paris to respect the independence of the two Sultans in Muscat and Zanzibar. He concluded from this that no agreement placing restrictions on Sultan Faisal's independence could be concluded without consulting the French, which he did not want to do. An exclusive protectorate arrangement, such as existed with the Trucial Shaikhs, was therefore not on the cards. Ross accordingly negotiated and signed with Sultan Faisal, in March 1891, a Commercial Treaty which re-asserted many of the provisions of the 1839 Treaty, adding a number of details relating to customs dues and exemptions. The Treaty also extended extraterritorial privileges for British subjects, granting their consular authorities the responsibility for hearing not only civil but also criminal cases involving British subjects. The Treaty also had attached to it a secret annex in which the Sultan promised not to cede any territory except to the British Government. The British considered this to be equivalent to a "quasi-protectorate", with influence that was paramount but not exclusive, this being taken to mean that the Sultan was legally free to conduct his own foreign affairs. The secrecy, incidentally, was of only moderate duration: the text was included in the edition of Aitchison's Treaties published in 1909, and was probably known about before that.

The relationship deteriorates

Sultan Faisal showed signs of determination to retain his freedom to conduct his own foreign policy. Indeed, it seems curious that he agreed to sign either the overt Commercial Treaty or the secret annex, given his negative attitude towards the British in these early years of his reign. He may have seen some commercial advantage to Omani merchants, since the 1891 provisions were properly mutual and balanced, and Omani ships needed to continue to trade with India. He would have felt it strategically useful to have an up-to-date treaty relationship with the main regional power. And he was under pressure from Ross, who delayed British recognition of his succession as Sultan in order to persuade him to negotiate.

After dismissing his pro-British *wazir*, Sultan Faisal went on to be difficult over an issue which he would have well known would be sensitive to the British – the continuation of the slave trade. At the time he was concerned to cultivate the more conservative religious elements in Omani society, probably in an attempt to cement a kind of national solidarity, or at least a wider sense of loyalty to himself as both political and religious leader, without having to pay out large subsidies which his Treasury could no longer afford. He styled himself "Imam" as well as "Sultan" on coins he had minted, and non-Omani Ibadis referred to him as "Imam of Muscat and Oman". Whatever the reason, and while generally he maintained the more moderate approach to religion with which the British were familiar and content, the outcomes on slavery were not satisfactory in the eyes of his British allies. In practical terms they meant that Sultan Faisal turned a blind eye to continued slaving activities in dhows from Muscat and Oman, and also allowed Omani dhow-owners to sail under the French flag, which put them outwith his jurisdiction. By the end of the 1890s reports suggested that it would no longer be feasible to press for the abolition of slavery in Oman, since Sultan Faisal would do no more than the bare minimum to respect his Treaty obligations, and in any case had lost control of much of the interior of the country.

The deterioration in the relationship in the 1890s cannot be laid simply at Sultan Faisal's door. External events imposed their pressure: in a decade which saw a noticeable rise in the intensity of competition between the imperial powers of Britain, France, Russia and Germany, the Gulf became an area where rivalries were inevitable. In Oman's case, it was a renewal of the rivalry between the French and the British which placed Sultan Faisal between powerful opposing forces. The situation was not helped by the neglect shown by the British in staffing the Resident and Agent posts in Bushire and Muscat. After the departure of Ross and Miles, in 1891 and 1887 respectively, with their deep and sympathetic knowledge of the language and culture of the region, and their ability to get on well with the local Rulers, these two posts suffered from a succession of poor appointments, and a lack of continuity. Between 1892 and 1900 there were four Residents, and four Agents; and in the closing years of the decade, when Captain Fagan (who spoke no Arabic) was in his mercifully short tenure at Muscat, the relationship with Sultan Faisal broke down completely. The situation was fortunately retrieved when the renowned Major (later Sir Percy) Cox took over first at Muscat in 1900 and then in Bushire in 1904.

Between the British and the French in Oman there were two bones of contention in the 1890s – use of the French flag on slaving vessels, and a request for a coaling station; and to this must be added one bilateral issue between Oman and Britain – that of gun-running. Let us take the last one first, although it was not solved until the very end of Sultan Faisal's rule. Muscat had become a regional centre for the munitions trade, as a substitute commodity after the virtual collapse of the more general commercial traffic which had brought prosperity until the 1860s, and the decline in the slave trade. Trading in arms became a useful money-earner. It was worth over £100,000 in 1900. At first Sultan Faisal connived in it, as the trade brought in revenue from customs duties. Later he came to regret the trade, because – as might be expected – not all of the imported guns were exported; and the inland tribes, who later became hostile to the Sultan, were able to make sure they became better armed and equipped. By 1897 the British had gathered the exasperating evidence that English-made rifles traded through Muscat were ending up in the hands of the Pathans whom they were fighting on the North-West frontier of India! Efforts were made to get Sultan Faisal and other Gulf Rulers to restrict the trade through their territories. But it was only in 1912 that an arms trade agreement was signed with Sultan Faisal; it put an end to the trade, but at a price of an additional *lakh* (100,000) of rupees, equivalent then to £6,666, to the Zanzibar subsidy. Since, with the weakening of the price of silver, the sterling equivalent of the subsidy's $MT 40,000 was by then worth barely £4,000, this was a significant addition, whose continuation was to become a significant issue between Britain and subsequent Sultans.

The clash with the French
We turn next to those issues which involved France. This was a period which saw a resurgence of rivalry between colonial powers, most especially in Africa. French policy – in the 1880s but notably in the 1890s under their Foreign Minister Hanotaux until he was replaced in 1898 – was aimed at competing with the British in several regions, including the Gulf and the Indian Ocean. In Oman this took the form of the appointment of a Vice-Consul at Muscat: M Ottavi, who had experience in Zanzibar and spoke Arabic, took up his post in November 1894, and soon established a good relationship with Sultan Faisal. He had to overcome initial suspicion on the part of Faisal, but his task was made that much easier by clumsy British handling of Faisal's campaign against an attack by conservative Ibadis in early 1895. Faisal had become irritated by abuse of the extra-territorial status enjoyed by subjects of British India resident in Muscat (the provisions for extra-territorial jurisdiction had existed for some time, and had been extended in the 1891 Commercial Treaty); but when he had made complaints to British officials they barely took notice, and in fact became irritated themselves.

The relationship between Sultan Faisal and the Agent, Major Hayes Sadler, deteriorated hopelessly. Thus it was that, when the Ibadi conservative coalition of tribes moved on Muscat in early 1895, and actually succeeded in getting aid – in the form of cash, guns and gunpowder – from Sultan Hamud of Zanzibar, the British, having attempted too late to press Hamud to stay out of Omani affairs then held back from giving Faisal active support. Ottavi meanwhile managed to arrange for a French gunboat to be sent to Muscat; this also arrived too late to be of military use, but the political effect was positive, and set the French on an improving trend while Sadler and his successors were on a downward path.

Worse was to come. The attacking force, mainly composed of Hinawi tribesmen, advanced on and occupied Muscat, forcing Sultan Faisal to take refuge in one of the forts. They hoisted the white flag of the Imamate over the Sultan's palace; and claimed they wanted friendship with the British Indian Government. Hayes Sadler stayed neutral, which was not a lot of help to Faisal, holed up in the fort. At this point Faisal called in aid from Ghafiri tribesmen, and some inconclusive fighting took place. The incident ended when Faisal concluded an agreement by which he pardoned the attackers, and promised resumption of the subsidies which he had previously been paying. Unfortunately, while evacuating Muscat the attackers stole or damaged a lot of property, causing huge losses to Indian traders, many of them British Indian subjects. The British, coming to their defence, claimed nearly $MT 78,000 in damages – almost two years' worth of the Zanzibar subsidy. This did not endear them to Faisal, who moved further into the arms of the French. Ottavi took every opportunity to drive wedges between his host and his rivals.

Tension turned to crisis as a result of a visit to Muscat by another French gunboat in March 1898. On this occasion Sultan Faisal agreed to a French request for a concession to establish a coaling station at Bandar Jissah, then a convenient natural harbour a few miles south of Muscat, and now the site of a diving centre and – nearby – a modern hotel complex. Then in October 1898 yet a third French gunboat arrived: the French exchanged valuable gifts and held secret conferences with Faisal, and went to inspect Bandar Jissah. The British looked as though they were about to be displaced. They also took offence when Faisal refused to fire the customary salute on the occasion of Queen Victoria's birthday.

166

Events in London and Paris on the one hand, and in Muscat, Bombay and Calcutta on the other, then moved quickly – although not consistently, since policy-makers in Europe were not co-ordinated with actors in the region. In Paris, Theophile Delcassé had replaced Hanotaux as Foreign Minister; he embarked on a policy of smoothing over the problems of colonial competition created by Hanotaux, and began the process of improving the relationship with London, which later led to the Entente Cordiale of 1904. Prime Minister Salisbury also wanted to end the difficulties with the French. When news of the coaling station concession at Bandar Jissah came out in November 1898, Delcassé denied knowledge of the affair and Salisbury decided to take a soft line in order to allow Delcassé an escape route. But no such conciliatory mood was to be found in Calcutta. There, George Curzon, who since 1892 had been pressing the need to reassert the British position in the Gulf, as a buffer zone in the system of defence for India, took up his post as Viceroy in January 1899 and immediately instructed Fagan in Muscat to protest to Faisal. Presumably he felt he had right on his side, as well as political advantage, since the non-cession clause in the annex to the 1891 Commercial Treaty committed Sultan Faisal and his heirs and successors "never to cede, to sell, to mortgage, or *otherwise give for occupation*, save to the British Government, the dominions of Muskat and Oman or any of their dependencies".[1] It was a fatal mix of personalities – Curzon, with his determined imperialist views of British interests in the region; Fagan, with his lack of understanding of Arabic and Arab culture, and his inability to cultivate a relationship with the Sultan; and Faisal, trying to run an impoverished Sultanate and to navigate a course between powerful rivals.

Needless to say, the interview between Fagan and Faisal was unproductive. Curzon instructed that a British flag should be hoisted at Bandar Jissah if a French warship appeared there, withheld the Zanzibar subsidy, and sent the Resident, Colonel Meade, to Muscat with an ultimatum – that Sultan Faisal should cancel the French concession. Although he agreed, on 13 February 1899, Meade and Curzon demanded a public announcement of the cancellation, suggesting that they wanted to embarrass both Faisal and the French. A British flotilla arrived off

---

1 Authors' emphasis. This commitment was in the first paragraph of the annex to the 1891 Treaty, given in Aitchison, Vol XII, pp 240-241

Muscat the next day, under the command of Admiral Douglas, and stood by threatening to bombard the city. Faisal gave in, and went on board Douglas's flagship to give his formal agreement. As he was rowed back to Muscat, Douglas's men fired the 21-gun salute appropriate for an independent sovereign – we do not know whether the irony was deliberate.

The incident had repercussions in Paris and London. The French protested against Douglas's action (the threat to bombard, not the salute); and Salisbury thought that Curzon's handling of the affair had been a "serious mistake". He and Delcassé sought to play it all down. Talks rumbled on for over a year about the French needs for a coaling station, Curzon and his people insisting that they should not be allowed a facility which could be developed into a naval base, and in the end the French agreed to share British coaling facilities within Muscat harbour.

It is easy, and tempting, to make a caricature of Curzon. Looking at his portrait, with his impeccable uniform and imperious nose, we may think there is some justification for the aphorism: "My name is George Nathaniel Curzon, I am a most superior person". But he knew the region extremely well, having travelled extensively in the Middle East for five years, 1887-92, including a year in Persia in 1889-90. He well understood the problems faced by Persian, Arab and Indian rulers and peoples, however much he can be faulted for his view that these problems had British solutions. His zealous advocacy on behalf of the defence of the Indian Empire, at almost whatever cost, would have stemmed partly from this view of the world of his time, and partly from his wish to do right by his position first as Under-Secretary in the India Office, then as Parliamentary Under-Secretary for foreign affairs, and finally as Viceroy.[2]

The other British-French issue of this time was not so critical, but contentious enough to end in a court of arbitration. It related to the use of the French flag on a number of Omani ships, mostly from Sur. We have to speculate on why this practice had grown up. The Sur sailors may have calculated that they stood a better chance of continuing some dubious trade, particularly in slaves, if under a French rather than Omani flag, since British ships might intercept Omani vessels (enforcing Omani Sultans' commitments to end the slave trade) but could be expected to

---

2 For more on Curzon, sea Sarah Searight: *The British in the Middle East*, London and The Hague, 1969, revised 1979; especially pp 148-9 and 190

hesitate from provoking an incident by intercepting an apparently French boat. The French practice went back to the 1860s, when there would have been more trade between Omani ports and the Mascarene Islands. Whatever the origins, questions about the practice arose in the late 1890s, when Ottavi claimed that these seamen should be granted French juridical protection – an extension of extra-territorial jurisdiction rights similar to those enjoyed by subjects of British India. Sultan Faisal objected to this, claiming that the seamen were being detached from their rightful allegiance – ie to himself. The British supported him, fearing that the presence in Muscat of a number of people owing allegiance to France would give Ottavi more opportunities to intervene in Omani affairs. They also resented the possibility granted to these seamen from Sur to continue a trade in slaves that should long have been ended. Local discussion of the issue failed, and it was referred to the Tribunal at The Hague. Judgement was not handed down until 1905. It maintained the Omani-British view, but by this time the issue was barely of any importance and French-British rivalry in the region had in any case faded.

The competition between the British and the French in Oman in the 1890s was of little significance beyond the local, and had small effect also on the strategic discussions in progress in London and Paris. Salisbury and Delcassé handled matters prudently, in the interests of the more important discussions on European stability, involving Russia and Germany in particular. But for Oman the outcomes were crucial. The policies and actions of Hanotaux and Ottavi had the immediate effect – by provoking Curzon into action – of leaving Sultan Faisal firmly in a British embrace. At the same time, French actions resulted in implicit confirmation of the commitment in the Declaration of 1862 – a reminder that Sultan Faisal's independence had to be respected. This was not to be taken for granted. It will be recalled that the British had considered declaring a protectorate during the discussions leading to the 1891 Commercial Treaty, and the possibility had been mooted again, but again dropped, in 1897. Curzon himself had said, earlier, "I have little doubt that the time will come ... when the Union Jack will be seen flying from the castles of Muscat".[3] At least, as he emerged from the 1899 crisis, Sultan Faisal could console himself that he was still an independent

3 Quoted by Skeet: *Muscat and Oman – the end of an era*, p 50

sovereign with control over his own foreign policy, and not a "protected ruler" as were the Trucial Shaikhs.

This did not mean that he could entirely escape the mixed blessing of the imperial embrace. British policy-making at this time was coloured by a pre-occupation with South Africa, following the outbreak of the Boer War in October 1899. There were fears that the other European powers – France, Germany and Russia – might in one way or another take advantage of the pressure Britain faced. In fact only the Russians contrived threats to British paramountcy in the Gulf, through a number of moves aimed at enhancing their diplomatic, commercial and strategic interests in Persia and Mesopotamia. They also tried – but unsuccessfully – to open a consulate in Muscat. This activity alarmed the British, afraid that the security of their Indian Empire would be put at risk by the Russian search for a "warm-water port", ie easier access to the Gulf or the Indian Ocean for their commercial or naval vessels. As Prime Minister, Salisbury preferred to deal with the Russian threat through quiet diplomacy, in order to minimise the risk of provoking a military build-up or even an actual attack which the British would not be able to counter because of the South African war. Lord George Hamilton, Secretary of State for India, favoured more positive action, but like Salisbury he wanted minimum exposure to risk in the face of Russian power. Indeed he considered that Indian security could be guaranteed by Britain maintaining paramountcy in the lower Gulf, and that it was prudent to acquiesce in a growth of Russian power in Persia and Kuwait. Curzon, who as we have seen felt strongly that the whole Gulf and its coasts should be under British influence, argued the case with Lord Lansdowne, Foreign Secretary and himself a former Viceroy, and succeeded in getting public opinion behind him. In fact no definite action was taken by either side in the argument, as it went on for two years, for most of 1900 and 1901. As the South African war was coming to an end, the Curzon position strengthened, as the Government in London saw that they could more easily afford to face down the Russians. In January 1902 they privately warned the Persians that Britain would not agree to a Russian base on the Gulf, and in May 1903 Lansdowne announced in the House of Lords that the Government would regard the establishment of a naval base in the Gulf by any other power as a very grave menace to British interests.

This was naturally to the huge delight of Curzon. In January 1903 he had hosted the Coronation Durbar in Delhi, to which Sultan Faisal sent his son Taymūr to represent him. In Muscat, on the day of the Durbar, Faisal had a salute of 101 guns fired in honour of the King-Emperor. Later in the year Curzon undertook a kind of triumphal parade round the Gulf. He came first to Muscat, where he presented Sultan Faisal with the insignia of the Grand Cross of the Order of the Indian Empire, and assured him (as the British had assured his father, Sultan Turki, in the 1886 Declaration) that Britain would uphold his rule, by force if necessary. But he made clear his view of the nature of the relationship in his despatch home afterwards, describing Faisal's behaviour as that of a "loyal feudatory of the British Crown rather than that of an independent sovereign".[4] Curzon went on to hold a *durbar* for all the Trucial Shaikhs on board ship at Sharjah, near Dubai. Although there was a turbulent swell running, he delivered a speech to them in which he referred to the order brought to the region by the British, and insisted that the influence of the British Government must remain supreme.

Improvement in relations led by Percy Cox

At another level, the atmosphere had in fact been improving after the coaling station crisis of 1898-9. Major Percy Cox, who later achieved distinction as Resident in Bushire and subsequently in Mesopotamia and Persia, replaced Fagan as Political Agent in October 1899, and soon established a good personal relationship with Sultan Faisal. Sa'id bin Muhammad, who had been removed from office in Faisal's early period, was re-appointed as *wazir*, and the administration took on a more pro-British tone. It was to Cox that Faisal turned for support in the matter of the French flags, a matter in which the British were only too happy to oblige. Nevertheless, this was a handy signal of Faisal's wish to turn to the British for advice in foreign affairs. Another area where there was mutual interest in co-operation was over finance: during this period, Faisal was granted loans by the British as a way of bringing some stability to his Treasury.

The 1900s were a decade of calm both internally in Muscat and Oman and in the relationship with Britain. Cox's advice, as well as the loans

---

4 Landen: *Oman since 1856*, p 267, quoting Lorimer

from the British Indian Government, helped Sultan Faisal stay solvent. Other issues in the relationship were satisfactorily resolved – for example the French flags issue, when judgement was given at The Hague in 1905, and the gun-running problem, through the agreement signed in 1912. The administration was also improved by the energy of Sulaiman bin Suwailim, a former slave who replaced Sa'id bin Muhammad as *wazir* in 1902. Because of dissension among the leadership of the conservative Ibadis, Faisal was not troubled by disorder or rebellion among the tribes of the interior.

Rebellion by religious conservatives

But the calm was superficial. The loans had enabled Sultan Faisal to tide things over, but the substantive problems remained: income and expenditure did not match, and the Sultan in Muscat had still not succeeded in winning, or buying, the loyalty of the tribes and villages of the Omani interior. His exchequer had been earning substantial import duties (£14,500 in 1907) from the munitions trade, and it was in order to keep up this revenue that Faisal had fended off or ignored British requests to end the trade. In the interior, the conservative leadership made common cause – and one of the issues which united them was complaint to Faisal over his handling of the arms trade agreement. They saw his capitulation to British demands, both now on munitions and earlier on the slave trade, as representing a failure to protect the Muslim *umma* (community) against foreign Christian domination. Back in 1901, the conservative tribal leader of the al-Hirth, Shaikh 'Isa bin Ṣāliḥ had protested to Sultan Faisal about the freeing of escaped slaves by the British. In addition, on the arms commerce, they accused Faisal of acquiescing in a British scheme aimed at preventing them from acquiring weapons to which they had a right of access. Here they were half-right: but Faisal also had a personal interest, quite separate from that of the British, in restricting the supply of arms to tribesmen who might use them against him.

In early 1913 the opposition to Faisal gathered in the Ibadi heartlands of Nizwa, the Jebel Akhdar area, and the Sharqiyah. In the 19th century we saw a number of tribal movements, with more or less religious impetus, gathering in rebellion against the Sultan or Ruler of Muscat. What distinguished the movement on this occasion was the coalition of both Hinawi and Ghafiri tribes, and its combination with a strong religious agenda and leadership. In May 1913, Shaikh Himyar bin Nāsir al-Nabhāni, the most influential of the Ghafiri leaders, called an assembly at Tanuf, his home town, which decided to revive the Ibadi Imamate and elected Shaikh Sālim bin Rāshid al-Kharūsi as Imam – the first since the death of 'Azzan bin Qais in 1870. The assembly also declared that Faisal was deposed and 'dissociated from the affairs of Muslims (ie Ibadis)'.[5] Shaikh 'Isa bin Sālih al-Harthi, still the most influential Hinawi leader, whose father had led the attack on Muscat in 1895, did not take part in the election but rallied to the Imamate cause shortly afterwards. The revived Imamate was to last for over forty years and to be a central part of the political architecture of the country throughout that time.

At this point the British authorities considered that they needed to make their position clear, in accordance with Curzon's undertaking to Sultan Faisal ten years earlier. In May 1913 Major Knox, the Political Agent, wrote to the Imam and his leading supporters, now established in Nizwa, with a statement that the British Indian Government would not allow Muscat and Matrah to be captured. In July 1913 Faisal requested support from British troops and the following month the first detachment of British Indian soldiers arrived, first in Matrah and shortly afterwards at Bait al-Falaj, a fort inland from Matrah which was to be the base for British troops till 1921 and later became the headquarters of the Sultan's Army and the Ministry of Defence.

The Imam sent Knox a roundly defiant reply, warning the British not to interfere in the affairs of the Ibadis and not to commit aggression against them. The Imam's supporters took control of the Wadi Samail, on the direct route between Nizwa and Muscat. Knox, supported by Cox (now Sir Percy), the Political Resident, argued that the British forces should if necessary be deployed proactively into the interior to counter the threat to Muscat, but the Government of India stuck firmly to the traditional line that British force should be used only in direct defence of the Sultan's territories on the coast.

It was in fact the Royal Navy which was again first in action. The Imam and his allies, growing in confidence, sought to spread their

5 Declaration quoted by Landen: *Oman since 1856*, p 394

influence over coastal towns and tribes of the Batinah traditionally loyal to the Sultan. In the course of 1914 Faisal received direct help to counter this in the form of gunfire from ships attacking coastal positions, which helped to reduce Imamate influence in Barka and Qurayyat.

Succession of Sultan Taymūr bin Faisal

As the crisis was intensifying, in October 1913, Sultan Faisal died. He was succeeded by his eldest son, Taymur, then aged 27. His reign between 1913 and 1931 was the last in which the fortunes of Oman were played out with little direct foreign influence save from Britain, and before the prospect of oil became a significant factor. During this period Britain found herself reluctantly compelled to become even more deeply involved, both militarily and administratively. In the first part of Faisal's reign, up until 1920, his régime became a fixed if minor component of the security strategy of British India, and faced its most serious threat from its tribal opponents, surviving only thanks to direct British military intervention. In the second, from 1920 to 1931, British officials played an active and effective role in sustaining the government through a period of weak administration.

Several of Sultan Taymur's al-Busa'idi forebears had ascended a throne beset by political uncertainty and financial difficulty, but none previously had taken over in mid-rebellion. Both inclination and prudence gave him some sympathy with the conservative arguments of the Imam and his supporters. He explored the prospects for a political accommodation with them, but found the Imam in unyielding mood. He was also left in no doubt about his position of dependence on the British Indian Government, being obliged to sign a letter which stated '...it is not hidden from me that I shall continue in my rule by the continuance of their help and assistance...I have accepted all the obligations [to the British Indian Government] descending to me from my father ...I rely on the help of the Government .. and will be guided by its views in important matters.'[6]

Some months of stalemate followed but the Imamate leaders gained new confidence from the outbreak of World War One in September 1914. They were prompted by German propaganda from East Africa, and

---

6 Similar letter signed by Sultan Sa'id bin Taymur in 1932 set out in J Peterson ' Oman in the twentieth century' (1978) p224

religious resentment of the British declaration of war on the Ottoman Sultan, who was also regarded as the Caliph or ultimate authority for all Muslims. They concluded that the preoccupations of war would prevent a robust British response, and it was indeed the case that in the autumn of 1914 the Political Agent, now Major Benn, had to argue against withdrawal of the detachment at Bait al-Falaj. They also, wrongly, believed that morale among the Indian troops was poor.

In October 1914 the Imamate leadership took the decision to move from Samail ready for an attack on Muscat and Matrah. There is some evidence of divided counsels amongst the leadership of the Imamate, Shaikh 'Isa bin Salih consistently being more in favour of negotiation, using the British as intermediaries, than of direct military conflict with the Sultan. The assault was not in fact launched until 5 February 1915, by which time the British detachment had been reinforced and was deployed in an arc round Muscat and Matrah with the ends on the coast and the centre at Bait al-Falaj. The outcome was catastrophic for the Imam's forces. They believed they were fighting for a religious cause and had a strong advantage in numbers (3000 as against the 700 mainly British Indian troops fighting for Sultan Taymur). However they used the traditional approach of a massed frontal assault (at night) against the centre of the British line – its strongest point. As a result they were exposed to murderous fire and use of the bayonet from the well-armed, disciplined, and well-entrenched soldiers of the 102nd Prince Edward's Own Grenadiers. British casualties were 7 dead and 15 wounded (including one British officer). The estimated casualties on the Imamate side were 186 dead and 146 wounded. The survivors withdrew in confusion.

Sultan Taymur wanted to use his British troops in their pursuit. This was refused by the Viceroy, Lord Hardinge, who coincidentally visited Muscat a week later on his return voyage from visiting the much larger British Indian force by now deployed in Mesopotamia. Hardinge warned Taymur that in wartime circumstances Indian troops could not be kept in Muscat indefinitely, confirming at the same time that the Sultan could count on continuing assistance if necessary. He urged Taymur to seek a political solution. He offered the services of the Political Agent as a mediator between the two sides. In the event reaching a settlement took another five and a half years, for all of which the imperative of continuing support for a weak Sultan necessitated the ongoing presence of a British Indian battalion at Bait al-Falaj. The underlying problem – that the al-Busa'idi ruler had once more lost the support of the religious conservatives of the interior – remained unsolved. Militarily there was stalemate given British refusal to allow the use of their troops in an attacking role. Imamate suspicion not just of Taymur but of the Political Agent remained strong: after all it was British Indian troops who had just weeks before ensured their military defeat, so they might reasonably question the impartiality of a British mediator.

Nonetheless, after some written exchanges, talks took place in September 1915 led by Shaikh 'Isa bin Salih al-Harthi, for the Imamate, and Major Benn, the first of three Political Agents with whom he was to confer at Seeb[7] over the next five years before agreement was finally reached. No agreement was possible on this occasion. The positions of the two sides were far apart. Sultan Taymur sought recognition of his authority in the interior and the return of key forts in the Samail Gap. The Imam's negotiators predictably based much of their position on religious foundations. They complained that Taymur did not comply with correct Ibadi practice; and that the British allowed what should be forbidden, such as the import and sale of alcohol and tobacco, and prohibited what the Qur'an permitted, such as trading in slaves and munitions. Their more secular demands were that the British should remove their troops from Oman, and should desist from claiming command and control of the high seas. They blamed the British, and Taymur, for worsening economic conditions, caused by the fall in the value of the Maria Theresa dollar and the resulting inflation in the price of imported goods.

It was to be four years before further negotiations took place. Militarily the stalemate continued, though the Imam was able to extend his hold on key areas of the interior, notably Rustaq. Sultan Taymur made little headway till 1920 in eroding these gains with the limited non-British forces available to him. In the meantime the economic situation deteriorated sharply throughout Oman. The World War was sharply reducing trade in the Gulf. Trade was at half its pre-war level by 1918 and Taymur's Government, despite loans from the British Indian

---

7 The village about 40 km West of Muscat near which is Muscat's international airport.

Government in the form of advances on the Zanzibar subsidy, was seriously in debt, notably to the Indian merchant community in Muscat. The position in the interior was made worse still by the blockading of trade with Muscat, which brought about shortages of essential goods and further price rises. Both parts of the country were also badly hit by the global flu epidemic of 1919, in which about 20,000 Omanis died.

British intervention in the administration; and agreement at Seeb.

Before negotiations resumed with the Imamate a significant new element in the British relationship with Oman began to develop. It was one which was to last in different forms until 1970 and beyond. Though the Royal Navy had been called into action several times, and British Indian troops were deployed in Muscat in 1914, British advisers and officials had not to this point been seconded or contracted to work directly for the Sultan to reinforce his military or civil administrations, let alone make decisions in his name. The British relationship with the Sultan had been managed exclusively by the Political Agent, backed up from time to time by the Political Resident from Bushire. Sir Percy Cox was the first to propose in 1914 the secondment from India of a confidential adviser and a military officer as well as the creation of a military unit on western lines, but these ideas were put on hold for the duration of the war. By 1917 the situation was becoming pressing. Finance and administration were both in dire straits. Major Haworth, the Political Agent, concluded in May 1917 that Taymur's Government 'is so bad that to continue to support it in its existing condition is nothing short of immoral'. He put forward a plan for complete reform of the administration, his proposal including an additional loan to get rid of Taymur's debts to the Indian merchants, a force of 600-1000 men to enable the Sultan to take the military initiative in the interior, a programme of education, and the appointment of a British Adviser and a European superintendent of customs. With the war continuing these ideas were again shelved in India.

Once the war was over in November 1918 the British wish to end the Muscat commitment of British troops became more pressing. Renewed efforts to secure an agreement with the Imam were the key to this, but administrative reform and the creation of a proper military capability for the Sultan were also essential if stability was to be restored without the presence of British troops. By now it was clear that Taymur was in no position to insist on recognition by the Imamate of his authority in the area under their control. Correspondence between Haworth and Shaikh 'Isa initiated in March 1919, and discussion at a further meeting in Seeb in September that year, was based on recognition of the status quo between Imamate and Sultanate and the resumption of normal commerce between the interior and the coast. The only territorial issue was the restoration of key 'gardens' (date plantations) in the Samail area which the Imamate had seized from leading supporters of the Sultan. Shaikh 'Isa would probably have agreed to a deal including this but, after protracted discussion, the Imam vetoed a settlement on these lines in February 1920.

Shortly after the Seeb meeting Haworth was succeeded by Major Ronald Wingate, an Arabic-speaking Indian Civil Service officer. He regarded the situation as untenable, and considered that Britain could neither quit Muscat nor deal with anyone other than the Sultan, who would be driven into the sea in 24 hours without British backing. He arrived with a firm brief to reach a settlement between Sultan and Imam, and to bring about administrative reform. The British Indian Treasury agreed to a loan of 650,000 rupees, which was enough to settle Taymur's debts. In return Taymur was to accept the appointment of a British Adviser to implement administrative reform. Captain McCollum, formerly Political Agent in Kuwait, arrived in March 1920 and set briskly about reform of the customs and other key departments. Shortly thereafter Taymur departed for what turned out to be a protracted stay in India (see Chapter 12) and McCollum was effectively in charge of the Government in Muscat. Wingate was nervous that McCollum's role could be interpreted as a prelude to British occupation and urged McCollum to wear native dress, be tactful, and try to make his reforms popular.

In the spring and summer of 1920 events rapidly created the conditions in which Wingate could make a further determined effort to secure an agreement between Sultanate and Imamate. Economic pressure on the Imamate was stepped up when Taymur agreed to a proposal from Wingate to impose a penal tax of 25-50% (rather than the normal 5%) on dates and pomegranates exported from the Imamate through the Sultan's territories. Shaikh Himyar bin Nasir al-Nabhani, the leader of the Ghafiri tribes, died in March and was replaced by his teenage son, thus greatly strengthening the influence of Shaikh 'Isa. Imam Salim al-Kharusi was coming under increasing criticism from the tribes for the economic predicament of the interior, and was finding increasing difficulty in securing their support for further military operations. In July he was assassinated. This time it was Shaikh 'Isa who moved swiftly to ensure the election as Imam of Muhammad al-Khalili, a respected Ibadi jurist who was also his father-in-law. Wingate took immediate steps to position himself as an impartial figure rather than the spokesman of the Sultan, and McCollum, who was on leave, was told not to return so that it could appear that leadership on the Sultanate side was in Arab not British hands. At the same time Wingate made it clear to Shaikh 'Isa that negotiations leading to removal of the penal tax could open only after the disputed gardens had been returned.

Shaikh 'Isa secured the agreement of the new Imam to this. Wingate, escorted by 50 men of the 117th Mahrattas, and Shaikh 'Isa, accompanied by over twenty other Shaikhs, then met at Seeb between 23 and 25 September 1920. The agreement reached was signed by Shaihk 'Isa and other tribal leaders and subsequently ratified by both the Sultan and the Imam. The text is in the box below. Under it Sultan Taymur agreed to remove the penal taxes and lift the ban on trade between interior and coast, and not to interfere in the internal affairs of the interior. The Imam's régime agreed not to attack the coast, to remain in peace with the Sultan, to allow trade into the interior, not to protect fugitives from the Sultan's justice, and to hear claims against Omanis of the interior according to Shari'ah law.

The Seeb Treaty, of 25 September 1920

In the name of God, the Compassionate, the merciful.

This is the peace agreed upon between the Government of the Sultan, Taimur bin Feisal, and Sheikh Isa ibn Salih ibn Ali on behalf of the people of Oman whose names are signed hereto, through the mediation of Mr Wingate, I.C.S., political agent and consul for Great Britain in Muscat, who is empowered by his government in this respect and to be an intermediary between them. Of the conditions set forth below, four pertain to the Government of the Sultan and four pertain to the people of Oman.

Those pertaining to the people of Oman are:

1. Not more than 5 per cent shall be taken from anyone, no matter what his race, coming from Oman to Muscat or Muttra or Sur or the rest of the towns of the coast.
2. All the people of Oman shall enjoy security and freedom in all the towns of the coast.
3. All restrictions upon everyone entering and leaving Muscat and Muttrah and all the towns shall be removed.
4. The Government of the Sultan shall not grant asylum to any criminal fleeing from the justice of the people of Oman. It shall not interfere in their internal affairs.

The four conditions pertaining to the Government of the Sultan are:

1. All the tribes and sheikhs shall be at peace with the Sultan. They shall not attack the towns of the coast and shall not interfere in his Government.
2. All those going to Oman on lawful business and for commercial affairs shall be free. There shall be no restrictions on commerce, and they shall enjoy security.
3. They shall expel and grant no asylum to any wrongdoer or criminal fleeing to them.

The claims of merchants and others against the people of Oman shall be heard and decided on the basis of justice according to the law of Islam.

Written on 11 Muharram, corresponding to 25 September 1920

Whether this document should be called an Agreement or a Treaty has been much debated. It is an important distinction since treaties are signed normally only between independent sovereign states. The ambiguity was deliberate (Wingate himself describes it in his official report as a Peace). 'The Omanis may say', he observes, 'that they have complete independence, and the Sultan may say that they have only dominion home rule'.[8] What mattered was that it could not be interpreted as acknowledgement by the Sultan or by Britain of the Imamate as a separate state. In practice Muhammad al-Khalili (whose Imamate lasted

8 Wingate to Deputy Political Resident Bahrain 14 October 1920

180

till 1955) and his tribal supporters were content to allow successive Sultans to conduct on their behalf such external relations with the British and others as were necessary. The issue was to become significant only in the 1950s when Egyptian and Saudi supporters of the then Imamate were trying to represent the resumption of control over the interior by the Sultan as a breach of the sovereignty of the Imamate.

However described, the Seeb document turned out to be one of unusual permanence in Omani affairs. It secured internal peace for 35 years, effectively drawing a political map which throughout that period allowed Sultan Taymur (and his son Sa'id) undisturbed control over Muscat, Matrah, the Batinah, and the coast going further south and east, while the Imam and his supporters had similar freedoms in the interior. Tribes in other parts of what makes up modern Oman owed less clear-cut allegiance and support to either. Those who had wished over previous decades to challenge successive Sultans on the grounds that the Sultan's contacts with Britain were un-Islamic became less influential. The tribal leaders of the interior were content that the agreement protected their modest economic contacts with the outside world.

It is interesting that the text uses the term "Omanis" to refer to the people of the interior, and that their signatory and representative was not the Imam but Shaikh 'Isa. This choice would have reflected the differentiation between the religious authority, held by the Imam, and the leadership exercised by Shaikh 'Isa in non-religious affairs. It may also reflect an agreement between Wingate and Sultan Taymur that it would be unacceptable for the Imam to sign. It is also interesting that the text mentions the role of Wingate as a mediator.

The result of the Seeb document is that the heartlands of interior Oman remained completely cut off to travellers from the outside for over three more decades. In his memoirs, published only in 1959, Wingate records that he was invited to visit the Imamate before his final departure and was conscious how unique the opportunity was. Sadly he seems to have left no detailed record of it.

20. Lord Curzon,
Viceroy of India, 1899-1905

21. Sayyid Faisal bin Turki,
Sultan, 1888-1913

22. Indian Army reinforcements arriving in Muscat 1913

CHAPTER 12

Reluctant Ruler (1921-1931)

Thanks to the results of the negotiations at Seeb in September 1920, the decade that followed was much less troubled than those which had gone before. The Sultanate of the coast and the Imamate of the interior coexisted with minimal contact. Sultan Taymur was a most reluctant and largely absentee ruler and his long term aim was to be allowed to abdicate. The financial situation remained dire and the administration ineffective. The result was a decade in which Britain wanted to disengage but could not allow the country to relapse into instability.

* * * * * * *

Muscat and Oman as perceived by British policy makers
To policy makers in India at the start of the 1920s, Muscat and Oman seemed a backwater. Once peace was secured between Sultanate and Imamate, there was no residual threat to British Indian security from Oman, or indeed from all the lower Gulf. The immediate priority could thus be to terminate the military commitment in Muscat, and make the finances and security of the Sultanate work at minimal cost to the Government of India.

To policy makers in London, the Gulf area, including Muscat and Oman, was a peripheral part of a Middle East which was as a whole becoming much more prominent in British foreign policy. Broader forces which would in due course redefine the whole way Britain thought about

183

Oman were however beginning to come into focus. The challenges facing the Government of India itself were mainly internal and the process which would ultimately lead to the independence of India in 1947 was under way. India's external security was unchallenged at this time. In terms of imperial communications air routes to India from Cairo and Baghdad were replacing the security of shipping routes as an active concern. Even before World War One, Britain had been deeply involved in the affairs of Egypt and Persia (later Iran). The defeat and collapse of the Ottoman Empire led to the assumption of British responsibility for Mesopotamia (later Iraq), Transjordan and Palestine. The 1920s were the apogee of British involvement in the Middle East, and policies were increasingly driven by perceived British interests in those areas rather than by the security of India alone. The importance to the Royal Navy of secure oil supplies from the Gulf had become a major factor and support for the interests in the area of British oil companies also became a significant driver of policy in London.

Later in the 1920s policies potentially inimical to British interests pursued by Reza Shah in Persia and King Ibn Saud in the newly emerging Kingdom of Saudi Arabia led to renewed concerns about the area. One result was that by 1928 the Gulf had its own Sub-Committee of the Committee of Imperial Defence which concluded that 'the maintenance of British supremacy in the Persian Gulf is ever more essential to the security of India and Imperial interest at the present time than it was in the past' and 'it should be a cardinal feature of our policy to maintain our supremacy in the region.'[1] From 1925 Ibn Saud began to extend his influence over tribes in Buraimi and the Dakhiliyah – the part of the interior, west of Muscat, controlled directly by neither Sultan nor Imam. This was an echo of the pattern of much of the 19th century. Some like Sir Percy Cox, the former Resident in Bushire now retired, believed that Ibn Saud considered that he was entitled to reassert authority anywhere where his Wahhabi predecessors had exercised it in the past. This caused alarm to some in the Imamate, notably Shaikh 'Isa bin Salih, who led a force westwards out of his own tribal areas in 1925 in a demonstration against this new Wahhabi threat. It also troubled the British authorities with their direct responsibilities for the Trucial States of the lower Gulf,

---

1 Quoted in Owtram: *A modern history of Oman*, 2004, p57

though Sultan Taymur himself was unconcerned. Thereafter British attitudes to tribal developments in Oman were increasingly determined by how they might relate to this new perceived threat.

Another significant change which would come to have an effect on British activity in Oman was the decision, after the Cairo Conference called by Churchill as Colonial Secretary in 1920, to place responsibility for the defence of British interests in Iraq, and subsequently in Aden, in the hands of the RAF. This was considered to be significantly cheaper, and also reflected the fact that small-scale military interventions to support British policy came not just to involve coastal areas, as had generally been the case hitherto, but also to involve political and tribal developments in the interior of countries like Iraq and Aden (and subsequently, as we shall see, Oman). The fact that the interests of oil companies were generally in the interior of the countries concerned also contributed to the final end of the principle, which we have seen applied several times in Oman, that any military involvement should be confined to coastal areas, and normally left in the hands of the Royal Navy. Thus the small Persian Gulf Squadron of the Royal Navy remained an asset which could be deployed to support the Sultanate, but by the end of the 1920s the RAF could also be drawn on.

Parts of modern Oman began to feature more prominently in the thinking of the Air Ministry towards the end of the decade. Earlier attention focussed on the choice between alternative routes on the Persian and Arab sides of the Gulf to support passenger and mail services to India. These touched Omani territory only in Gwadar, the Omani enclave on the coast of what is now Pakistan. By the end of the decade however the RAF was recognising a need, for its own purposes, for a route which would link its commands in Basra and Aden following the coastline of the Arabian peninsula and thus the whole coast of Oman.

The paradox of ever-increasing British involvement
This was the context in which successive Political Agents in Muscat and Political Residents in Bushire operated in the 1920s. Only in his early 30s at the time he was appointed in 1918, Ronald Wingate was one of the two key British figures in Oman in the 1920s. The strategy which seized swiftly on the changing balance of forces within the Imamate to redefine the relationship between it and the Sultanate at Seeb in

September 1920 was his. Similarly, although key elements of the plans for reform – the Indian loan, the creation of the Muscat Levies, and the introduction of British (and other) advisers, had been put forward by his predecessor, it was Wingate who oversaw their implementation following agreement by the Indian authorities. The long-cherished objective of ending the deployment of a British Indian battalion was achieved. He also set out to establish a decision-making structure which would permit a minimal level of governance to continue in the Sultan's increasingly lengthy absences. This took the form of persuading Taymur to appoint a four-man Council of Ministers, chaired by one of his uncles, which would work closely with the Political Agent and British Advisers.

This was arduous work in very difficult circumstances. The Political Agent was the only civilian British official in the Sultanate. Wingate summarised the situation on his arrival trenchantly in his memoir *Not in the Limelight*.... 'A bankrupt Sultanate, an indifferent Sultan, a beleaguered capital, no Europeans except the officers of the distant battalion (the Bombay Grenadiers then the Mahratta Light Infantry) whom one could visit about once a fortnight, the worst climate in the world, and contact with civilisation consisting of, with luck, one ship a week.' Travel was by four-oared whaler, the only conveyance provided for him, or by camel. He describes sleeping in the 'gharbi' (westerly) winds of summer. 'I used to sleep on a canvas camp bed on the roof. I lay on a Japanese grass mat with a wooden block as a pillow and, of course, without a stitch of clothing, as one could not bear the touch of cotton or linen. The bed was on a foot of sand, which was continuously soaked with water. And in between me and the wind was stretched a cotton sheet which was taken down every half hour and dipped into a bath of water and put up again'.[2]

There is a paradox in the British position faced by Wingate and his successors in Muscat in the 1920s. The efforts of the period between 1917 and 1921 to reduce British Indian commitments, when coupled with Taymur's determination to take no active part in the rule of his Sultanate, in fact led inexorably to greater direct control by British officials than at any time before or since. Formally Muscat was an independent state in treaty relationship with Britain, which by request conducted the Sultan's foreign relations save those with France and the United States. As we

---

2 These two quotations from Wingate are from his *Not in the Limelight*, xx, 1959, pp 79-82

saw, a formal protectorate was excluded well before World War One, and the Union Jack never flew over Oman (save over the Political Agency). Visiting Royal Navy ships exchanged the salutes due to a sovereign Head of State. The British position had evolved to protect commercial interests and to make Muscat part of a *cordon sanitaire* to protect those interests but outside the periphery of the British Empire itself. Over the years this could be achieved only by supporting a series of politically and financially weak Sultans against increasing disillusion among the tribes, who felt that their interests were being surrendered in favour of British ones, and undesirable and un-islamic practices permitted.

A number of terms have been used to describe this situation, for example informal empire, client state, or veiled protectorate (a term used by senior officials in India in the 1920s). Wingate was blunt about the position. 'Our influence' he wrote in his report on Seeb 'has been entirely self-interested, has had no regard to the peculiar political and social conditions of the country and its rulers, and by bribery of the Sultans to enforce unpalatable measures, which benefitted no-one but ourselves, and permitting them to misrule without protest, has done more to alienate the interior and to prevent the Sultans from establishing their authority there, than all the rest put together... The result is that we have been reduced to supporting by armed force under our treaty obligations a ruler against whom most of his subjects were in open revolt, who was theoretically independent and yet who would be driven into the sea in 24 hours if it were not for us'.[3]

The agreement at Seeb would, he believed, change this. But it was equally imperative to find a way of circumventing Taymur's unwillingness to rule and to reform the administration of Muscat. Between 1915 and 1918, Wingate believed, 'the Sultan's government sank from bad to worse, became involved in hopeless debt, and reached an unparalleled degree of ineptitude'. The reforms he implemented in 1920-21 were designed to tackle this, but had only limited success. By 1924 weak rule and maladministration, by Taymur and his Council of Ministers alike, caused Wingate's successors to conclude that there was little alternative but to allow themselves to be dragged into a more direct role, not least to assure the repayment of the 1920 loan.

3 Wingate to Deputy Political Resident Bahrain 14 October 1920

Taymur's personality and his reluctance to rule were an important factor in this unsatisfactory situation. Wingate's judgements of Taymur were harsh. He singled out his vanity and his idleness. He described Taymur as 'not unintelligent, particularly vicious or absurdly extravagant but a fool in many matters... determined to be as idle as possible.' He also concluded that Taymur disliked both his position and his country (Muscat) and hankered after civilisation.[4]

Bertram Thomas, who played a prominent part in the affairs of the second half of the 1920s, had a softer view. 'Sultan Taymur', he wrote looking back in the 1930s, 'was a man of much natural ability and enlightenment, was moreover of pleasing personality, but was the victim of his times'.[5] The experience of the early years of his reign left their mark. He was only too well aware from his accession – not least from the conditions imposed on him by the British Indian Government – that he was in real control neither militarily nor financially. That dependence was graphically underlined by the events of 1915. He is said to have suffered ill health and depression during World War One, when he was also unable to travel away from Muscat. When he did try to take the initiative during that period the British refused to support him. By the end of the war he was broke, and apathetic about the responsibilities of government. His disinclination for rule, and his lack of resources, disposed him to neglect the essential but time-consuming business of maintaining relationships with tribal leaders.

By the time the British Indian Government invited him to pay an official visit to the Viceroy in 1920 his mind was set on being allowed to abdicate and live in India. The fact that he had recently married an attractive Circassian Princess who would have been totally out of place in Muscat can only have reinforced this determination. On Wingate's advice, the Viceroy, Lord Chelmsford, firmly rejected the idea – as well as the proposal that Taymur should live in India with a Regent ruling in his place on behalf of his young son Sa'id. Taymur, who had by this time bought a house in India, remained obstinate and did not return to Muscat for eighteen months. Negotiations dragged on as to how many months a year he would agree to spend there. (He finally agreed to four whereas

4 Wingate to Deputy Political Resident Bahrain 14 October 1920
5 Bertram Thomas: *Arab Rule under the Al Bu Said Dynasty'*, 1938

the British wanted six, but failed to keep even this commitment.) In the meantime he endorsed Wingate's plan for a Council to govern in his absence. When he did return in 1921 he accompanied Wingate on a Royal Navy ship for the first time to Salalah which, like his son, he came to prefer greatly to Muscat even when he was in the country. Moreover, as we shall see, he had not given up on the idea of abdication.

After McCollum's swift departure in 1920 (see chapter 11), no new British Financial Adviser was appointed, though experts of other nationalities were installed to try to increase revenues. Slightly oddly, after the formation of the Muscat Levies in 1921, its British Commander was pressed into service to support the efforts of the Political Agent to get some order into financial affairs. Little headway had been made by 1923, in a time of continuing economic depression, and 'imminent bankruptcy' (and with it default on loan payments to India) was forecast. This led to the appointment of the other key British figure in Muscat in the 1920s, Bertram Thomas. At Taymur's request a decision was made in 1924 to appoint a new full time Financial Adviser. Thomas, who was serving as a revenue officer in Transjordan, jumped at the otherwise unattractive post because of the prospects it offered to fulfil his passion for exploration (see box on page 192), for which he became much better known.

At the outset Thomas was not a member of the Council of Ministers, though Taymur envisaged from the start that he would act as his *wazir* (Minister) in his own absence. The British agreed in 1926 that he should become a member of the Council and Thomas began to exercise a role over an ever widening range of non-financial issues. Towards the end of his five years in Muscat he described himself as 'virtually regent'. He was closely involved in the first tentative steps to look for oil in Oman, under an agreement signed with the D'Arcy Company in 1925 (see chapter 18).

His relations with successive Political Agents became notably tense both on policy issues and because the Political Agents believed, probably correctly, that Thomas was using situations of unrest to promote his plans for travel and exploration. In 1927 the Political Agent described him as 'impatient of control, with little inclination for humdrum routine and the detail of administration'. They also believed that he was usurping the functions of the Council and rubbing in the fact that it was British officials who were making key decisions. They felt that he had no idea of keeping slightly in the background and allowing Omanis to appear to run the state. The 'Men on the Spot', as one author describes them, could see that they were on a hiding to nothing. They could not control Thomas, but well knew that, in local eyes, he was assumed to have their sanction in whatever he did.

There were several episodes in the 1920s where Shaikhs owing allegiance to Taymur stepped out of line, usually over the payment of taxes, leading to the deployment of ships of the Royal Navy's Persian Gulf Squadron to help to reassert the Sultan's authority. Events in Sur were more complex. Sur had been, with Muscat, the major port for trade between Oman and East Africa. Some of the Shaikhs there consistently accepted the Sultan's authority. Others, notably the senior Shaikh of the Bani Bu Ali tribe, Shaikh 'Ali bin Abdullah al-Hammouda, whose territory stretched well inland into the Sharqiyah and the borders of the Imamate, were more ambivalent. They were also resistant to the authority of the Imam because they were not Ibadis but Wahhabis. As such their actions had broader implications in the light of Ibn Saud's renewed interest in Oman. In the absence of any steps by Taymur to exercise influence over the 'independent' tribes, Shaikh 'Ali saw an opportunity to flex his muscles and demonstrate his independence. He refused to collect customs dues for the Sultan and provocatively flew the Saudi flag over one of his forts. Dealing with his aspirations took some five years spanning the end of Taymur's reign and the beginning of that of his son. It saw British forces deployed twice, the Royal Navy in 1927 (though the authorities in India rejected advice from the Political Agent to accompany this with the deployment of an Indian infantry battalion) and both the Royal Navy and, for the first time the RAF, in 1932. Sur was a significant bone of contention between Thomas and the Political Agents, with the latter far more inclined to treat the Bani Bu Ali activity as a proxy threat from Saudi Arabia.

Events in Sur and Musandam underlined the degree to which Taymur and his family had distanced themselves from the on-going necessity to maintain relationships with (and offer financial support to) key tribes outside the Imamate heartland. This element in Taymur's neglect of the responsibilities of rule in a tribal state had already been identified by Wingate who commented that 'his vanity, in an Arab state where geniality and good manners towards high and low alike are mandatory, has alienated many of those who by conviction are his supporters'.[6]

In 1930 Thomas extended a period of leave without permission (though he claimed that Sayyid Sa'id bin Taymur, the Sultan's son, who was now effective Regent, knew of his plans) to make his pioneering crossing of the Empty Quarter. It had already been agreed that his contract would not be renewed. His successor, Captain Hedgcock, arrived as a new broom, accusing Thomas of providing misleading figures and arguing that bankruptcy was again imminent. He succeeded in crossing almost everyone in Muscat during his six months in the post, including the Political Agent, who felt that Hedgcock was exaggerating the situation, and, most significantly Sayyid Sa'id, who from this moment seems to have decided to dispense with British Financial Advisers whenever he had the opportunity to do so.

Another development of the 1920s which was to be increasingly significant in the future was the first step in the development of proper armed forces in Oman, which saw British officers in command of Omani and other soldiers in the service of successive Sultans continuously until the late 1980s. The object, as the British Indian battalion left, was to replace ineffectual groups of personal retainers supported by tribal levies with a more effective force. Proposals had been made during World War One to replace the Indian battalion with a British-officered force. At the time this was seen in India as itself prolonging an unwanted commitment and turned down. By 1921 however the desire to find a basis on which the Indian battalion could be withdrawn without leaving the Sultan defenceless had increased. Captain E R McCarthy, formerly of the now disbanded South Persia Rifles, was recruited to command the Muscat Levy Corps of 300-500 Baluchis soldiers, initially from Seistan (in Iran) but latterly from Omani-controlled Gwadar or from within Oman. This remained Oman's only regular military force until the 1960s.

By the end of the decade Taymur's reign was moving towards its end. In 1928, accompanied by Thomas, he paid the first ever official visit by a Sultan of Muscat to Britain. In the course of a three week tour he travelled throughout Great Britain and Southern Ireland (and went to the theatre seven times!). In 1928 his eldest son Sayyid Sa'id, now aged 18

6 Wingate to Deputy Political Resident 14 October 1920

and with his education in India and Iraq complete, returned to Muscat and took over the Chairmanship of the Council of Ministers from Taymur's uncle, who had recently died. Taymur may well have been consciously biding his time until his son came of age to raise the issue of abdication again. He did so in 1930. This time the proposal was not rejected, and in November 1931 he told the Political Resident that he would abdicate the next day and transfer his powers to Sa'id.

British travellers in the Empty Quarter

The Rub' al-Khālī, the Empty Quarter, is a huge expanse of sand desert and high dunes in the southern half of the Arabian peninsula, straddling the borders of modern Oman and Saudi Arabia but mostly in the latter. For many centuries it has been crossed by, and offered a sparse living to, bedu tribes whose lives revolve around their camels. Until 1930 it had however remained closed land to Europeans.

The three pioneer travellers who crossed it between 1930 and 1950 were all English: Bertram Thomas, St John Philby, and Wilfred Thesiger. Thomas and Thesiger entered the dunes from the south – Oman, and Phiby from the north – Saudi Arabia. All three wrote extensively about their travels. These writings are important sources on the mindsets and way of life of the bedu of Oman and Saudi Aabia before they were touched, and later transformed, by modernity.

Chronologically Thomas was the first to make the crossing. His role as Financial Adviser to Sultan Taymur in Muscat is described in chapter 12. It was the prospect of travel and exploration which had drawn him to accept the post. From the start he sought opportunities to travel outside the areas fully controlled by the Sultan. In 1927 he accompanied an RAF team from Abu Dhabi to Buraimi and Sohar looking for prospective landing grounds. Amazingly this was a journey only twice made by Europeans before. In 1928 he made an overland journey from Ras al-Hadd to Dhofar. At the beginning of 1930 he journeyed 200 miles north-east from Salalah to the edge of the Empty Quarter. In October that year he slipped away from his duties in Muscat, his plans apparently known to nobody but Sayyid Sa'id, at that time acting as Regent for his father.

He returned to Salalah to await guides from the Rashid tribe whom he had met at the beginning of the year. He set out on 30 December and took 58 days to travel across the Empty Quarter from Salalah to Doha (in modern Qatar), photographing and collecting specimens assiduously as he went.

Philby was a former Indian Civil Servant who had spent much of his career in the Middle East and had started to explore the Arabian peninsula in 1917. Aged 45 in 1930, he had settled in Riyadh and become a Muslim. King Ibn Saud would not permit him to enter the Empty Quarter in 1930 and he was bitterly disappointed that this allowed Thomas to get a year's start on him. In 1931 he started from close to where Thomas had completed his crossing but kept generally further west. At Naifa conditions and disaffection among his guides forced him to turn directly to the west and leave the Empty Quarter not south into Oman but west towards Sulayil and ultimately Mecca.

Thesiger's roots were in Africa and it was a role researching locust swarms in the Arabian Peninsula which first took him to Oman in 1946. The lure of continuing the exploration of the Empty Quarter was in his mind from the start. He crossed the Empty Quarter twice. In 1946 he journeyed from south to north on a route to the east of Thomas's, before swinging back through Oman to Salalah. His 1948 crossing started much further west in modern Yemen. He crossed to Sulayil, which had been where Philby left the sands, and where Philby, still living in Riyadh, had to use his influence with Ibn Saud for him to be allowed to continue. He then made the longest crossing from west to east ending in Abu Dahbi. Later that year and in 1949 and 1950 he also continued to travel extensively in interior Oman but was thwarted by Imam and Sultan alike in his desire to cap these travels by climbing the Jebel Akhdar.

23. Sultan Saʿid bin Taymur with British officers

24. Council of State, 1920s

25. Bertram Thomas   *26. Sultan Taymur bin Faisal*

27. Wilfred Thesiger

CHAPTER 13

New Broom and the impact of War (1931-1945)

During the first part of the reign of Sultan Sa'id bin Taymur, the British maintained a close relationship with Oman, an alliance of strategic value to Britain in facilitating air communications during World War Two, in which Oman was otherwise little involved. Sa'id knew he needed the continuing relationship, but looked for ways of asserting his freedom of action.

* * * * * * *

Sultan Taymur finally notified the British authorities in November 1931 that he was abdicating and handing over his responsibilities to his son Sa'id. Taymur was only 45, and he lived till 1965, mainly in India, but he also travelled extensively, including to Britain and to Japan. He revisited Oman once, for three months in 1945-6, but relations with Sa'id were poor and he did not go back again.

At his accession, Sa'id was already the effective Ruler in Muscat. Captain Alban, the Political Agent noted just before Taymur's abdication that Sa'id had 'acquired an ascendancy not approached for a hundred years. He has taken on the full control of the administration, including the duties formerly carried out by the Adviser [Thomas].' Though Sa'id was only twenty-one the Indian authorities decided that the moment had come to allow Taymur to have his way. Formal British recognition to Sa'id's accession was given in January 1932 and the transition was announced in Muscat in February 1932 at the end of Ramadan.

Sultan Sa'id's thirty-eight year reign until his deposition in 1970 was a story of two halves. The first twenty years, until 1952, saw few events which stand out in the historical record, whereas the last eighteen were to be tumultuous and full of drama. In the first two decades the country remained divided between Imamate and Sultanate, impoverished, and virtually unknown to the outside world. Apparent change was minimal between 1920 and 1950. The ways of traditional Arabia prevailed, even in Muscat. Sa'id was nonetheless working throughout this period cannily and systematically to reduce wherever possible his dependence, especially financial dependence, on Britain and India. The peaceful co-existence created at Seeb between, on the one hand Muscat and Dhofar under his control, and on the other Interior Oman under the Imam and the major tribal leaders, continued. At the same time Sa'id used his growing freedom of manoeuvre to build relationships which he could in due course build on to reassert a role in Interior Oman when the Imam died.

In 1931 the Political Resident in Bushire summarised British policy in the Gulf, including Oman, as being to maintain the Rulers of the region so long as they were acceptable to their subjects, to avoid being drawn into internal affairs wherever possible, but to prevent any other foreign power gaining influence or privilege. Gulf policy was increasingly being driven by issues of concern to London – aviation, oil, and the activities of Ibn Saud – rather than to India. When World War Two broke out, Oman was disconnected from active theatres of operations – Egypt, Iraq, Iran and East Africa – but her position on lines of sea and air communication with the Gulf, India and beyond increased her strategic importance to Britain and the United States as the war unfolded.

The strategic context which governed Britain's relationships with Sultan Sa'id was thus gradually changing over these years. Oil was becoming an increasingly significant factor. The search for oil in Arabia, and the complex relationships between the British (and other European) and American companies involved became active issues following the discovery of oil in Bahrain in 1932. Sa'id signed his first concession agreements with British oil companies in June 1937, having first dallied with an American option. One covered Dhofar and the other, after some deliberation on the British side, the rest of Oman, Sultanate and Imamate territory alike. The reality was that virtually all the promising areas for oil exploration lay in areas of Interior Oman outside Sa'id's control. He nonetheless obtained significant and immediate financial advantage just from signing the concessionary agreement. It was to be nearly twenty years before significant exploration could begin, and before then issues stemming from the competition for oil had become central to the future of Oman, and to Britain's relations with her. (For the story of oil exploration in Oman see chapter 17).

Sultan Sa'id was educated in the 1920s at Mayo College, a school in Ajmer principally created for the education of Indian princes, which his father had also attended. He subsequently studied for a year in British-dominated Iraq in order to bring a stronger Arabic element to his studies. One result was that he thought instinctively of himself as much more akin to Rulers of Indian princely states than to the Rulers of the neighbouring Gulf states under British protection. British officials and visitors commented favourably on his sophisticated command of English, something no other Arab Ruler of the day could demonstrate. By instinct and by choice he was a quiet man satisfied with a modest and private lifestyle, and he lived a frugal life governed by affordability. Whereas Sultan Taymur had a number of wives (both before and after his abdication), Sultan Sa'id had two, both the daughters of middle ranking tribal Shaikhs in Dhofar, where by preference he spent as much of his time as his father had in India.

Before he left for a world tour in 1937 he had been in Salalah for 15 months. In his early years he was not above using as a negotiating card with British officials the threat to leave Muscat for good and let them sort out affairs there. For the last twelve years of his life he did not visit Muscat at all and left central government affairs in the hands of a small group of trusted advisers. He cut himself off from his people, even most of his own family, and both dealt and socialised with a very limited circle, a large proportion of them not Omanis. He discouraged aspiration for change save where it was prudent, politic, and affordable. Nonetheless, wherever he was, from the first he kept detailed personal control of the minimal structures of finance and administration. Even in the 1930s the Political Agent had to make a special journey by sea from Muscat to Salalah to secure Sa'id's approval to the appointment of a new Commanding Officer for the Muscat Levies.

Sultan Sa'id bridled at the conditions he had to accept from the British Government on his accession. He was both resentful and sceptical of the work of the British Advisers imposed on his father, notably Bertram Thomas, though the two men seem to have enjoyed a good personal relationship when Sa'id first returned to Muscat. His Letter of Accession – drafted by the British Political Agent – was couched in similar terms to those his father had had to accept in 1913 (see page 174). He set out from the start to assert his independence of British advice whenever he could. He swiftly moved to scrap the Council of Ministers, which had been set up to fill the governance vacuum during his father's prolonged absences, and which he had himself chaired since he returned to Muscat in 1928. Whilst he could not instantly do without a Financial Adviser and accepted two more short-term British appointments to this role (one of them a former Political Agent), he dispensed with their services as soon as he could and increasingly took control of all financial matters himself. In this he was supported by Asian and Arab officials whose roles, whatever their titles, were essentially clerical.

By 1940 he had achieved a position where he was no longer in thrall to Britain on financial matters, despite the termination in the mid-1930s of the subsidy paid to his father and grandfather to compensate them for loss of revenue from the arms trade through Muscat, which they had agreed at British insistence to end. By the end of World War Two his Government had significant assets invested overseas. This was partly achieved by his close and conservative personal control of spending, including cuts in the stipends paid to members of his family, who not infrequently took their grievances to the Political Agent, as well as his refusal to spend more than an absolute minimum on infrastructure or modernisation. He also showed himself adept at exploiting new situations to obtain additional sources of revenue from Britain, for example in the context of the first oil concessions signed in 1937, and of British requirements for facilities at Masirah and elsewhere, notably at the beginning of World War Two.

The greater freedom of manoeuvre which he enjoyed as a consequence was applied first and foremost to the development of what has been called his 'policy of peaceful penetration', that is positioning himself to be able to move when the right moment came to reassert his authority over the tribes, and therefore territories, of the interior. How this eventually played out in the 1950s will be seen in the next chapter, but the foundations were being laid before 1945. Sultan Sa'id's wish to reduce his dependence on Britain did not extend to internal security. He was well aware that his ability to turn to Britain for help was his strongest card. He had no hesitation in doing so when challenged by tribal leaders in territories he considered his, and he considered it as no more than keeping their side of the bargain that the British should respond. The major example came at the very beginning of his reign with the need to bring to a definitive end the on-going attempt by Shaikh 'Ali bin 'Abdullah al-Hammouda of the Bani Bu 'Ali to establish his own customs post at Sur. Sa'id was in active discussion with the Political Agent on ways to bring this about before his accession was announced. Both a Royal Navy ship of the Persian Gulf Squadron and, for the first time, Singapore flying boats of the RAF were on hand to give decisive backing to his demands. The Senior Naval Officer Persian Gulf and the Commanding Officer of 203 Squadron RAF were in Muscat in connection with this operation when the Political Resident formally acknowledged Sa'id's accession in March 1932, and took part in the ceremony.

This ability to turn to Britain for support was a key element in Sa'id's policy of setting himself up as the most powerful figure in the whole of Oman, and thus in a position to determine where oil companies could explore. As and when he could, notably as a result of the arrangements he made with Britain at the beginning of World War Two, he also strengthened the Muscat Levies both in numbers and equipment as a force which tribal leaders would be unable to match. At the same time Sa'id took care not to move prematurely; and the period up to 1945 was devoted to a more subtle policy of building up his political standing with key tribes, bypassing the Imam. Particularly important was his developing relationship with Shaikh 'Isa bin Sālih al-Harthi, who had long seen a negotiated relationship with the Sultan as an element in securing his own position and that of his tribe. In these talks he adroitly represented the proposed improvement of relations as being in the interests of both sides by reducing their dependence on Britain.

Sa'id understood the importance for the success of this policy of following tribal custom by backing his conversations up with gifts in cash and kind, something his financial progress now allowed him to do. He acknowledged the cultural conservatism of the Ibadi tribes of the Imamate by emphasising his respect for Shari'ah law and appointing respected figures from the Imamate as *wālīs* (local governors) and *qāḍīs* (judges) in the Sultanate. Gradually he built up a position where he could be seen to mediate and resolve major inter-tribal disputes, a major attribute of leadership and authority in the tribal system. He was careful not to challenge the Imam directly or personally, but was more than ready to capitalise on tribal disillusionment with him. A key element in his discussions as early as the mid-1930s was what would happen when the Imam died. At one stage Sultan Saʿid appeared to be considering putting himself forward for election as Imam, but by 1945 the focus of the discussion was on an approach whereby the major tribal leaders would agree in advance not to move to elect a new Imam when the moment came.

There were other issues where British officials became acutely aware that they were now dealing with a Ruler who firmly regarded himself as Head of an independent state. In 1937-38 Sultan Saʿid made a world tour, which took him to India, where he was received by the Viceroy, Lord Linlithgow; Japan, to see his father; Washington, where he was received by President Roosevelt; and France, as well as London. He started to make his plans for the tour without consulting British officials first, and reacted robustly to their expressions of pained surprise, pointing out that Oman enjoyed Treaty relations with the United States and France and that he was fully entitled to deal directly with them.

In addition to the 1937 oil concession agreements themselves, which Sultan Saʿid personally negotiated, he intervened forcefully on issues relating to the parallel political agreement between the Iraq Petroleum Company (IPC) and the British Government, following the signature of the concessions. He also immersed himself in the details of the talks leading up to the signature of a revised Anglo-Omani Commercial Treaty in 1939. The Commercial Treaties with Britain went back exactly 100 years to 1839 and regulated Britain's privileged trading position in Muscat and, importantly, the extra-territorial rights of British subjects in the Sultanate, most of whom were Indian merchants. Saʿid conducted the review of these arrangements personally, having no ministers to whom to delegate them even if he had wished to do so, and his London visit included no less than five negotiating sessions on the revised Treaty.

We saw in the previous chapter that aviation matters in the Gulf first came to prominence in the 1920s in the context of the search for routes

201

for civil flights from Egypt via Iraq to India. This impinged on Oman only in relation to landing facilities in the north of the country, and a staging post in Gwadar. A formal Civil Aviation Agreement regulating these was signed in 1934. We also saw the increased prominence of the RAF in the defence of British interests in both Iraq and Aden. This had led to the establishment of two RAF Commands in Basra and Aden. Thinking about a route between them began as early as 1926. By 1930 a safe route between them became a firm objective. Flying directly across the Arabian Peninsula was ruled out both politically and because of the limited range of the aircraft of the time, so a route around the coast of the peninsula, much of it Omani controlled, would have to be followed. Before his abdication Sultan Taymur had been keen on the idea of a route which would link Muscat with his preferred home in Salalah. Sa'id was also ready to consider RAF use of a string of landing grounds. Two of these, on Masirah Island, and at Salalah, were to remain in RAF use at various levels of intensity for forty years from their establishment in the 1930s until 1977.

Two routes were in fact developed in the course of the 1930s, one for flying boats and one for fixed wing aircraft. Having tracked down the Gulf from Basra, both routes crossed into Oman from Ras al-Khaimah and Sharjah. They then followed the coastline to Muscat, where the Royal Engineers first cleared a landing strip at Bait al-Falaj in 1930, Ras al-Hadd and Masirah, thence down the coastline to Dhofar and into Aden. Reconnaissance of possible sites began by sea from Aden in 1930. Initial operations involved flying boats, Singapores and then Rangoons of 203 Squadron based in Basra. Their first flight to Masirah in March 1931 was accompanied by HMS *Penzance*, a sloop of the Royal Navy's Persian Gulf Squadron. This was the islanders' first encounter with the modern world. Facilities were set up for petrol supplies (in four-gallon drums which had to be manhandled to the aircraft and the fuel individually poured through muslin filters) to be transferred by sea from Muscat, Khor Jarama (a lagoon near Ras al-Hadd), and Masirah from the north and into Dhofar from Aden. In November 1933 two Rangoons made the first continuous flights from Basra to Aden, on to East Africa, and back.

Both Sultan Sa'id and successive Political Agents were directly involved in setting up these arrangements. In some of the areas involved there was no administrative structure with whom the Political Agent or the RAF could deal. Muscat and Dhofar were firmly under the Sultan's control; but Ras al-Hadd and Khor Jarama were close to Sur, where the Bani Bu 'Ali challenge to the Sultan's authority had only just been brought to an end. Indeed the security of the landing sites was a factor in ensuring the deployment of British forces in 1932. The Janaba tribe which directly controlled the Ras al-Hadd area as well as Masirah and much of the coast southwards towards Dhofar owed direct allegiance neither to the Sultan nor the Imam. They were nonetheless accommodating towards approaches from the Sultan and from British officials. Major (later Sir) Trenchard Fowle was Political Agent at Sa'id's accession and made the initial journey to Masirah in 1931. He later moved to become Political Resident in Bushire. Captain Alban, who had briefly been the Sultan's Financial Adviser, negotiated the arrangements for the first fuel depot with the Masirah islanders the following year. Fowle's successor Captain Bremner was personally involved in 1935 in resolving labour and other issues with the islanders. All three enjoyed Sa'id's support in these efforts, and the resources of the Royal Navy and the RAF to move around. They had however to have the personality and skills to negotiate in colloquial Arabic with local Shaikhs to secure what was needed.

Bremner was also involved over several years in discussions with Sultan Sa'id about filling in the gap between Ras al-Hadd/Masirah and Dhofar with landing grounds which would permit a fixed wing route to be opened. In 1934 he surveyed the coast with Sultan Said's permission on HMS *Bideford*, accompanied by Sayyid Shihab, one of the Sultan's two trusted Omani advisers. In 1935 the RAF made the switch in emphasis from flying boats to fixed wing aircraft. Responsibility for the route was taken over by 84 Squadron based at Shaiba near Basra, using Vincent aircraft. This was a single engine biplane with a crew of three in open cockpits with a range of up to 1250 miles at a speed of 120 mph.

By the end of the year a new landing ground and fuel store had been established at Masirah, on the site which was to be used by the RAF till 1977 and by the Royal Air Force of Oman to this day. A landing ground with fuel supplies was also created at Khor Garim on the mainland coast between Masirah and Mirbat in Dhofar. This was later shifted to Shuwaimiyah further along the coast. A detachment of Wapiti fighters flew this route to join up with a similar detachment from Aden in 1936, a year which also saw the first deployment of fixed wing aircraft all the way from Iraq to Aden and beyond. In October 1937 a Vincent crashed at Khor Garim, killing its three crew. This was the only reported fatal accident along this route before the Second World War. One of the casualties was a Wing Commander known to Sultan Sa'id, who sent a personal note of condolence to the Political Agent. They were buried on the spot and the location of their graves was unknown until they were rediscovered in 2006 and the Royal Air Force of Oman made arrangements for them to be disinterred and moved to Muscat for burial in the Christian cemetery there. At the end of 1938 the most spectacular journey using the route was made by a full squadron of twelve Vincents as part of a 'grand tour' from Iraq to Aden, East Africa, Egypt and back to Iraq. They arrived in Masirah in thick mist and were fortunate to be able to locate the landing ground and get down safely.

World War Two swirled around Oman, in the Indian Ocean, Iraq and Iran but touched it directly very little. Only one direct attack was made on Omani territory, by a Japanese miniature submarine which destroyed a Norwegian merchant ship in Muscat harbour in 1943 (see box on page 207). Most Omanis of the coast and interior alike were cut off from the dramatic events of the war and for the most part totally unaware of what was happening.

Sultan Sa'id was quick to establish that, while cooperative, he was not to be taken for granted. Negotiations in the autumn of 1939 led to an exchange of letters in which he offered to consider British requests for additional facilities. In exchange the British offered to defend and assist him in the event of internal disturbances. They promised him that he would be a party to any Peace Treaty affecting his interests. They accepted that any additional facilities granted in wartime would be terminated when it ended. They committed themselves to consult him on any political matters affecting Oman and not to enter into direct communication with tribal leaders without consulting him. They promised him some free war stores and, most important, significant one-off payments and a monthly subsidy for the duration of the war. The difference in tone compared with the accession agreement of eight years earlier is striking.

In the event Oman was little involved for the first two years of the war. It was 1942 which saw a sharp build-up of activity to support both flying boat and fixed wing operations from Oman. These were directed against both German and Japanese submarines and for the escort of convoys, particularly those carrying supplies to the Gulf for delivery to Russia via Iran. The original RAF seaplane base on Masirah was reactivated and from the end of 1942 Canadian, British and Dutch Catalina flying boats used it, first on an occasional basis, but soon as a permanent base, for operations of many hours' duration far into the Indian Ocean. The runways at Masirah, Ras al-Hadd and Bait al-Falaj were improved in 1942. The RAF landing ground on the northern tip of Masirah became a base for shorter range anti submarine patrols by Bisley aircraft (a variant of the Blenheim) described by one commentator as 'a truly disgraceful aircraft' because of its poor performance and reliability. 244 Squadron in Masirah had 50 aircraft issued to it in 16 months to maintain 12 aircraft in the air. The only recorded 'kill' was in October 1943, when a Bisley flying from Sharjah sank UBoat 533 off the northern Omani coast near Shinas.

In Dhofar the main focus of air operations switched from Mirbat to a new airfield on the plain between Salalah town and the encircling hills. This was used by transit aircraft of the RAF and also by BOAC as one of eight stages on the 'Hadramawt Route' from Cairo to Karachi flown by Lockheed Lodestar aircraft. Late in 1942 US aircraft also began to transit Oman in significant numbers and by early 1943 the US Air Force had established its own staging post in Masirah, sharing facilities with what in July 1943 became RAF Masirah with the deployment of the first permanent RAF detachment there. At this stage of the war, most of the Pacific area was too much at risk from attack by Japanese forces, and US aircraft destined for the Pacific had to travel via the Caribbean, Brazil, Ascension Island, the Gold Coast (modern Ghana), Sudan, Aden, Oman and India. PANAM were keen to follow BOAC in opening up a passenger service along the Omani Coast but had their knuckles severely rapped by Sultan Sa'id for assuming that they could do so in time of war without his specific consent. By September 1943 the flying boat base on Masirah had 140 personnel and the RAF base 750. The logistical problems of an operation on this scale were huge. In September 1943 the Americans alone used 66000 gallons of petrol, all brought in and transferred to aircraft in 4 gallon tins. It was only later in the war that the fuel drum size was increased to the now standard 44 gallon drum.

In 1944 five 'Miami' high speed rescue launches supplied to the RAF by the Americans under 'lendlease' arrangements were deployed along the Omani coast, at Muscat, Masirah, and Raysut near Salalah. In early 1944, 244 Squadron, the only RAF Squadron ever to deploy wholly to Oman, moved from Sharjah to Masirah to replace the Bisleys with Wellingtons and intensify anti-submarine and convoy escort operations in the Gulf of Oman. In early 1945 operations in this theatre ran down swiftly. The Catalinas and Wellingtons were withdrawn and the Americans closed down their staging post. The flying boat base was used by the Miamis till they were disbanded in 1947. For a while there was a flow of aircraft and personnel back from the Far East but by 1946 the RAF stations in Salalah and Masirah were on a care and maintenance basis with the residual low-scale activity limited to a few civil and charter flights. BOAC ceased to operate the Cairo-Karachi service on this route in February 1947.

Once World War Two was over, priorities both for Sultan Sa'id and Britain began to change again. Sa'id was swift to remind the British authorities that his agreement to additional facilities had been for the duration of the war only. So far as on-going British use of the facilities was concerned his agreement to this was forthcoming, but he was insistent on the removal of troops from the Aden Protectorate Levies who had been introduced into Dhofar to guard the facilities at Salalah. He had a consistent and tenacious eye to his own position and advantage in his dealings with British officials and authorities. The Political Resident of the time noted that he was 'a supremely able negotiator who will agree to nothing in a hurry'. The British in 1944 considered offering to buy or lease the whole island of Masirah, but the idea was dropped on grounds of cost, and the RAF settled for renewal of their rights to continue to use the facilities on the island.

With these transitional issues settled, the focus turned back over the next ten years to the Sultan's aim to regain authority in interior Oman, the wish of the oil company to commence serious prospecting, and the aspirations of King Ibn Saud (and the US oil companies operating in Saudi Arabia) around the north western corner of Omani territory.

Japanese daring in Muscat harbour

A naval action displaying considerable seamanship took place right in Muscat harbour in June 1943. A merchant ship, the *Dah Puh.* sailing under the Norwegian flag, Captain Adolf Buhre, was anchored in the harbour in order to discharge cargo – 500 tons of bitumen in drums. She had sailed from Bahrain on 24 June, en route from Basra to Karachi. On the morning of the 28th, the Japanese submarine *Fukumura* approached the Duweira Gap, a narrow and shallow sea passage beneath Jalali Fort, east of the harbour, which nowadays lies at anything between half a metre and 2 metres deep, depending on the tide, and is no more than 10 metres wide. The submarine's captain, carefully calculating the depth of the water at the state of the tide, fired a torpedo through the narrow gap between the rocks, and over the sand bar, and hit the *Dah Puh*, whose mainly Indian crew no doubt thought they were safely protected by the high hills on three sides.

The torpedo caused a horrendous explosion on the starboard side, almost splitting the ship in two. The after part sank in a few seconds, while debris and the cargo of bitumen were scattered round the harbour. Witnesses reported that the bitumen melted in the sun and ran down from the rooves of houses. About 60 people were reported as having been on board when the torpedo struck. The ship's life boats, and other boats provided by the British consul, assisted in the rescue work. But 14 crew and 26 local workers (who were on board to help unload the cargo) died.

There was correspondence afterwards between the British Agent, the Muscat authorities and Gray Mackenzie, the shipping agents who arranged salvaging of the wreck. There seems to have been some urgency about this, probably because of the risk of pillaging. A 12-pounder gun was salvaged and presented to the Sultan. The fine brass bell of the *Dah Puh* was also salvaged, and at the time of writing (end 2005) hangs in the social club of the British Embassy in Shatti al-Qurm, Muscat. Initially the wreck was left to block the Duwaira Gap, but this was later found to be an inconvenience to shipping, and – following a personal request from Sultan Sa'id bin Taymur to the British Consul – the wreck was removed by a British salvage crew under an RNVR commander in December 1946.

28. RAF Flying Boat

29. RAF Vincent

CHAPTER 14

Reuniting Imamate and Sultanate (1945-1955)

With virtually no change or economic development in the country, absence of external pressures enabled Sultan Sa'id to position himself to unite Sultanate and Imamate, which he appeared to have achieved in 1955. The path to this was not straightforward, and was made additionally difficult by the renewed assertiveness of Saudi Arabia on his north-western borders. The growing interest of the oil companies, in Oman as in other Gulf territories, increasingly played a part in Sa'id's calculations.

* * * * * * *

Superficially, an Omani, whether living in Muscat, the Imamate, or elsewhere, would have seen and felt very little change in the first fifteen years of Sultan Sa'id's rule. There had been little or no economic growth or development. Indeed the restrictions resulting from World War Two and consequent reduction in trade had made the economic situation even harsher. The co-existence between Imamate and Sultanate established at Seeb in 1920 continued largely unruffled. Compared with the years around World War One the internal situation was calm and there was a striking absence of any external threat. The Sultan was a largely invisible Ruler. The role of the British Political Agent as the only diplomat in Muscat, the dependence on British India Line ships for communication with the outside world, and occasional visits by Royal Navy ships and RAF aircraft underlined the exclusive nature of the Sultanate's links with

Britain. (The World War Two movements in and out of Masirah were unknown to most Omanis.)

What had in fact changed was evident only to Sultan Sa'id and a few trusted advisers, and to British officials. His extreme financial prudence coupled with additional revenues from concessions granted to the Iraq Petroleum Company (IPC), and from the British wartime subsidies (the latter to an extent to be replaced by income from a civil aviation agreement signed in 1947), had greatly reduced his financial dependence on Indian merchants and the British Indian Government. He had been shrewdly using this greater freedom of manoeuvre to build links with tribal Shaikhs to position himself to assert his authority in the interior in due course, though his personal respect for the Imam meant that this would be deferred so long as the latter lived. The route to the apparent achievement of this goal at the end of 1955 is the main theme of this chapter.

Evolutionary changes in British policy towards Oman

Sultan Sa'id and British officials alike faced three fundamental international changes in navigating a way through the decade after 1945. With the British grant of independence to India in 1947, the main reason for Oman's importance to British interests could be said to have disappeared. However the Middle East as a whole remained central in British global strategy. Changes in policy affecting Oman were therefore evolutionary rather than radical, for three sets of reasons. First, Britain had major political commitments in Palestine (until 1948), Egypt, and Aden. Iran and Kuwait were vital sources of oil, and the spectre of the Gulf as the possible scene of aggressive policies by Stalin was a very real one. As a result no major reorientation of British defence policy away from the area took place. Second, the development of oil reserves in the Arabian peninsula gathered pace and drew in the United States ever more directly. ARAMCO, the consortium of American companies operating in Saudi Arabia, was formed in 1948. Third, as the decade proceeded, other Arab Governments began to pursue policies and interests which impacted directly on Oman. Saudi Arabia reasserted and extended earlier claims in the area where Saudi Arabia, Qatar, the Trucial States (notably Abu Dhabi), and Oman meet. Following overtures from tribal leaders who had hitherto nominally accepted the Sultan's authority, this resulted in a fully-fledged international crisis around Omani-controlled villages in the Buraimi oasis. After King Farouq of Egypt was overthrown in 1951, Arab nationalism with a strong anti-colonial and anti-British element was a potent force in the Middle East. Both Saudi Arabia and Egypt came to be sources of backing for political groups in Oman opposed to the régime of Sultan Sa'id, who continued to be supported by Britain.

It is important to set Sultan Sa'id's moves with tribal leaders in the geographical and political context of traditional Oman. A map of Oman in 1930 would have shown three distinct areas, not two. Sa'id controlled the Batinah coast from the borders with the Trucial States to Sur, as well as Dhofar in the south. Imamate authority clearly ran from the Sharqiyah area in the east (the territory of the al-Harthi tribal confederation) to Nizwa and the Jebal Akhdar, or Green Mountain, the major peak in the Western Hajjar mountains. But in most areas there was a buffer area between them in which the writ of neither Sultan nor Imam ran unequivocally, and there were large parts of the rest of the country which were under 'no overall control'. These included the south-eastern area around Ras al-Hadd and Masirah, the vast expanse of desert between Imamate territory and the borders of Dhofar, Musandam in the north, and the Dakhiliyah, the area to the north-west of Nizwa running to the Buraimi oasis and the interior borders of the Trucial States. These areas were dominated by the leaders of the tribes living in them, who were often in a state of rivalry if not conflict with each other, and neither Sultan nor Imam appointed *walīs* (local governors) or *qādīs* (judges), or collected taxes.

We should also remember that the Imamate was an elected, primarily spiritual, office. But his selection was ultimately under the control of the tribal leaders, notably the tamimas, the normally hereditary supreme leaders or paramount Shaikhs of the major tribal groups, which themselves formed the two shifting confederations of the Ghafiri and Hinawi. The balance of influence among them at the moment of election of an Imam ultimately determined who was elected and the political direction the Imamate would take.

By 1945 Sultan Sa'id appears to have concluded that he would not succeed in reuniting Sultanate and Imamate by seeking to have himself elected as Imam, and that he should instead work to avoid the election of another Imam, leaving the way open to proceed politically through his relationships with the tamimas. In April 1945 he was visited in Muscat by the tamima of the Bani Bu 'Ali, 'Ali bin 'Abdullah al-Ḥamūdi, and Sulaiman bin Ḥimyār, tamima of the al-Riyami tribe and leader of the Ghafiri confederation. They had previously met in the interior with 'Isa bin Ṣāliḥ al-Harthi, the leading figure of the Hinawi and the leading signatory on the Imamate side at Seeb in 1921. As reported to the British authorities the two tamimas declared that they would take no part in the choice of a new Imam and had placed themselves 'under the orders' of the Sultan; and it was reported that 'Isa bin Salih would also take little part in choosing a new Imam. This was followed by a successful mediation by the Sultan between 'Ali bin 'Abdullah al Bu 'Ali and 'Isa bin Salih. This all seemed more immediately significant than it proved to be because the Imam was seriously ill and not expected to live, though he did not in the event die until 1954.

Despite his apparent success with the tamimas Sultan Sa'id believed that his objective would not be secured without military strength to support his authority. In early 1946 he sought agreement from the British for a plan of action to be put into effect when the Imam died. This would have involved the provision by the British of weapons and other military supplies, and of one British and several Indian officers and NCOs, together with agreement to the use of the RAF as had been done against the Banu Bu 'Ali in 1932. Against the advice of the RAF, the Political Agent and the Political Resident, London and India turned down the use of the RAF on grounds of possible diplomatic reaction at the newly formed United Nations. They advocated instead a programme of financial largesse to the tribes, some of it to be funded by IPC to advance the company's growing interest in the interior. This was a severe disappointment to Sa'id who did not want the oil company dealing direct with interior tribes until his authority there was unequivocally accepted. He reacted by disappearing to Salalah to bide his time till events strengthened his hand in seeking British support on his own terms.

The importance of oil, and territorial sovereignty
In the years after World War Two, Sultan Sa'id's aspirations to reassert his authority in Imamate territory came to interact directly with those of Petroleum Development Oman (PDO – IPC's operating company in

212

Oman), which became an additional major player in the events of the next decade. Elsewhere in the Gulf oil issues had already drawn British Governments, traditionally concerned with sea routes and uninterested in the tribal hinterland, into the politics of control of those hinterlands. Oil concessions, with their major investment requirements as well as the need to guarantee revenue from any production achieved, required the traditional structures of tribal control in inland Arabia to give way to Western concepts of sovereignty and contract. In 1920, at Seeb, Britain had been happy to leave ambiguous the question of the sovereignty of Imamate-controlled territory. After 1945 they were obliged to judge whether the territory of the Imamate or that under 'no overall control' could evolve into political units with which PDO could deal. If not, they had no option but to continue to back Sa'id's aims in the interests of PDO.

By 1948 the dilemma was being starkly put by R E R Bird of PDO. 'It is time that HMG faced facts and, if upholding the Sultan's sovereignty over Oman implies refusing to allow the de facto rulers of the interior to negotiate concessions with the Company, there is no prospect whatsoever of developing Oman's probably very considerable resources.' That year Bird initiated discussions with a number of tribal groups and reached agreement with three. Acceptance of these as they stood would effectively have treated them as independent Rulers and excluded the Sultan. Sa'id, who had always refused to let the Company see the terms agreed at Seeb, was predictably alarmed. He had meetings with a number of Shaikhs from the Buraimi area and dispensed considerable sums to them, claiming that they had in return acknowledged his authority. When Bird returned to Buraimi in 1949 however the Shaikhs denied this claim. Sa'id then said he would agree to PDO negotiating with individual tribes, and payment of a per barrel sum to them, if the agreements made clear their acceptance of his authority. Predictably this was refused by the tribes and the way to oil exploration in interior Oman and Buraimi remained blocked.

The stakes were raised in 1950 by Sulaiman bin Himyar, who was by this stage the most powerful tribal leader in the Imamate, and controlled the Jebel Akhdar area at its heart. He used Wilfred Thesiger (see box on p 192) who was seeking his help to enable him to visit the Jebel Akhdar in the course of his journeys in northern Oman (which were approved of

213

by neither the Sultan nor the Imam), to ask the British Government to acknowledge him as an independent Ruler, with a view to concluding an agreement with PDO. This necessitated an explicit decision in London as to whether to back Sa'id's wider aspirations or to revert to the pre-1921 approach of supporting him only on the coast and in Dhofar, and as a consequence dealing piecemeal with other leaders in the interior. The former policy was called 'fictitious' by Thesiger and others because it depended on acknowledging the Sultan's non-existent authority in the interior; the latter was called 'realistic'.

Sir Rupert Hay, the Political Resident in the Persian Gulf, argued for continuing support for Sa'id, to avoid alienating him, to preserve the validity of PDO's concession agreement which was written to cover all his dominions (and which would have been of little value if limited to the coast and Dhofar), and to avoid creating a political vacuum in interior Oman which could be exploited by Saudi Arabia. Hay's advice was accepted, with the result that PDO had to bide their time until Sa'id was in a position to offer adequate protection for exploration activity in the areas they were interested in. The pain of continuing exclusion from the Dakhiliyah/Buraimi area was however mitigated by the fact that PDO's attention was increasingly focussed not on that area but on Fahud (see map 6 on p xiv), in Duru-controlled territory much further south. This was a classic example of a geological formation under which the chances of finding oil were deemed very high. It had been spotted accidentally from an overflying oil company plane in 1948 and was from that time on the real object of the Company's activities. It was however to be 1954 before geologists could get to it on the ground.

The Buraimi crisis

To the 21st century visitor to the twin towns of Al Ain in Abu Dhabi and Buraimi in Oman, the thought that this was the focal point of a major international crisis in the 1950s involving extensive military activity, and occupying the time and attention of Kings, Presidents and Prime Ministers, is hard to comprehend.

The 'crisis', which lasted for three full years from 1952 to 1955, was in part the result of a clash between western 20th-century notions of determining land borders and traditional bedu Arab views of territory and tribal allegiance. Historically, tribes had grazed camels and herds freely over wide tracts of land, owing allegiance to Shaikhs or tamimas wherever they might be. The realisation that oil and gas lay below the mostly barren sands brought with it the entirely new need to delimit the land and attribute ownership. This was one of the last areas of the globe in which formal state boundaries were settled. The colonial scramble of the late 19th century which resulted in so many arbitrary but durable frontiers being created in Africa had passed Arabia by. The absence of modern states and the resilience of informal bedu tribal authority in desert areas with tiny, often nomadic, populations meant that borders had simply not been an issue.

Two things had been important in the earlier history of the area. If formal borders were of no consequence, control of major oases certainly was. It was no accident that places like Buraimi and Ibri played such a prominent role. The assets and lands of tribal leaders were concentrated there, often with several tribes sharing influence in a single oasis. In a multi-layered structure of influence and authority, Rulers such as the Sultan of Muscat and the Rulers of the Trucial States also sought to assert suzerainty over the desert tribes and their lands. In the case of Buraimi, a cluster of nine villages around a series of natural and artificial water channels, six were of tribes owing a degree of allegiance to the ruling family of Abu Dhabi and three to the Sultan of Muscat.

As we saw earlier the influence of the Wahhabi movement, spreading from the central areas of the peninsula, had extended to this area over much of the 19th century. Holding it at bay was a central strand in the relationships between successive Sultans and the Government of British India. For much of the century until 1870 Buraimi had intermittently been a Saudi outpost; and Wahhabi influence had spread further through parts of interior Oman as far as Ras al-Hadd. At times Rulers in Muscat were forced to concede Wahhabi suzerainty over a number of tribes in the interior. In a world where hold over people not land was the primary consideration, this provided a basis for later Saudi leaders to assert their claims right across the area.

It was almost fifty years after 1870 before the process of creating the modern state of Saudi Arabia resulted in a renewed if modest pole of attraction there for tribal leaders in Buraimi and the surrounding area. From around 1925 emissaries from what was later the eastern province of Saudi Arabia began to be active around Buraimi and to seek acknowledgement through the collection of religious tax, the *zakāt*. This caused some alarm in the Imamate, which felt more directly threatened than the Sultanate, but it remained a fairly minor phenomenon, though 'Isa bin Salih raised tribal levies in 1925 for what turned out to be an abortive plan to reassert the control of the Imam.

The discovery of the first oil in the lower Gulf, in Bahrain in 1932, created a new situation. The companies making up the IPC on the one hand, and those of the consortium of American companies outside IPC on the other, both moved to consolidate their positions in areas of interest to them. Thanks to exclusive agreements secured by the British in the 1920s with the Trucial States, Qatar and Muscat, IPC had a commanding position there. The American companies were dominant in Saudi Arabia. The Buraimi issue was thus a modest part of a game being played out over a much wider area. The frontier-less and virtually unpopulated area between the Trucial States and Muscat, whose foreign policies were managed by Britain, and the recently unified Saudi state, became a critical element in this competition.

The result was a series of Saudi-British negotiations in the 1930s. These discussions had failed to reach a conclusion when they went into abeyance with the outbreak of World War Two in 1939. Differing lines had been put on the table by the two sides as bases for negotiation, the British side taking as their point of departure arrangements tentatively reached with the Ottoman Turkish Government before World War One. The Saudi position was based on the 'Hamza Line' of 1935 named after the Saudi official who tabled it (see map 8 on p xvi). The British line developed in the 1930s was variously called the 'Ryan Line' after the British negotiator or the 'Riyadh Line' after the venue of the talks. This incorporated a line drawn between the Sultan's territories and those of Saudi Arabia through the Empty Quarter to the border with Aden beyond which Sa'id cautiously and with some misgivings accepted that he had 'no claims'.

It was the abrupt Saudi extension of the 'Hamza Line' in 1949 to incorporate much of the territory of Abu Dhabi as well as all of Buraimi which was the trigger for turning the issue from problem to crisis. This was coupled, menacingly for Sultanate and Imamate alike, by statements that Saudi relations with the Shaikhs of the Dakhiliyah concerned them alone, not the Sultan or the British. Behind the specific claim lay a belief on the part of Ibn Sa'ud that he could if he chose also claim authority over all of Muscat and Oman. He never extended his specific claim beyond Buraimi but was more than ready to seek to exploit developments in Oman to extend his influence as far as the Imamate.

Since the creation of the Saudi state in the 1920s (the new Kingdom was proclaimed in 1932) Saudi claims had not been backed up with military activity, and many were sceptical that any significant threat could emerge across the 400 miles of desert between Buraimi and the nearest inhabited point in Saudi Arabia. The British and the Arab rulers of the area, including Sultan Sa'id, were alike slow to appreciate the threat. The Trucial Oman Levies was created in 1950 to give some military capability to the Ruler of Abu Dhabi. It was however only in 1951 that Britain began to appreciate the implications of the more hawkish positions taken by the Saudis in fruitless discussions, conducted by Amir 'Abdullah, Ibn Sa'ud's brother. Sultan Sa'id too was slow to appreciate the need to reinforce his nominal authority and jurisdiction in Buraimi. Matters were complicated by ongoing pressure from PDO to be allowed to negotiate direct with the tribes of the area which led to Sa'id being at serious cross purposes with PDO and British officials on the ground in Buraimi.

Matters came abruptly to a head in October 1952. Following a request for Saudi support from Omani Shaikhs from Buraimi who had previously pledged allegiance to Sultan Sa'id, a Saudi official, Turki bin 'Atayshān, arrived in Hamasa, one of the Omani villages of the Buraimi oasis, with a force of 40 men, vehicles and radio equipment. He also had lavish funds to distribute both in Buraimi and more widely, and was able to claim with some plausibility that he had come at the request of the people. This was a clear threat to both Imamate and Sultanate. In the former there was a vigorous response to the threat of the extension of Wahhabi influence. The Imam took the initiative to write to the Sultan about a joint response. With the full support of most tribal leaders Sultan and Imam agreed together to send a two-pronged force to reassert Omani authority in Hamasa. An Imamate force of 400 was prepared, whilst a Sultanate tribal force of 1000 was assembled at Sohar and Sa'id travelled there to launch it on its mission to Buraimi.

There followed one of the most climactic moments in the whole British relationship with successive Sultans. The initial British response was to encourage the steps Sultan Sa'id was taking to reassert his sovereignty. Then there was an abrupt volte-face. Fearful of American reactions to direct engagement with Saudi forces and in the light of Saudi agreement to a 'standstill' whereby neither side would introduce more forces into the oasis, Anthony Eden personally instructed local British officials, against their own judgement, to dissuade Sa'id from launching an assault which could not have failed to succeed. The latter, dependent as he was on the British for the conduct of his foreign relations, had no option but to accept, but insisted that the British advice be put in writing. Major Leslie Chauncy, the British Consul in Muscat, drove to Sohar with the letter. Deeply frustrated and feeling humiliated in front of the assembled tribes, Sa'id insisted that Chauncy should formally read the ultimatum aloud in front of the force to underline that it was a British choice, not his own. He then retired to Salalah for two years, speaking two months later of 'the great cost to myself' of accepting this British advice.

The subsequent diplomatic intricacies of the Buraimi dispute need not concern us here. In the short term the standstill agreement provided that neither side would reinforce its troops in Buraimi (a small force of the Trucial Oman Levies had been installed in one of the villages loyal to Abu Dhabi to balance the continuing Saudi presence in Hamasa). In November 1952 after exchanges involving Churchill as Prime Minister, King Sa'ud and the British Government agreed that the claims of the two sides should be submitted to arbitration in Geneva. Sultan Sa'id reluctantly accepted the standstill and the arbitration, making it very clear that it was for Britain to uphold the Omani interest they had denied him the chance to defend. Vast compilations of documents were prepared (with significant support from the American oil companies on the Saudi side). When the arbitration finally got under way in September 1955 it became apparent that the Saudis were engaged in vigorous activities both on the ground and in the margins of the arbitration process, hoping to influence the outcome. The British Government decided to withdraw from the process and, in effect, itself to take the action that it had prevented Sultan Sa'id from taking three years earlier. We shall take up that narrative later.

Oil again

The British Government continued to steer PDO firmly away from the Dakhiliyah/Buraimi area as the crisis developed. This was no time to be undermining Sultan Sa'id by further direct dealings with the tribes. But both they and he saw fewer objections to the beginning of exploration activity in an area on the southern coast of Oman. This too was an area of 'no overall control' but it was more distant from the heartlands of the Imamate, and the major tribes had reasonably cordial relationships with Sa'id. As always the Sultan's reactions were cautious and incremental, and correspondingly frustrating to PDO. In 1951 he had considered the area unsafe for the Company but after the Saudi incursion into Buraimi the value of an assertion of his sovereignty into an area not controlled by the Imam became more apparent to him. In 1952 he indicated that the Company could explore a strip of the southern coast up to a limit of 50 miles inland, with Duqm as its centre. It was however mutually agreed that it would need its own security force to protect it and that Sa'id had no current force capable of this. At first the Company bridled at picking up the cost. Protracted negotiations took place with the Sultan. He began by seeking British Government support to raise an additional 1500 men. In the end he settled for agreement to recruit 400 non-Omanis to the Muscat and Oman Field Force (MOFF). This would be responsible to the Sultan but paid for by the Company and armed and trained by the British Government. Colonel Pat Waterfield, who had been recruited in 1952 to command the Muscat Infantry, was given the task of raising the Force after the first British officer recruited to do so walked away. Waterfield was to serve Sa'id in various capacities until 1970.

The appointment of a British commander, the raising and elementary training of the Force, and the assembly of shipping and equipment for what was effectively an amphibious landing on a coast with no port, occupied most of 1953. It was February 1954 before the Force and the Company's expedition of three landing ships converging from Muscat and Aden arrived in Duqm. The party, including a Shaikh of the local Janaba tribe loyal to the Sultan, the General Manager of IPC, and its local representative Edward Henderson, was much more warmly received than an earlier party had been in 1926. Expecting early drilling activity, the Sultan and his British Foreign Minister Neil Innes, together with Chauncy, arrived on a Royal Navy ship a month later. The Sultan was disappointed that prospection did not lead immediately to drilling and was unimpressed with the Force. PDO, for its part, felt that he remained excessively restrictive in defining where they could work. For

Henderson in particular the prize was not the southern area itself but a springboard to mount an expedition across the desert to Fahud without having to touch on Imamate territory. Nonetheless for the first time in Oman outside Dhofar systematic mapping and surveying could begin.

A new Imam

In May 1954, three months after the PDO expedition went ashore in Duqm, Muhammad al-Khalīlī died; he had been Imam since before the conclusion of the arrangements at Seeb in 1921. Whatever assurances about the election of a new Imam the major tamimas had given Sultan Sa'id in 1945, a successor, Ghālib bin 'Ali al-Ḥinā'i was swiftly elected. Ghalib had been a well-respected *qādī* under the former Imam, and was believed to be the latter's preferred successor. His support was however limited; even the tamima of his own tribe did not support him. It became immediately apparent that he was very much in the hands of his ambitious brother Ṭālib and of Sulaiman bin Himyar. Their aim now, following the British rejection of Imam Ghalib's bid to secure recognition as an independent Ruler, was to work with the Saudis and other Arabs to turn interior Oman into a separate state, with an oil deal with an American company as a major potential prize if this happened. The restraints of the Seeb Agreement, which Muhammad al-Khalili had always scrupulously observed, were swiftly jettisoned. The Imamate began to issue its own passports for the first time and overtures were made for the Imamate to join the Arab League.

In this situation the interests of Sultan Sa'id and PDO were in fact closely aligned. The Sultan sought to fend off the threat of a new and expanded Imamate in alliance with Saudi Arabia, and if possible to reassert his own authority in the interior. For PDO the overriding aim was the ability to access Fahud. For this the key was the support of the leaders of the nomadic Duru tribe who exclusively controlled the Fahud area, and who had the option of aligning themselves with either the Sultanate or with the Imamate and the Saudis.

Sultan Sa'id had been greatly frustrating PDO by refusing to allow them to approach the Duru directly and at the same time failing to engage them effectively himself. The election of Imam Ghalib was seen by the Duru Shaikhs as a potential threat, and they travelled to Muscat to discuss the terms on which they would agree to take the Sultan's side. While

Sa'id and PDO were seeking to go to Fahud, the Duru wanted an assurance that the Sultan would support them, militarily if necessary, against the Imam. This Sa'id had in fact declined to give, but enough ambiguity was left by Henderson and Sa'id Ahmad bin Ibrahim, the Sultan's representative in Muscat, for the Duru to agree to join an expedition from Duqm to Fahud.

The expedition to Fahud

Preparations had been made over the summer of 1954 for the overland journey of nearly 200 miles from Duqm to Fahud, a route never before travelled by foreigners and never undertaken by vehicles. In October 1954 the party set out, taking four days to get to Fahud. For PDO this was its destination. For the Duru the end-point was their centre of Tan'am, some 70 miles to the north. Colonel Percy Coriat was the Commander of the MOFF escorting the Company team, the first British officer to command Omani forces operationally on behalf of the Sultan. He had explicit orders not to enter Tan'am or Ibri except by invitation. The Duru Shaikhs insisted on proceeding from Fahud to Tan'am, threatening otherwise to defect to the Imam. Henderson agreed with Coriat that the hundred or so soldiers of MOFF would accompany Henderson and the Shaikhs to Tan'am but would remain just outside the village. In the event it proved not to be occupied by Imamate forces, and the Imam's *qāḍī* in Ibri surrendered the town to the Sultan's representative. Other tribal leaders in the area hastened to offer their allegiance to the Sultan, replacing the white flag of the Imamate with the red of the Sultanate. Though this was a tremendous boost for the Sultan's prestige he felt it had been made against his wishes. At this stage he saw the MOFF as a tool with which to build his prestige with the tribes, but he was not yet ready to risk a direct confrontation with the Imam. He accepted the position only reluctantly and even threatened Coriat with disciplinary action. He was certainly not at this stage ready to exploit it further.

In the early months of 1955 the situation remained finely poised for control of interior Oman. The MOFF remained in control of Ibri and, though he continued to veto moves to secure other towns in the Dakhiliyah between Ibri and Buraimi militarily, Sa'id did permit the Force's deployment for punitive strikes designed to remind wavering Shaikhs that he had the potential to use organised military force in the area.

Sultan Sa'id now had a foothold which could be used to achieve his long-held goal of extending his authority throughout the interior. But any move eastwards towards the Imamate capital at Nizwa would need to be carefully prepared. The Imam was known to be landing arms on the Batinah coast and moving them though the mountains towards Nizwa. The MOFF was still a poorly trained and equipped force and the ground had to be prepared politically among the tribes to minimise opposition when the move was made. Sa'id made one of his rare extended visits to Muscat in the summer of 1955. He secured the all-important backing of Shaikh Ahmad al-Harthi, a major Hinawi leader, who had assumed the leadership of the Harthi tribe on the death of 'Isa bin Salih. Even Sulaiman bin Himyar was hedging his bets by talking to Sa'id. Shaikh Zaid, later the Ruler of Abu Dhabi and at this stage the Governor of Al Ain on behalf of his father Shaikh Shakhbut, was helpful in securing for Sa'id the formal allegiance of key Dakhiliyah tribes who had hitherto not rallied to his support.

Sultan Sa'id's initiative on the interior
On the basis of these developments, and of discussions in London in summer 1955, the Sultan began in secrecy to plan his move on Nizwa. The British authorities were nervous that he was underestimating the risks from the Imamate (which still had Saudi support), and that their consistent refusal to get militarily involved in interior Oman could again be put to the test. However they did not seek to resist his plans which were fully coordinated with the British authorities in the Gulf. One critical factor from the British viewpoint was the need to secure international public support for the Sultan against propaganda for the Imam now emerging from Saudi Arabia and Egypt. Neil Innes, the Sultan's 'Foreign Minister', was charged with coordinating this and the decision was made for the first time ever to invite selected international journalists to observe the operation. The *Times* was to be the chosen vehicle in the shape of Peter Fleming who was to join the first move to Nizwa, and James (later Jan) Morris who was to observe Sultan Sa'id's own role in what was planned.

As the operation was being set up Sultan Sa'id's position was boosted by the restoration of his undisputed authority in the traditionally Omani-controlled parts of Buraimi. In September 1955 the British Government concluded that the arbitration proceedings in Geneva were leading nowhere and that the Saudi presence in Buraimi should be terminated firmly but without bloodshed. On 26 October two Squadrons of the Trucial Oman Scouts, supported by a Lincoln bomber, moved on the Saudi position in Hamasa village. They were supported late in the operation by a troop of the Muscat Infantry. The Saudi Representative Major Na'imi offered the only resistance and was slightly wounded before being captured. He and his men were then flown out via Bahrain to Saudi Arabia. Meanwhile other elements of the Scouts were engaged in much brisker fighting with the tribesmen of the Na'imi tamima and other Omani Shaikhs who had supported the Saudi position. Edward Henderson, though still an employee of the oil company, had been appointed by the Political Resident to conduct negotiations with the tribal groups on the ground. By the end of the day he had managed to negotiate the surrender of the rebel Shaikhs on the basis that they too would get safe conduct to Saudi Arabia.

Boosted by this, in December 1955 Sultan Sa'id launched the move of a force of 340 MOFF troops with eight British officers, accompanied by Innes, from their base at Fahud to Adam, Firq, and Nizwa under the command of Bill Cheesman, who had succeeded Percy Coriat. In parallel with this the Batinah Force launched an operation against the Imam's stronghold at Rustaq on the Batinah side of the mountains. This force had been recruited after 1952, under the command of Colin Maxwell, another British officer who would serve the Sultan faithfully till 1970, to give him some modern military capacity on the Batinah coast to respond to any moves the Saudis might make or sponsor. It was not known if the Imam was in Nizwa and opposition had to be anticipated. In the event he was not and the Sultan's forces were welcomed without resistance into the 'capital' of the Imamate on 13 December. The following day Shaikh Ahmad al-Harthi arrived with a force of camel-mounted warriors to take control of the town in Sultan Sa'id's name. After some fierce fighting against supporters of Talib, the Imam's brother, Maxwell took control of Rustaq for the Sultan on 19 December.

On the same day Sultan Sa'id left Salalah on the overland journey from Dhofar through the interior to Nizwa (the only time he ever visited this part of his realm), the Batinah Coast and Muscat, which is so vividly described in Jan Morris's *Sultan in Oman*. The first part of the journey, with Sa'id personally in charge of navigation, covered nearly 500 miles of trackless but firm desert never before traversed by vehicles. He briefly visited Fahud and, on 24 December, he ceremonially entered Nizwa. His aim of reuniting the entire country under his authority appeared to have been achieved. The Imam was allowed to retire to a mountain village in the custody of a tribal kinsman, and Sulaiman bin Himyar made an ignominious submission to the Sultan. Of the three key players in the Imamate the only one remaining unaccounted for was Talib, who made his escape from Rustaq and made his way to Saudi Arabia. Before travelling down the Batinah Coat to Muscat (there was as yet no direct road link between Nizwa and Muscat) Sa'id visited Buraimi and met Shaikh Zaid.

Over this decade Sultan Sa'id's relations with the British 'men on the spot' were always immaculately polite. Further steps were taken to meet his continuing wish to be clearly seen as the Ruler of an independent state. He had always addressed the British Representative in Muscat as 'my dear friend', but using the title of Consul, not Political Agent, which implied in his view that Muscat was being treated as a protected state like the other states of the Gulf. When the bilateral Treaty of Commerce was renegotiated at Sa'id's insistence in 1951, British use of the title also ended; it was after all a remnant from the days when Agents were appointed by the Governor of Bombay. From then on until the early 1970s the British Representative in Muscat was designated simply as Consul (later Consul General). The new Treaty was otherwise substantively unchanged from its predecessor (which dated from 1939) save that the extra-territorial jurisdiction with which the Consul was empowered was limited to 'citizens of the United Kingdom and colonies' instead of 'all British subjects', with more limited jurisdiction over Commonwealth citizens. Sultan Sa'id declined an invitation to the Queen's Coronation in 1953, but he visited London in 1953 (for the first time since 1938) and 1955. The 1953 visit was seen in London as important in restoring his confidence after the Sohar episode the previous year.

Sultan Sa'id remained obstinate over this period in his dealings both with the British Government and PDO in pursuit of his own strategy and timing for extending his authority in interior Oman. There were frustrations among British officials about his long absences in Salalah and his manifest preference for his life 'as a country squire' there. At the same time the British recognised that continuing financial prudence, which they encouraged, did indeed come more easily if he was not accessible to the importunities of tribal leaders all too ready to trade their support for financial backing. In 1954 Sultan Sa'id still bore the wounds of Sohar and felt that the British had failed to establish for him secure boundaries and a stable relationship with Saudi Arabia, as well as believing that Government and oil company together had failed to provide the financial support he was entitled to expect to enable him to modernise his army to the point where success would be guaranteed. By the end of 1955 however he appeared to have succeeded in his determination to 'do down the Imam' and reassert his own authority, and vindicated in the approach he had adopted with moments of assertiveness punctuated with quite long periods of diplomatic preparation with the tribes. Chauncy described the events of December 1955 as 'a personal triumph'. However British doubts about the resilience of the Saudi-backed triumvirate controlling the Imamate, as well as their fear of being drawn into direct operational involvement in the interior, proved, as we shall see, all too well founded.

A colourful military career in Oman – Jasper Coates

A few British officers served in Oman for as long as Jasper Coates did, continuously or in separate appointments. Others served both as British and as contract officers at different times. What made Coates's career remarkable was that it involved service in all three services, in the air, on land, and at sea.

A Yorkshireman, born in 1908, Coates served in the RAF from the late 1920s until 1957. Much of his service was in Iraq and the Gulf, and his Arabic was of interpreter standard. His early career was spent principally in Iraq based flying-boat Squadrons, notably 203 Squadron. He flew Rangoons of 203 Squadron on some of the pioneering flights to Muscat and Masirah in the early 1930s, including the first ever flight between Basra and Aden in 1933. He was involved with the Political Agents of the period in negotiating with the islanders the setting up of refuelling facilities in Masirah, and was then given specific responsibility for the development and supply of the chain of landing grounds between Muscat and Salalah for fixed wing aircraft.

By 1957 Coates had become, as a Group Captain, the Senior RAF Officer in the Gulf, based in Sharjah, responsible for RAF support for the Trucial Oman Scouts (TOS) in Buraimi and elsewhere. Over these two decades he had come to know Sultan Sa'id bin Taymur personally and when he decided to retire from the RAF he wrote directly to the Sultan asking for a job as a contract officer. This involved his first change of service. As the revolt led by Talib and Sulaiman bin Himyar was gathering strength in the summer of 1957 he was appointed as a Major to command the HQ Company of the Oman Regiment at Firq near Nizwa. It was on his rear party that the remnants of the Companies ambushed at Bilad Sait in July 1957 fell back. He was then involved in the withdrawal of these elements to the Oil Company base at Fahud and, after the decision was taken to disband and withdraw the Oman Regiment, he was transferred to the Northern Frontier Regiment (NFR). He was appointed personally by Sultan Sa'id, on the strength of his Arabic, as the political officer attached to the force led by Colonel Carter of the TOS which advanced from Fahud to retake Nizwa. His primary – highly exposed – job was to approach successive villages of uncertain allegiance under the red flag of the Sultanate and seek the support of the village elders for the Sultan. He is also recorded as having acted as a sniper at Firq (where he had previously been based) to draw rebel fire and enable the Cameronians to pinpoint the objective they would need to take in their night attack.

When this operation was over and the leading rebels retreated to the Jebel Akhdar, Coates, with only nominal control from his Commanding Officer, undertook initial probes into the jebel – at this stage never visited by any European in the 20th century, to assess the chances of pursuing the rebels. He rapidly concluded that substantial forces would be needed and that animal transport would be essential to get supplies, above all water, up the mountain. He appointed himself NFR's Animal Transport Officer and raised a force of donkeys and asses which became known as Jasper's Horse.

His unorthodox style and tendency – as a retired Group Captain – not to suffer fools gladly did not fit easily with the more orthodox methods favoured by Colonel Smiley and other Loan Service Officers who arrived in Oman after the Amery Agreement of 1958. Coates was transferred from NFR to help strengthen anti-smuggling activities on the northern side of the Hajjar Mountains along the Batinah Coast. Nominally this involved reorganising the Baluch Guard which had been established in the area after the Saudi incursion into Buraimi in 1951. Again he showed his flair for unorthodox ways of getting the job done, recruiting Iranian smugglers who had sought refuge in Oman from the regime of the Shah to try to catch the local Omani arms smugglers. He returned to the Jebel Akhdar to lead a small force of Abriyin tribesmen, with whom he had worked the previous year, on a diversionary attack on the northern slope of the mountain from Awabi as the SAS launched their assault from the south in January 1959.

As the process of transforming the Baluch Guard into the Oman Gendarmerie got under way, Coates found himself making his final change of service when he was invited to take responsibility for another recommendation arising from the Amery Agreement, the creation of a separate navy for the Sultanate. In the first instance this consisted of just one patrol boat, based on the Batinah Coast as part of the operation to deter the infiltration of men and arms. Having been noted for his highly informal appearance both as an airman and a soldier he now metamorphosed into the very model of a naval officer. He remained in this role for the final years of his service in Oman, his final recorded operation being linked to the very early stages of the Dhofar War in 1965. The Iranians had intercepted a dhow load of Dhofari rebels in the Shatt al-Arab setting out from Iraq to infiltrate themselves back into Oman. The Shah agreed that they should be handed over to the Sultan and Coates was sent to take charge of them from the Iranian navy and bring them to Muscat.

Jasper Coates was a colourful and larger than life character, of rumpled appearance till his days as a naval officer, and with a flair for dealing with Arabs. He had a highly original and sometimes irregular approach to meeting military objectives. Smiley noted wryly that he tended to regard decisions not as orders to be obeyed but as the basis for extensive and critical discussion. He was noted as a good companion with a supply, whatever the circumstances, of malt whisky specially brewed for him in Strathspey, and as the man who had always hoarded from somewhere the bit of kit he needed. He stands as well as anyone for numerous British officers who threw themselves with dedication and enthusiasm into the service of in the field of successive Sultans.

30. Jasper Coates accepting the surrender of rebels at Izz, 1957

31. Sulaiman bin Himyar and Imam Ghalib

32. Sultan Saʿid with Sayyid Qaboos

33. Sultan Saʿid's Desert convoy, 1954

34. Sultan Sa'id signing agreement with Political Resident

35. Sultan Sa'id with Sh Zaid, 1955

CHAPTER 15

Rebels from the Jebel (1956-1959)

The seemingly decisive events of December 1955 proved to be far from the end of the story. The period of just over three years between then and January 1959 saw the struggle for control of inner Oman between Sultan Sa'id and the Imam and his supporters seesaw back and forth several times. Sultan Sa'id commented at the end of 1956 that it had been the most peaceful year of his reign. In the summer of 1957 however Saudi support for his opponents produced a sharp shock. The Oman Regiment (as the Muscat and Oman Field Force had been renamed) was destroyed as a fighting unit by rebels skilfully controlled by the Imam's brother Talib, and the white flag of the Imamate was rehoisted over Nizwa.

Within weeks it was removed again by a combined British and Omani force and Sultan Sa'id's opponents retired to the fastnesses of the Jebel Akhdar. Through most of 1958 they both repulsed efforts by the Sultan's Armed Forces (SAF) to make any military impression on their secure base, and increasingly seized the initiative in disrupting the communications of the army and the oil company around the foot of the mountain. At the end of 1958 and early in 1959 this phase of Oman's history reached its conclusion. With the Sultan's own forces stiffened by serving British officers, British troops were needed again – for the last time outside Dhofar – to seize control of the Jebel Akhdar once and for all.

* * * * * * *

At the beginning of 1956 it seemed to the Sultan and to the British Government alike that PDO's funding of the MOFF had achieved the twin aims of securing his control of inner Oman and allowing the company to establish the communications it needed between Fahud, Nizwa and Muscat to permit a serious drilling campaign to get under way in Oman for the first time. The Imam had returned to his home village and the protective control of the tamima of his own tribe, the Bani Hina. Sulaiman bin Himyar had made his act of submission to Sultan Sa'id during his brief visit to Nizwa. Salih bin 'Isa, having lost out to Ahmad bin Muhammad for the position of tamima of the Al Harth, was noisily but ineffectually promoting the cause of the Imamate both in Saudi Arabia and in Egypt. He and other Imamate spokesmen got a ready hearing This was the year of British withdrawal from the Suez Canal Zone, and of the brief but inglorious campaign by Britain and France to seize control of the Canal back from President Nasser.

Talib, the Imam's brother, was also thought to be in Saudi Arabia, but was less evidently active. In fact, with support and funding from the Saudi authorities he was building up and training a rebel army recruited from young Omanis from tribes traditionally opposed to the Sultanate who had gone to Bahrain or Kuwait to seek the jobs which were not available in Oman. The equipment provided by the Saudis consisted mainly of modern American weapons and landmines provided by the US to help build up Saudi Arabia's own armed forces.

Rebel success in Nizwa
Early in 1957 it began to be rumoured that Talib had slipped back into Oman. There was however little evidence of significant tribal support for him, and little awareness of the existence of his Saudi trained force. In fact and in secret Sulaiman bin Himyar and Talib on the one hand, and Salih bin 'Isa on the other, were planning joint risings in the Jebel Akhdar/Nizwa area and in the Sharqiyah respectively. In the spring of 1957 Ibrahim bin Ahmad, Salih bin 'Isa's partner on the ground in planning the Sharqiyah rising, showed his hand prematurely before Talib had arrived, failed to gain much tribal support, and surrendered to Sultan Sa'id. Sulaiman bin Himyar was summoned to Muscat as a precaution and held loosely there under house arrest. In June however Talib and a group of supporters landed on the Batinah Coast, and made their way to his home town of Bilad Sait, where he was reunited with his brother.

The Oman Regiment (formerly the Muscat and Oman Field Force), unaware of the equipment and training Talib's supporters had acquired, decided on a reconnaissance in force from its base at Firq to Bilad Sait which lay in a bowl up a rocky wadi bed. The outcome was a debacle for the Sultan's forces. Initially there was something of a standoff between the Oman Regiment and the Bani Hina in the town. However Sulaiman bin Himyar slipped his house arrest in Muscat, murdering some wounded Oman Regiment soldiers as he travelled inland. He then led his Bani Riyam tribesmen to join the Bani Hina in Bilad Sait.

Trapped between hostile tribal forces the two companies of the Oman Regiment had no option but to attempt to retreat to their base at Firq. The distance was only some 20 miles but the way was a mixture of mountain defile, open wadi beds and streets winding through hostile villages. Not many made it – only the British officers of the companies involved and a few Baluch NCOs and soldiers. Those who regrouped at Firq were still in a perilous position and withdrew swiftly to the oil company base in the desert at Fahud, outside the tribal area of the hostile tribes and with its own airstrip. The whole Nizwa area, the heartland of the traditional Imamate, was lost to the rebels. Another company of the Oman Regiment which had been garrisoning Nizwa was taken prisoner.

British officers were able to fly to Muscat to report the situation. Sultan Sa'id reportedly accepted the position phlegmatically. It was evident that this was not just a tribal uprising but an externally organised threat, of a kind which his armed forces were not capable of dealing with on their own. In his mind it was part of his unwritten deal with the British that in these circumstances their broader interests in the area would require them to intervene on his behalf. He decided more or less on the spot to seek direct British military assistance for the first time since the Agreement of Seeb. This was on 16 July 1957.

The prospect of direct British military involvement in Arabia, only months after the humiliation of Suez, and the hostility which that operation had generated across the Middle East, was deeply unwelcome in London. But whatever the diplomatic and political complications, failure to sustain Sultan Sa'id against a Saudi and Egyptian backed uprising was unthinkable. The decision in principle was swift. Action was urgent and plans were drawn up within four days, involving forces and headquarters in Kenya, Aden, Cyprus and the Gulf.

On the ground the operation to retake Nizwa was to be carried out by two columns. One, based around the Muscat Regiment of the Sultan's Armed Forces, would move through the Samail Gap from Muscat to the interior along a road which had been opened up over the past eighteen months for oil company traffic. This came to be known as Haughcol after the Commanding Officer of the Muscat Regiment. A second and larger force would be assembled at Ibri and Fahud with the primary task of retaking Firq and Nizwa. This was known as Carterforce after the Commanding Officer of the Trucial Oman Scouts, based in Sharjah, who was to be its Commander. It consisted of several elements. The Trucial Oman Levies had British officers and were under direct British control. Its soldiers were Arabs from mixed tribal backgrounds, at one stage mainly from Aden but by 1957 principally bedu from Oman and the Trucial States themselves. Two Trucial Oman Scouts squadrons of 120 men were part of the force. It also included a squadron of Oman's Northern Frontier Regiment (formerly the Batinah Force) commanded by Lt Col Colin Maxwell, who had captured Rustaq in 1955. Britain flew in a troop of the 15/19 Kings Royal Hussars from Aden with Ferret armoured cars, and a company of the Cameronians from Bahrain together with the battalion's mortar and machine gun platoons from Kenya. Brigadier Robertson, the senior British Army officer in the area, was based at Fahud in overall command of the British forces involved. The oil company's airstrip there became for a brief period a major military airfield handling many different kinds of transport aircraft, notably the huge Beverly freighters recently put into service with the RAF.

The RAF played a major part in operations in Oman over the next eighteen months. The doctrine and experience of the 1920s under which tribal dissent could be dealt with by air action alone, largely unsupported by troops on the ground, no longer worked thirty years later. In the Arabian Peninsula however the RAF still played a very prominent role in British military thinking in a situation where there was great reluctance to keep troops in significant numbers permanently based in the region. Aden and Bahrain were the RAF's main bases in the area with forward operations in Oman conducted from Masirah and Sharjah. Leaflet dropping and the destruction after warning of fortified buildings were the main operations undertaken. Considerable efforts were made to avoid civilian casualties wherever possible. By the late 1950s Venom fighters were the main aircraft deployed with Lincoln, later Shackleton, bombers in support. Large numbers of sorties were flown against rebel strongholds and positions in late July and early August 1957. The results were mixed. The great mud brick tower of the fort at Nizwa for example was barely dented, but many less heavily fortified buildings were badly damaged and the message that retribution was planned must have been clear both to the rebels and perhaps more important to tribes deciding which side to back.

Nizwa recaptured

After this warming-up process Carter gave the order to advance from Fahud across the desert towards Firq and Nizwa on 6 August 1957. The campaign was brief and decisive. With RAF support Carterforce had overwhelming fire power. Villagers were quick to appreciate this and in most places the white flag of the Imamate was rapidly again replaced with the red of the Sultanate. Progress across the desert was steady and a forward airstrip was established near Izz to permit resupply from the air. Stiff resistance at Firq however required some three days to overcome. The oasis and village was commanded by a spur of the Jebel Akhdar called Crown Hill which was occupied by rebels. This had to be captured to permit entry into the village and access to the road to Nizwa beyond. There was an initial delay while Carter sought permission from London to change his rules of engagement to allow the dropping of bombs by the RAF Venoms as well as use of their machine guns. The clearing of Crown Hill was entrusted to the Cameronians who scaled it by night. The rebels quickly fell back and the village was taken by the Trucial Oman Scouts and the Northern Frontier Regiment on 12 August. The way to Nizwa was open and on the same day patrols from Carterforce and Haughcol, both as it happened led by seconded Captains of the East Surrey Regiment, linked up at Birkat al-Mawz.

Haughcol, only some 100 men strong, had made good and largely unopposed progress through the Samail Gap and had had to mark time at Izki while Carterforce captured Firq. It was accompanied by Sayyid Tariq, the Sultan's half-brother. He had been appointed by Sultan Sa'id as his representative in the interior, and had the specific task of organising tribes loyal to the Sultan in support of the small military forces available. He accepted the surrender of Nizwa and the symbolic destruction (with Royal Engineer help) of the major buildings and fortifications owned by the leading rebels. The latter all escaped however towards the heights of the Jebel Akhdar, and the Government in London insisted on the immediate withdrawal of the Cameronians back to Muscat and then Sharjah, which precluded any serious immediate hot pursuit.

The year following the recapture of Nizwa was one of increasingly unacceptable stalemate. The rebel leaders and a few hundred active supporters remained in the villages on the top of the Jebel Akhdar plateau. Of the British units deployed in July only the armoured cars of the Hussars remained. The Trucial Oman Scouts followed the Cameronians back to Sharjah. In the autumn of 1957 Sultan Sa'id, with the forces left to him, ordered probing operations to seek a foothold on the Jebel Akhdar, but without success. The rebels for their part set about bringing in more men and arms, and mounted an increasingly active programme of covert mine-laying on the roads at the foot of the Jebel which took a growing toll of military vehicles and seriously inhibited the drilling work of the oil company. The instability was dangerous; and the British Government, anxious to avoid being drawn in again directly, agreed to support the further build-up of the Sultan's forces, including the appointment for the first time of a serving British officer to command them.

Regaining the Jebel Akhdar
Up till this time only one European had ever penetrated the Jebel Akhdar – Wellsted in the 1830s (See p 121). It had however been extensively overflown by the RAF, who had identified a number of scalable approaches to the inhabited plateau some 20 miles by 10 in extent, surrounded by vertiginous cliffs and crags. Most could be climbed only in single file. A few only could be passed by donkeys carrying loads. The climb took several hours and in many places involved long flights of rock steps. All had points where they were overlooked and were likely to be militarily suicidal. Moreover all supplies, crucially water, would have to be carried with them by any force making the ascent. The initial probes of some of these ways up the mountain by Omani forces, involving minor skirmishes with rebels, learned important lessons, but progress was minimal.

Late in 1957 Sultan Sa'id decided that a more determined and structured effort had to be made to try to break through to the plateau. The British Government agreed to the renewed deployment of two squadrons of the Trucial Oman Scouts to piquet the mountains on either side of the wadi through which the Northern Frontier Regiment (NFR) would pass to seize a supposed water hole. Once this was done tribal supporters organised by Sayyid Tariq would move through to occupy a foothold on the plateau itself. The piquets climbed successfully into position but arrangements to supply them, above all with water, broke down. One of the two British officers with the NFR got lost at night and was presumed dead (though this happily turned out a day or so later to be wrong). Water supplies for this force too were inadequate and the operation was aborted.

Efforts to make an impact on the rebels by intense bombing were equally unsuccessful. The villages were off limits to the RAF because of the civilian occupants, and there were many caves in which the rebels could shelter. For some months the initiative lay with them as they built up their resources and developed their mining and bombing campaigns with the support of tribesmen in the villages below. The Batinah coastal area on the opposite side of the Jebel Akhdar from Nizwa had been denuded of troops. Security was in the hands of the Sultan's walis and of tribal leaders, many of whom actively or passively turned a blind eye to rebel reinforcement through the area. The rebels also enjoyed significant support in the Gulf port of Sharjah, which was ironically also the base for the Trucial Oman Scouts and the RAF aircraft operating over the Jebel. One daring rebel operation involved the assembly in Sharjah of some forty rebels and a quantity of modern equipment from Saudi Arabia. The party set off from Sharjah in a three ton truck, unloaded it close to the Omani border and infiltrated men and equipment across on foot with pack animals while the empty truck drove through the Sultanate's customs post. Reloaded, it drove openly through the Sultanate to the foot of the Jebel, at times challenged by security forces. The Commander of the Sultan's Armed forces in person joined the chase but the truck eluded them and its occupants duly climbed the Jebel to reinforce the rebels.

In the meantime, despite the permanent stationing of a Trucial Oman Scouts squadron at Izki, where the Wadi Sumail road from Muscat emerges onto the flatter area round Nizwa, mining became a daily occurrence, taking a steady toll of military vehicles, if only limited human casualties, as the mines available at that time were fairly small American anti-personnel mines with limited capacity to penetrate even soft-skinned vehicles. Measures to deter mine-laying, often carried out by local villagers, by reprisals against their villages, had little effect. In mid-1958 the rebels became more daring. They planted a bomb at an oil company store near Muscat, and they also succeeded in detonating a bomb at the home of the Foreign Minister Neil Innes in Muscat itself as he was about to entertain the Political Resident in the Persian Gulf, Sir Bernard Burrows, to dinner.

From late in 1957, after the failure of the initial probes against the Jebel Akhdar, both Sultan Sa'id and the British Government could see that the status quo was precarious and likely to worsen. The Sultan had just two effective regiments of troops, the Muscat Regiment and the Northern Frontier Regiment. Their officers were a handful of British officers directly employed under contract. Apart from the Trucial Oman Scouts their only British support was the Ferret armoured cars (where the 13th/18th Hussars had replaced the 15th/19th), a few signallers, and one Royal Marine officer and a handful of NCOs attached to the Northern Frontier Regiment to improve its operational effectiveness. The RAF was invaluable in support but could not secure or hold ground alone.

For the British Government it was becoming important to find a way of putting an end to the revolt without further deployment of British troops on a scale that would bring down a torrent of international criticism. The Trucial Oman Scouts, where all the soldiers were Arabs, were less sensitive than British units. Sultan Sa'id and the British Government appreciated however that the key requirement was to strengthen the Omani armed forces. In January 1958 Prime Minister Harold Macmillan sent his son-in-law Julian Amery, Minister of State at the War Office, and himself a veteran of World War Two Special Forces operations, to Muscat. There ensued a series of negotiations, concluded with an exchange of letters when Sultan Sa'id was in London that summer. The British Government persuaded him to relinquish control of Gwadar, the Omani enclave on the coast of Baluchistan, and to accept the need to begin to tackle seriously the issue of real economic development in the hope that oil, which was not in the end discovered in commercial quantities for several years, would provide the necessary finance. In return Sultan Sa'id was to receive financial support to fund the expansion of his army and the creation of a small air force, some modern equipment, and the provision of seconded British Army officers in key positions. In the summer of 1958 Colonel Pat Waterfield, who had acted as the Sultan's overall commander in Muscat in 1957, gave way to Colonel David Smiley. Smiley, from the Household Cavalry, had been on special operations in Yugoslavia with Amery a decade earlier and was Amery's personal choice for the job. He remained in Oman for three years and in the 1960s played a crucial role in the so-called 'Secret War' in the Yemen.

It was rapidly clear to Smiley, on his arrival in Oman, that the forces available to him were barely sufficient to contain the rebels and not enough to prevent mine-laying, let alone assault the Jebel Akhdar. To help deal with the mine-laying, it was agreed that the two troops of Ferrets of the 13th/18th Hussars would be replaced by a full squadron of the Life Guards, which arrived in September. However, turning the tables on Talib and Sulaiman bin Himyar clearly necessitated an assault on the Jebel Akhdar itself. Various plans involving British forces of different strengths were formulated and discussed during the autumn of 1958. Smiley finally presented a plan for an assault by a Brigade with two British battalions, one to be either from the Royal Marines or the Parachute Regiment. This was rejected by Ministers in London in October.

Arrival of the SAS

A number of alternative options were then considered by Smiley and others. The 22nd SAS Regiment was at that time coming to the end of several years of operations in Malaya and, in a period of army cuts following Defence Secretary Duncan Sandys's post-Suez White Paper, was frankly looking for a role. Oman was to form not one but two significant chapters in the SAS's subsequent history. Smiley spotted an opportunity to use one squadron in Oman on its return journey from Malaya to Britain. On 18 November 1958 D Squadron under Major Johnny Watts, who was to feature prominently in Oman three times over a thirty year period, arrived in Oman. Three weeks before they had been in the jungle on the Malay-Thai border.

A crucial first step had taken place before their arrival. A patrol of the Muscat Regiment had discovered an unguarded route on to the Jebel. It led from the village of Hijar near Awabi and involved six hours' hard climbing and the ascent of 80 steps cut into the rock face by Persian

239

attackers 1000 years earlier. Crucially it could be negotiated by donkeys. A week after their arrival the SAS climbed the track by night and established themselves, despite opposition, on the Jebel. A firm foothold was then created, held by the Muscat Regiment supported by mortars from the Trucial Oman Scouts and machine guns dismounted from their Ferrets by the Life Guards.

It was judged however that the combined British and Omani forces available were still insufficient to clear the Jebel. In January 1959, Lt Col Anthony Deane Drummond, Commanding Officer of 22 SAS, arrived with an additional squadron. A number of brisk engagements took place with the rebels in the next few weeks, both on the Jebel from the base above Kamah, and in the area around Tanuf (Sulaiman bin Himyar's home village) where there was a significant concentration of rebels. Their attacks were beaten back only with difficulty. It was decided that surprise could best be achieved by an assault from the south, the opposite side of the Jebel from Awabi (see map on page 242). Successful deception tactics (notably broad hints deliberately dropped to tribal donkey drivers) convinced the rebels that the now inevitable SAS assault would be launched from the Tanuf area. In fact, after a 24 hour delay due to weather, it was launched on the night of 26 January up an untried route near Hijar which the rebels had guarded with just one outpost manned by only two defenders.

Final assault on the Jebel Akhdar

Surprise was effectively achieved. Opposition was light. It is as a physical feat, a barely credible climb against the clock, that the operation is principally remembered. After a climb of nine and a half hours the SAS were firmly established on the Jebel with resupply possible by air. By mid-morning the two squadrons, one having had to ditch most of their equipment and the other to use ropes to access the base of a high ridge, had consolidated in a single position. Elements of the NFR and the Life Guards followed them up onto the Jebel. Over the next few days patrols of the SAS and the Sultan's Armed Forces pushed out across the rest of the Jebel, the rebels and their leaders melted away, and the villages on the plateau were brought for the first time under the direct control of Sultan Sa'id.

36. The Cameronians in camp, 1957

37. RAF Shackleton over Jebel Akhdar

38. SAS on Jebel Akhdar 1959

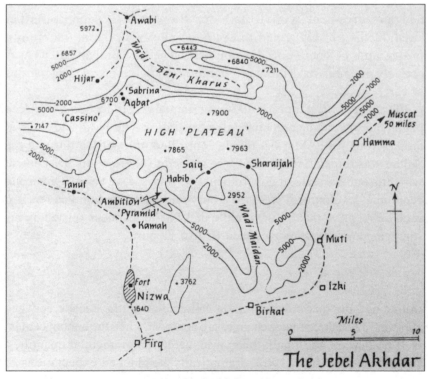

39. Jebel Akhdar map

CHAPTER 16

Downward to deposition (1959-1970)

By early 1959 the threat of a revival of the Imamate was much reduced and never renewed. Sultan Sa'id's position was more secure than any Ruler in Muscat had known for 50 years or more. He had an agreement with Britain for the latter to support further strengthening of his armed forces in parallel with the initiation of a programme of economic development. The oil company PDO was actively pursuing its drilling programme with widespread expectations of early success.

Eleven years later, in early 1970, substantial oil production had indeed begun but in Britain and Oman alike frustration with Sa'id had reached a dangerous level. Marxist rebels controlled most of Dhofar and the Sultan was refusing to do what was needed to reverse this. Discontent with him and his style of government was widespread across Oman and economic development was still embryonic. The situation had reached such a low point that by the middle of 1970 he had been ousted by his son in a coup which enjoyed tacit British support.

* * * * * * *

In tracing how this transformation came about in the decade between 1960 and 1970 three major changes are apparent. First, the announcement in 1964 that oil had finally been discovered in commercial quantities, and would flow from 1967, dramatically heightened expectations of improved lives among Omanis, many of whom had been working in other Gulf states and so had first-hand experience of what this could mean. Second, Harold Wilson's Labour Government in Britain took two major policy decisions: to withdraw from Aden at the end of 1967 and, as soon as this had taken place, to withdraw militarily from the whole Gulf area by the end of 1971. Third, the nature of the international threat to Oman changed radically. Relatively low level support from Saudi Arabia and Egypt for the Imamate leaders had been seen off in the 1950s with British backing. In the 1960s it was replaced by something quite different.

Until the early 1960s British control in Aden and the Aden Protectorates effectively sealed off any external threat to southern Oman. Nationalist and Marxist forces gradually made the British position in Aden untenable and, after British withdrawal in 1967, Dhofar became Oman's soft underbelly. Saudi Arabia on the other hand fell out with Egypt over developments in Yemen, to the north of Aden, and became a supporter of the status quo rather than an agitator for change in the east of the Arabian Peninsula. With the prospect of British military withdrawal from the Gulf in 1971, the creation of architecture which would maintain stability in the region, including Oman, became an increasingly urgent priority not only in London, but also in Washington. The stakes became greater than the nature of government in Oman. Dhofar became an active manifestation of Cold War rivalries, with Russian, Chinese, Cuban and East German support for the rebels matched against active British support for the Sultanate. Washington and London came to fear that, if Dhofar and with it Oman fell under Communist control, the Trucial States (not yet formed into the Emirates) would be perilously vulnerable, and even the eastern parts of Saudi Arabia, with their huge reserves of oil, would be at risk. (The conduct of the Dhofar War is described in chapters 18 and 19.)

Sultan Sa'id, now in his 50s, failed to adjust to these challenges. From 1958 he ruled by choice exclusively from his palace in Salalah and never visited Muscat again. "Rule" is the right word. The issue was not neglect but a rigid determination to keep all the levers of power in his own hands despite his remoteness, working by radio telephone through a tiny group of Omani and expatriate advisers. He constantly kept his foot on the brake of development, both because of ingrained financial caution, and because he judged, accurately enough, that significant development would be incompatible with the kind of minimal state he sought to maintain. He had become reclusive, mistrustful, and controlling. He regarded Dhofar as his personal fiefdom and, in contrast with his sophisticated methods of dealing with tribal Shaikhs in northern Oman, treated the Dhofaris, including their tribal leaders, autocratically. The initial seeds of revolt in Dhofar in the mid-1960s were largely due to his highhandedness. His obstinacy, and his resentment of British tutelage which went right back to his accession in 1930-31, also continued to drive his behaviour. He was a great procrastinator. People who dealt with him recorded that his most frequent reaction to an idea for change was 'I see'. The uninitiated interpreted this as a preliminary to action: the experienced became familiar with reading it as 'I understand but have no intention of doing it'.

British relationships with Sultan Sa'id became increasingly frustrating, both for Ministers in London and for the 'men on the spot' in Bahrain and Muscat who had to conduct them with him. Dealings mostly concerned four issues: the nature of the state and government in Oman, Oman's capacity to maintain her own security without again sucking in British forces, diplomatic defence of the Omani-British relationship, and the pace of development.

Sultan Sa'id's views on the appropriate nature of the Omani state began to diverge sharply from those of his British interlocutors. The Sultan had spent the first 25 years of his reign seeking to assert his authority over the tribal heartland of northern Oman. So long as Imam Muhammad al-Khalili lived, little changed. Behind the minimal leadership of the Imam, the two tamimas who stood at the pinnacles of the great tribal confederations which had persisted since the 17th century, Sheikh 'Isa bin Salih and Sheikh Sulaiman bin Himyar, were effectively impregnable. In 1954 they permitted if not encouraged the selection of an Imam of much less spiritual repute and sought to sustain their position with Saudi and Egyptian support. This gave Sa'id the opportunity over the next five years gradually to assert his authority with British support. He had no intention however of replacing the basically tribal basis of governance with the bureaucratic apparatus of the modern state. He successfully rendered impotent the two tamimas (who were both in exile), and with them the two confederations. He believed profoundly nonetheless in the continuance of governance of local tribal communities

245

through their individual Shaikhs. The power of the state, which basically meant himself with his network of *wālīs* (governors) and *qāḍīs* (judges), was largely limited to the arbitration of frictions and disputes, with all major issues running back to him personally over the radio telephone line to Salalah.

In 1959 the British Government's principal concern in Oman was to ensure that the Imamate threat did not revive with Saudi support and again threaten British interests not just within Oman but elsewhere in the Gulf. This in turn required in their eyes more proactive government and development in interior Oman up to and including the border with Saudi Arabia. In one sense the 1959 Jebel Akhdar operation had failed. The rebel leaders were neither killed nor captured. They soon became diplomatically active again within the Arab world, and the British view of the risk of a renewed revolt within Oman was less sanguine than Sultan Sa'id's. There were sharp exchanges in 1959-60 about the treatment of the tribesmen on the Jebel Akhdar, the British view that he should seek a political accommodation with the rebel leaders, and the need to strengthen governance and development amongst the other tribes of northern Oman. At one stage in 1959 the British Government was considering involving itself directly, as it had at Seeb in 1920, to broker a new agreement – the Treaty of Nizwa – between the Sultan and the rebels. The Sultan for his part was obdurate. He would have nothing to do with any confederation of tribes and would allow the rebel leaders to return only to resume their positions as Shaikhs within their own individual tribes.

On the risk of a renewed Imamate revolt Sultan Sa'id's instinct, held from 1959, that the threat would not be reactivated with the same degree of vigour, proved accurate. The Saudis continued to provide training and equipment for low-level but irritating mining and bombing campaigns within Oman until 1962. From 1960 there was also a series of attacks launched by the 'Oman Resistance Movement' outside Oman. Of these the two most serious were the blowing up of a Gulf Air DC3 en route to Sharjah in July 1960 with the loss of thirteen lives, and, much more spectacularly and tragically, the sinking of the British India Line ship SS *Dara* off Dubai en route for Muscat in April 1962, in which 338 people died. A major blow to the rebels' activities was the interception of a dhow in July 1962 by HMS *Loch Ruthven* off Suwaiq on the Batinah coast and the capture of five rebels and a substantial quantity of arms. Information from those captured led to a series of operations over the next six months which effectively broke the back of the rebel structures developed within Oman since 1959. By the time the revolt in Dhofar began to gather pace from 1964 the Imamate threat to the security of northern Oman had effectively ended.

The British and the Sultan diverge

Sultan Sa'id's approach was rooted firmly in the assumption that the British would for their own interests continue to provide the wherewithal for him to maintain internal security against any tribal indiscipline. They would also, he assumed, come to his aid to ensure the defeat of any externally supported threat. To a degree these were accurate assumptions in the 1960s. At the same time, from the late 1950s the British authorities had an increasingly divergent view of what Sultan Sa'id should be doing to fulfil his side of the bargain. Most centrally the Macmillan Government was determined that Oman would in the future have to ensure her own security without British military intervention. There was to be no repeat of 1957.

The field in which Sultan Sa'id's views and those of the British authorities intersected most clearly was thus the strengthening of Oman's armed forces. The need to create adequate forces to maintain internal security without British involvement was apparent from the events of 1957-1959. This was a period in which British military activity elsewhere in the Gulf was increasing. British troops were deployed to support Kuwait against threatened Iraqi invasion in 1961. The 1962 Defence White Paper was the basis for an increase in permanently deployed forces in Bahrain and Sharjah. Following the 1959 Jebel Akhdar operation Brigadier Hope Johnson was sent to Muscat to oversee an assessment of what the future strength of Oman's armed forces should be. This served as the basis for a major Cabinet level policy review in 1960 in which the need to be able to reinforce Kuwait without overflying Iraq or Saudi Arabia was a critical concern. This looked at and rejected several radical options: disengagement, allowing the recreation of a separate 'state' in the interior, and guaranteeing the Sultan's security but without a programme of support for the build-up of his own forces. All of these were considered to involve unacceptable risks to regional British interests.

The outcome was agreement in August 1960 between the Sultan and the Lord Privy Seal, Edward Heath, on an enhanced version of the Amery programme for civil and military development and a bigger British financial subsidy to enable it to happen. The two existing infantry battalions were to be expanded into a force of some 2300 with many more Omani recruited soldiers to reduce the dependence on Baluchis, with both seconded and contract British officers in command positions above platoon level. The small Air Force, initially of three piston-engined Provosts and two Pioneer light transport aircraft, which had been agreed in the Amery negotiations of 1958, became operational in 1960. The critical weakness of the Batinah coast as an easy route for rebels to smuggle in men and weapons was plugged with the creation of the Gendarmerie, later converted to become an additional infantry battalion. The first seeds of the Royal Omani Navy were also planted in this period with the commissioning of a British-officered coastal patrol boat.

British deployments to Oman in the 1960s were frequent but not operational. An important element of the 1958 Exchange of Letters following the Amery negotiations had been Sultan Sa'id's agreement for the RAF to use the base on Masirah Island for 100 years. Some of the sorties flown in support of operations on the Jebel Akhdar were flown from Masirah, though the majority came from Sharjah or from aircraft carriers in the Gulf of Oman. Masirah was however an important element in British strategic thinking in relation to the Gulf, the Indian Ocean, and routes to South East Asia and the Far East. Both Masirah and Salalah were given concrete runways for the first time in the 1960s, as was Sharjah. Nuclear-armed Vulcan bombers deployed regularly from Cyprus to Masirah. Oman was also used regularly for exercises from the enhanced base at Bahrain, notably by the Parachute Regiment. All of this was welcome to Sultan Sa'id as a demonstration to his own people and the wider international community that Britain's military underpinning of the Sultanate remained intact.

Supported only by Brigadier Waterfield, who had become effectively the Minister of Defence when Colonel Smiley was appointed to command the Sultan's Armed Forces in 1958, the Sultan personally conducted the negotiation of these arrangements down to the last detail, of which he showed an amazing grasp. Many of the discussions were in London and Ministers in the Conservative Government – Selwyn Lloyd as Foreign Secretary and John Profumo as Secretary of State for War as well as Heath – found themselves negotiating with an experienced and wily leader with a very clear sense that he held more cards in his hand than his British interlocutors. Though the Sultan's regular visits to London came to an end after 1964 these detailed discussions with Sultan Sa'id became an annual event until the British subsidy was terminated, at Treasury insistence, in 1967, shortly before oil revenues began to flow.

An issue on which the Sultan remained absolutely firm till the last year or so of his reign was his expectation that the nature of his relationship with Britain meant that she would conduct his foreign affairs for him. This was the corollary of the expectation that Britain would defend him against both internal and particularly external threats. It was rooted in his experience in 1953 when Britain overrode his plans to resist the Saudi incursion into Buraimi. Thereafter Buraimi was for him a British problem and he was extremely reluctant to be drawn into any face-to-face dealings with the Saudis or indeed the other Gulf Rulers. Apart from an Indian Consul, the British Consul General was the only diplomatic representative in Muscat; and he reported to the Foreign Office through the Political Resident Persian Gulf, now based in Bahrain. Sultan Sa'id never left Oman again after his visit to London in 1964, and virtually never received foreign visitors. Oman's only 'diplomatic representative' overseas was Charles Kendall, a British businessman who handled much of the Sultan's procurement in Britain and was appointed Consul in 1964.There had been two successive British 'Foreign Ministers' between 1948 and 1958, and subsequently an uncle of the Sultan, Sayyid Shihāb, held the title. The post-holders' purview was however limited to the recruitment of British contract officers, the administration of Gwadar, and, under Shihab, the issue of passports and permissions to travel. They certainly did not deal with other foreign governments.

The "Question of Oman" at the United Nations
After the Imamate leaders were forced to leave Oman in 1959 they spent much of the next decade pursuing, often at loggerheads with each other, campaigns based in Saudi Arabia, Egypt, Syria or Iraq, to promote the case for the Imamate and to maximise international criticism of Britain and the Sultan .The Sultan regarded it as no responsibility of his to deal with these pressures. He would have nothing to do with the Imamate

leaders and would accord them no status beyond their immediate tribal group if they returned to Oman. Between 1958 and 1971 'the question of Oman', pursued at length in New York at the UN, thus became an on-going responsibility of British diplomacy. The argument revolved around the Agreement of Seeb of 1920 and whether it acknowledged the Imamate as a separate state. If so, did it render illegal the measures taken by the Sultan and the British to suppress the Imamate in the mid-1950s? Opponents of the Sultan and the British Government argued that an Imamate state should be created and recognised, and that Oman was in effect a British colony and thus a legitimate subject of concern both of the UN and of the strong body of anti-colonial opinion articulated in New York.

The most threatening diplomatic attack came in the form of an effort to put the issue on the agenda of the Security Council in 1958. This was only narrowly defeated, with the United States abstaining. Opponents had more success in getting it regularly inscribed on the agenda of the General Assembly each year from 1959 to 1971. Resistance to these moves became a major, and highly frustrating, responsibility for the British UN Mission in New York, who were often in a small minority, forced to use up valuable and limited credit with other delegations, and thoroughly irritated by the Sultan's refusal to lift a finger to appoint anyone else to speak for Oman. The issue was on different occasions remitted to other UN Committees such as the Political Committee. In 1962-3 Herbert de Ribbing, the Swedish Ambassador to Spain, was appointed by Dag Hammarskjoeld, the UN Secretary General, to examine the situation. He had previously been a scrupulously fair and unbiased UN mediator on the Buraimi issue and was acceptable both to the British Government and the Sultan. He visited London, Oman, and Saudi Arabia. His report broadly endorsed the views put forward by Sultan Sa'id and by Britain, and he also recommended UN assistance for development. This did not however satisfy the opposition in New York and at Arab insistence an 'ad hoc' Committee was set up in December 1963, with membership from Afghanistan, Costa Rica, Nepal, Nigeria, and Senegal. The Committee visited a number of Arab capitals and London, but Sultan Sa'id refused to receive them in Oman on the grounds that de Ribbing had settled the issue. Their report in January 1965 was predictably more negative. They concluded that Oman was indeed an international issue as a result of 'imperialistic policies and foreign intervention'. The General Assembly 'noted' the report, but took no further action, and the annual discussion led to no further initiatives in succeeding years.

Slow economic development in the Sultanate

If security and foreign policy were areas of broad agreement between Sultan Sa'id and the British authorities in the first half of the 1960s, the pace and direction of development certainly was not. The Sultan was not necessarily the cynical and uninterested Ruler he has sometimes been made out to be. He was strongly influenced by his wish to sustain Oman as a tribally organised society, and by his long practised financial prudence. He also retained to the end a deep conviction that to allow educated Omanis to return from overseas to take over key civil or military positions from Britons and Indians or Pakistanis would inevitably undermine his position and the kind of state he was determined to maintain. He described his views on development to the American oil man and archaeologist Wendell Phillips in 1958. 'Certain conditions in Oman inherited from the past are not really my fault, and if I do not have the funds to change these conditions, where change is desired, that is still not my fault. If however I do have the means and do not improve my people and my country then I should be ashamed.' By 1970 many believed that that was exactly the situation, and that he should indeed be ashamed.

Realistic about Sultan Sa'id's inhibitions on development, Julian Amery had insisted in 1958 on the creation of a development budget and the appointment of a Development Adviser, as a balance to British commitment of further military support. Britain also assumed that the money recently received from Pakistan for the cession of Gwadar could be applied to kick-start the development process, but the Sultan was equally firm that he wanted to use it to build up Oman's reserves and, as usual on financial matters, he prevailed. For the post of Development Adviser the British Government nominated Colonel (later Sir) Hugh Boustead, an Arabic speaker who had brought about great change over the previous decade in an area of the East Aden Protectorate with a comparable tribal society and a comparable level of poverty. The problems in Oman were huge: a representative of the British Government's Middle East Development Division told Sultan Sa'id that in 20 years' experience he had never seen a people so poverty stricken, or so debilitated by diseases capable of treatment and cure.

Boustead had an annual budget of £250,000 from the British Government but was deeply frustrated by Sultan Sa'id's constant wish to control and slow down the programme. He threw himself into his role with huge personal enthusiasm, spending much of his time away from his desk overseeing road building and negotiating with tribal leaders. There were particular arguments with Sa'id over the villages on the Jebel Akhdar, where there was keen British appreciation that enhancing the standard of living of the villagers was the best insurance against renewed temptation to harbour rebels, while the Sultan refused to be seen to be rewarding rather than penalising those who had done just that in 1958-59. He refused outright to allow Boustead to be involved. After three years Boustead was glad to accept a proposal that he should move to Abu Dhabi as Political Agent. His legacy was a Department with 122 staff, and embryonic road building, health, agriculture and educational programmes.

After a brief and unsuccessful interregnum, Boustead was succeeded by Major D N R Ogram, who held the post from the end of December 1962 until British funding for the post was withdrawn in March 1967. Ogram was much more sympathetic to Sultan Sa'id's views on the right pace of progress. 'The most important principle', he wrote in reviewing his period of office 'is that the rate of progress should not be too rapid.' This he justified, again echoing the Sultan, on the grounds that there were insufficient Omanis to run a major programme, and a large influx of migrants could undermine traditional values and be politically unsettling. The work of the Department was carried on a British budget until the subsidy ended in 1967. Thereafter the Sultan's control over it became even tighter. By then it had overseen the construction of some 600 kilometres of graded road, nine health centres, two experimental farms and a single school in Muscat.

After the British Government's review of 1960 and the decision to extend the subsidy there was effectively an annual three-sided negotiation between the Treasury, the Foreign Office and the Sultan about its continuation, its level, and the balance between military and civil expenditure. The Sultan constantly emphasised the military, the British side the civil. On one occasion the Sultan testily commented that, while denying him funds for what he regarded as essential military expenditure, the British were forcing on him more money for civil projects than he could appropriately (in his eyes) use. Successive Political Residents and Consuls General in this period expressed their frustration with the Sultan's capacity to slow down and postpone the start of the most basic civil projects. From 1964 the two programmes were separated, the civil projects being funded from the budget of the Overseas Development Administration, controlled by the Foreign Office, whereas the Treasury kept its stranglehold on the level of the subsidy, and with it the military programmes. In 1965, once Shell had announced the commencement of oil production in 1967, the Treasury insisted that the subsidy should come to an end at the end of the 1966-7 financial year. In all these negotiations the Sultan insisted that his own contribution could only be minimal because his other revenues were insufficient to do much more than meet the other expenditure of his minimal state. The British Government believed that he was understating the surpluses he was in fact making but, short of accusing him directly, they had insufficient evidence to prove this because the Sultan resolutely refused to divulge, even to them, the details of his budget and expenditure.

Up to 1967 Sultan Sa'id had some justification for the position he took because of the failure for some years of oil exploration to discover oil in commercial quantities. This is dealt with at greater length in chapter 17. Suffice to say here that at the beginning of the decade the British authorities shared the expectation and assumption, based on oil company predictions, that oil, and therefore oil revenues, would be flowing early in the1960s. In the event it was 1964 before Shell announced that proven reserves had been discovered, and 1967 before the necessary pipeline had been built and oil began to flow. Thereafter Sa'id did begin to move slowly to put in place the machinery to utilise the consequent revenues. A Development Board was set up in place of the Development Department 'to execute such plans as we decide upon' and a Secretary to the Board and a Development Director were appointed. These plans were accompanied by the issue of a lengthy document, written by the Sultan himself, entitled 'The words of Sultan Sa'id about the history of the financial position of the Sultanate in the past and the hopes for the future' which set out his defence of the slow progress of the previous 38 years, and his aspirations for the future, still however stressing that there would be a gap before significant benefits began to appear. By this time however measures which would have seemed of an appropriate scale and ambition in the early years of the decade seemed too little too late.

In the middle of the 1960s Sultan Sa'id might have viewed with some satisfaction the evolution of his tussle with his British 'partners' on these issues – the nature of the state, dealing with rebels and foreign critics, and the funding of civil and military development. Oman was being ruled to his prescription. Two of his brothers, Sayyid Tāriq and Sayyid Fahr, who had favoured more active policies of change, had retired into self-imposed exile. The pace of development was being slowed to what he deemed acceptable. Efforts by the Imamate leaders to rebuild a significant following within Oman seemed to have run definitively into the sand. Diplomatic pressure at the UN was contained if not repulsed. The main cloud on the horizon was already unrest in Dhofar, which entered into a new and more organised phase with the first Congress of the Dhofar Liberation Front in 1965.

Three years later the picture looked very different. The Dhofar rebellion is examined in more detail in chapter 18. By 1968 it had passed from being a largely tribal uprising with Arab nationalist support to being an ideologically Marxist campaign actively managed and supported from Aden with the involvement of several Communist Governments. In April 1966 a rebel infiltrated into Sultan Sa'id's personal Dhofar Security Force had come within a whisker of a successful assassination attempt. Sa'id's governance by remote control through his small group of Omani and expatriate advisers was increasingly resented. Expectations for development remained largely unfulfilled though oil revenues were now known to be coming in. Returning Omani workers were increasingly reluctant to accept the limitations of the tribal state. The risks from disaffection in the north as well as the south were growing. His brother Sayyid Tariq, from exile, and his son Sayyid Qaboos, despite being cut off from contact with the outside world in Salalah, began to discuss alternative ways forward.

British involvement in the Sultan's administration
Before we turn to the events of 1970 and the end of Sultan Sa'id's reign, it is worth summarising who from Britain was involved on the ground in Oman in various elements of the very particular set of relationships which

existed during the 1960s. Before the mid-1950s the number of Britons anywhere in Oman was tiny: the Consul General, the Commander of the Muscat Infantry, and a handful of advisers to the Sultan. The relationship with Britain was critical to what happened in Oman outside the territories of the Imamate but was almost totally intergovernmental. Until the British Bank of the Middle East (BBME) was permitted to open in 1948 there were no British businesses, though there was a significant number of merchants and businessmen from British India, both Muslim and Hindu. There were tiny RAF detachments at the staging posts in Salalah and Masirah. The 1950s saw a significant expansion, particularly of contract officers helping with the build-up of the Sultan's Armed Forces, and the exploration staff of the oil company. After 1958 and the conclusion of the 'Amery Agreement', additional civilian advisers, like Boustead, and the first Loan Service Officers on secondment from the British Army and RAF began to arrive. Loan Service numbers were in the low 30s in the first instance, but increased later in the 1960s with the additional demands of the Dhofar War. Oil company numbers had also increased sharply. But both these groups lived entirely away from the Omani community as a whole and interacted only with their Omani counterparts. The numbers also remained very small by comparison with the influx (from Britain and elsewhere) following Sultan Qaboos's accession in 1970.

Notable among the handful of Britons dealing directly with the Sultan were Waterfield, who was his right hand man in all the negotiations about military matters, and Leslie Chauncy, described as Principal Adviser, who had been a long serving Consul General in the 1950s and returned to Oman in 1961. Both were among the very small group who had frequent radio telephone discussions with the Sultan in Salalah. Chauncy was regarded by his successors a decade later as someone who shared with the Sultan an Indian background and who encouraged his inclination to live in the past and change only by minuscule and incremental steps. The British Commanders of the Sultan's Armed Forces (SAF) also dealt directly with the Sultan on operational matters, more frequently once operations in Dhofar got seriously under way. Other Advisers such as Boustead were in direct contact much more rarely, and in some cases hardly at all. By the late 1960s two key business figures also dealt regularly with the Sultan: Peter Mason, the Manager of the BBME in Muscat, and Francis Hughes, the Managing Director of PDO, who found himself being turned to by the Sultan rather more than he wished. Given the very personal nature of Sultan Sa'id's rule, with so little delegated to others, the principal burden of carrying forward all the facets of the complex intergovernmental relationships fell on the Consul General, or more occasionally the Political Resident. Consuls General travelled regularly to Salalah with a long agenda of issues to raise over several days – one records a visit where he had 34 separate issues on his list. In the period between 1958 and 1964 the Sultan also visited London more or less annually and key negotiations were organised to come to a head in direct meetings with Ministers.

Pressure rises in Dhofar

By the early months of 1970 the rebels controlled all of Dhofar save the plain immediately around Salalah. Security even there was tenuous. Harrassing attacks on RAF Salalah were frequent. The chances of the rebels being able to overrun the air base and the camp of the Sultan's Armed Forces' units conducting the campaign against them were slight. But military stalemate was highly embarrassing for the Sultan, and for the British Government. In March 1970, unknown in advance to the Sultan, the Commanding Officer of 22 SAS Regiment, Lt Col John Watts (who as a Major had won an MC on the Jebel Akhdar in 1959) visited Dhofar. His conclusions were stark. No progress would be made until the population was given some reason to support the Sultan and his forces rather than the rebels. Humanitarian activity and development needed to go forward alongside military action. Sultan Sa'id summarily rejected these conclusions. He showed no sign of varying his hard line approach not just to the rebels but to the population as a whole in the rebel-held areas. 'Those people on the Jebel are very bad. I want you to kill them all' were his words to the new seconded Commander of the Sultan's Armed Forces, Brigadier John Graham, when he paid his initial call on the Sultan. The weak military position was also in good measure the Sultan's doing. He had for several years refused to authorise the additional infantry battalion and helicopter force which his commanders believed were essential if the tide was to be turned. He had finally relented in late 1969 but improvements were still in the pipeline.

Early in 1970, Ministers in London reviewed the Dhofar situation and the policy to be followed in Oman, and concluded that a serious and high-level official approach, perhaps to be followed by a ministerial visit, should be made to Sultan Saʻid, in order to extract from him a commitment to development of his country and reform of his Government. At one stage in the official correspondence this was called the "grand remonstrance", later considered as "too minatory" a term and tempered to "Oman review". Acting on carefully written instructions, Sir Stewart Crawford, the Political Resident Persian Gulf, travelled to Salalah to make this further attempt to persuade Sultan Saʻid to change his approach, but to little avail. The British authorities, preoccupied with the implementation of withdrawal from the Gulf by the end of 1970, and the legacy they would leave, were now additionally alarmed by evidence of growing discontent in the rest of Oman, driven by resentment at Saʻid's isolation in Salalah, the continuation of petty restrictions on travel, and the absence of discernible benefits from the flow of oil money. Much of the discontent was passive but Sultan Saʻid did nothing to rally even the tribal leaders on whom his view of Oman depended. More ominously, an organised Iraqi-backed group, the National Democratic Front for Liberation of Oman and the Arab Gulf (NDFLOAG) had emerged among Omanis who had left the country for work or for education. A significant number of these had been radicalised or ended up in Communist countries as a result of Saʻid's refusal to allow Britain and the US to offer educational places to them. Sayyid Tariq, the Sultan's exiled brother, was known to be in touch with this group. Intelligence assessments were however that, at a time when the armed forces were seriously stretched by operations in Dhofar, an active uprising was unlikely.

It came therefore as a serious shock when, on 12 June 1970, explosions were set off at the Muscat Regiment's base in Nizwa, and rockets and machine gun fire were directed at the Northern Frontier Regiment's (NFR) camp at Izki. The NFR gave chase to the dozen attackers and, as a result of some exemplary basic soldiering, eleven of the twelve were killed or captured as they tried to escape into the Jebel. Interrogation of the prisoners led to the identification and arrest of large numbers of other NDFLOAG supporters across northern Oman. Sayyid Tariq later revealed to Brigadier Graham that the attacks had been intended as the first steps in a campaign to neutralise the army and its leadership, including the killing of British officers, to remove the main obstacle to a successful general uprising.

Sa'id's system of rule ensured that it was very difficult to make any move against him other than rebellion or assassination. There was effectively no political process. The activities of NDFLOAG apart, the reputation of his intelligence system ensured that most people kept their views well concealed.

The need for action

Within Oman the one person who could act was Sayyid Qaboos. Born in 1940, he had been sent ten years earlier to Britain, first to learn English with a clergyman in Suffolk, and then to Sandhurst. Following a short attachment to learn something of local government, and an attachment of several months to the Cameronians in Germany, he returned to Salalah. Apart from a world tour in 1964, escorted by Leslie Chauncy, the Sultan's senior British Adviser, he was kept cut off not only from other Omanis but from his father, with no involvement in public affairs, and was permitted few and controlled contacts with Omanis or expatriates. British officials repeatedly raised with the Sultan the desirability of Qaboos learning more of the rest of his country, and getting experience in governance. Sa'id equally regularly recognised the strength of the argument but never got to the point of making any specific arrangement. The point was never pushed. The issue of succession was not on the agenda and the Sultan himself was only in his early fifties.

Sayyid Qaboos himself was clearly aware of the deteriorating situation from the few Omani friends permitted to him, and from his exchanges with Captain Tim Landon, a fellow cadet at Sandhurst and now, as a contract officer, the Intelligence Officer of the Dhofar Brigade of the Sultan's Armed Forces. He also had a number of frank conversations, especially about Dhofar, with successive Political Residents and Consuls General. By the summer of 1970 plans for a move against his father were well under way. The events of 12 June in the north were probably a catalyst in terms of the timing of his move.

On the British side the Political Resident was writing in June of a possible Ministerial visit to Salalah in the autumn as the next step in trying to persuade the Sultan to change his policies. By early July however it was clear to Brigadier Graham that Sayyid Qaboos intended to remove his father. His two principal Omani supporters in Salalah were

Shaikh Braik bin Mahmoud, the son of the Sultan's *wālī* in Dhofar, and Shaikh Hilal bin Sultan al-Hosni, the commander of half of the armed guard force at the Sultan's Palace, who came from the al-Hosni tribe which had traditionally provided men for this role for successive Sultans. Landon and certain other contract officers, notably Brigadier Hugh Oldman, a predecessor of Brigadier Graham's and from the beginning of 1970 the Military Secretary in Muscat in the place of Pat Waterfield, were involved in the plans. Graham and Lt Col Turnill, the Commanding Officer of the Desert Regiment based in Dhofar, were also made aware of them. As seconded British officers they were in a difficult position, but Oldman made clear to them that their primary responsibility in their current roles was to Oman not to Britain. Graham was well aware that the outcome of the planned coup would depend as much on the actions of the forces under his command as on those directly involved. Sounded out by Qaboos on what the attitude of the Armed Forces might be to a coup he replied guardedly, 'I am confident that the Armed Forces will do whatever is best for the country.' His own judgement on what that meant was clear and the messages he was getting from London through the Consul General were that he should ensure the success of any move by Qaboos. The Labour Government had lost a General Election on 14 June to the Conservatives led by Edward Heath, and Julian Amery had returned to the Government as Minister of State at the Foreign Office, so the new Government had within it at least two Ministers very familiar with Oman and with the Sultan.

On 23 July Qaboos wrote to Turnill announcing his intentions, and calling on Turnill to rally to his support in the interests of the country and the avoidance of bloodshed. Graham, who had located himself in Salalah at the critical moment, instructed him to agree. The outcome was swift. Though Sultan Sa'id had been warned of what was being planned he was caught off guard. Shaikh Hilal's men secured the Palace without intervention from the other (Baluch) element of the guard. Shaikh Braik with a small party entered by a small unguarded door, closely followed by a party from Desert Regiment led by Lt Sa'id Sālim al-Wahaibi. A few slaves who attempted to oppose them were disarmed and one was killed. Shaikh Braik's party then pursued Sultan Sa'id through the Palace. Shaikh Braik was wounded by the Sultan. Cornered in a locked room Sa'id called out that he had wounded himself by accident and was willing to surrender but only to a senior British officer. Turnill was summoned and, when Sultan Sa'id pointed a gun at him, replied 'Sir, put that gun down, I have come to save you.'

Sa'id was carried in a closed vehicle, without being identified by the crowds which had gathered, to the RAF base. There he signed an instrument of abdication and was flown on 24 July to Bahrain and subsequently to London, where he lived with a small group of personal retainers in the Dorchester Hotel till his death from a heart attack in October 1972. He and Qaboos never saw each other again.

The father's deposition, the son's accession

Though Qaboos's accession as Sultan was known and acclaimed in Salalah immediately, it was announced to the rest of Oman and the world only on 26 July. Five days later, on 31 July, Sultan Qaboos flew for the first time in his life to Muscat. A new, and still unfinished chapter in the history of Oman and in the British relationship with Oman, had begun. Oman swiftly emerged as a full member of the international community. Within 18 months the British withdrawal from the Gulf was complete and Britain was no longer in a position to act as the sole guarantor of Omani security. The relationship could no longer be the exclusive one which it had been for a century.

The story after 1970 is therefore part of a different and wider picture, in which the two Governments and peoples developed a mature and more balanced partnership in Gulf and world politics. 1970 is therefore a good date to regard as the terminal point of the series of relationships between successive Sultans and the British Indian and British authorities which we have sought to narrate. There are however two, linked points on which it is appropriate to carry the story forward. The first is the story of the Dhofar War, in which Britain was integrally engaged. This is outlined in chapters 18 and 19, and extended over the first five years of Sultan Qaboos's rule. The second, treated much more briefly, is the termination of the basing rights at Masirah and Salalah granted to Britain as part of the Amery package of 1958. Following the withdrawal from the Gulf, and once the Dhofar War was over, Britain had no more need of these and they were terminated in 1977. 1975, when the Dhofar campaign was concluded, and 1977, when Masirah was handed over, both have some claim to be the precise dates at which the unique relationships of previous decades ended and a new era began. In practical terms, however, an entirely new style of relationship came into effect from the moment of Sultan Qaboos's accession.

It was clear to British Ministers and officials, and to Omanis concerned about the future, that by 1970 Sultan Sa'id, though a known quantity and loyal to the cause of working closely to support British interests, had shown conclusively that he was no longer the man for the times. This should not detract from the achievements of the first 35 years of his reign in putting Oman back on to a financially stable position, and then reunifying it. British officials began to talk about the necessity of replacing him some ten years before his abdication, but this was as much because of his strengths in resisting British demands with which he did not agree as because of weakness. Until the Dhofar Revolt became serious his judgements that the threat from the Imamate was over, and that his version of the tribal state was working, were supported by the facts on the ground, however uneasy British officials might be about its sustainability. Until 1970 there was no alternative which would better serve British interests. At the same time his skill, tenacity and judgement in pursuit of the Omani interest in the conduct of his negotiations with British Ministers and officials cannot but command admiration.

But British doubts about him, which were shared by Government and senior officials at Shell worried about threats to the security of their operations in Oman, were well-founded in the longer term. The pressure for change from Omanis, more and more of whom were familiar with the outside world, escalated in the north and in Dhofar alike, reinforced in Dhofar by the doctrinally driven Marxist revolt. Sultan Sa'id's very traditional view that revolt should be countered by repression alone, and his vindictive streak not only towards those who had led revolt but to the communities which had supported them, had proved bankrupt; but the Sultan still adamantly refused to resile from them. Oman had in the 1960s become the last country in the Arabian peninsula to begin to move into the modern world. David Holden, a respected British writer on the area, described the country in the mid-1960s as still in a long sleep. Once the decision was made that Britain's military presence in the area would have gone by the end of 1971, Sa'id's trump card – that at the end of the day Britain needed him to sustain her interests even more than he needed them – was simply no longer valid. The loss of Dhofar, and even more damagingly the overthrow of the Sultanate by radical groups in the north of the country were both real threats. A new approach under new leadership had become imperative for Oman and Britain alike.

40. Sultan Qaboos meeting British officers, 1970

CHAPTER 17

Economic transformation – the creation of Oman's oil industry

The discovery and production of oil was to prove the major transforming factor in the politics and development of Oman in the 20th century. It became important in British and British Indian policy much later in Oman than in Iran and Iraq. From the moment that the Royal Navy became dependent on oil rather than coal in 1912 it was a major strategic concern underlying British policies. If the Anglo Persian Oil Company (later BP) and its offshoots, or the Iraq Petroleum Company (of which it was part), developed an interest in oil prospects anywhere they became a policy interest for the British authorities. In Oman that began to take place in the 1920s but did not translate into significant work on the ground till well after World War Two, led by Shell from 1960. Oil wealth only began to come on stream at the very end of the period covered in this book.

* * * * * * *

A disclaimer may be appropriate here. British military and political relationships with Oman before 1970 were more or less exclusive. The story of Oman's oil however involves not just British oil companies, and certainly not just Britons. At the same time its evolution, along with that of the oil industries of the Trucial States and Qatar, was a central thread in British assertion of its interests in the Arabian peninsula in the decades following the collapse of Ottoman power at the end of World War One.

The process was led by the Iraq Petroleum Company from London. The network of Treaties signed with the Trucial States and Oman in the late 19th century gave Britain monopoly rights over the foreign economic and political relations of the states concerned. British based companies continued to lead the development of the oil industries in these states, but the monopoly came under significant stress from the 1930s onwards from the activities of the American oil companies by then established in Saudi Arabia.

The point of departure in Oman was one in which the British Government took the precaution of concluding an agreement in 1923 with Sultan Taymur (and with other Gulf Rulers) giving Britain exclusive rights to control oil exploration in the Sultan's territories. The pioneer of British oil interests in the Gulf region had been William Knox D'Arcy who, following many ups and downs, discovered commercial quantities of oil in Southern Iran in1908. This was commercialised under the name of the Anglo-Persian Oil Company. D'Arcy died in 1917, but Anglo-Persian retained his name in that of its exploration company, the D'Arcy Exploration Company Ltd. In conformity with the 1923 Agreement with Sultan Taymur, the company signed an accord with him in 1925 which granted it a licence to explore in Oman for two years, with an option to continue for a further two. Under this agreement, in 1925-6 the D'Arcy Company sent a team under George Lees, an Irish geologist who had conducted earlier surveys for them in other parts of Arabia, to conduct the first serious evaluation of Oman's oil prospects.

This was the period of maximum British involvement in the affairs of the Sultanate. The 1923 Agreement gave the Political Agent a right of veto on where exploration could take place. Lees and his team were accompanied on part of their journey by Captain Eccles, the Commander of the Muscat State Levies, and by Bertram Thomas, the Sultan's British Finance Minister. They travelled by camel up the Batinah coast and crossed the Hajjar mountains to a point where they could look down on much of the interior plain. However, not only was much of it Imamate territory, and thus not under the Sultan's control, but further north and west of the Hajjar there was tension between the Imamate and the tribes of the Dhahirah, who owed allegiance to neither Sultan nor Imam. The Dhahirah tribes were also being wooed for the first time since 1880 by emissaries of the Saudis.

The D'Arcy party's welcome was very mixed. 'Isa bin Salih, the tamima of the al-Harthi tribe, gave formal written warning that he would be unable to control his tribesmen if the party entered their territory, and D'Arcy could also not enter areas under Imamate control. When Lees and his party subsequently explored the coastline between Muscat and Dhofar they landed at Duqm to face an attitude of complete non-cooperation from the bedu tribes of the area. 'Our welcome could not be described as cordial, nor were any regrets expressed on our departure', Lees wrote. His report was at best tentative. The Sultan and the British authorities would have liked to see it followed up but the D'Arcy Company's conclusion, endorsed by its Chairman Sir Arnold Wilson, was pessimistic about the prospects and their agreement was allowed to lapse.

The Iraq Petroleum Company and the origins of Petroleum Development (Oman)

No further activity took place for a decade by which time Sultan Sa'id was well established in Muscat and determined to be less dependent, especially financially, on Britain. In the meantime the main player in eastern Arabia had become the Iraq Petroleum Company (IPC). This was the successor to the earlier Turkish Petroleum Company (TPC) set up in 1912 to explore for oil in then Ottoman Mesopotamia (now Iraq). From 1929 IPC's shareholding was 23.75% each for Anglo-Persian, Shell, Compagnie Francaise des Petroles (CFP), and Near East Development Company (NEDCO), a subsidiary of what later became Esso and Mobil. Calouste Gulbenkian, who had been centrally involved in setting up the original TPC, held 5% through his company Partex. A crucial element of the IPC arrangement was the 'Red Line Agreement' whereby the partners agreed not to pursue concessions individually in the Arabian peninsula. Standard Oil of California, not an IPC partner, was the first to challenge this arrangement when it concluded an agreement with Ibn Saud of Saudi Arabia in 1934.

The search for oil in Arabia became more competitive after the discovery of oil in commercial quantities in Bahrain in 1932. The British Government was content to use Petroleum Concessions Ltd (PCL; IPC's subsidiary set up to pursue concessions outside Iraq) in Gulf states where it had signed exclusive oil agreements in previous decades. PCL was active in the Trucial States in 1935 and 1936, and then turned its attention to Oman. The Sultan was keen to start to derive some income from oil exploration. It was already clear that the best prospects lay to the west of the Hajjar, in the Dhahirah and in Imamate territory. In the absence of any British or company contacts with the Imam or tribal leaders, agreement with the Sultan was accepted, after some reflection in London, as the necessary springboard. It was recognised that 'certain parts of the Sultan's territory are not at present safe for operations', and the Sultan's good offices were accepted to enable the company to enter such areas when he judged it safe to do so. On this basis agreement was reached in June 1937 on separate 75-year options for Oman and for Dhofar (which was regarded as in effect the Sultan's personal fiefdom). These were assigned to Petroleum Development (Oman and Dhofar), IPC's subsidiary in Oman, to manage, initially for five years. They were accompanied by a parallel 'political agreement' between the British Government and IPC, setting out the rules of the game, and the Sultan was reluctantly obliged to confirm that he had seen and accepted this.

Following some initial coastal surveys from Dubai in the winter of 1937-8, a geological expedition was mounted in 1938-9 into the Dhahirah (but not the Imamate). Despite efforts by the Sultan to prepare the ground most of the tribes remained determined to keep European prospectors out of their territory. Wilfred Thesiger summarised their attitude a decade later 'the discovery of oil ... has raised the cupidity and suspicion of the nearby tribes and has made them increasingly jealous of their rights. Involved in intrigues to preserve or increase their territorial claims, they are at present agreed only in the policy of excluding all Europeans from their land.' The 1937 party was attacked while trying to get to Ibri and had to divert northwards to Buraimi where it met up with another IPC party from Abu Dhabi. There were hopes of being able to undertake more systematic work in 1939-40 but the outbreak of World War Two put a stop to all activity. The 1937 agreement options were extended in 1942, and the concessions formally taken up in 1944, but it was 1948 before work resumed.

The Sultan was impatient to see some activity under the agreements he had signed. But Oman was a low priority for IPC, and the British authorities were continuing to steer them away from territory not under Sa'id's control and where they did not have his specific agreement to go.

Dhofar was a different case and IPC agreed to mount a survey there in January 1948. This was conducted by two geologists, Mike Morton and Rene Wetzel, who undertook a tough 600 kilometre reconnaissance by camel over six weeks (following an even longer and more arduous journey through the eastern Hadramawt over the previous three months). This pioneering journey proved however to be a dead end. They concluded 'Dhofar can therefore be rejected as a possible oilfield.' Following this IPC formally terminated their Dhofar concession in 1950 and the local operating company became Petroleum Development (Oman) – PD(O).

The interaction between the emerging interests of PD(O) and the Sultan's strategy for reasserting his control over the territories of the Imamate was outlined in chapter 14 . In the course of 1947 the company appeared to be getting signals from Sultan Sa'id that he was prepared for them to begin work in areas west of the Hajjar in the Dhahirah, outside the area controlled by the Imam. The company's representative, Dick Bird, himself a former Political Agent in Muscat, was led to believe that the Sultan had told the current Political Agent that it could deal direct with tribal groups in the area at its own risk. Bird drove into Ibri in March 1948 – the first car to be seen there. He made agreements with several tribes for three year exploration licences with a right to two year extensions. When Bird subsequently visited Muscat the Sultan was extremely angry about these direct negotiations, though he ultimately accepted that they had taken place on Government advice. He insisted however that the tribes acknowledge his authority and that the company should work through him.

In February 1949 Bird set off again for Buraimi, accompanied by representatives of the Sultan, to discover the Shaikhs in an uncooperative mood and the previous year's agreements torn up as a result of the Sultan's position. The strategy of seeking agreements with the tribal leaders of the Dhahirah was taken no further though it was reassessed as an option from time to time both by officials and IPC. The Sultan's influence in the Dhahirah at this time was in fact extremely limited. The area was increasingly tense from 1949 as a result of Saudi claims and incursions, and the British Government banned the company from going into the disputed areas. To be told to look elsewhere was not however entirely unwelcome to the company. Also in 1949, a chance over-flight of the Fahud area, in the desert 100 miles south west of Ibri, and in the territory of the Bedouin Duru tribe rather than any of the settled tribes of the Dharihah, had attracted the attention of a senior IPC geologist who described it as 'a beautiful anticline'. Thereafter Fahud became the company's primary target as an area to explore.

The move to Fahud

It was to be five years before Fahud could be seriously investigated. The Sultan first agreed in 1952 that the company might explore a strip of the southern coast up to a limit of 50 miles inland, with Duqm as its centre. As described in chapter 14 the Muscat and Oman Field Force (MOFF) was formed at the company's expense to protect its activities. By the time it had been recruited and trained, and the company's own resources assembled, it was February 1954 before the expedition of three landing ships converged on Duqm from Muscat and Aden. In addition to Edward Henderson and the General Manager of IPC the party also included Mike Morton, one of the geologists who had made the pioneering survey of Dhofar in 1948. It received a much friendlier reception at Duqm than the Lees party in 1926.

Despite Company frustration with Sa'id's limits on where they could work, for the first time in Oman, systematic mapping and surveying could be carried out before the operation, dependent on supply over the beach at Duqm, had to be scaled back with the onset of the Indian Ocean monsoon in June. By the autumn of 1954 progress in assuring the support of the Duru, in whose tribal area Fahud lay, opened the way for the company's cherished objective of moving from Duqm across the Jiddat al-Harāsīs to Fahud to be fulfilled. The death of Imam Muhammad al-Khalili in May and the election of Imam Ghalib in his place had created a situation in which this move was also able to serve as a platform for Sultan Sa'id to enhance his authority in the interior radically over the next year. The pioneering journey across the Jiddat al-Harasis took place in October 1954, and the company element of the expedition established itself in Fahud and set about the task of assessing the actual potential of the formation. The political dimension of these events was considered in chapter 14.

At this time the concession to the IPC shareholders had been in place for 17 years but no serious exploration work, let alone drilling, had been possible because of the turbulent internal conditions in what were regarded as the promising areas of the country. This could now change, though another seven years were to pass before oil was discovered in significant quantities. Soon after the dash for Fahud, Stephen Gibson, the Managing Director of IPC, visited the newly established camp to evaluate the possibilities for himself. All concerned were enthusiastic about the prospects. A decision in principle was taken to drill, subject only to certain geological conditions being satisfied. Perhaps for one of the last times in oil industry history this was done on the basis of surface data alone without seismic testing.

It took a year to get to the point of 'spudding' the first well. During 1955 prospection began to take place at other locations also but the lead time was long, largely due to the problems of getting heavy equipment in to this extremely remote location, far from the sea, with continuing tension between Sultan, Imam and independent tribes, and with no road network. The decision was made to air freight equipment from Qatar in a prototype Blackburn Universal Freighter, later the RAF's Beverley freighter. Politically the Sultan continued to move cautiously through 1955, building up the body of Dhahirah Shaikhs owing him allegiance, a process helped by tribal disaffection with the overtly radical policies being pursued by the new Imam and his brother Talib. What turned the balance of forces decisively within Oman was the breakdown in October 1955 of the arbitration proceedings on Buraimi in Geneva between Britain and Saudi Arabia, and the subsequent swift ejection from Buraimi of the Saudi contingent and their leading supporters among the local tribal leaders.

Following the occupation of Nizwa in December 1954 Sa'id embarked on his historic drive from Dhofar via interior Oman to the Batinah coast and Muscat. The first leg took him across the desert to Fahud where he inspected the derrick already in place for drilling to start just a few weeks later, before going on to make a triumphal entry into Nizwa.

Drilling did begin at Fahud on 18 January 1956. Fahud-I has been described as 'the unluckiest and most ill-fated wildcat well in the history of Middle East oil'. Though the location appeared to be an ideal oil-bearing formation, the well ran into technical difficulties through 1956, and then hit a fault of very hard rock so that it penetrated only a short distance into what later proved a prolific oil bearing formation. It was abandoned in May 1957. No Fahud-2 was drilled to test the structure more fully though proposals were put forward from the men on the ground to drill again on the other side of the fault. It subsequently turned out that the well was only some 200 metres from where oil in large quantities was later discovered. What impact a discovery in 1957 might have had remains one of the great might-have-beens of modern Omani history.

Other wells were drilled at Ghabah and Hayma in 1958-60 but they too proved unsuccessful. Painfully slowly the infrastructure to permit larger scale operation began to be put in place. With Saudi departure from Buraimi some road access from Dubai became possible. Work began to install port facilities on the coastline near Muscat. A connecting road from Muscat through the Samail Gap toward Izki and Nizwa brought about an unlamented end to the use of Duqm as the company's main landfall from the sea. But these were still disturbed years in interior Oman, and even in Muscat. Though the balance of forces never swung decisively back towards the Imamate after 1955, British military intervention proved necessary in Nizwa and the Jebel Akhdar in June 1957, and it was not until the beginning of 1959 that the last rebels were dislodged from the upper fastnesses of the mountain. Even after that, company convoys had to be escorted, and on at least one occasion in 1959 a vehicle was blown up by a mine.

These were years of reflection among policy makers within IPC. In 1950, piqued by the withdrawal of PD(O) from the Dhofar concession, the Sultan awarded it to Wendell Phillips, an American archaeologist working in Dhofar, who had no experience of the oil industry. He brought in a company called Cities Services to conduct the exploration work, later handed over to John Mecom – Pure Oil. In 1957 the Sultan unilaterally redefined the boundary between the Oman and Dhofar concessions, and awarded part of PD(O)'s territory to Phillips Petroleum. This put significant stress on relations between the Sultan and the company. Its representative in Muscat, Sir William Lindsay, a former Chief Justice of Sudan, put out feelers direct to Phillips and was declared persona non grata by the Sultan. The American companies spent more than a decade, and many millions of dollars, drilling north of Salalah and to the north-east near Marmul, close to the boundary between the two concessions. Wells drilled at Marmul in 1957/8 produced oil, but it was deemed too heavy to be commercial, and Phillips finally withdrew in 1967, after their personnel and installations had become frequent targets in the early years of the Dhofar revolt (see chapter 18).

PD(O) restructured, and Shell's profile raised

Lindsay's situation, uncertainties on the ground, rising costs, and failure to discover oil led to serious questioning within IPC as to whether work should continue, and ultimately to a major restructuring of PD(O). It was a time when low oil prices and ample supply of cheap oil were leading companies to review a number of seemingly unprofitable operations. At the end of 1959 BP, CFP and NEDCO all decided to withdraw from the IPC Oman venture. Shell, with much less Middle East oil of its own, and Partex, decided to continue. Shell took over the operation of the company from 1 October 1960 and cut back the scale of operations drastically, leaving just one base and materials at Afar.

It took nearly seven years, now under the control and direction of Shell, not IPC, to move from this sense of an uncertain future to the emergence of Oman as a significant exporter of oil on world markets. At the outset the Sultan would not permit the company to set up an exploration office in Oman and operations had to continue to be directed from Qatar. The initial view within the company was that if revived exploration effort did not produce positive results in a specific time-frame a judgement would have to be made whether to carry on or not. Through 1961 the existing data was reviewed and expanded by teams of geologists backed by British Arabic-speakers. Yibal, 45 kilometres southwest of Fahud, was selected as the most promising structure and the Yibal-I well was 'spudded' in March 1962. Conditions were primitive and the environment exceptionally harsh with summer temperatures up to 58° C (136.4°F).

Relations with the Duru tribesmen of the area were generally good. A number were employed by the company and they also benefited from the company's ability to drill deeper and better wells for water than they could for themselves. A driller at Yibal summarised the relationship 20 years later. 'The people then were as they are now – friendly, polite and proud and very easy to get on with.' The company's Arabic-speaking 'liaison representatives' had a crucial part to play, in liaison with the tribal Shaikhs, in ensuring good labour relations. The early representatives of the company, first Henderson, replaced in 1955 by Stuart Watt, and then the liaison officers over the next decade, have a good claim to be the first Britons, indeed the first foreigners, ever to deal and work with the interior tribes of Oman and their Shaikhs.

Yibal-I suffered a dramatic blowout after some months' work and had to be abandoned. But a second well was more promising and other wells were started at Natih, and, from December 1963, at Fahud itself where seismic studies had made the nature of the field much clearer. Oil was first found some 1500 metres from the original dry well of seven years earlier. While this work went on in considerable secrecy, known only to the Sultan among Omanis, extensive surveying work was being undertaken across much of the rest of northern Oman. In July 1964 the Sunday Times leaked the story that Shell had what it called a 'major oil find', and in November Shell finally announced that oil in commercial quantities had been discovered at Fahud, Natih, and Yibal.

The pipeline to Mina al-Fahal
The next two and a half years saw an operation of an entirely different scale to anything seen thus far, to turn these discoveries into producing fields, and to link them with the sea. After Duqm had been rejected as a terminal because of the swell during the summer monsoon, the Sultan gave permission for the construction of a 376 kilometre pipeline from Fahud through the Samail gap to Mina al-Fahal near Muscat, which was selected as the main base for the company and the site where mooring buoys would be installed for tankers to load. Nothing like this had been seen in Oman before, and it was at the time quite unmatched by any other area of development. It involved risk-taking and local solutions to unexpected problems; 'pioneering spirit at its best' one participant called it. Omanis and expatriates working together made it possible. Perseverance had paid off. There had been a good deal of scepticism along the way as to whether it would succeed. A mixture of growing objective information with a mix of persuasiveness and stubbornness on the part of key individuals over these years saw the process brought to fruition. On 27 July 1967 the *Mosprince* loaded Oman's first export cargo, 543,000 barrels of oil destined for Japan.

Francis Hughes, appointed the company's General Manager in 1966, oversaw the final stages of the work and kept tirelessly in touch with the

Sultan as it unfolded. He often travelled to Salalah for several days at a time with an agenda ranging well beyond technical issues. He was, in the view of the British Consul General of the time, liked and trusted by Sultan Sa'id. In a publication issued a few days after the first cargo was loaded, he said '[This] is a cause for celebration for the peoples of the Sultanate of Muscat and Oman for whom, in certain respects, the oil era starts today. It is my earnest wish and that of PD(O) that the people of the Sultanate will never have any reason to regret this, but will look back on it in the months and years to come as the beginning of a new era of prosperity and happiness in the long history of the country.'

The early years of production were a transitional period. Though significant resources were now coming into Oman the way of life changed little and non-oil development was slow to begin. The interaction of the public impatience with this with the growing insurgency in Dhofar over the last three years of Sultan Sa'id's reign is covered in chapter 18. The Sultan was also reluctant to relax his restrictive attitude to what expatriates working for the company could do. They were not permitted to travel up the Batinah coast, and wives were restricted to a very small area around the company base, Matrah and Muscat. Francis Hughes was very aware of the frustrations the situation was bringing about among Omanis. 'Lack of development is the most glaring aspect of the country', he wrote, 'What is lacking is the encouragement of private development of any kind. Houses may not be built, cars may not be bought, and local people may not travel abroad except for work. The flow of an already sparsely settled population from here to Kuwait, Saudi Arabia, Dubai and Abu Dhabi continues despite the opportunities one would have thought oil would bring. The lack of education facilities drives others, illegally, away.'

The story of PDO after 1970 is properly part of the history of modern Oman, of the renaissance of the country under Sultan Qaboos. The company 'became part of the social and economic structure of Oman' with 'measured interdependence' reflecting high popular expectations and 'a desire to be taken note of and listened to by the new Government in contrast to its predecessor which was considered as remote and uncaring'. The structure of the company changed radically. Already in 1967 the concession agreement had been radically revised to reflect changing relationships between oil companies and the states where they operated. This provided for the company's concession area to be reduced by over 80% by 1990. At the same time CFP became a shareholder again, taking 10% of the company with Shell holding 85% and Partex 5%. In 1969, the insurgency notwithstanding, Dhofar was brought back within the company's concession area, Phillips having renounced any interest there. By the mid 1970s the whole concept of concessions had become unacceptable to the members of OPEC, to be replaced either by nationalisation or 'participation'. Though not an OPEC member, Oman decided to follow the participation path. In 1973 the state acquired a 25% stake in PD(O) and this was increased to 60% a year later. With the end of the Dhofar insurgency in 1975, operations there became possible for the first time and from 1978 oil production began in Marmul and Amal.

Production rose steadily but not spectacularly from that first cargo in 1967. With oil prices remaining low Shell kept PD(O) on a tight rein till after the price leap of 1974. Even with the discovery of new fields in the centre of the country and the production from Dhofar, it was estimated at the end of the 1970s that overall a production plateau of 320,000 barrels a day could be attained and sustained for 20 years till 2000. At that stage the levels actually attained of 600,000 barrels a day in 1988 and 840,000 in 2000, together with Oman's diversification into gas and its associated downstream industries would, one company official involved at the time said, have been considered the proposal of a complete lunatic.

41. *D'Arcy Petroleum Company survey party, 1928*

42. *The Fahud anticline*

43. *The MOFF en route for Duqm, 1954*

CHAPTER 18

Downhill in Dhofar 1965-1970

The war in Dhofar brought Oman into an international conflict which, if it had had a different outcome, would have had major repercussions for stability in the Gulf in the last quarter of the 20th century. Beginning as a series of acts of insurgency directed against Sultan Sa'id, it later involved troops from Iran and Jordan as well as Britain in support of his son, and widespread communist assistance to the rebels. To begin with, the insurgents – using guerrilla tactics, and facing weak opposition – attained a position where only Salalah and its surrounding plain remained loyal to the Sultan.

* * * * * * *

The Dhofar War of the 1960s and 1970s was much more protracted than the episodes in northern Oman in the 1950s. From the earliest small scale incidents to the mopping up of the last rebels some fifteen years elapsed, though the major events were concentrated in the decade between 1965 and 1975. It originated as an internal campaign for the redress of regional grievances. By 1968 it had become the on-going front line of a struggle between Marxist and western approaches to the future of the whole region and its crucial oil fields and shipping routes. When it threatened to spill dangerously into northern Oman, the inadequate responses of Sultan Sa'id became the catalyst for his deposition and replacement by his son Qaboos in 1970. The non-military story of how Sa'id's reign arrived at that point is set out in chapter 16.

For successive British Governments the Dhofar War raised difficult questions. The 1960s were the decade when issues about the affordable scale of defence effort 'east of Suez', which had rumbled on since the end of the Second World War and the Independence of India in 1947, came to a head. Withdrawal from Aden in November 1967 was followed swiftly by the decision – in the face of mounting economic pressures – to withdraw militarily from the whole Gulf region, for which a date of 1971 was set. However this merely raised the importance of leaving behind stable and viable regimes in Oman and the Gulf. Continuing Cold War rivalries, and the security of British and other western oil supplies from Oman itself and the wider Gulf region, ensured that Dhofar was not a region on which Britain could lightly turn her back.

With oil revenues now flowing in, Oman was expected to bear the brunt of the costs of the war herself, but a sustained if low-cost programme of helping her to overcome the rebellion was little challenged within Whitehall, though kept as discreet as possible. International concern within the region and more broadly about the implications of failure also came to play an important role. The Unites States, whose interests had sharply differed from those of Britain in the 1950s, was alarmed by the prospect of British departure and shared the objective of a stable Omani buffer between Marxist-dominated Aden and the choke point of the Straits of Hormuz for shipping entering and leaving the Gulf. At the same time, the Governments of Presidents Johnson and Nixon were both militarily and politically too involved in Vietnam to have any appetite for direct engagement. After 1970 other regional leaders, notably the Shah of Iran and King Hussein of Jordan, came to accept the case for military as well as diplomatic support for Sultan Qaboos, to ensure the future of a stable and pro-western monarchy in Oman.

Dhofar – background
In area Dhofar is about the size of Wales. It has a coastline of some 200 miles, facing south across the Indian Ocean, stretching from the border with Aden to the point where the Jiddat al-Harasis, the gravel plain of central Oman, meets the sea. In the centre of this coastline lies Salalah, Dhofar's principal town, and its adjacent plain some 30 miles by 10 in extent. Other smaller towns occupy lesser flat areas along the coast. However most of Dhofar is occupied by three blocks of tangled

mountains up to 4000 feet in height and cut by deep valleys or wadis. These are the Jebel Samhan to the east of Salalah, the Jebel Qara behind it, and the Jebel Qomar to the west. Salalah, and a limited and clearly defined area of the Jebel Qara, are unique in the Arabian peninsula in having a wet season from July to September, known as the *kharīf*, part of the massive monsoon system of the Indian Ocean. This transforms the area into a cool and verdant oasis among the parched rocks and deserts of the rest of the province. During the Dhofar war, this affected campaigning. Both movement and flying were more difficult during the kharif. Much of the description of the campaign comes in yearly episodes, starting in October and going through to June. Behind the Jebel Qara stretches the Nejd, a featureless gravel plain stretching north to the sand dunes of the 'Empty Quarter' and the borders of Saudi Arabia.

Dhofar is inhabited by two main ethnic groups, both distinct from the major tribal groups of northern Oman. The principal Sunni Arab tribe of the Salalah area is the Bani Kathir (also called *Bait Kathir*). The jebalis (literally "mountain people") of the three jebels, from whom the majority of the rebels came, are of three largely settled groups, the Qara, Mara, and Shara, in the 1960s still mainly dependent on their cattle and goats. Slighter and wirier in build than most Arabs, they are regarded as descendants of some of the pre-Arab population of South Arabia, speaking their own Semitic languages which are quite distinct from Arabic. The rebels were always known by the British military as the *'adu*, or *adoo*, "the enemy".

Control of Dhofar from Muscat goes back only to the reign of Sayyid Sa'id bin Sultan, who annexed it in 1829 as part of the spread of his influence across the western Indian Ocean. The al-Busa'idis' control through most of the 19th century was minimal until reasserted by Sultan Turki in 1879. Successive 20th century Sultans, Faisal, Taymur and then Sa'id, made Salalah their refuge both from the Muscat climate and from the pressures of tribal politics. To the frustration of British representatives in Muscat, Sultans Taymur and Sa'id spent more and more time there. The latter was in Salalah throughout the Second World War and made it his permanent home in 1958 after which he never revisited Muscat. Until Sultan Sa'id made the desert journey to northern Oman in 1955 described in chapter 14, contact between Muscat and Dhofar was almost exclusively by sea.

The origins of the revolt and the war

What happened in Dhofar from the early 1960s has been called a revolt, a rebellion, a revolution, an insurgency, and a war. Its scale and its international dimensions justify the use of the word 'war'. The Dhofar War falls into four broad phases: a gathering local and nationalist revolt between 1962 and 1967; a much more serious uprising based on Marxist principles and sustained from across the border with Aden, which by 1970 effectively controlled all of the province other than the Salalah plain; a period of stand-off between 1970 and 1972 during which Omani forces were strengthened and reorganised to begin to reassert Government control area by area; and the gradual rolling back of the uprising between 1972 and 1975 when Sultan Qaboos was able to declare that victory had been achieved.

Sultan Sa'id treated Dhofar as a personal estate. Its revenues went directly to him. He was in general contemptuous of jebalis, though his wife, Sultan Qaboos's mother, was a Qarawi. He hedged Dhofaris' lives round with petty restrictions, doing nothing to encourage any kind of economic development. As a result many left to find work elsewhere in the Gulf. Several groups angered by his approach were set up in the early 1960s within Dhofar and elsewhere – the Dhofar Benevolent Society, the Dhofar Soldiers Organisation (a disaffected group of Dhofaris within the Trucial Oman Scouts), and Dhofari groups within the Arab Nationalist Movement. Early dissident activities between late 1962 and the end of 1964 had three main targets. The first was sabotage against the RAF base at Salalah. The second was attacks against the 'Midway' (or Thumrait) Road which led from the Salalah plain up on to the Jebel Qara. The airbase at Thumrait was built only later, in 1974, but the Midway road from Salalah to the plateau was of strategic significance, being the only road link between Dhofar and the rest of Oman. The third linked target was the oil exploration activities of the American John Mecom – Pure Oil company, whose operating base was at Midway. Many of these activities were carried out by a group led by Musallam bin Nafl (also known as Musallam al-Kathīri), a Kathiri former driver, who had worked for Sultan Sa'id. He secured support, in the form of training and of arms and vehicles from Saudi Arabia organised for him by Tālib bin 'Ali, brother of the former Imam. He visited Saudi Arabia at least twice, crossing the Empty Quarter to recruit and to collect materiel. This group's activities in 1964 provoked Sultan Sa'id to erect a barbed wire fence round Salalah and deny the jebalis entry, as well as making arbitrary arrests and destroying water holes. This only caused further economic hardship and swelled support for what was at this stage essentially a local movement, albeit also supported verbally by other Arab nationalists who had given help in the 1950s to Sa'id's opponents in the north, as well as the Saudis.

At this time the Sultan's Armed Forces (SAF) did not operate in Dhofar, a further example of Sultan Sa'id's view of it as quite separate from the territories of Muscat and Oman. There was a small, British-officered unit called the Dhofar Force, many of whom were Dhofaris, but its functions were a combination of ceremonial duties and local security in Salalah. In 1964 the level of insurgent activity reached the point where the Commander of SAF, Colonel Anthony Lewis, was ordered to lead a company of the Northern Frontier Regiment on to the jebel from the north. It failed however to draw the rebels into any form of engagement. At the end of 1964 a small SAF reconnaissance party was sent to Dhofar on a permanent basis. Regular overland SAF deployments to Dhofar began in 1965, when two companies of the Muscat Regiment were deployed to patrol the Jebel Qara. Being better equipped they came off best in two encounters with rebel groups, but had to withdraw at the beginning of the monsoon in July, leaving the rebels with freedom of movement throughout the jebel areas. In June 1965 the Sultanate of Oman Air Force (SOAF) began to operate in support of operations from the RAF base at Salalah. The security of the base was an increasing British preoccupation. In the spring of 1965 the Political Resident Persian Gulf was sufficiently concerned about it to deploy a platoon of the Parachute Regiment to enhance security.

The start of insurrection
At a Congress at Wadi al-Kabir in central Dhofar in June 1965 the Dhofar Liberation Front (DLF) was created, bringing together elements of the different dissident groups. The Congress elected an 18-man leadership executive. A Declaration was issued on 9 June to coincide with an attack on a Government patrol. 9 June was subsequently used by the DLF and its Marxist successors as the anniversary of the formal beginning of the uprising. The Declaration stressed the DLF's aim as 'the liberation of

Dhofar from the rule of the despotic Al Bu Said Sultan whose dynasty has been identified with the hordes of the British imperialist occupation', a blending of finite local aims with Arab nationalist rhetoric typical of the period. DLF members were a mixture of tribesmen from the jebel and people from Salalah. There were from the outset clear fault lines between Dhofari nationalists, more likely to have links with the Imamate movement and Saudi Arabia, and radicals whose ties were with Egypt or Iraq. The capture by the Iranians in May 1965, in the Shatt al-Arab at the head of the Gulf, of a dhow-load of Dhofaris trained and equipped in Iraq, underlined this multiplicity of sources of support for the rebels.

With one spectacular exception 1966 was a year of continuing low level attacks. The exception was an assassination attempt against Sultan Sa'id in April which very nearly succeeded. He was reviewing a guard of the Dhofar Force at Arzat near Salalah when the guard commander and some of its members, apparently infiltrated by the DLF, started firing at him. Sa'id was uninjured but the Pakistani Commander of the Force was wounded before personal retainers shot dead the guard commander and disarmed the others involved. Sa'id's response was twofold, to retire into his Palace, which he rarely left again, and to strengthen repressive measures against the jebalis. He rejected all arguments for political concessions to reduce support for the rebels. From then on a SAF presence was permanently maintained in Dhofar, based at Umm al-Ghawarif ('the mother of mosquitos') outside Salalah.

By the end of 1966 Colonel Lewis concluded that the military situation was at a stalemate and that SAF's weaknesses of manpower, leadership, intelligence, and mobility meant that it could not destroy the DLF. At the same time SAF was too strong for the DLF to destroy, and it was short of supplies in 1966-67. For the next year and a half the stalemate continued. The prospect of this situation changing for the worse following British withdrawal from Aden at the end of 1967 was however an increasing concern. Much of the area of the East Aden Protectorate adjacent to Dhofar was already controlled by Marxist elements of what would become the Government of the People's Republic of South Yemen (PRSY), and in 1969 the People's Democratic Republic of Yemen (PDRY). It was evident that the DLF were increasingly able to use Hawf, just across the border, as a safe haven and the source of arms and supplies. In the autumn of 1966, as the area was still nominally under

British control, the Labour Government of Harold Wilson authorised the landing of troops from the Irish Guards and the Special Air Squadron (SAS) from HMS *Fearless* to search Hawf and detain a number of DLF members (who were subsequently incarcerated by Sultan Sa'id in Fort Jalali in Muscat).

The rebel movement strengthens

Between 1968 and 1970 stalemate gave way to clear advantage for a revitalised and restructured rebel movement, which also began to infiltrate groups of rebels into northern Oman to put added pressure on the Sultan. These were dark days, the dog days of Sultan Sa'id's reign where the issue was the avoidance of defeat – a complete rebel takeover of Dhofar with implications much farther afield – rather than the development of a strategy for victory. Tactical ingenuity and courage on the ground could not conceal this reality, whose backdrop was the control of the PDRY by a Marxist-led Government and the implications of the British decision to withdraw British forces completely from east of Suez by 1971.

The new context was swiftly reflected in a complete restructuring and renaming of the DLF, and the imposition of doctrinaire ('revolutionary') and often brutal control over the civilian communities in the areas they controlled. Up to 1968 the DLF leadership contained both those who subscribed to the basically nationalist aims set out in 1965 and an increasingly radical element whose model became the Marxist doctrines of the National Liberation Front (NLF) in Aden. At a second Congress at Hamrin in September 1968 the latter seized complete control. Only three of the previous DLF leadership remained and most of the 'nationalists' were expelled. Military support from Communist Governments largely replaced that from other Arab states. The organisation was renamed the People's Front for the Liberation of Oman and the Arab Gulf (PFLOAG), making its broader strategic aims very plain. Over the next eighteen months the new leadership, many of whom had trained in Russia or China, established effective control over virtually the whole of Dhofar except the Salalah Plain. The Front was liberally supported with weapons and supplies from PDRY, which it could move freely by camel along routes in the jebel parallel with the coast. Policy towards civilians reflected the training provided by communist countries.

Neither Islam nor tribal authority had a place in these doctrines. Those who opposed these moves, tribal Shaikhs in particular, were treated with great brutality. Discipline was rigid and children came to be separated from their families and sent to Aden for 'education' prior to becoming rebel fighters in their turn. For the moment these policies were effective in a situation where Sultan Sa'id for his part obdurately refused to consider any 'hearts and minds' strategy to offer an alternative focus of loyalty. Militarily the rebels built up a network of fighting units estimated at some 2000 strong, supported as required by some 3000 further men organised in local militia units.

The SAF's resources to counter this surge of confidence and capability were minimal. Sultan Sa'id had finally agreed in 1966 to raise a third infantry battalion, the Desert Regiment, to add to the Muscat Regiment and Northern Frontier Regiment created in the 1950s. One battalion at a time, reinforced by a company from one of the others, was deployed in Dhofar and its Commanding Officer was the Commander on the ground, reporting to the SAF Commander in Muscat. From April 1967 this was Brigadier Corran Purdon. From Muscat Brigadier Purdon and Colonel Pat Waterfield, who had been in Oman as a contract officer since 1953 and was now the Military Secretary responsible for resources and procurement, had the unenviable task of organising support for the forces on the ground. Equipment, even clothing, was scarce. Lt Col Peter Thwaites described the battalion he took over in mid-1967 as a 'pathetically ragged little army'. Sultan Sa'id did agree to some modest improvements in the equipment available to the infantry battalions. Belgian made rifles and the British General Purpose Machine Gun (GPMG) were introduced.

Purdon made the case that the war could not be won without more infantry, artillery, armoured cars and above all helicopters. However Sultan Sa'id remained resistant to any further increase in the size of the SAF, and to the introduction of a helicopter force, arguing that the British subsidy had just been withdrawn and oil revenues had yet to flow. He also continued to refuse to take the political decisions which could have transformed the military situation. As it was, SAF had to operate, thinly stretched in an area of extreme terrain, on foot or by track with air support from fixed wing aircraft, operating only within range of Salalah or where rough landing strips could be constructed. These limitations were particularly acute when it came to casualty evacuation. Complete operations had at times to be aborted because of the need to concentrate resources on carrying wounded soldiers through enemy territory with the chances of survival or recovery sharply reduced by long delays before casualties could be brought back to Salalah for medical treatment. One factor which changed in the summer of 1967 was the decision of the John Mecom Company to terminate its search for oil in Dhofar. This meant that its base at Midway, and its vehicles on the road between there and Salalah, no longer needed protection. However the strategic importance of the road as the only land communication link with the rest of Oman, remained a major factor till the end of the war.

The battalion operating in Dhofar in the latter part of 1968, as the changing nature of the rebel movement became apparent, was the Northern Frontier Regiment commanded by Lt Col Mike Harvey. Harvey had won a Military Cross for leading out the survivors of the Gloucestershire Regiment after the Imjin River Battle in 1953. He knew and thoroughly disliked the Chinese and their ways and was very comfortable to have a Chinese-trained force as the enemy. He was a restless, driven Commander, in agreement with Sultan Sa'id's hard-line policies; these included blowing up the precious water resources of communities who backed the rebels. Col Thwaites describes this period as one where 'the NFR spent the latter half of 1968 dashing about Dhofar biffing the enemy'. Wherever possible Harvey operated as far to the west as he could, on the principle that this was where rebel resupply and reinforcement could be most effectively impeded.

Salalah almost under siege
The reality nonetheless was that these operations were pinpricks, and that by the beginning of 1969 the rebels could operate with impunity and in great strength almost anywhere in Dhofar. The SAF might come off best in individual encounters but the rebels were winning the war. They had also begun to bombard Salalah itself from the Jebel Qara. An operation to open the Midway Road to permit a roulement of battalions from the north, which had needed a company a year or so earlier, now needed a battalion. In August 1969, during the monsoon, the rebels launched a full scale assault on Rakhyut, the principal town on the coast between Salalah and the border with PDRY, killing the Sultan's governor

in the town. The Muscat Regiment, under Lt Col Peter Thwaites and with Ranulf Fiennes among its officers, had taken over in Dhofar that summer. Thwaites told Purdon that with a single reinforced battalion he had to have realistically limited aims, which should be to defend Salalah, keep open the Midway Road, and to do as much to frustrate rebel resupply in the west as could be achieved with a single company. By the end of the Muscat Regiment's tour however, rebel strength in the west was such that operations there could not be sustained and the whole of western Dhofar between Mughsayl (at the western end of the Salalah plain) and the Aden border had to be abandoned to the rebels.

Those involved in these operations had every reason to be proud of what they achieved on the ground. The one major step forward in 1969 was the delivery of jet Strikemaster aircraft to take on the role of close air support from the propeller-driven aircraft on which SOAF had until then depended. At the strategic level however, the situation when Brigadier John Graham of the Parachute Regiment arrived to take over from Brigadier Purdon in the spring of 1970 was dire. Sultan Sa'id had finally agreed in the autumn of 1969 to the raising of a fourth infantry battalion – the Jebel Regiment – and to make an order for helicopters. These had not yet arrived and he remained resolutely set against any change of policy, although this could have undermined support for the rebels. Rebel strength was increasing; SAF's was static. Purdon's appeals for more direct support from Britain went unheeded, and the rebels effectively controlled the whole jebel from west to east. One of Graham's first decisions was to withdraw the last company based off the Salalah plain along the Thumrait Road. The situation was visibly unsustainable to Graham and to the British Government, reluctant as were the latter to be drawn in further. This was a primary factor in the events leading up to the deposition of Sultan Sa'id described in chapter 16. With the accession of Sultan Qaboos many things began to change swiftly, even if it would take many months to shift the balance of military advantage substantially.

*44. Said Hof, former Dhofari rebel who
declared for the Sultan*

45. Operation to clear the Midway Road

CHAPTER 19

Ascent to victory in Dhofar 1970-1975

S ultan Qaboos took on a battered inheritance. Development in all Oman was sadly neglected, and the military situation in Dhofar was still precarious. A number of factors enabled him and his allies to turn the tide. These included the Sultan's own determination to see the best done for the people of Dhofar, and his recognition of the mistakes made in the past. Combining firm strategy with a spirit of reconciliation, adding to his own military capacity and drawing on assistance from British and other allies, Qaboos worked towards an outcome that would give Dhofar – and therefore the rest of the Sultanate – a basis for peace and prosperity.

* * * * * * *

The situation faced by Sultan Qaboos on his accession was far from comfortable. The rebels were well established on the jebel, and although it must have been clear to them quite soon that Qaboos was going to be a far more enlightened ruler than his father, they were not inclined to give up. They believed that their Marxist propaganda had sunk in, and for them, the enemy – an autocratic Sultan and the imperialist British – were still in place. But the accession of Qaboos in 1970 transformed policy-making on the Dhofar War in three crucial respects: resources, hearts and minds, and international support. All had significant lead times before they could make a real difference, and 1970-72 were years of preparation. Stalemate on the ground thus masked a fundamental change

287

in the making. There was soon no longer a risk that the rebels could win, and the SAF now moved on to the front foot in readiness for more decisive moves from 1973 on.

A start on "hearts and minds"

It was in the field of 'hearts and minds' that Sultan Qaboos's accession allowed the swiftest adoption of radically different approaches. Dhofar was above all a war about people. Sultan Sa'id's animosity to the jebalis had been unshakeable. But time would show that PFLOAG had also made fundamental misjudgements in this respect in 1969-70. The jebalis were far from natural communists. Islam was an integral part of their way of life, and they were shrewd and independent. The regime of terror which PFLOAG introduced rapidly produced its own reaction, and even before July 1970 dissent was widespread and acting as a brake on the Front's ability to exploit to the full the military superiority which it briefly enjoyed. Hearts and minds were there to be won. Sultan Qaboos had a totally different mind-set; his mother was a jebali and had been brought up in Dhofar, and he himself had never visited Muscat before his accession. He grasped very clearly the prime importance of winning the support of the people of Dhofar as the key to winning the war, principally through a totally different approach to civil development. He swiftly introduced an amnesty to induce a substantial flow of Surrendered Enemy Personnel (SEPs), who were then treated as returning brothers not defeated enemy, and put a temporary halt to operations on the jebel whilst new approaches were considered.

Ideas were readily available. The late 1960s, following the decision to leave Aden, had been a lean period for the SAS. After the relatively recent experience of the Jebal Akhdar campaign, and despite the successes of the rebel movement, senior officers had sensed that Dhofar could yet be won back for the Sultan. With Purdon's agreement the then Commanding Officer of 22 SAS, Viscount Slim, visited Oman in 1968, but given the rigidity of Sultan Sa'id's thinking, nothing came of this. The ideas which emerged from the visit of the new CO of 22 SAS in early 1970 were rejected by Sultan Sa'id but were readily available to Sultan Qaboos when he took over just months later. Now they fell on much more receptive ears. They revolved around four key aims: the improvement of intelligence; the conduct of psychological operations;

the winning of hearts and minds; and the development of a strategy for counter-revolution on the jebel.

The SAS, the BATTs, and the firqas

Within days of Sultan Qaboos's accession in July 1970 the SAS was providing close protection for him. Within two months the first elements of the SAS force to conduct what was called Operation Storm had arrived. Immediate tasks were to help with training and to lay, with the SAF, the foundations of a detailed and dependable intelligence system. Small groups were also swiftly deployed, under the name of British Army Training Teams (BATTs), in coastal communities to the east of Salalah such as Taqa and Mirbat, which were among the few slim footholds off the Salalah plain not under rebel control, but nonetheless under severe pressure from them. Key to their activities was the provision of basic medical and veterinary services. To these were added, as the Civic Action Programme was gradually extended area by area on to the jebel, help with livestock and with the provision and improvement of water supplies. In parallel with the work of the SAS, Qaboos approved for the first time the setting up of a civilian Development Department for Dhofar, headed by a British civilian.

Sultan Qaboos's amnesty – with incentives – for rebels who came over to the Government side offered for the first time good reasons for rebels to consider defection. His policy was helped by growing jebali disillusionment with the brutality and hostility to Islam of the foreign-trained commanders of PFLOAG. By March 1971 over 200 rebels had defected. Musallam bin Nafl was among those who decided to change sides. With the help of one defector who had been trained at Mons Officer Cadet School in Britain to become an officer in the Trucial Oman Scouts, the defectors began to be organised into irregular units called "firqas" (Arabic *firqāt*, singular *firqah* or *firqa*), trained by the SAS and increasingly operating alongside the SAF to share real knowledge of the terrain and communities among whom the war was being fought. It became swiftly apparent that they were most effective if each was made up of men from a single tribal group and operated in its home area. Alongside the development and propaganda programmes this was the key element of the 'counter-revolution' prompted from then on alongside military operations. They were unpredictable and difficult to command but were to make an essential contribution, under SAS guidance, to the gradual defeat of the rebels.

In parallel with these early initiatives on the ground Brigadier Graham was working hard with Brigadier Hugh Oldman to expand the SAF to a force of 10,000 men by 1972. Oldman had replaced David Smiley as a Loan Service Officer in the role of Commander of the SAF in 1961. On leaving the British Army he returned as a contract officer in early 1970 to replace Pat Waterfield as Defence Secretary. In addition to the extra battalion, Strikemasters and helicopters finally approved by Sultan Sa'id, Sultan Qaboos agreed to the formation of an Armoured Car Squadron and the expansion of artillery to regimental strength, as well as to further expansion of the Air Force and Navy. An active Omanisation programme was also initiated; by the end of 1971 it had already turned out over 100 junior officers. Modest but psychologically important additional British help was also forthcoming, especially for the defence of RAF Salalah.

In 1970-71 the SAF could operate on the jebel but not maintain a permanent presence there. Doubts about the future remained in British official circles. Progress was however sufficient for Brigadier Graham to conclude early in 1971 that the rebels would not succeed in conquering the whole of Dhofar by military means, but that major operations to regain the initiative would have to wait until after the *kharif*, not least because helicopters would then be available for the first time to support operations on the ground. Two full battalions were now deployed in Dhofar at any given time. In January 1971 an initial base was established north of the jebel, subsequently moved further west to Akut. The pace of operations against the rebels in the eastern jebel was stepped up. At the same time the command structure in Dhofar was strengthened with the creation of a separate area headquarters, whose first Commander was Col Mike Harvey, who had commanded the Northern Frontier Regiment to good effect in 1968.

Breakthrough on the jebel

Two operations mounted in the autumn of 1971 were effectively the first steps in a four year campaign to break the rebel stranglehold on the jebel, which they had been able to establish between 1967 and 1970. The first, Operation Jaguar, was to establish a secure base for the SAF on the eastern jebel, an area chosen as that where jebali resentment at the

Marxist policies of PFLOAG was strongest and had produced the most defections, and where the SAS was best established. For the first and only time Graham entrusted the leadership of this operation to the SAS and, for the first time in Oman since January 1959, two full Squadrons of 22 SAS (120 men) were involved, with two SAF companies. Whilst an SAS detachment made a noisy incursion from Mirbat into a different area to divert the rebels, half the force marched overnight across country to secure an airstrip (called Lympne) into which the rest of the force could be flown. Two weeks of sharp fighting followed at the end of which some 100 square kilometres of jebel had been secured, including a site initially called White City but later renamed Medinat al-Haq, which became the site of the first Government centre on the jebel from which medical and other services could be delivered. Watts wanted to follow-up by moving west but his firqas insisted on a pause for Ramadan, and it was decided to consolidate the gains already made, not least by facilitating with military transport and protection the removal of goats and cattle to market on the coast.

Supplies were still reaching the rebels in the eastern area from the Hadramawt in the west and it was decided in the second operation to hinder them by establishing a series of positions running inland from the sea at Mughsayl at the eastern end of the Salalah plain. These positions were known as the Leopard Line, and the line was the precursor of a series of lines, progressively further west, designed to cut the rebels off from their sources of supply in the PDRY. The initial Leopard Line remained porous and from the autumn of 1972 operations began to link these positions in a permanent barrier, known as the Hornbeam Line.

At the beginning of 1972 the situation remained precarious. Though he judged it unlikely, Graham could still not be absolutely confident that without further reinforcement Dhofar might not have to be abandoned. Continuing concerns about the threat of a serious uprising in the north meant that up to half of the SAF's capacity had to be retained there. The SAS and other British forces from Sharjah had also been used to counter tribal dissent in Musandam in the autumn of 1970. The beginnings of civil development throughout the country were making Omani recruitment more difficult because more civilian jobs were now available. Progress on the eastern jebel was encouraging but SAF resources in men and materiel were very limited when set against the task of regaining the rest of Dhofar. With the final departure of British Forces from elsewhere in the Gulf in December 1971, the British Government was under increasing pressure to run down British support for Oman still further. One of the two SAS squadrons was due to be withdrawn in April 1972 though some modest extra help was agreed from the RAF Regiment and the Royal Engineers. On the other hand one very positive consequence of Sultan Qaboos's accession had been the rapid establishment of Oman as a full member of the international community, a step Sultan Sa'id had always refused to take. By the end of 1971 Oman had joined both the Arab League and the United Nations, and Britain no longer had to bear the diplomatic strain of defending the situation in Oman.

This created for the first time the potential for supplementing British support with help from other nations in the region whose appreciation of the significance of Dhofar in the broader political rivalries of the Cold War was similar to Sultan Qaboos's. The newly constituted United Arab Emirates (which brought together the former Trucial States), Iran, Saudi Arabia and Jordan all potentially fell into this category. Graham and Oldman concluded that both political and military arguments pointed towards a high profile operation as close as possible to the border with Aden, designed to demonstrate that the SAF's efforts in a wider cause were robust and worthy, but at the same time needing further support if they were to prevail.

This consideration was to be a major factor in the decision to launch the most spectacular operation undertaken in 1972. Colonel Harvey, and the new Commanding Officer of 22 SAS, Lt Colonel Peter de la Billiere, another Jebel Akhdar veteran, both favoured building on the regaining of a foothold on the central jebel at Akut with an offensive from there to the north in the direction of the rebels' principal stronghold and supply base in the Shershitti caves. Lt Col Nigel Knocker, commanding Desert Regiment which held Akut, had grave doubts about the feasibility of attacking the rebels head on in their strongest position with the limited forces available. He considered that as much damage to their operations could be achieved by seizing a position very close to the PDRY border and so cutting their key supply lines. Such a position would have to be supplied entirely from the air but the presence of helicopters made it possible to consider such an operation for the first time in 1972. The result was the plan for Operation Simba, originally proposed by Knocker, which was to seize and hold a position at Sarfait only four miles from the rebels' base at Hawf in PDRY. Provided that a separate feature called Capstan at the top of the coastal escarpment could be held, Sarfait could interdict the routes which all the rebels' supply lines were obliged to use. This chimed with Brigadier Graham's conclusion that it was essential to attract the attention of potential backers for Oman in the Arab world with a bold and striking initiative as well as the Sultan's wish to operate as far west as was feasible. Despite the drain the operation would have on air support for operations elsewhere, Graham gave it his support and it was approved.

The campaign pushed westward

The risks were high and the operation only a partial success. The Sarfait position was exposed to enemy bombardment from within PDRY, and totally dependent on supply from the air. The Desert Regiment force was successfully landed by helicopter on 12 April 1972 but bad weather and stiff resistance delayed the attack on the Capstan position, and when it was finally attacked it was discovered that the expected water supply to allow it to be held was non-existent. Effort was also diverted away from Sarfait by a rebel attack on a Sultanate fort at Habrut on the border further to the north, which led to the withdrawal of the small SAF garrison there and the destruction of the Sultanate fort. This episode so infuriated Sultan Qaboos that he decided on direct retaliation against the rebels and their backers in the form of air attacks conducted over two days on known and suspected PFLOAG targets in Hawf. The Sultan's initiative led to tense diplomatic exchanges between London and Muscat about the use of British loan service personnel in cross-border operations. The authorities in London refused to let them take part directly. Graham circumvented these restrictions by getting the orders signed by Colonel Colin Maxwell, his Deputy, who was a contract officer. Fortunately, enough of the pilots at Salalah were also contract officers to mount the attacks.

The impact of these events, in the form of political support for the Omani position from Iran and within the Arab world, was huge, ironically generated as much by the PDRY's response at Habrut and what followed as by Operation Simba itself. It led to the delivery a month later of 25 Jordanian 25-pounder guns, and in August by the first of 60 C130 loads of Iranian arms and equipment. These developments provided powerful justification for the concentration of effort in the west even at the expense of slowing down the process of consolidation in the east. Sarfait itself remained an isolated outpost for three more years subject to constant bombardment from across the border. The rebel supply lines had not been cut. But its existence was an important symbol of determination, and it absorbed a huge amount of rebel ordinance which would otherwise have been available for use elsewhere.

Repulse at Mirbat

The summer of 1972 produced one other spectacular engagement, this time at rebel initiative. In order to show that they were still capable of operating at strength in the east, they decided to launch a large sale 'prestige attack' on Mirbat, a small town with an old fort, on the coast about 45 miles east of Salalah. Some three hundred rebels from a number of units closed in at dawn on 19 July, when the monsoon had begun. This was the biggest rebel force deployed in the whole war. Its aim was to take the town by storm and kill Government supporters. Mirbat was garrisoned by a firqa, most of whose personnel the rebels had lured away on a diversion, a platoon of the Dhofar Gendarmerie (the Baluch force recruited to replace the Dhofar Force after the 1966 assassination attempt on Sultan Sa'id), a single 25-pounder gun, and an eight-man SAS detachment. Led by Captain Mike Kealy, the SAS team held off the much stronger attacking force for several hours. At one stage an SAS Trooper from Fiji was firing the 25-pounder at point blank range over open sights. By about mid-morning the monsoon cloud lifted just sufficiently for three Strikemasters to relieve the pressure by attacking the assaulting rebels in the open. Fortuitously a second SAS Squadron had arrived in Salalah the previous day to relieve the detachments scattered round eastern Dhofar. This was flown in by helicopter to relieve the town and drive off the rebels, for whom the outcome was catastrophic. Around one third of the attackers were killed or wounded. Deep recriminations and further defections followed and this was to be the last time the rebels sought to mount a major attack off the jebel. From this point they were limited to guerrilla war.

The autumn of 1972 saw changes in command, both in Muscat, where Major General Tim Creasey succeeded Brigadier Graham, and in Dhofar, where Brigadier Jack Fletcher succeeded Col Harvey, now as Brigade rather than Area Commander, each one rank more senior than his predecessor. General Creasey's initial assessment was sombre. Final victory over the rebels was as yet by no means assured, though defeat was now improbable without a dramatic increase in external support for them. The close air support provided by SOAF's Strikemasters, the ability to deploy and resupply by helicopter, SAF's superior artillery, and the build-up of the armoured car squadron for patrolling on the ground, all contributed to this. Casualty figures were very much in the Sultanate's favour. Between July 1970 and the end of 1972 the SAF lost 90 men killed and 216 wounded. Estimates of rebel casualties were 1000 dead and wounded and 570 defections. At the same time a long war of attrition and stalemate was still very possible. Too much manpower was tied down in static positions. Salalah itself remained vulnerable until, at Colonel Knocker's suggestion, defensive positions on the jebel – the "Diana" positions – were installed in the summer of 1973 to prevent rockets being fired into Salalah. At the same time PFLOAG had by no means given up on its attempts to undermine Sultan Qaboos's position in northern Oman. The stakes were high, since the Straits of Hormuz and the passage of much of the west's oil were at risk if the unity and alignment of Oman were threatened.

But both Creasey and Fletcher were accomplished commanders, much respected by the men they led. They were able to seize the opportunity they had been given to capture the initiative, and to provide a platform for their successors to mount the operations which would bring the war to an end. 1973 was a year of much hard work at many levels but the strategic situation changed little. Making Dhofar secure for development was now acknowledged as the key to the whole military effort – the objective of the war. In the east development activity could now expand but only in limited areas. West of the Midway Road the rebels could still operate fairly freely. The two battalions deployed at any given time were fully occupied in trying to keep them on the back foot and deny them supplies, as well as garrisoning Sarfait, though it proved possible to maintain a presence on the jebel throughout the 1973 monsoon for the first time. The war was the first charge on Oman's budget, something not generally appreciated in northern Oman where it was seen as a remote conflict. Modest additional British support was now being provided. It was however still the case that, even with this, Oman's own resources were insufficient to secure a decisive outcome over forces supported and supplied by several other nations. Sultan Qaboos and his British military advisers still badly needed additional allies before victory could become a probability, still less a reality.

The arrival of allies

From about mid 1972, help in the shape of men and not just materiel had begun to be forthcoming. Several Arab nations preferred to keep their support for Sultan Qaboos at the diplomatic level. However Jordan and Iran, both of whom had appointed sympathetic Ambassadors to Muscat, with whom Brigadier Graham had quickly developed good relations, emerged as more active allies. King Hussein quickly concluded that success for Sultan Qaboos was a crucial factor in preventing the risk of increased communist penetration of the region. He provided first an engineer regiment and then a small but effective Special Forces Unit at the beginning of 1974 to operate with the SAF. The Shah of Iran saw himself in the 1970s as an equal partner of Britain and the US in holding the line against communism. Iran controlled the northern shore of the Straits of Hormuz and had the strongest possible interest in ensuring that Musandam and the Straits' southern shore never fell under communist control. The first Iranian Special Forces Unit arrived in late 1972. In 1973 the Shah agreed to deploy to Dhofar a battle group of first battalion and then brigade level, eventually some 5000 men, doubling the infantry capability facing the rebels at a stroke. At the end of 1973 this permitted General Creasey to mount an operation to secure and hold the line of the Midway Road once and for all.

The Hornbeam Line

Though the road still had to be patrolled, and low level attacks continued in the east, SAF efforts could thereafter be concentrated on the central and western jebel. In 1974 the Hornbeam Line from Mughsayl north into the central jebel was completed, with more permanently manned outposts and a major exercise to close the gaps between them with minefields and barbed wire. It was by no means impermeable but made rebel resupply very much more difficult. Political pressures on the rebels were also increasing. Chinese support had essentially come to an end. Developing relationships in Iran had become more significant for her. The effort to create serious unrest in the north had effectively failed, thanks to the impact of Sultan Qaboos's development policies, and enlarged and more effective intelligence and security services. This was acknowledged by PFLOAG at a conference in May 1974 which led to the dropping of the words 'Arab Gulf' from the organisation's name, focussing its aims solely on Dhofar as the Peoples Front for the Liberation of Oman (PFLO).

In the autumn of 1974 Brigadier John Akehurst, who had replaced Brigadier Fletcher as the Commander of the Dhofar Brigade, formulated a plan comprising: the continuation of operations in Salalah, Sarfait and on the Hornbeam Line; the replacement of the Iranians along the Midway Road, freeing them for operations further west; and active operations in the central and eastern jebel aiming to establish tribal firqas in their own tribal areas backed by enhanced civil development programmes. At the same time Sultan Qaboos had authorised the building of a major airfield at Thumrait and work began to create a two-lane surfaced road south from there to Salalah. Sir Gawain Bell was appointed by the British Government to assess the longer term needs and governance of Dhofar. By the end of November 1974 the Iranian taskforce was flown into an airstrip at Manston, west of the Jebel Qomar, as a prelude to the construction of a second fortified line, 15 miles from the PDRY border and 25 miles west of the Hornbeam Line. This would run down to the sea at Rakhyut and cut the rebels' supply routes to the central and eastern jebels. These operations were a close run thing, and significant setbacks were narrowly averted on two occasions. The inexperienced Iranians took significant casualties. Plans for a diversionary attack on the Shershitti caves had to be abandoned and the full Iranian force concentrated for the attack on Rakhyut. The Shershitti attack was instead put into the hands of the SAF who in turn suffered casualties when firqa guides led an advancing company off the planned route and into a rebel ambush. The objective of capturing the caves was abandoned, though the SAF were left poised to develop operations further west later in 1975. Rakhyut, the administrative centre of western Dhofar, captured by the rebels at the beginning of 1969, was retaken by the Iranians on 5 January 1975. Operations to install the proposed Damavand Line from there to the north could then get under way.

In these and other operations closer to the Hornbeam Line the rebels still fought with ferocity and skill. They continued to receive from their backers modern weapons, including SAM 7 ground-to-air missiles, and were reinforced in the west by significant numbers of PDRY troops. However their casualties were high and, in Brigadier Akehurst's view, they never fought again with quite the same tenacity, and became increasingly reluctant to engage with the SAF. In the extreme west it began to be possible for patrols to climb down the escarpment from Sarfait on to the Capstan plateau to create chances to attack rebel supplies almost as soon as they crossed the border. By May 1975 Brigadier Akehurst was also able to report to Sultan Qaboos that he did not believe the 150 or so remaining rebels on the central and eastern jebels could interfere significantly with development activities.

Final operations

General Ken Perkins succeeded General Creasey as Commander of SAF at the beginning of 1975. The decisive operations of the final phase of the war followed the end of the *kharif* in the second half of October 1975. Troops from Sarfait captured the Capstan position unopposed and thus definitively cut the rebels' supply route from Hawf. This had been planned as a diversion with the main operations taking place further east, but reinforcements were swiftly moved to make it the decisive strike. The artillery fire from Hawf which had been brought to bear on Sarfait since its occupation three years before was at the same time countered, at Sultan Qaboos's command and with some unease on the part of his commanders, by intensive attacks using artillery and Hunter aircraft provided to SOAF by King Hussein in the course of the summer. Further east, between Sarfait and the Damavand Line, operations were conducted to clear the area around Shershitti and take the caves themselves. SAF troops were able to advance simultaneously from there and from Sarfait along the Dara ridge parallel with the sea, joining up on 2 December 1975. Mopping up operations continued in both the eastern and western jebels for some months, and the SAS BATT teams continued to reassure jebali communities and get development work under way. On 4 December 1975 Brigadier Akehust was however in a position to signal to Sultan Qaboos 'Dhofar is now secure for civil development'. In December the Sultan announced publicly that the war was over, though shelling of Sarfait from PDRY continued till March 1976 when PDRY accepted a cease-fire under diplomatic pressure from Saudi Arabia. In

May 1976 Qaboos visited Salalah for a firepower demonstration followed by a guest night where the assembled British officers entertained him for dinner.

The Dhofar War: an assessment

The conduct of the Dhofar War was an international effort. As well as Omanis, increasingly as junior and middle-ranking officers as well as NCOs and other ranks, there were still substantial numbers of Baluchis as there had been since the earliest days of organised military units in Oman. There were Jordanians and Iranians in some numbers in the latter stages of the war. The bulk of the tactical and strategic leadership was however British, and this was the principal British contribution to the war. Over the ten years of active operations there were five British Commanders of the Sultan's Armed Forces, Dhofar Brigade Commanders from 1971, and Lt Colonels, Majors and Captains in Regimental and Staff posts throughout. Unlike the wars fought by the British Army in the 2000s this was, by mutual agreement, largely a secret war. These officers and NCOs had none of the public support and sympathy later enjoyed by the troops on the ground in Iraq and Afghanistan. They were never very numerous. In 1974 there were 110 Loan Service officers and 43 NCOs, and 156 contract officers and 19 NCOs. Some of these were in Muscat and elsewhere in the north, not in Dhofar. The Loan Service personnel were serving members of the British Army and RAF, administered as such with their costs defrayed by Oman to the Ministry of Defence. The more junior among them were often volunteers looking for active soldiering and a change from the tedium of service in Germany. The junior officers served for 19 months in Oman, usually at a rank higher than that held in the British Army. Those of the rank of major and above served for two and a half to three years. The contract personnel often shared the desire for active service but with the additional spur of employment once regular service in the British forces had come to an end. They were recruited and paid directly by the Omani Government.

In the years between 1970 and 1974 10 British officers and 11 NCOs were killed, and 18 officers and 9 NCOs wounded (some of whom were from the SAS and other British detachments). British deaths over the whole active period of the war between 1965 and 1975 numbered 35. On the ground this was primarily counter-insurgency infantry soldiering against a skilled, determined, and well equipped enemy. Artillery and armoured car operations were also important. It was a tough and dangerous operation. Conditions were harsh and the terrain off the Salalah plain rugged and arduous. In the 1960s the SAF units were poorly equipped and supported. Oman has shown – particularly through the support of the SAF Association – that the country recognises what she owed to these men at a time when, as a result of Sultan Sa'id's policies and international pressures, her own military leadership capacity was embryonic.

The same is true in the air. SOAF grew from just 4/5 aircraft in the early 1960s to 60 in the mid-1970s. All were flown, during the years of the Dhofar war, by Loan Service or contract pilots. Air Marshal (later Lord) Stirrup, Britain's Chief of Defence Staff between 2008-11, cut his teeth as a Strikemaster pilot in Dhofar in the early 1970s. One difference between the Army and RAF Loan Service personnel was that the Army taught its officers and NCOs Arabic as a matter of course whereas the RAF did not. Three categories of aircraft, all requiring nerve, skill, and not infrequently daring in the conditions and terrain, were involved. The piston engine Strikemaster, based on the RAF Provost, gave way in the late 1960s to the jet version. Between them they provided ground attack support for a decade to the units on the ground. Caribous and Skyvans provided essential links between Salalah and dispersed units with rough landing strips. Helicopters, desperately needed from about 1968, made their appearance in 1971 but then transformed what SAF could do.

In a decade of retrenchment the British Government's direct contribution to the Dhofar War was grudging – at least on the part of the Treasury; Ministers and officials in the Ministry of Defence and the Foreign Office were steadily supportive. Until the change of Government in 1970, there was also unease among Labour Ministers about the extent of Britain's commitment to Sultan Sa'id's regime. After 1967 Oman was expected to fund her war for herself, whatever the impact on the pace of much needed civil development elsewhere in the country. Loan Service officers and NCOs continued to be made available, though numbers were restricted and some units at least were firmly of the view that their brightest and best should gain their experience exercising in Germany, not fighting in Dhofar. Until the withdrawal of British Forces from bases in the rest of the Gulf in 1971 much informal help was given by British forces there, but the deployment of British units remained a neuralgic point in London. The RAF Regiment and the Royal Artillery sent detachments for the direct defence of RAF Salalah. Whitehall would have liked to give up the Salalah commitment but Sultan Sa'id was firm that it was part of a package with the (to Britain) more important base at Masirah. Otherwise British deployments were limited to the SAS, after 1970 Army and RAF medical and surgical teams, a Royal Engineers detachment tasked to support civil development as well as the conduct of the war, and for a year a squadron of Wessex helicopters. In 1974 there were just over 450 serving British personnel in Oman. After the Gulf withdrawal in 1971 plans existed for the deployment of a British battalion battle group if complete collapse threatened, but the most uncertain times were already past by then.

The SAS operation in Dhofar is probably unique in the history of the British Army. Its first Commander, Major Tony Jeapes (like Lt Cols Watts and de la Billliere, winner of an MC on the Jebel Akhdar in 1959) called it the best conducted counter-insurgency campaign fought. Under the title of British Army Training Teams, their combat role not avowed, a force of normally less than 100 save in 1971-2, was deployed for over five years. The prescriptions set out by Watts in 1970 were built into the plans of Sultan Qaboos and his Commanders from very soon after the coup in July. In Operation Jaguar in 1971 they played a key combat role with two squadrons deployed. Over the longer period they played a crucial role in expanding and exploiting the capacity of SAF as a whole to seize the initiative back from the rebels. From the autumn of 1970 they started to give reality in various ways to the argument that improvement in the lives of the people of the jebel could be brought about by the Government, not the rebels. This led the BATT detachments into a whole range of non-military activities, notably dispensing basic medical services in places where none had ever been available, and providing veterinary assistance for the tribesmen's all-important animals. From 1970 they were also the mainspring in turning the increased numbers of defectors from the rebels into the firqas to work alongside SAF units. This was at times a frustrating and unpredictable task, at least once requiring the personal intervention of Sultan Qaboos to secure their cooperation. But they made an essential contribution to the outcome of the War, and the SAS can be justly proud of them.

By 1975 the British involvement in Oman as it had existed under Sultan Sa'id had already changed radically. Oil revenues were being used to fund development across the country. A proper Government structure had been created. Oman had become a full member of the international community. From 1975 the military relationship too changed in nature, focussing on the creation of effective and Omani-led armed forces for the future. The latter years of the Dhofar War thus straddled the early years of Sultan Qaboos's policies of national rebirth, and were at the same time an essential enabler of their application across the whole country.

46. SAF positions at Sarfait

*47. Sultan Qaboos in military
uniform, 1972*

48. SOAF Strikemaster in operation

Afterword

By the time the fighting in Dhofar came to an end Sultan Qaboos had already moved a long way down the road of transforming Oman into a modern state, based on the flow of revenue from the export of oil and, later, gas. Oman had become a full member of the Arab League and of the United Nations, and swiftly built up her Foreign Ministry and diplomatic network so that British diplomats no longer acted as her mouthpiece on the world stage.

Relations between Oman and Britain from the mid-1970s remained very strong but no longer exclusive. The Dhofar War meant that British military and security advice from both seconded and contract officers remained crucial, and in the early years of the reign British officers continued to command at all but the most junior levels. A programme was put into place very quickly to build Omani leadership in all the Omani armed forces, a process basically complete by 1990 around when the last senior British commanders handed over their responsibilities to Omani officers.

Relationships at political level between Sultan Qaboos and successive British governments have remained close. Sultan Qaboos has been a key partner for Britain and other western governments in the security of the highly sensitive Gulf region. It was Britain not he who decided to withdraw from the RAF's bases at Masirah and Salalah in 1977. He welcomed large tri-service British exercises in Oman in 1986 and 1999 to test British ability to deploy complex forces in the region. He offered practical support for British involvement in the freeing of Kuwait from Saddam Hussein in 1990 and in Afghanistan after 2002. His personal relations with Queen Elizabeth have also been strong. The Queen has paid two State Visits to Muscat, the most recent in 2010, when their pleasure in each other's company was very evident.

British companies thrived in the initial wave of economic development between 1970 and 1985. By that year the British community in Oman had grown to some 10,000. Since then many British companies have continued to do good business in Oman. As with other relationships in the educational and cultural fields, Britain, while enjoying advantages of history and language (a striking number of educated Omanis speak excellent English), now has to show a new generation of Omanis why the continuation of close links with Britain remains relevant for twenty-first century Oman. The 'Oman with Britain' programme, mounted across many sectors in 1988, was an initial attempt to do this. In 2000 the Ambassador of the day marked the 200th Anniversary of the Agreement, from which we drew our title, with a similarly ambitious event.

On the British side more and more people are taking advantage of the development of Oman's tourist industry to see the country for the first time. One of our hopes is that this book may help them to understand something of the length and depth of the contacts between the two countries. But the modern ties, as well as the Oman they visit, are qualitatively different from the country and the relationships over several centuries which we have tried to present. At the same time the words of our title remain apt for the world of 2012.

49. Queen Elizabeth II and Sultan Qaboos, 2010

Annex A
Notes for further reading

General:

The inquisitive reader looking for more material will find a reasonable selection of books in English on Omani history. Many of those mentioned below are out of print, but second-hand copies are often available through web-sites. A few published primary source books have become available through print-on-demand publishing, using either photocopying of the original text or reproduction by optical character reader.

For general background on Oman and its history, see:

Hawley, (Sir) Donald: *Oman*, Stacey International, London, 1977, which has an informative text and is extensively illustrated. A new edition, revised and updated by Richard Muir (like Hawley, a former Ambassador in Muscat) was published in 2012.

McBrierty, Vincent, and al-Zubair, *Mohammed: Oman – Ancient Civilisation: Modern Nation*, Trinity College Dublin and Bait al Zubair Foundation, 2004

Phillips, Wendell: *Oman – a short history*, Longmans, London, 1967

There are several books about Oman in the twentieth century, many of which cover the periods both before and after 1970. They include:

Skeet, Ian: *Muscat and Oman: the end of an era*, Faber, London, 1974

Townend, John: *Oman: the Making of a Modern State*, Croom Helm, London, 1977

Peterson, John: Oman in the Twentieth Century, Croom Helm, London, 1978

Owtram, Francis: *A modern history of Oman*, IB Tauris, London, 2004

Joyce, Miriam: *The Sultanate of Oman; a twentieth century history*, Praeger, London, 1995

Chapters 1-3:

For early travellers, and indeed visitors to Oman and the Gulf through history, see:

Bidwell, R: *Travellers in Arabia*, Hamlyn, Reading, 1994

Hamilton, A: *An Arabian Utopia: the Western Discovery of Oman*, Arcadian Library and OUP, 2010. (Contains details on Wellsted, and on many travellers to Oman, with some fine illustrations.)

Searight, Sarah: *The British in the Middle East*, Weidenfeld and Nicholson, London, 1979

Kiernan, R H: *The Unveiling of Arabia*, Harrap, London 1937

Palgrave, W G: *Central and Eastern Arabia*, Macmillan, London and Cambridge, 1865

Ward, P: *Travels in Oman*, Oleander Press, Cambridge UK and New York USA, 1987 – a fine compendium of photo-reproduced extracts from accounts by travellers and visitors.

Lorimer, J G: *Gazetteer of the Persian Gulf, Oman and Central Arabia*, originally published in Calcutta, 1908-15; republished with translation into Arabic, by Sultan Qaboos University and St Antony's College, Oxford, Garnet Publishing 1995

Quotations from or about early travellers in the text are taken from:

Moseley, C W R D (tr and ed): *The Travels of Sir John Mandeville*, Penguin, London, 1983 and 2005

Buckingham, J S: *Travels in Assyria, Media and Persia*, London, 1829

Fitch: *The Voyage of Ralph Fitch by way of Tripolis in Syria*, London, 1598

Hamilton, A: *A new account of the East Indies*, ed J Corfield and I Morson, 1727. Reprinted by Edwin Mellen Press, New York, USA, 2001

Fryer, J: *A New Account of East India and Persia, in eight letters*, 1698, quoted in Bidwell, R: *Travellers in Arabia*, Hamlyn, Reading, 1994

Ovington, J: *A voyage to Surat*, 1696. Reprinted, ed H G Rawlinson, Oxford, 1929

Parsons, Abraham: *Travels in Asia and Africa*, London, 1808

The connection between Oman, Britain and India (with particular reference to the perception of Gulf countries as a part or an extension of the Indian Empire) is well analysed in J Onley's *The Arabian Frontier of the British Raj*, OUP, Oxford, 2007

Chapters 4-9:

A masterly account of Britain's relations with Oman and other Gulf countries in the 19th century is in J B Kelly's *Britain and the Persian Gulf*, 1795-1880, Oxford, 1968.

The pirate campaigns of 1809-21 are vividly related in H Moyse-Bartlett's *The Pirates of Trucial Oman*, Macdonald, London, 1966.

The history of Indian Ocean slavery is not widely covered in either academic or general readership books. Useful material is to be found in Sir Reginald Coupland's two books, *East Africa and its Invaders*, Oxford, 1938; and *The Exploitation of East Africa*, 1856-1890, London, 1939.

Published primary sources from which quotations are in the text include:
Owen, William: *Narrative of Voyages to explore the shores of Africa, Arabia and Madagascar,* London, 1833
Maurizi, V: *History of Seyd Said, Sultan of Muscat*, reprinted by Oleander Press, Cambridge and New York, 1984
Salil-ibn-Razik, tr G P Badger: *History of the Imams and Seyyids of Oman*; London, Hakluyt Society, 1871, available in Kessinger Publishing's Rare Reprints. As the historian J B Kelly remarks, in his introduction to S B Miles's book, *Salil ibn Razik* (correctly Ḥamad or Ḥumayd bin Muḥammad bin Razīq, or possibly Ruẓayq) took much of his material from an earlier history entitled *Kashf al-Ghummah* ("Dispeller of Grief"), composed by Shaikh Sirhān bin Saʿīd of Izkī in about 1728. Col E C Ross, Political Resident, translated and published *Kashf al-Ghummah*, in the Journal of the Asiatic Society of Bengal in 1874. It is now more easily available in a reprint, as *Annals of Oman to 1728*, Oleander Press, Cambridge and New York, 1984

Chapters 10-13:
A good overview of the period following that covered by J B Kelly's book is in R G Landen's *Oman since 1856*, Princeton, 1967
For individual characters, including British Residents and Agents, useful biographies include:
Philip Graves: *Life of Sir Percy Cox*, London, 1939
Victor Winstone: *Capt Shakespeare*, Consul, 1906-07
Kaye, J W: *Life of Sir John Malcolm*, London, 1856
Hazell, A: *The Last Slave Market*, Constable, London, 2011; a biography of Sir John Kirk, Agent and Consul in Zanzibar
Wingate, Ronald: *Not in the limelight*, Hutchinson, London 1959; the memoirs of the British participant in the Agreement of Seeb in 1920

British representation in Oman and the history of the Agency, later Consulate, building in Muscat, are covered in:

Arbuthnott, Clark and Muir: *British Missions around the Gulf*, 1575-2005; Global Oriental, Folkestone, 2008

Chapters 14-16:

Readers interested in 20th-century British travellers in Oman and elsewhere in Arabia will want to read:

Sadlier, G F: *Diary of a Journey across Arabia (1819)*, Bombay, 1866 (reprinted Oleander Press, 1977)

Thomas, Bertram: *Alarms and Excursions in Arabia*, Allen and Unwin, London, 1931; and *Arabia Felix*, Jonathan Cape, London 1932

Thesiger, Wilfred: *Arabian Sands*, Longmans, London, 1959

Wellsted, J R: *Narrative of a Journey into the Interior of Oman*, Journal of the Royal Geographical Society, London, 1837

Wellsted, J R: *Travels in Arabia and Travels to the City of the Caliphs*, London, published in 1838 and 1840 respectively. (Vol 2 of each of these, but not Vol 1 of Travels in Arabia which contains the Oman journey, have been republished as print-on-demand.)

Monroe, Elizabeth: *Philby of Arabia*, Quartet, London, 1980

The Imamate, its twentieth century revival and its end in 1955 are covered in:

Wilkinson, John: *The Imamate tradition of Oman*, Oxford, OUP, 1987

Ghibash H: *Oman: The Islamic democratic tradition*, Routledge, London, 2006

Rabi Uzi: *The Emergence of states in a tribal society*, Brighton, Sussex Academic Press, 2006

Morris, James (later Jan): *Sultan in Oman*, Faber, London, 1957, (paperback Eland, London, 2008) describes first hand the journey of Sultan Sa'id from Salalah to Nizwa and beyond in 1955

British policy in the Gulf after World War Two, and the Buraimi dispute as part of this, are covered in:

Kelly, John: *Eastern Arabian frontiers*, Faber, London, 1964

Darby, Peter: *British Defence Policy east of Suez 1947-68*, OUP, London 1973

Burrows, Bernard: *Footnotes in the sand – the Gulf in transition 1953-1958*, M Russell, Salisbury, 1990

Wilkinson, John: *Arabia's frontiers: the story of British boundary drawing in the desert*, IB Tauris, London, 1991

Chapters 15-16
The fullest treatment of the events in Interior Oman between 1955 and 1959, and of the Dhofar campaign between 1965 and 1975, is given in:
Peterson, John: *Oman's Insurgencies*, London, Saqi, 2007.
A number of British servicemen have written about the military events leading up to the Jebel Akhdar campaign of 1959, including:
Coriat P: *Soldier in Oman*, Amalgamated Authors, London, Undated
Allfree, Peter: *Warlords of Oman*, London, Robert Hale, 1967 (paperback 2008)
Deane Drummond, *Anthony: Arrows of fortune*, Leo Cooper, London, 1992
De la Billliere, General Sir Peter: *Looking for trouble – an autobiography from the SAS to the Gulf*, 1994
Smiley, David: *Arabian assignment*, Cooper, London, 1975

Coverage of non-military events in the 1950s and 1960s is patchier.
Sultan Sa'id's British 'Foreign Minister' in the 1950s, Neil Innes, published his memoirs in *Minister in Oman*, Oleander, Cambridge, 1987.
Hugh Boustead has a chapter on his role in trying to start a development programme in Oman after 1959 in his memoir *Wind of Morning*, Chatto and Windus, London, 1971.
British journalist David Holden wrote an elegiac description of Oman in the dog days of the 1960s in *Farewell to Arabia*, Faber, London 1966
British relationships with Sultan Sa'id in the 1960s are summarised in a chapter in Miriam Joyce: *Ruling Sheikhs and Her Majesty's Government 1960-1969*, London, Frank Cass, 2003.
Ian Skeet: *Oman before 1970. The end of an era*, Faber, London, 1974 describes the Oman of the 1960s from the perspective of an oil man who was there.

Chapter 17
The major survey of the creation and development of Oman's oil industry is:
Clark, Sir Terence: *Underground to overseas – the story of Petroleum Development Oman*, London, Stacey International, 2007. (Clark was formerly British Ambassador to Oman.)

Chapters 18-19

Apart from Peterson's overview in *Oman's insurgencies*, first hand recollections of the Dhofar campaign in command and on the ground include:

Thwaites, Peter: *Muscat command*, Barnsley, Pen and Sword, 1995

Fiennes, Ranulf: *Where soldiers fear to tread*, Mandarin, London, 1975 (paperback 1995)

Purdon, Colum: *List the bugle – reminiscences of an Irish soldier*, Greystone Books, Antrim, 1983

Graham, John: *Ponder anew – reflections on the twentieth century*, Spellmount, Staplehurst, 1999 (which contains the fullest published account of the events of 1970)

Gardiner, Ian: *In the service of the Sultan*, Pen and Sword, Barnsley 2007

Akehurst, John: *We won a war*, Michael Russell, Wilton, 1982

Perkins, Ken: *Fortunate soldier*, Brasseys Defence, Oxford, 1988

Ray, Brian: *Dangerous frontiers – campaigning in Somaliland and Oman*, Pen and Sword, Barnsley, 2008

SAS activities in Dhofar, including the battle for Mirbat, are the subject of:

Jeapes, Tony: *Operation Storm – SAS secret war*, Harper Collins, London, 1996

Higgins, A: *With the SAS and other animals – a vet's war*, Pen and Sword, Barnsley 2011

White R: *Storm front*, London, Bantam Press, 2011

Air operations in Oman between the 1930s and the 1970s are surveyed in:

Richardson, Colin: *Masirah – tales from a desert island*, Lancaster, Scotforth Books, 2003

Lee D: *Flight from the Middle East*, London, HMSO, 1980

Archival records

Records of the correspondence between British Residents and Agents, and their superior officers in Bombay, Calcutta, and later Delhi, and also London, are in the India Office Records kept at the British Library. Consular and other correspondence between offices abroad and London are in the Foreign Office records at the National Archives, Kew; (see especially FO 54 (correspondence relating to Zanzibar and Muscat) and FO 84 (slave trade)), as are the records of the FCO and the Muscat Consulate General after 1947.

Large numbers of British official documents on Oman from 1867 onwards were published as *Records of Oman* in facsimile form by Archive Editions, Slough:
Vols 1-7, edited by Ronald W Bailey (1988-1992) cover 1867-1947
Vols 8-12 edited by Bailey (1988-1992) cover 1947 – 1960
5 vols, edited by Anita Burdett (1997) cover 1961-1965)
6 vols, edited by Burdett (2005) cover 1966-71

Other published primary sources, drawn on or quoted from in the text, include:
Burton, (Sir) Richard: *Zanzibar: City, Island and Coast*, London, 1872
Fraser, J B: *Narrative of a journey into Khorasan*, London, 1825
Malcolm, J: *Sketches of Persia*, London, 1845
Miles, S B: *The Countries and Tribes of the Persian Gulf*, London, 1919
Niebuhr, K: *Description de l'Arabie*, Copenhagen, 1773
Aitchison, C V: *A collection of Treaties, Engagements and Sanads relating to India and the neighbouring countries*, 12 vols, Calcutta, 1909. Vol XII contains those relevant to Oman.

Annex B
Imams and Sultans

Ya'ruba dynasty of Imams

1624 - 1649	Nasir bin Murshid bin Sultan al-Ya'rubi
1649 - 1668	Sultan bin Saif (cousin of Nasir)
1679 - 1692	Bil'arab bin Sultan (son of Sultan bin Saif)
1692 - 1711	Saif bin Sultan (brother of Bil'arab)
1711 - 1718	Sultan bin Saif II (son of Saif bin Sultan)
1718 - c1743	Saif bin Sultan (aged 12)(with periods of "split Imamate")
1718-20:	Muhanna bin Sultan;
1721:	Ya'rub bin Bil'arab
1724 - 1728:	Muhammad bin Nasir, of Bani Ghafir
1733-37:	Bil'arab bin Himyar
1741-1743:	Sultan bin Murshid

Al-Busa'idis

Ruled	Name
1749 (or 1744) – 1775	Imam Ahmad b Sa'id
1783 (or 1775) – 1779	Imam Sa'id b Ahmad
	Lived mainly at Rustaq; deposed as Ruler in 1793, but remained Imam*; died between 1811 and 1821
1779 – 1792	Sayyid Hamad bin Sa'id (did not take title of *Imam*)
1792 – 1804	Sayyid Sultan bin Ahmad
1804 – 1807	Sayyid Badr bin Saif, nephew of Sultan bin Ahmad, murdered at Barka, probably by Sa'id bin Sultan
1807 (or 1806) – 1856	Sayyid Sa'id bin Sultan, died on passage to Zanzibar,

*After the death of Imam Sa'id bin Ahmad, there was no Imam until 'Azzan bin Qays in 1868.

in Muscat		in Zanzibar	
1856 - 1866	Thuwaini bin Sa'id (murdered by son Salim, 1866	1856-70	Majid bin Sa'id
1866 - 1868	Salim bin Thuwaini		
1868 - 1871	'Azzan bin Qays, killed in battle at Mattrah by Turki bin Sa'id, 1871, also Imam	1870-88	Sultan Barghash bin Sa'id

1871- 1888	Sultan Turki bin Sa'id bin Sultan		
1888-1913	Sultan Faysal bin Turki	1888-90	Sultan Khalifa bin Sa'id
		1890-93	Sultan Ali bin Sa'id
		1893-96	Sultan Hamad bin Thuwaini
		1896-1902	Sultan Hamoud bin Muhammad*
		1902-1911	Sultan Ali bin Hamoud (abdicated)
		1911-1960	Sultan Khalifa bin Harub (grandson of Thuwaini bin Sa'id)
1913-1932	Sultan Taymur bin Faysal		
1932-1970	Sultan Sa'id bin Taymur	1960-64	Sultan Jamshid bin Abdullah
1970 -	Sultan Qaboos bin Sa'id		

*In August 1896 Sayyid Khalid bin Barghash seized the Sultanate, but was accused of poisoning Sultan Hamad, deposed after three days (after the 45-minute British naval bombardment sometimes called the "shortest war in history"), and exiled.

Imams after 1810

1868	'Azzan bin Qays, killed in battle at Mattrah, 1871
1871	No Imam for 42 years
May 1913	Salim bin Rashid al-Kharusi, murdered by a Wahiba tribesman
1920 - 1954	Moh'd bin Abdullah bin Sa'id bin Khalfan al-Khalili
1954	Ghalib bin Ali, of the Bani Hina (escaped to Saudi Arabia, October 1954)

Annex C
British Representatives in Bushire (later Bahrain), Muscat and Zanzibar

Note: the British Embassy in Oman has a fine collection of photographs of British Political Agents, Consuls, Consuls-General and Ambassadors in Muscat, complete except for the period 1932-39. The dates recorded on those photographs do not completely tally with those given below, since the 19th century custom was for officers to take long leave ("furlough") from time to time, during which a deputy would be Acting Resident or Acting Political Agent. Several of these acting appointments are recorded in the footnotes to the tables below.

* died in the appointment

a) 1763-1835: Bushire and Muscat

In Bushire	Resident	In Muscat	Political Agent[1]
1763			
1798	Mirza Mahdi Ali Khan	1800	Surgeon A H Bogle*
		1801-1809	Capt David Seton*[2]
		1808	Lt Watts (acting)*
		1809	W C Bunce (acting)*
1810	Nicholas Hankey Smith[3]	1809-1840	In abeyance
1812 - 22	Captain William Bruce (absent June 1820-July 1822)		
1822 - 23	Lt John Macleod*		
1824 -	Lt Col E C Stannus[4]		
1827-1831	Captain David Wilson		
1832-1834	D A Blane		
1835	Maj James Morrison		

b) 1837 - 1900: Bushire, Muscat and Zanzibar

In Bushire Resident	In Muscat	Political Agent	In Zanzibar Consul
			1822-36[5]
?1837-52 Samuel Hennell			1839 Capt Robert Cogan[6]
	1840	Atkins Hamerton	1841-57 Atkins Hamerton[7]
1852-56 Capt Arnold Burrowes Kemball	1843 on	Non-British Agents appointed	
1856-64 Capt Felix Jones		**Agent[8]**	1858-61 Capt C P Rigby
	1861	Lt W M Pengelly[9]	1861 Major Lewis Pelly
1864-72 Major Lewis Pelly[10]	1862	Maj M Green	1863-65 Col R L Playfair
	1863-66[11]	Lt Col H Disbrowe	1865-67 G E Seward (acting)
	1867-69	Capt G A Atkinson	1867-70 Henry Churchill[12]
	1869-70	Lt Col Disbrowe[13]	1870-86 Dr (later Sir) John Kirk[14]
	1870 - May 71	Maj A Cotton Way*	
	1871-72	Capt E C Ross	
1872-91 Maj E C Ross	1872-87	Lt Col S B Miles[15]	
	1887-89	Lt Col E Mockler	1887-88 Sir Claude McDonald
	1889	Lt W C Stratton	1888-91 Sir Charles Euan-Smith
	1889-90	Maj C E Yate	**British Agent and Consul-General**
1891-93 Lt Col A C Talbot	1890-91	Lt Col E Mockler	
1893-94 Maj J H Sadler[18]	1892-96	Maj J Hayes Sadler[16]	1891-92 Gerald Portal (Sir Gerald, 1892)[17]
1894-97 Col F A Wilson	1896-97	Capt F A Beville	1893 Rennell Rodd[19]
1897-1900 Lt Col M J Meade	1897-99	Capt (later Major) C J F Fagan	1894-1900 Sir Arthur Hardinge

c) 1900 - 1971: Bushire (Bahrain from 1946) and Muscat

In Bushire	Resident	In Muscat	Political Agent[1]
1900-04	Lt Col C A Kembell[20]	1899-1904	Maj P Z Cox
1904-20	P Z Cox[21]	1904-08	Maj W G Grey[22]
		1908-10	R E (later Sir Robert) Holland
		1910-11	Maj (later Lt Col) A P Trevor
		1911-14	Maj (later Lt Col) S G Knox
		1914-15	Lt Col R A E Benn
		1915-16	Maj H Stewart[23]
		1916-19	Maj L B H (later Lt Col Sir Lionel) Haworth
1920	A T Wilson (acting)	1919-23	Mr (later Col Sir) Ronald Wingate[24]
1920-24	A P Trevor		
1924-27	F B Prideaux	1924-26	Lt Col C G Crosthwaite
1927-28	L B H Haworth	1926	Maj C C J Barrett
1928-29	F W Johnston	1926-30	Maj (later Lt Col) G P Murphy
1929	C C J Barrett (acting)		
1929-32	H V Biscoe		
1932-39	Maj T C Fowle	1930-32	Maj T C (later Lt Col Sir Trenchard) Fowle
1939-46	C G Prior	1932-35	Maj C E Bremner
	Political resident	1935-39	Maj R P Watts
	Bahrain	1939-40	Capt T (later Lt Col Sir Tom) Higinbotham
1946-53	W R Hay[25]	1940-42	Capt J B Howes
		1942-43	Maj C J Pelly
		1944-45	Lt Col A C Galloway[26]
		1945-46	R I Hallows
		1946-48	Maj A C Stewart
			H M Consul General
1953-58	B A (later Sir Bernard) Burrows	1949-58	Maj F C L Chauncy
		1958-60	W N Monteith
1958-61	Sir George Humphrey Middleton	1960-63	J F S Phillips
		1963-65	J S R Duncan
1961-66	Sir William Luce	1965-69	D C Carden
1966-70	Sir Stewart Crawford	1969-71	D G Crawford
1970-71	Sir Geoffrey Arthur		**British Ambassador**
		1971-75	D F (later Sir Donald) Hawley

Notes

[1] Also referred to as "Political Resident". In this book we have used "Resident" for the official in Bushire, and "Agent" for the appointee in Muscat.

[2] on sick leave 1802-3. The Agency was closed in 1803, and re-opened (again by Seton) in 1805. Lt William Watts acted as Agent, May-August 1808.

[3] Hankey Smith acted as Agent in Muscat, January-April 1810.

[4] referred to as "Stanners" in Coupland: *East Africa and its Invaders*. He was the first to carry the title "Resident for the Upper Gulf" under Elphinstone's reform of Residency arrangements.

[5] Bennett (*History of the Arab State of Zanzibar*, p 20) says that an Omani subject was appointed British agent in Zanzibar under the Moresby treaty, 1822, and a successor appointed in 1826.

[6] On returning from accompanying Ali bin Nasir, Governor of Mombasa, on an official visit to England, bearing appointment of "Her Majesty's Commissioner and Plenipotentiary at the court of the Imam of Muscat".

[7] 1840 Hamerton accompanied Sa'id to Zanzibar; Bennett (*History of the Arab State of* Zanzibar, p 46) dates his arrival at 4 May 1841. He died in July 1857, and there was an interval of about a year before his successor arrived

[8] From 1861 until 1949 the appointment in Muscat was "Political Agent and Consul"

[9] After a gap since 1840, with Indian and local agents standing in.

[10] Protégé of Sir Bartle Frere, Governor of Bombay.

[11] The Political Agency was closed in early 1866 when Sayyid Salim seized power after killing his father, and reopened in January 1867 year, after recognition had been granted to Salim, under Atkinson.

[12] Churchill was appointed by the Foreign Office, unlike his predecessors, who were appointed by the Indian Government.

[13] The British Embassy in Oman has a photograph of Surgeon Lt Col Jayakar IMS, recorded as being Agency Surgeon 1870-1900, and as having acted as Political Agent "many times".

[14] John Kirk was first appointed to Zanzibar in 1866, as Agency Surgeon and Vice-Consul.

[15] P J C Robertson was acting as Political Agent in June 1877, Major C B Euan-Smith from July 1879 until January 1880, Major C Grant for periods in 1880 and1881-83, and Major E Mockler for periods in 1883 and 1886.

[16] For a period in 1893-94 Sadler stood in as Resident in Bushire; and for a period in 1895 Captain J F Whyte acted as Political Agent in Muscat.

[17] Portal stood in during Euan-Smith's temporary absence in Europe in 1889. Appointed as Consul in succession to Euan-Smith, he became British Agent and Consul-General in October 1891, soon after the British Protectorate was promulgated in November 1890.

[18] J A Crawford was acting Resident for part of 1893.

[19] Awarded KCMG in 1899, and in 1933 created Baron Rennell of Rodd.

[20] or Kemball

[21] Percy Zachariah Cox; Capt Cox when first appointed, later Sir Percy Cox

[22] Capt W H I Shakespear acted as Agent, July-Nov 1906. Capt N Scott and Capt F McConaghey acted as Agent April-July and July-November respectively, in 1908

[23] Filling the gap between Maj Stewart and Maj Haworth, Lt Col C Ducat, Maj A R Burton, Maj E B Howell and Maj A R L King-Mason acted as Agent.

[24] For periods in 1921-23, Major (later Lt Col) M E Rae was acting Political Agent.

[25] from 1952, Sir William Hay; from 1948 the Residency plus the Agencies at Muscat, Kuwait, Bahrain and Sharjah reported to the Foreign Office.

[26] The gap between Pelly and Galloway was filled by Capt R E Bird and Capt R D Metcalfe

Annex D
List of Treaties

The earliest formal agreements between the British and Muscat/Oman were:
1646 Agreement between Philip Wylde, on behalf of the East India Company, and the people of Sohar
1659 Agreement between Col Rainsford, on behalf of the East India Company, and Imam Sultan bin Saif

In 1863, C U Aitchison, Under Secretary in the Foreign Department of the Government of India, assembled a "Collection of Treaties, Engagements and Sanads relating to India and neighbouring countries". Subsequently, and even after his death (in 1896) the Government of India up-dated the collection and republished several revisions, the most recent edition being that of 1930. This compilation contains 23 treaties and engagements with Oman, including two concluded with the "Chief of Sohar" (see note (a) below), but not the two 17th century texts mentioned above. Of these the most significant are:

12 October 1798:	Cowlnamah - written engagement from the Imam of Muscat to Mehdi Ali Khan, representing the East India Company. (Aitchison describes this in the Contents as an "Agreement .. for the exclusion of the French from his territories".)
18 January 1800:	Agreement, signed by Imam Ahmad bin Sa'id and Captain John Malcolm
4 September 1822:	Treaty with the Imam of Muscat for the suppression of the slave trade (the Moresby Treaty)
31 May 1839:	Treaty of Commerce (including, in Article 15, provisions on the slave trade)
17 December 1839:	Additional Articles to the Treaty of Commerce, on the slave trade
2 October 1845:	Treaty concluded with the Sultan of Muscat prohibiting the export of slaves from His Highness' African dominions
14 June 1854:	Deed executed by the Sultan of Muscat ceding to the British crown the Kuria Muria islands
10 March 1862:	Declaration made by Great Britain and France engaging to respect the independence of Muscat and Zanzibar
17 November 1864 and 10 January 1865:	Agreement, and Convention, for the construction of telegraph lines
14 April 1873:	Treaty for the abolition of the slave trade

19 March 1891: Treaty of Friendship, Commerce and navigation, with the 20 March Agreement (originally secret) regarding the cession of territory by the Sultan of Oman

Notes

a) the Agreements with the "Chief of Sohar" relate to the conclusion of peace between Sayyid Sa'id bin Sultan, Ruler of Muscat, and Sayyid Humud bin 'Azzān, Shaikh of Sohar, through the mediation of Hennell in 1839; and to a commitment by Humud's son and successor, Sayf, to prohibit the slave trade.

b) although the 1930 edition of the compilation lists undertakings made by the Sultan in 1921 and 1929, it omits the 1912 undertaking on the suppression of the munitions trade.

c) in the course of the 19th century the designation used for the ruler of Muscat changed. From the Aitchison collection we can see the move away from the use of "Imam" and the extension of claimed authority, from "Muscat" to "Muscat and Oman". The following terms are used (note the variety of spellings for "Sayyid", viz, *Seid, Syud, Syed, Seyyid* and *Sayid*):

• in the Moresby Treaty of 1822: HH the Imam of Muscat
• in the 1839 Treaty of Commerce: HH Sultan Seid Saeed bin Sultan, Imam of Muscat
• in the 1845 slave trade abolition agreement: HH Syud Saeed bin Sultan, "the Sultan of Muscat"
• in the cession of the Kuria Muria islands, 1854: HH the Imam of Muscat
• in the 1864 telegraph Articles of Agreement, 1864: HH Syed Thoweynee bin Saeed bin Sultan, the Sultan of Muscat
• in the 1891 Treaty of Friendship, Commerce and Navigation: HH the Seyyid Feysal bin Turki bin Saeed, Sultan of Muscat and Oman
• in the prolongation of the 1891 Treaty: HH Sayid Sir Taimur bin Faisal KCIE CSI, Sultan of Muscat and Oman

In the period since 1930 we should note in particular:

1939, 5 February Treaty of Friendship, Commerce and Navigation, between HM The king of Great Britain, Northern Ireland and his Dominions beyond the seas, Emperor of India; and Sultan Saiyid Said bin Taymur, Sultan of Muscat and Oman and dependencies. (Lt Col Sir T C W Fowle, Political Resident in the Persian Gulf, signed for GB and Northern Ireland, and again for India.)

1951, 20 December Treaty of Friendship, Commerce and Navigation Treaty between the United Kingdom and the Sultan taking account of the Independence of India

Index

324